MARVEL STUDIOS
AVENGERS ENDGAME
PRELUDE

BASED ON THE SCREENPLAY BY **CHRISTOPHER MARKUS** AND **STEPHEN McFEELY**

WRITER: **WILL CORONA PILGRIM**

PENCILER: **PACO DIAZ**

COLOR ARTIST: **DONO SÁNCHEZ-ALMARA**

LETTERER: **VC'S TRAVIS LANHAM**

ASSISTANT EDITOR: **LAUREN AMARO**

EDITOR: **MARK BASSO**

FOR MARVEL STUDIOS

MANAGER, PRODUCTION & DEVELOPMENT: **BOJAN VUČIĆEVIĆ**

EXECUTIVE, PRODUCTION & DEVELOPMENT: **TRINH TRAN**

PRESIDENT: **KEVIN FEIGE**

AVENGERS CREATED BY STAN LEE & JACK KIRBY

COLLECTION EDITOR: JENNIFER GRÜNWALD

ASSISTANT EDITOR: CAITLIN O'CONNELL

ASSOCIATE MANAGING EDITOR: KATERI WOODY

EDITOR, SPECIAL PROJECTS: MARK D. BEAZLEY

VP PRODUCTION & SPECIAL PROJECTS: JEFF YOUNGQUIST

SVP PRINT, SALES & MARKETING: DAVID GABRIEL

EDITOR IN CHIEF: C.B. CEBULSKI

CHIEF CREATIVE OFFICER: JOE QUESADA

PRESIDENT: DAN BUCKLEY

MARVEL'S AVENGERS: ENDGAME PRELUDE. Contains material originally published in magazine form as MARVEL'S AVENGERS: ENDGAME PRELUDE #1-3, INFINITY GAUNTLET #1 and GUARDIANS OF THE GALAXY #19. First printing 2019. ISBN 978-1-302-91495-0. Published by MARVEL WORLDWIDE, INC., a subsidiary of MARVEL ENTERTAINMENT, LLC. OFFICE OF PUBLICATION: 135 West 50th Street, New York, NY 10020. Copyright © 2019 MARVEL No similarity between any of the names, characters, persons, and/or institutions in this magazine with those of any living or dead person or institution is intended, and any such similarity which may exist is purely coincidental. **Printed in the U.S.A.** DAN BUCKLEY, President, Marvel Entertainment; JOHN NEE, Publisher; JOE QUESADA, Chief Creative Officer; TOM BREVOORT, SVP of Publishing; DAVID BOGART, SVP of Business Affairs & Operations, Publishing & Partnership; DAVID GABRIEL, SVP of Sales & Marketing, Publishing; JEFF YOUNGQUIST, VP of Production & Special Projects; DAN CARR, Executive Director of Publishing Technology; ALEX MORALES, Director of Publishing Operations; DAN EDINGTON, Managing Editor; SUSAN CRESPI, Production Manager; STAN LEE, Chairman Emeritus. For information regarding advertising in Marvel Comics or on Marvel.com, please contact Vit DeBellis, Custom Solutions & Integrated Advertising Manager, at vdebellis@marvel.com. For Marvel subscription inquiries, please call 888-511-5480. **Manufactured between 1/25/2019 and 2/26/2019 by LSC COMMUNICATIONS INC., KENDALLVILLE, IN, USA.**

10 9 8 7 6 5 4 3 2 1

MARVEL'S AVENGERS: ENDGAME
PRELUDE #1

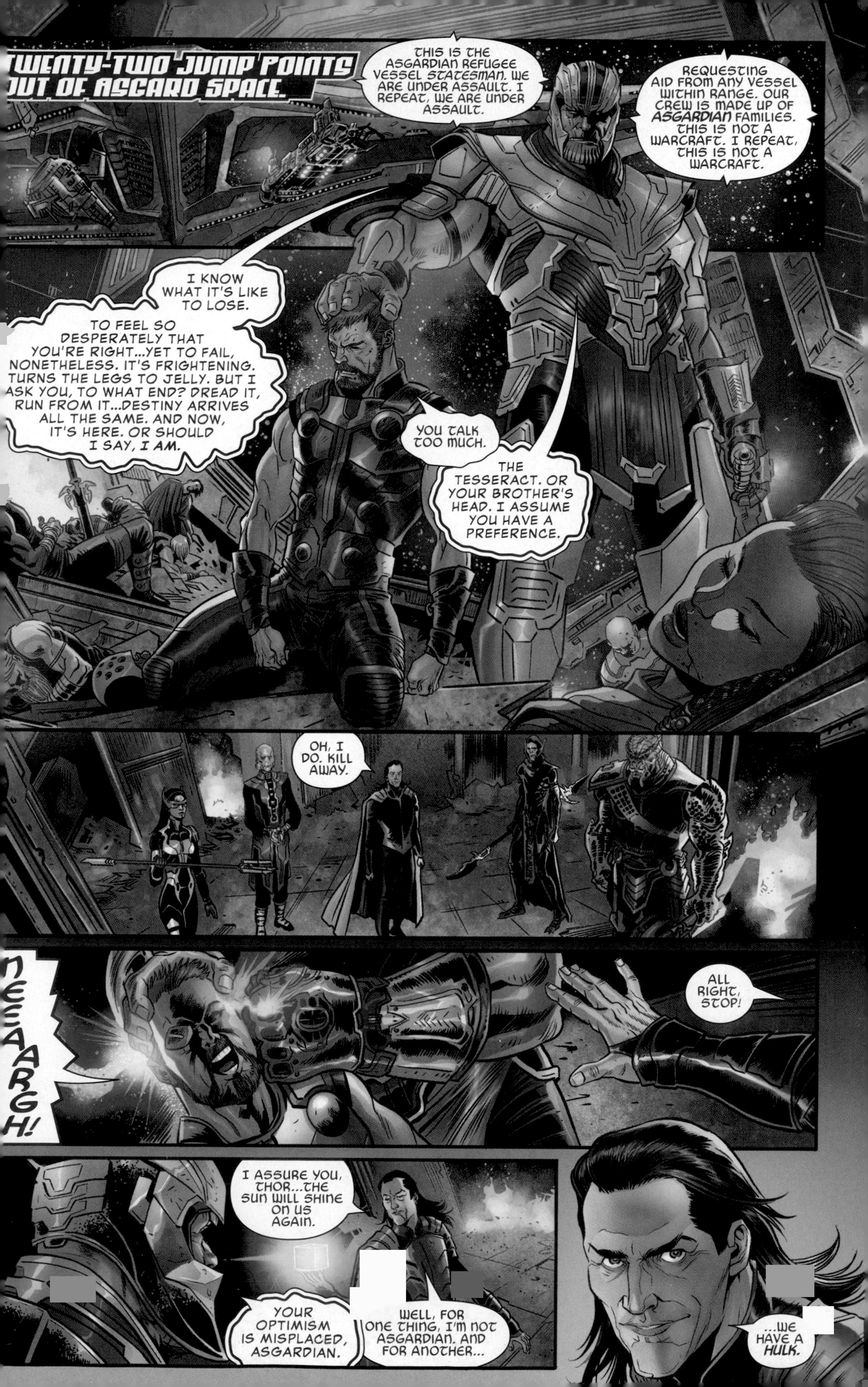
TWENTY-TWO JUMP POINTS OUT OF ASGARD SPACE.
THIS IS THE ASGARDIAN REFUGEE VESSEL STATESMAN. WE ARE UNDER ASSAULT. I REPEAT, WE ARE UNDER ASSAULT.
REQUESTING AID FROM ANY VESSEL WITHIN RANGE. OUR CREW IS MADE UP OF ASGARDIAN FAMILIES. THIS IS NOT A WARCRAFT. I REPEAT, THIS IS NOT A WARCRAFT.
I KNOW WHAT IT'S LIKE TO LOSE.
TO FEEL SO DESPERATELY THAT YOU'RE RIGHT...YET TO FAIL, NONETHELESS. IT'S FRIGHTENING. TURNS THE LEGS TO JELLY. BUT I ASK YOU, TO WHAT END? DREAD IT, RUN FROM IT...DESTINY ARRIVES ALL THE SAME. AND NOW, IT'S HERE. OR SHOULD I SAY, I AM.
YOU TALK TOO MUCH.
THE TESSERACT. OR YOUR BROTHER'S HEAD. I ASSUME YOU HAVE A PREFERENCE.
OH, I DO. KILL AWAY.
NEEAARGH!
ALL RIGHT, STOP!
I ASSURE YOU, THOR...THE SUN WILL SHINE ON US AGAIN.
YOUR OPTIMISM IS MISPLACED, ASGARDIAN.
WELL, FOR ONE THING, I'M NOT ASGARDIAN. AND FOR ANOTHER...
...WE HAVE A HULK.

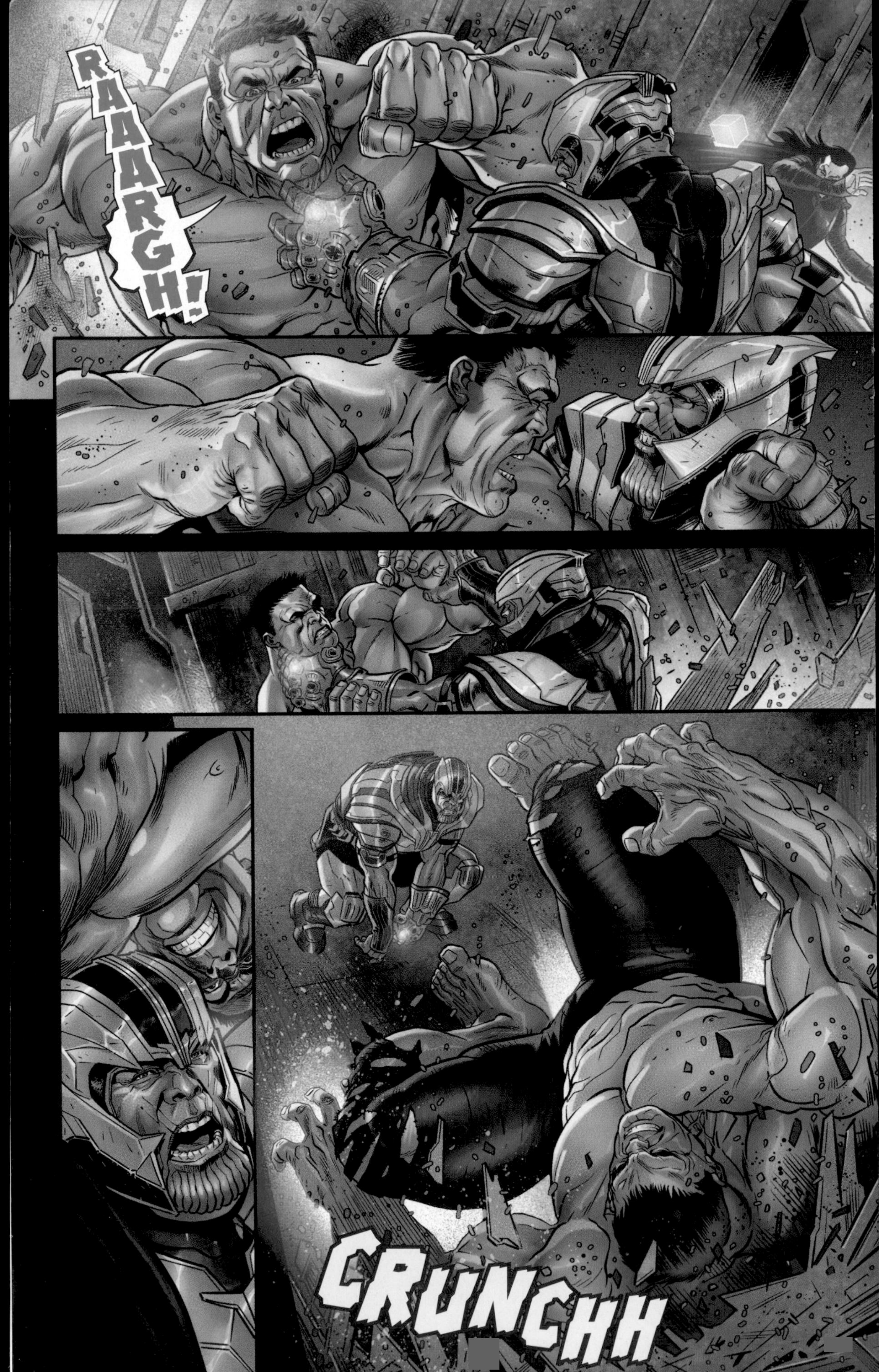
RAAAARGH!
CRUNCHH

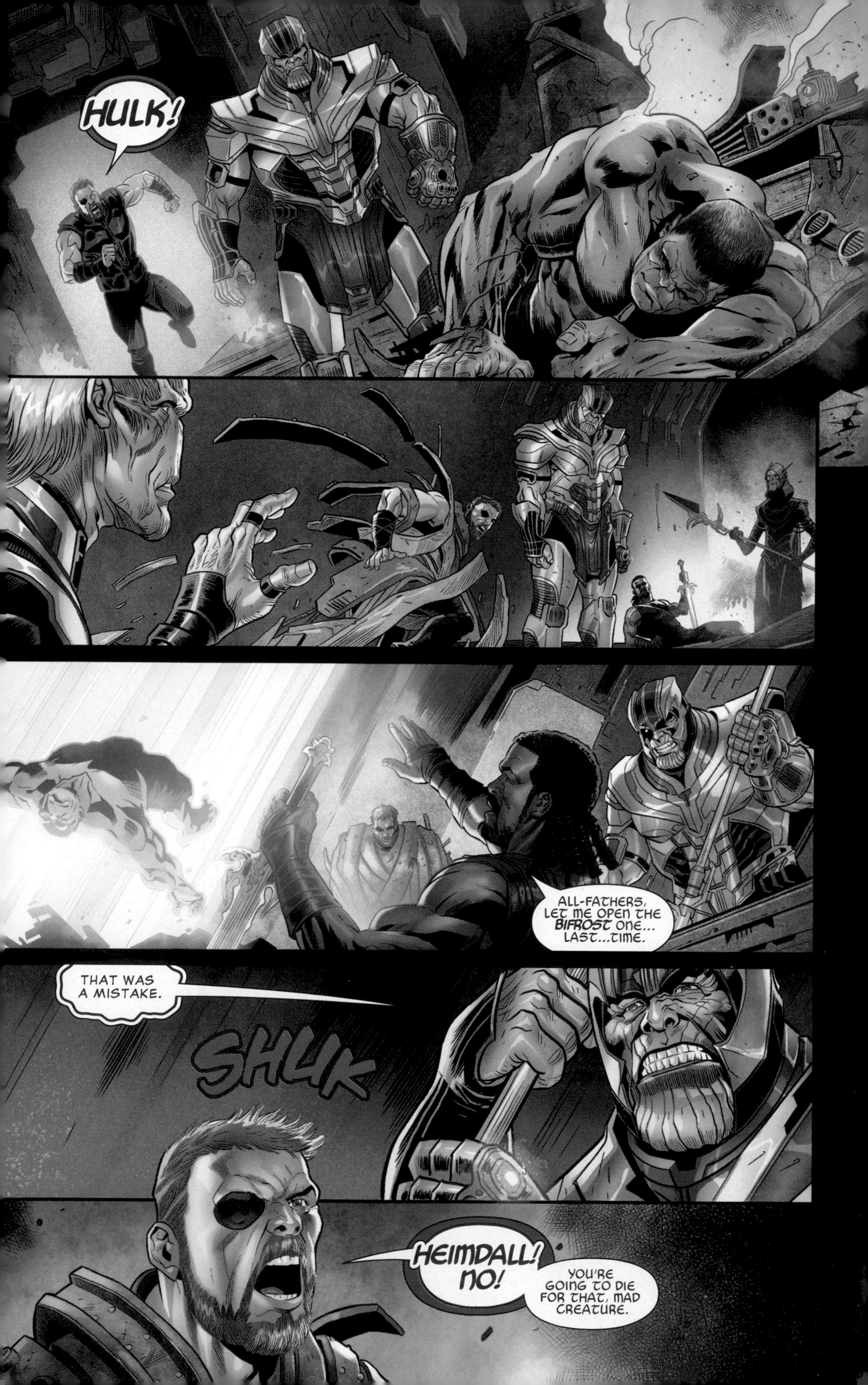

HULK!
ALL-FATHERS, LET ME OPEN THE BIFROST ONE... LAST...TIME.
THAT WAS A MISTAKE.
SHUK
HEIMDALL! NO!
YOU'RE GOING TO DIE FOR THAT, MAD CREATURE.

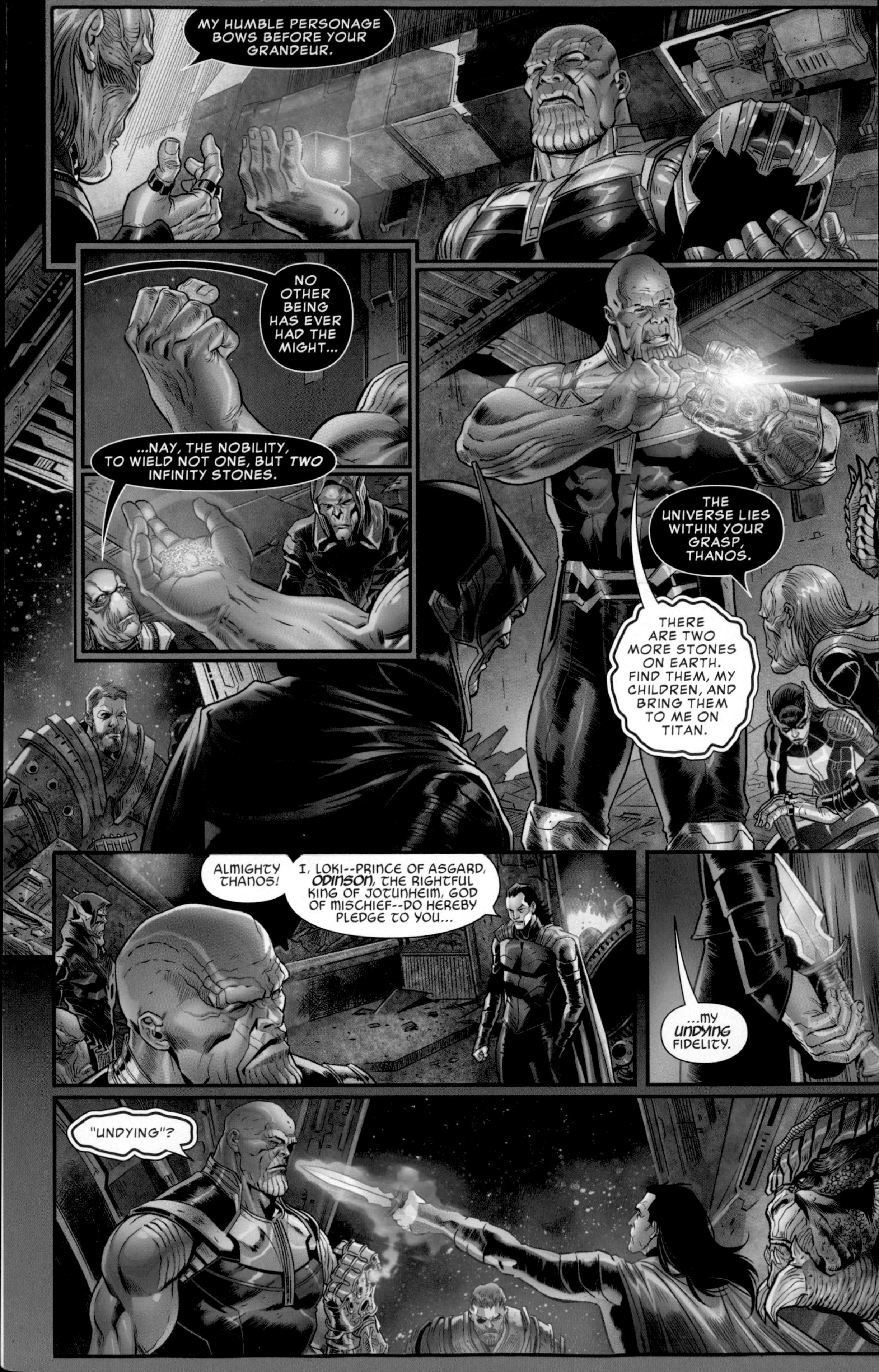
MY HUMBLE PERSONAGE BOWS BEFORE YOUR GRANDEUR.
NO OTHER BEING HAS EVER HAD THE MIGHT...
...NAY, THE NOBILITY, TO WIELD NOT ONE, BUT TWO INFINITY STONES.
THE UNIVERSE LIES WITHIN YOUR GRASP, THANOS.
THERE ARE TWO MORE STONES ON EARTH. FIND THEM, MY CHILDREN, AND BRING THEM TO ME ON TITAN.
ALMIGHTY THANOS!
I, LOKI--PRINCE OF ASGARD, ODINSON, THE RIGHTFUL KING OF JOTUNHEIM, GOD OF MISCHIEF--DO HEREBY PLEDGE TO YOU...
...MY UNDYING FIDELITY.
"UNDYING"?

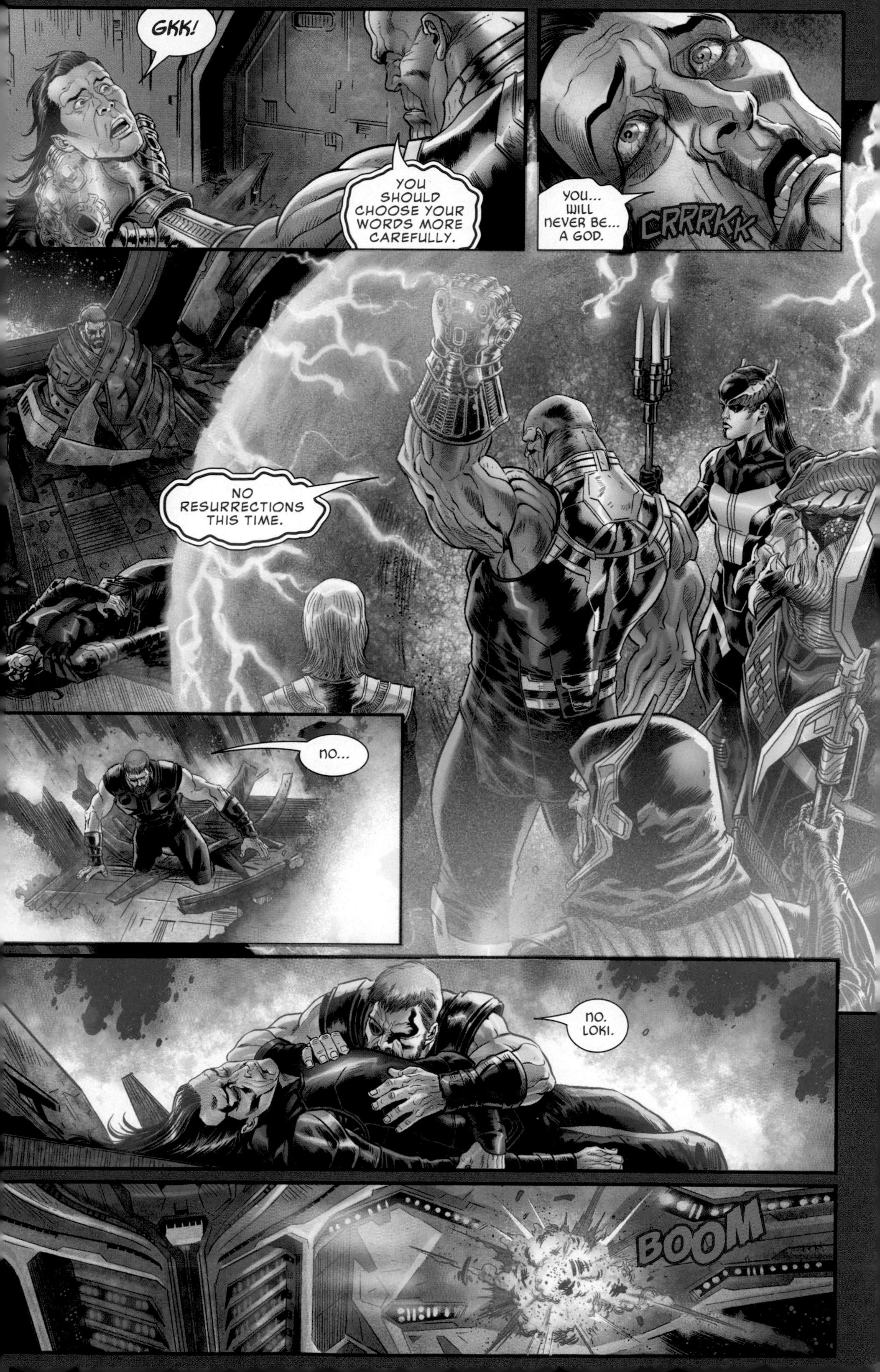
GKK!
YOU SHOULD CHOOSE YOUR WORDS MORE CAREFULLY.
YOU... WILL NEVER BE... A GOD.
CRRRKK
NO RESURRECTIONS THIS TIME.
NO...
NO. LOKI.
BOOM

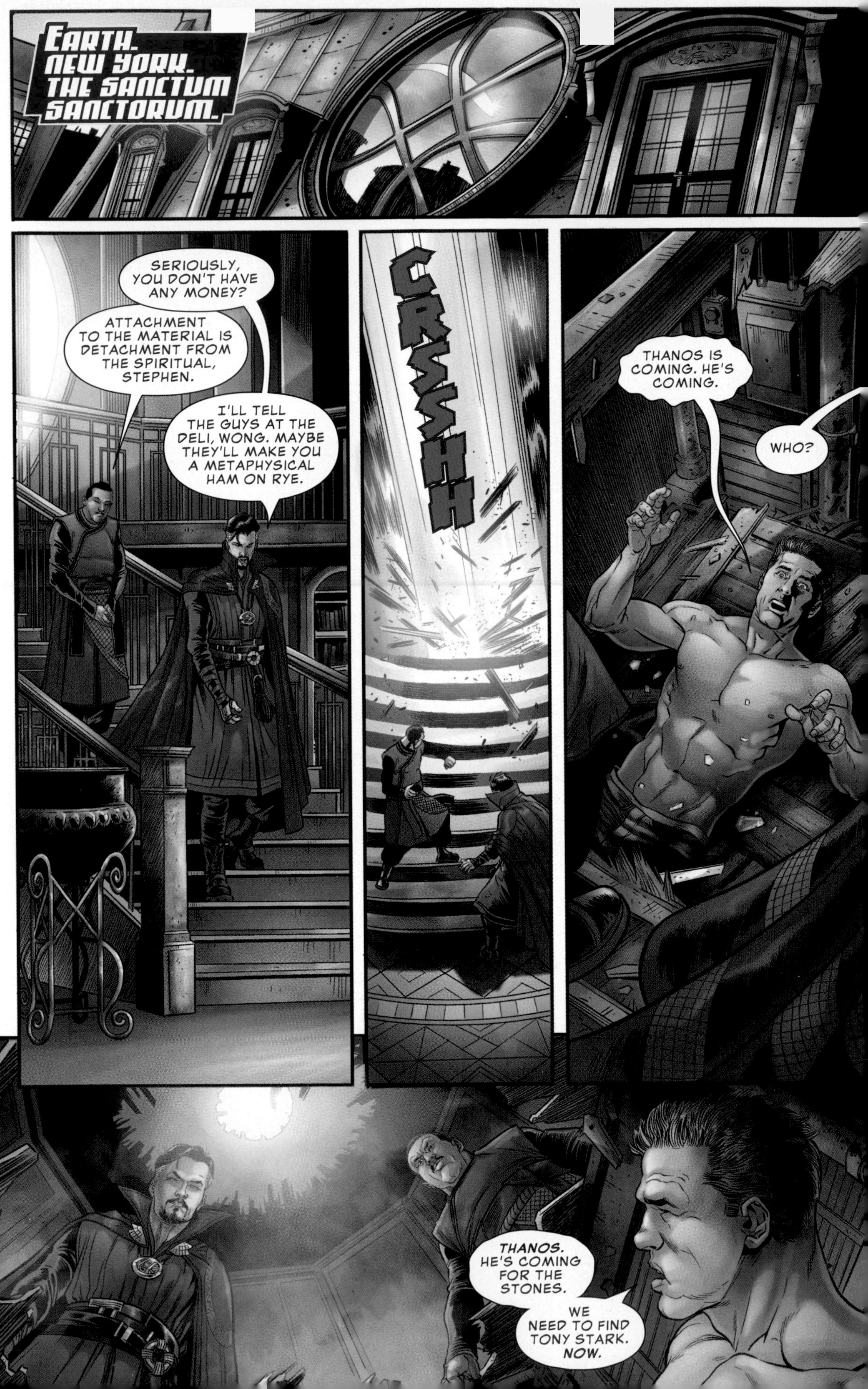
EARTH. NEW YORK. THE SANCTUM SANCTORUM.
SERIOUSLY, YOU DON'T HAVE ANY MONEY?
ATTACHMENT TO THE MATERIAL IS DETACHMENT FROM THE SPIRITUAL, STEPHEN.
I'LL TELL THE GUYS AT THE DELI, WONG. MAYBE THEY'LL MAKE YOU A METAPHYSICAL HAM ON RYE.
CRSSHH
THANOS IS COMING. HE'S COMING.
WHO?
THANOS. HE'S COMING FOR THE STONES.
WE NEED TO FIND TONY STARK. NOW.

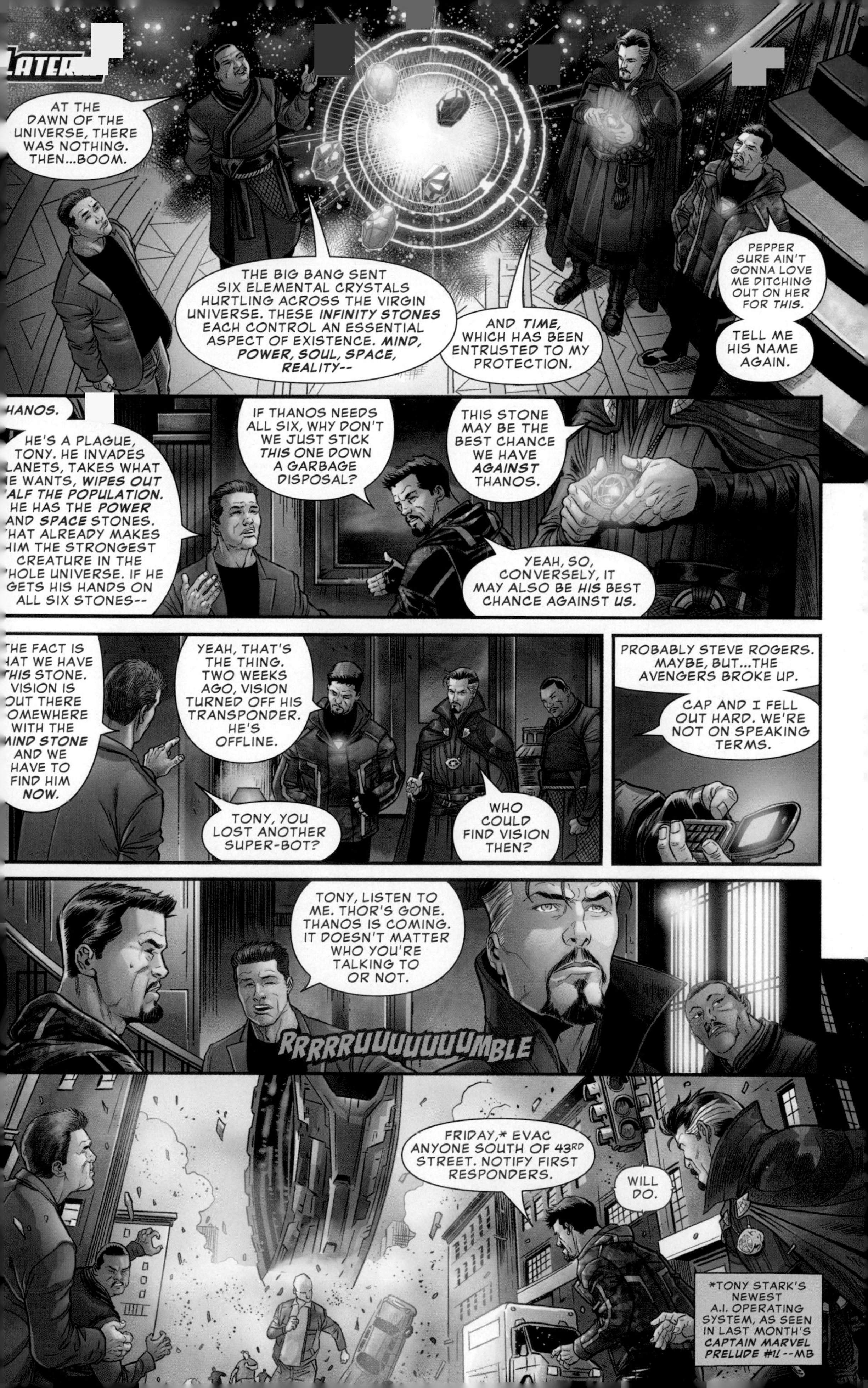
LATER
AT THE DAWN OF THE UNIVERSE, THERE WAS NOTHING. THEN...BOOM.
THE BIG BANG SENT SIX ELEMENTAL CRYSTALS HURTLING ACROSS THE VIRGIN UNIVERSE. THESE INFINITY STONES EACH CONTROL AN ESSENTIAL ASPECT OF EXISTENCE. MIND, POWER, SOUL, SPACE, REALITY--
AND TIME, WHICH HAS BEEN ENTRUSTED TO MY PROTECTION.
PEPPER SURE AIN'T GONNA LOVE ME DITCHING OUT ON HER FOR THIS.
TELL ME HIS NAME AGAIN.
HANOS.
HE'S A PLAGUE, TONY. HE INVADES LANETS, TAKES WHAT E WANTS, WIPES OUT ALF THE POPULATION. HE HAS THE POWER AND SPACE STONES. HAT ALREADY MAKES HIM THE STRONGEST CREATURE IN THE HOLE UNIVERSE. IF HE GETS HIS HANDS ON ALL SIX STONES--
IF THANOS NEEDS ALL SIX, WHY DON'T WE JUST STICK THIS ONE DOWN A GARBAGE DISPOSAL?
THIS STONE MAY BE THE BEST CHANCE WE HAVE AGAINST THANOS.
YEAH, SO, CONVERSELY, IT MAY ALSO BE HIS BEST CHANCE AGAINST US.
HE FACT IS HAT WE HAVE THIS STONE. VISION IS OUT THERE OMEWHERE WITH THE MIND STONE AND WE HAVE TO FIND HIM NOW.
YEAH, THAT'S THE THING. TWO WEEKS AGO, VISION TURNED OFF HIS TRANSPONDER. HE'S OFFLINE.
TONY, YOU LOST ANOTHER SUPER-BOT?
WHO COULD FIND VISION THEN?
PROBABLY STEVE ROGERS. MAYBE, BUT...THE AVENGERS BROKE UP.
CAP AND I FELL OUT HARD. WE'RE NOT ON SPEAKING TERMS.
TONY, LISTEN TO ME. THOR'S GONE. THANOS IS COMING. IT DOESN'T MATTER WHO YOU'RE TALKING TO OR NOT.
RRRRRUUUUUUUUMBLE
FRIDAY,* EVAC ANYONE SOUTH OF 43RD STREET. NOTIFY FIRST RESPONDERS.
WILL DO.
*TONY STARK'S NEWEST A.I. OPERATING SYSTEM, AS SEEN IN LAST MONTH'S CAPTAIN MARVEL PRELUDE #1! --MB

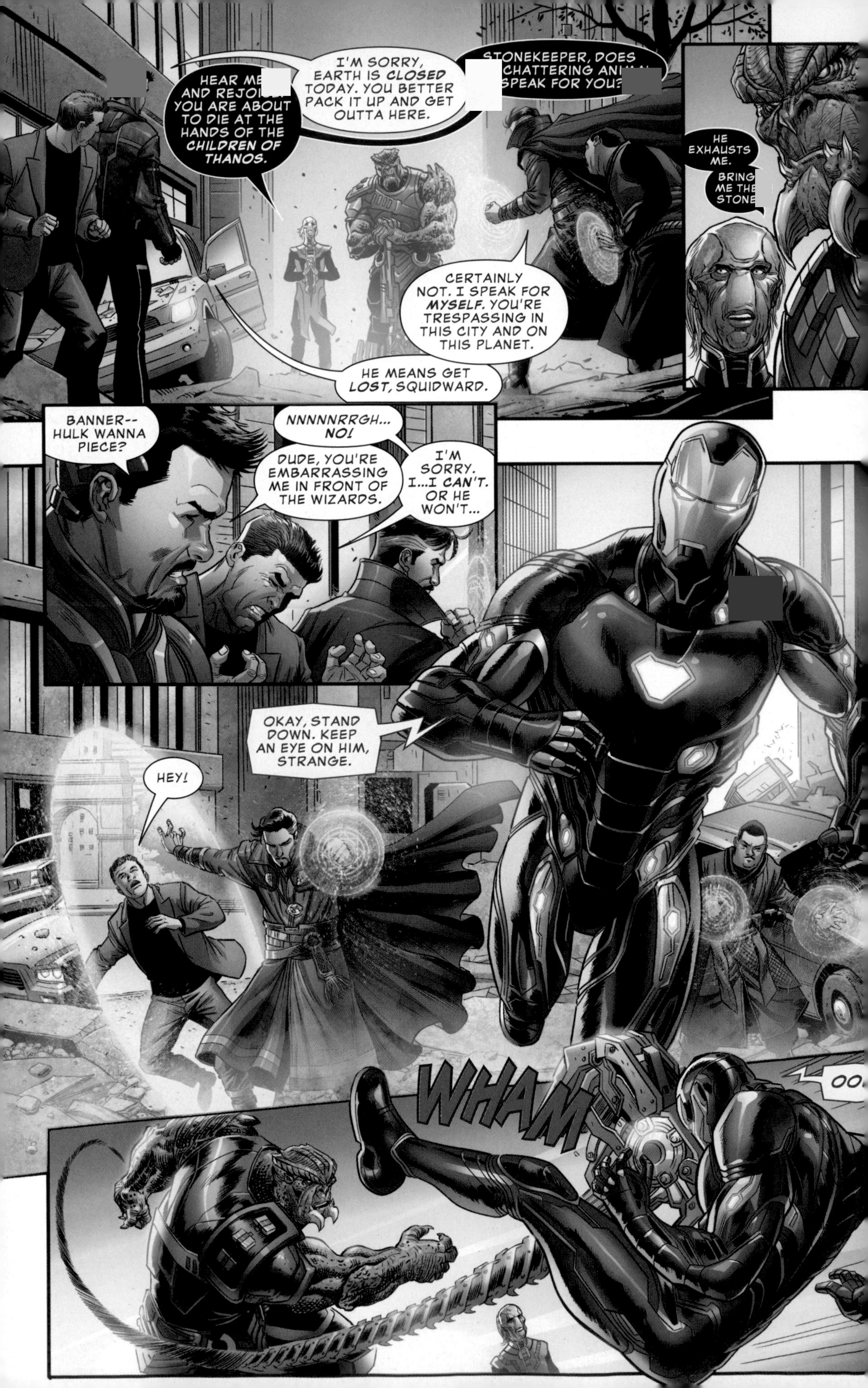
HEAR ME AND REJOI YOU ARE ABOUT TO DIE AT THE HANDS OF THE CHILDREN OF THANOS.
I'M SORRY, EARTH IS CLOSED TODAY. YOU BETTER PACK IT UP AND GET OUTTA HERE.
STONEKEEPER, DOES CHATTERING ANI AL SPEAK FOR YOU?
HE EXHAUSTS ME.
BRING ME THE STONE
CERTAINLY NOT. I SPEAK FOR MYSELF. YOU'RE TRESPASSING IN THIS CITY AND ON THIS PLANET.
HE MEANS GET LOST, SQUIDWARD.
BANNER-- HULK WANNA PIECE?
NNNNNRRGH... NO!
DUDE, YOU'RE EMBARRASSING ME IN FRONT OF THE WIZARDS.
I'M SORRY. I...I CAN'T. OR HE WON'T...
OKAY, STAND DOWN. KEEP AN EYE ON HIM, STRANGE.
HEY!
WHAM
OO...

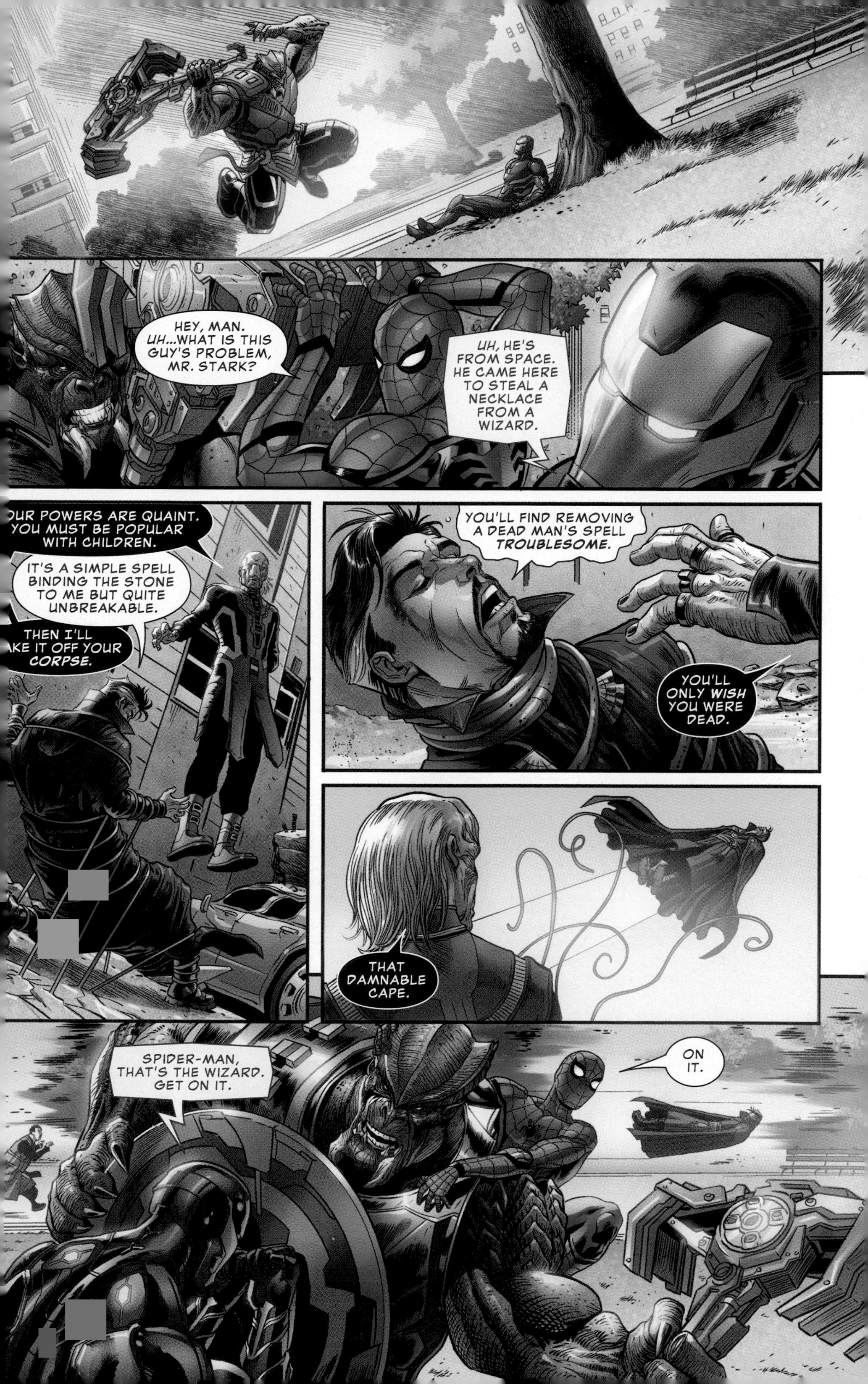
HEY, MAN. *UH...*WHAT IS THIS GUY'S PROBLEM, MR. STARK?
UH, HE'S FROM SPACE. HE CAME HERE TO STEAL A NECKLACE FROM A WIZARD.
OUR POWERS ARE QUAINT. YOU MUST BE POPULAR WITH CHILDREN.
IT'S A SIMPLE SPELL BINDING THE STONE TO ME BUT QUITE UNBREAKABLE.
THEN I'LL AKE IT OFF YOUR *CORPSE.*
YOU'LL FIND REMOVING A DEAD MAN'S SPELL *TROUBLESOME.*
YOU'LL ONLY *WISH* YOU WERE DEAD.
THAT DAMNABLE CAPE.
SPIDER-MAN, THAT'S THE WIZARD. GET ON IT.
ON IT.

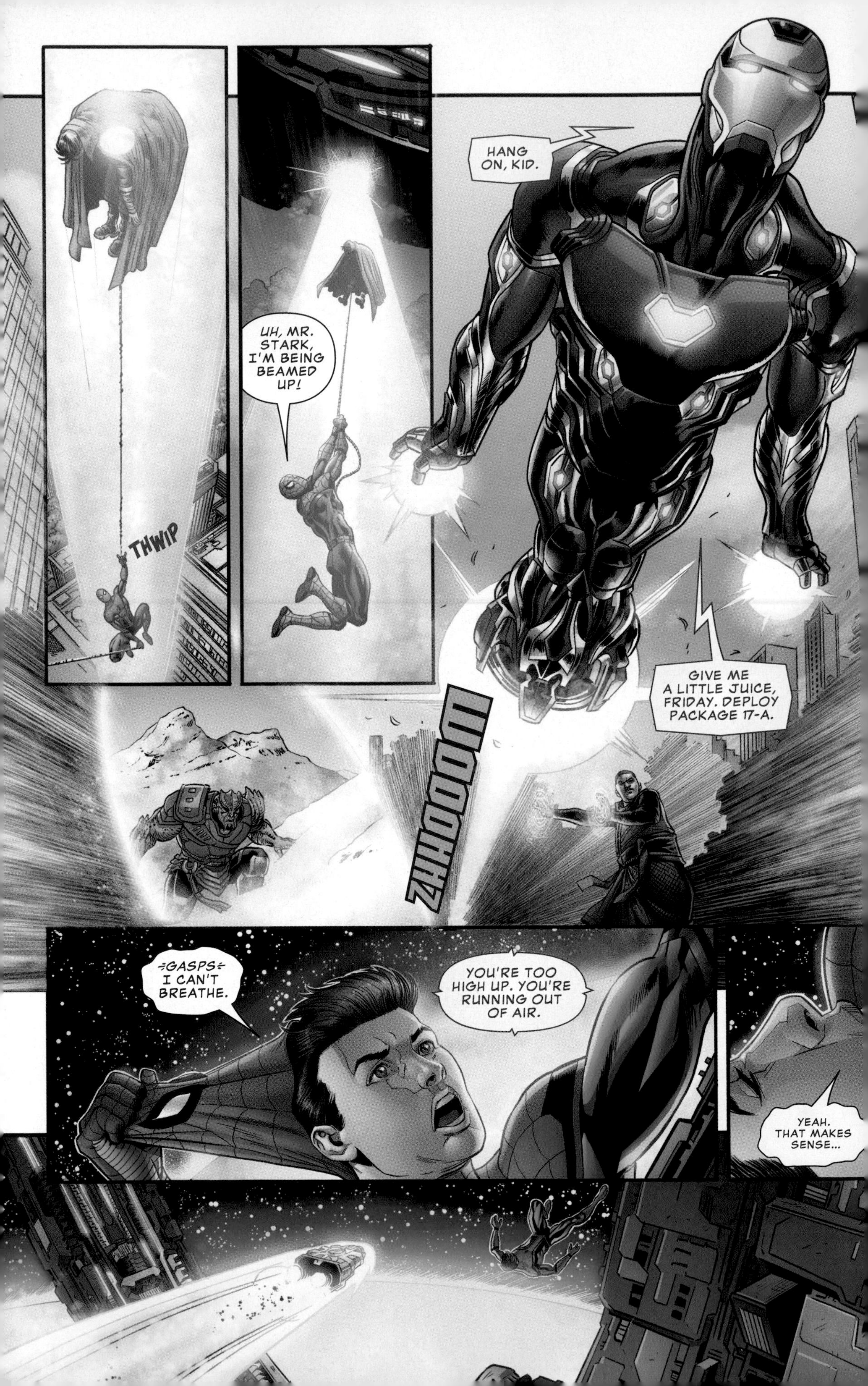
THWIP
UH, MR. STARK, I'M BEING BEAMED UP!
HANG ON, KID.
GIVE ME A LITTLE JUICE, FRIDAY. DEPLOY PACKAGE 17-A.
ZHOOOOOM
=GASPS= I CAN'T BREATHE.
YOU'RE TOO HIGH UP. YOU'RE RUNNING OUT OF AIR.
YEAH. THAT MAKES SENSE...

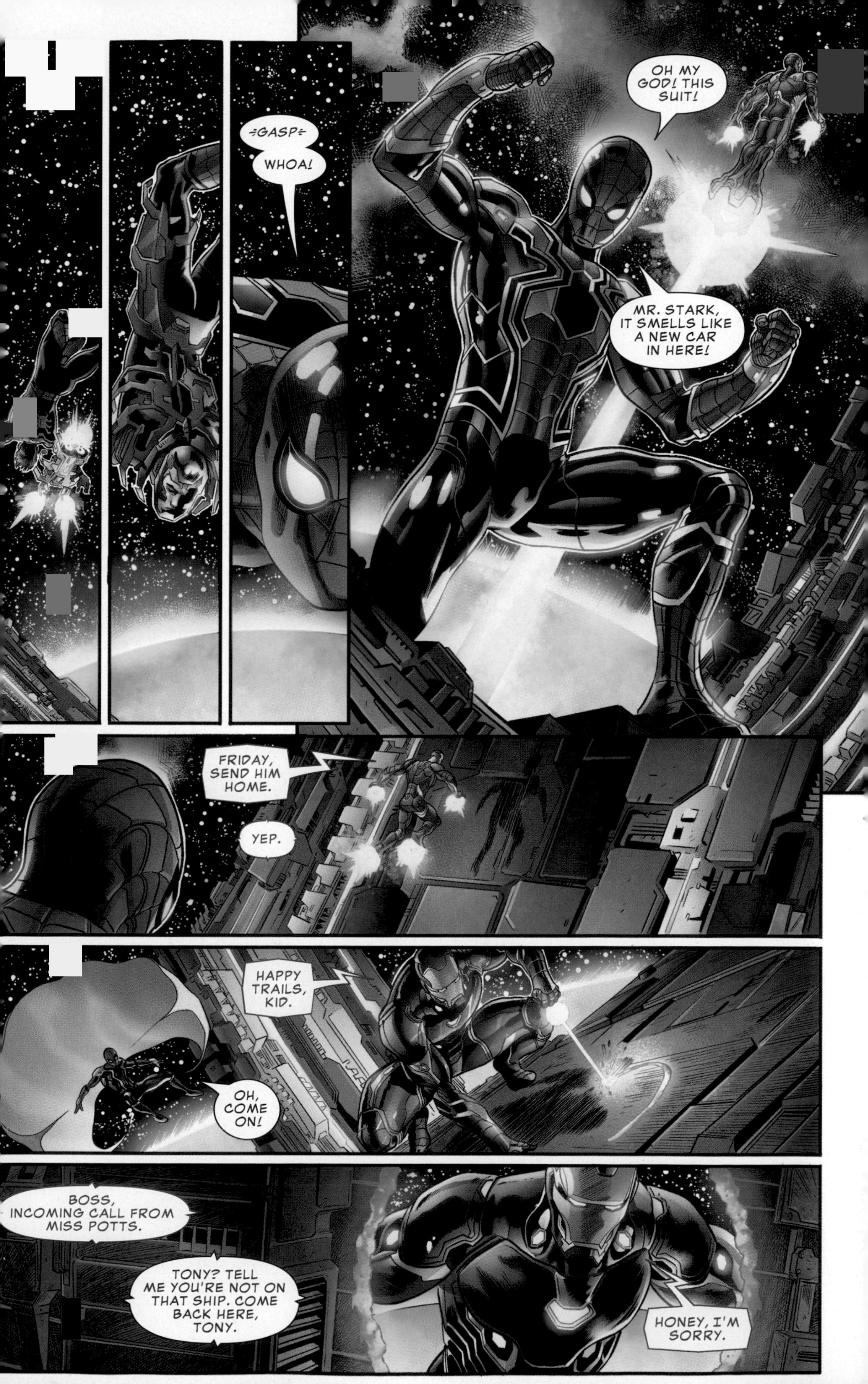

-GASP-
WHOA!
OH MY GOD! THIS SUIT!
MR. STARK, IT SMELLS LIKE A NEW CAR IN HERE!
FRIDAY, SEND HIM HOME.
YEP.
HAPPY TRAILS, KID.
OH, COME ON!
BOSS, INCOMING CALL FROM MISS POTTS.
TONY? TELL ME YOU'RE NOT ON THAT SHIP. COME BACK HERE, TONY.
HONEY, I'M SORRY.

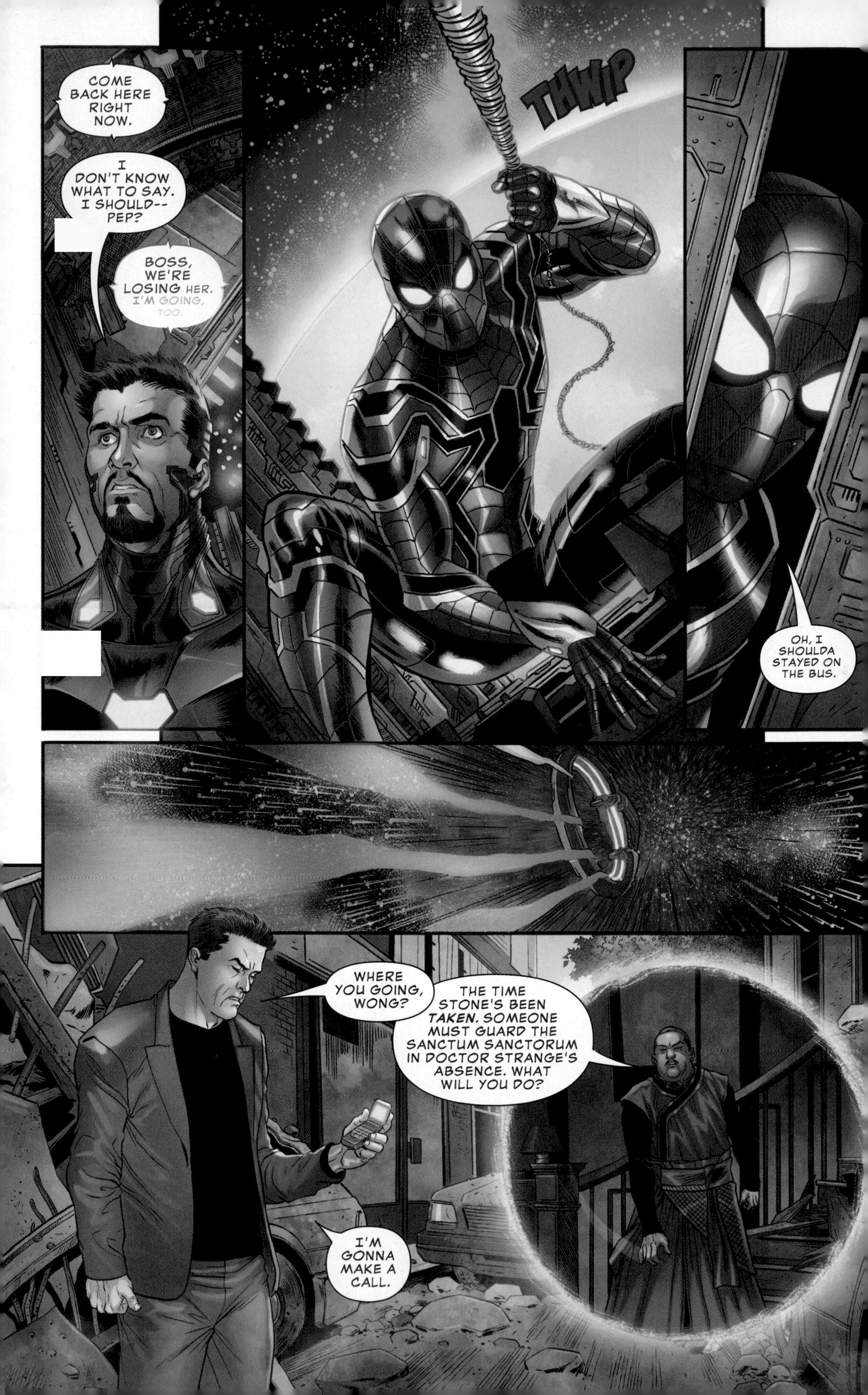
COME BACK HERE RIGHT NOW.
I DON'T KNOW WHAT TO SAY. I SHOULD-- PEP?
BOSS, WE'RE LOSING HER. I'M GOING, TOO.
THWIP
OH, I SHOULDA STAYED ON THE BUS.
WHERE YOU GOING, WONG?
THE TIME STONE'S BEEN *TAKEN.* SOMEONE MUST GUARD THE SANCTUM SANCTORUM IN DOCTOR STRANGE'S ABSENCE. WHAT WILL YOU DO?
I'M GONNA MAKE A CALL.

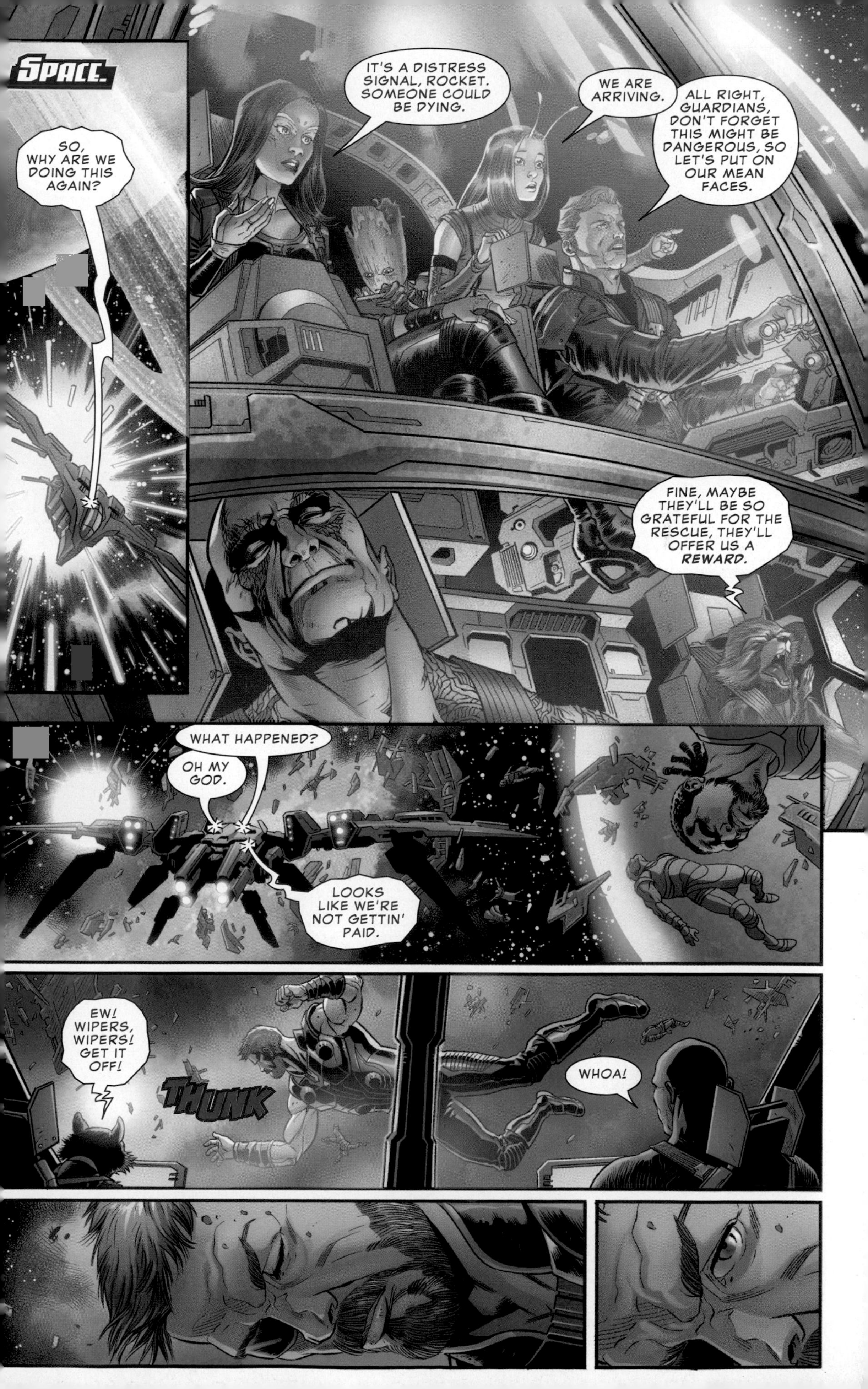
SPACE.
SO, WHY ARE WE DOING THIS AGAIN?
IT'S A DISTRESS SIGNAL, ROCKET. SOMEONE COULD BE DYING.
WE ARE ARRIVING.
ALL RIGHT, GUARDIANS, DON'T FORGET THIS MIGHT BE DANGEROUS, SO LET'S PUT ON OUR MEAN FACES.
FINE, MAYBE THEY'LL BE SO GRATEFUL FOR THE RESCUE, THEY'LL OFFER US A REWARD.
WHAT HAPPENED?
OH MY GOD.
LOOKS LIKE WE'RE NOT GETTIN' PAID.
EW! WIPERS, WIPERS! GET IT OFF!
THUNK
WHOA!

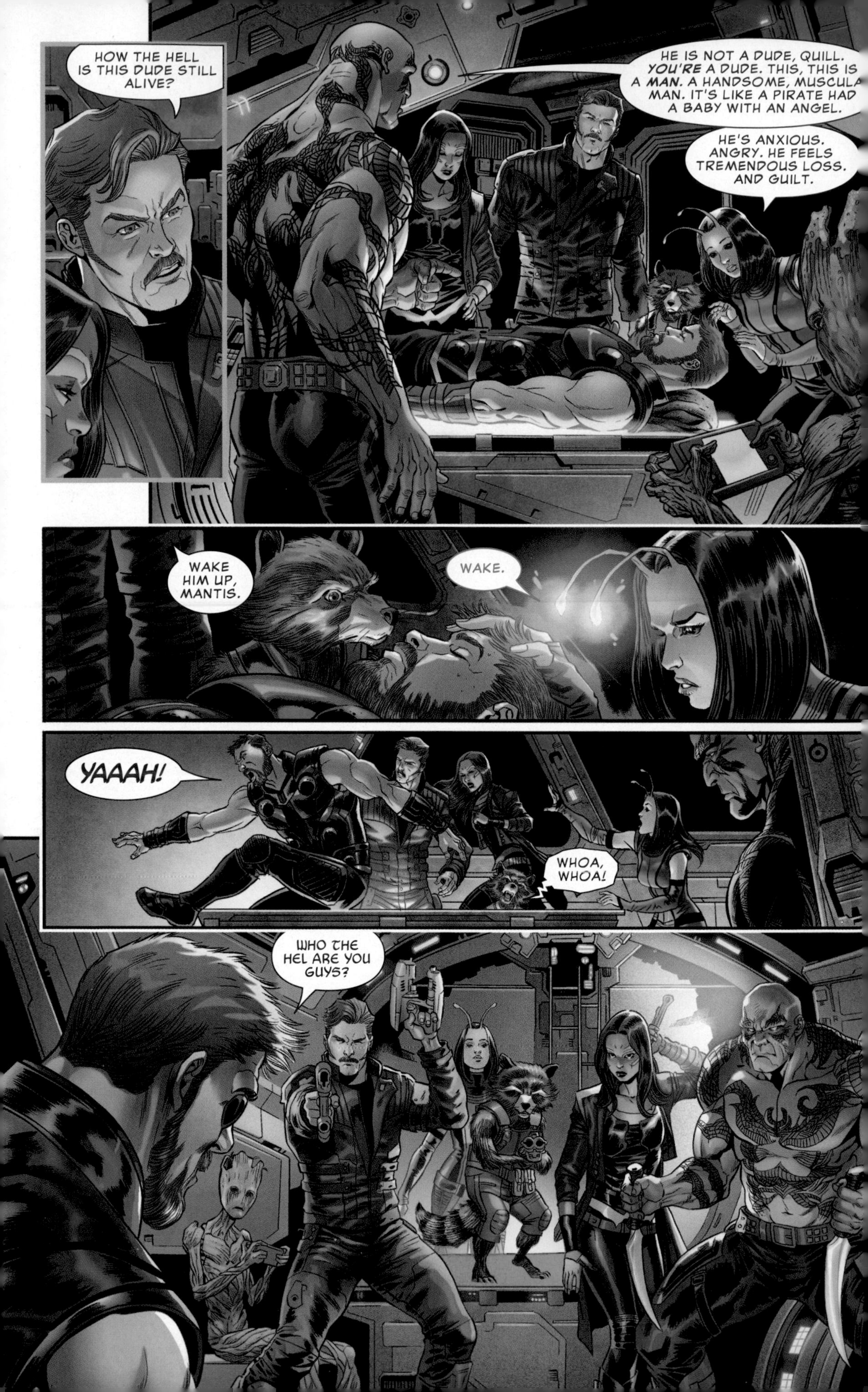
HOW THE HELL IS THIS DUDE STILL ALIVE?
HE IS NOT A DUDE, QUILL. YOU'RE A DUDE. THIS, THIS IS A MAN. A HANDSOME, MUSCULA MAN. IT'S LIKE A PIRATE HAD A BABY WITH AN ANGEL.
HE'S ANXIOUS. ANGRY. HE FEELS TREMENDOUS LOSS. AND GUILT.
WAKE HIM UP, MANTIS.
WAKE.
YAAAH!
WHOA, WHOA!
WHO THE HEL ARE YOU GUYS?

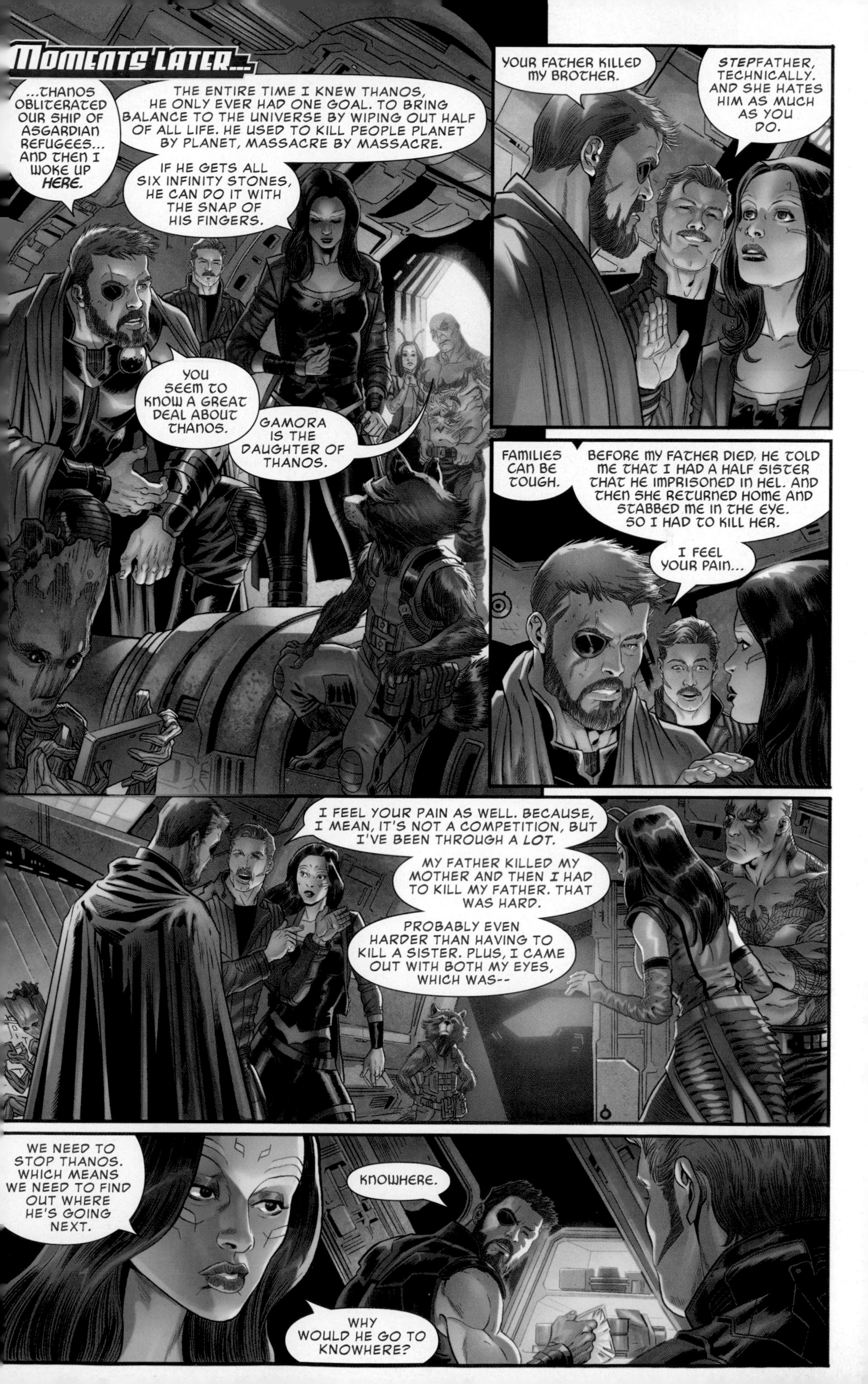
MOMENTS LATER...
...THANOS OBLITERATED OUR SHIP OF ASGARDIAN REFUGEES... AND THEN I WOKE UP HERE.
THE ENTIRE TIME I KNEW THANOS, HE ONLY EVER HAD ONE GOAL. TO BRING BALANCE TO THE UNIVERSE BY WIPING OUT HALF OF ALL LIFE. HE USED TO KILL PEOPLE PLANET BY PLANET, MASSACRE BY MASSACRE.
IF HE GETS ALL SIX INFINITY STONES, HE CAN DO IT WITH THE SNAP OF HIS FINGERS.
YOU SEEM TO KNOW A GREAT DEAL ABOUT THANOS.
GAMORA IS THE DAUGHTER OF THANOS.
YOUR FATHER KILLED MY BROTHER.
STEPFATHER, TECHNICALLY. AND SHE HATES HIM AS MUCH AS YOU DO.
FAMILIES CAN BE TOUGH.
BEFORE MY FATHER DIED, HE TOLD ME THAT I HAD A HALF SISTER THAT HE IMPRISONED IN HEL. AND THEN SHE RETURNED HOME AND STABBED ME IN THE EYE. SO I HAD TO KILL HER.
I FEEL YOUR PAIN...
I FEEL YOUR PAIN AS WELL. BECAUSE, I MEAN, IT'S NOT A COMPETITION, BUT I'VE BEEN THROUGH A LOT.
MY FATHER KILLED MY MOTHER AND THEN I HAD TO KILL MY FATHER. THAT WAS HARD.
PROBABLY EVEN HARDER THAN HAVING TO KILL A SISTER. PLUS, I CAME OUT WITH BOTH MY EYES, WHICH WAS--
WE NEED TO STOP THANOS. WHICH MEANS WE NEED TO FIND OUT WHERE HE'S GOING NEXT.
KNOWHERE.
WHY WOULD HE GO TO KNOWHERE?

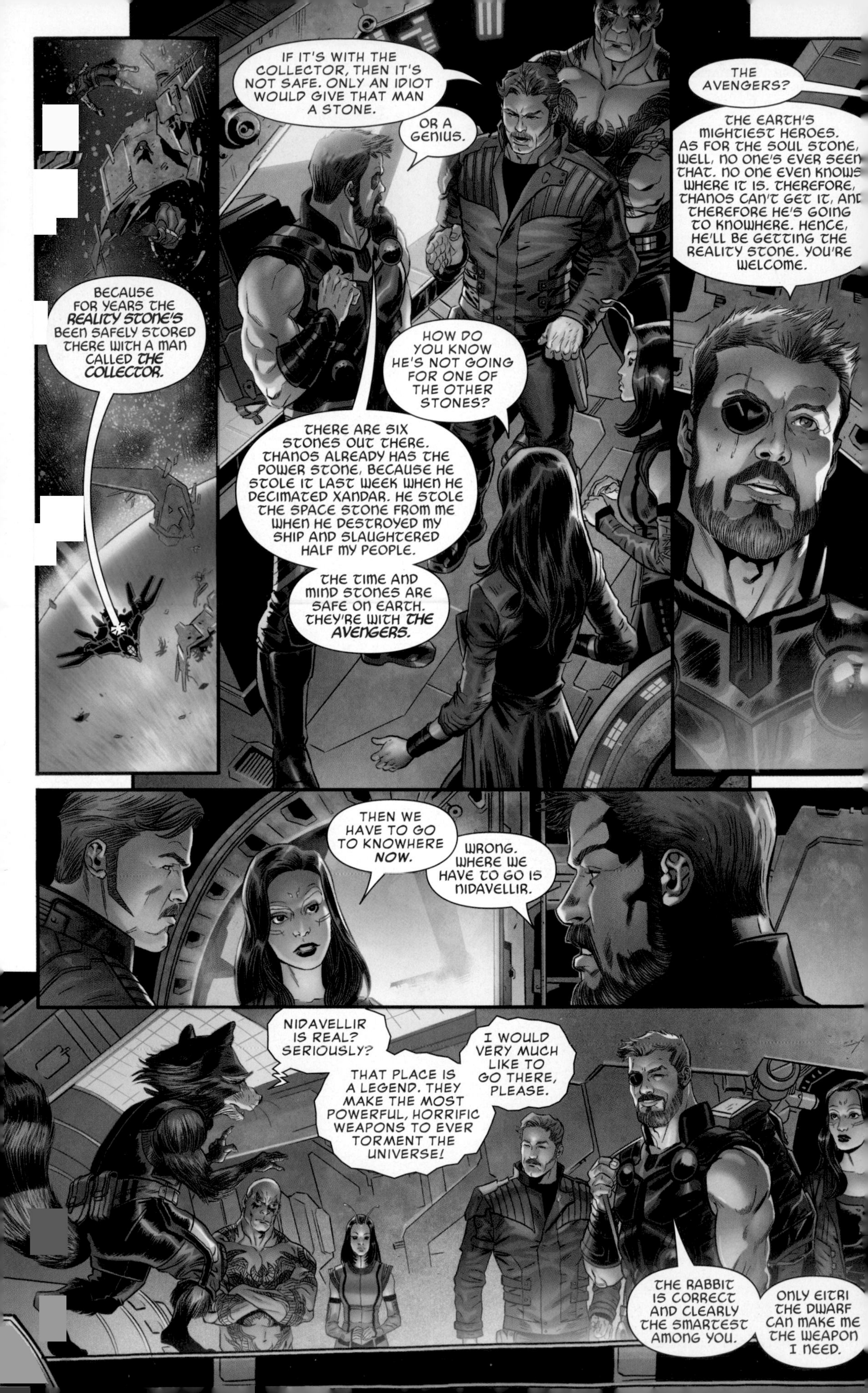
BECAUSE FOR YEARS THE REALITY STONE'S BEEN SAFELY STORED THERE WITH A MAN CALLED THE COLLECTOR.
IF IT'S WITH THE COLLECTOR, THEN IT'S NOT SAFE. ONLY AN IDIOT WOULD GIVE THAT MAN A STONE.
OR A GENIUS.
HOW DO YOU KNOW HE'S NOT GOING FOR ONE OF THE OTHER STONES?
THERE ARE SIX STONES OUT THERE. THANOS ALREADY HAS THE POWER STONE, BECAUSE HE STOLE IT LAST WEEK WHEN HE DECIMATED XANDAR. HE STOLE THE SPACE STONE FROM ME WHEN HE DESTROYED MY SHIP AND SLAUGHTERED HALF MY PEOPLE.
THE TIME AND MIND STONES ARE SAFE ON EARTH. THEY'RE WITH THE AVENGERS.
THE AVENGERS?
THE EARTH'S MIGHTIEST HEROES. AS FOR THE SOUL STONE, WELL, NO ONE'S EVER SEEN THAT. NO ONE EVEN KNOWS WHERE IT IS. THEREFORE, THANOS CAN'T GET IT, AND THEREFORE HE'S GOING TO KNOWHERE. HENCE, HE'LL BE GETTING THE REALITY STONE. YOU'RE WELCOME.
THEN WE HAVE TO GO TO KNOWHERE NOW.
WRONG. WHERE WE HAVE TO GO IS NIDAVELLIR.
NIDAVELLIR IS REAL? SERIOUSLY?
THAT PLACE IS A LEGEND. THEY MAKE THE MOST POWERFUL, HORRIFIC WEAPONS TO EVER TORMENT THE UNIVERSE!
I WOULD VERY MUCH LIKE TO GO THERE, PLEASE.
THE RABBIT IS CORRECT AND CLEARLY THE SMARTEST AMONG YOU.
ONLY EITRI THE DWARF CAN MAKE ME THE WEAPON I NEED.

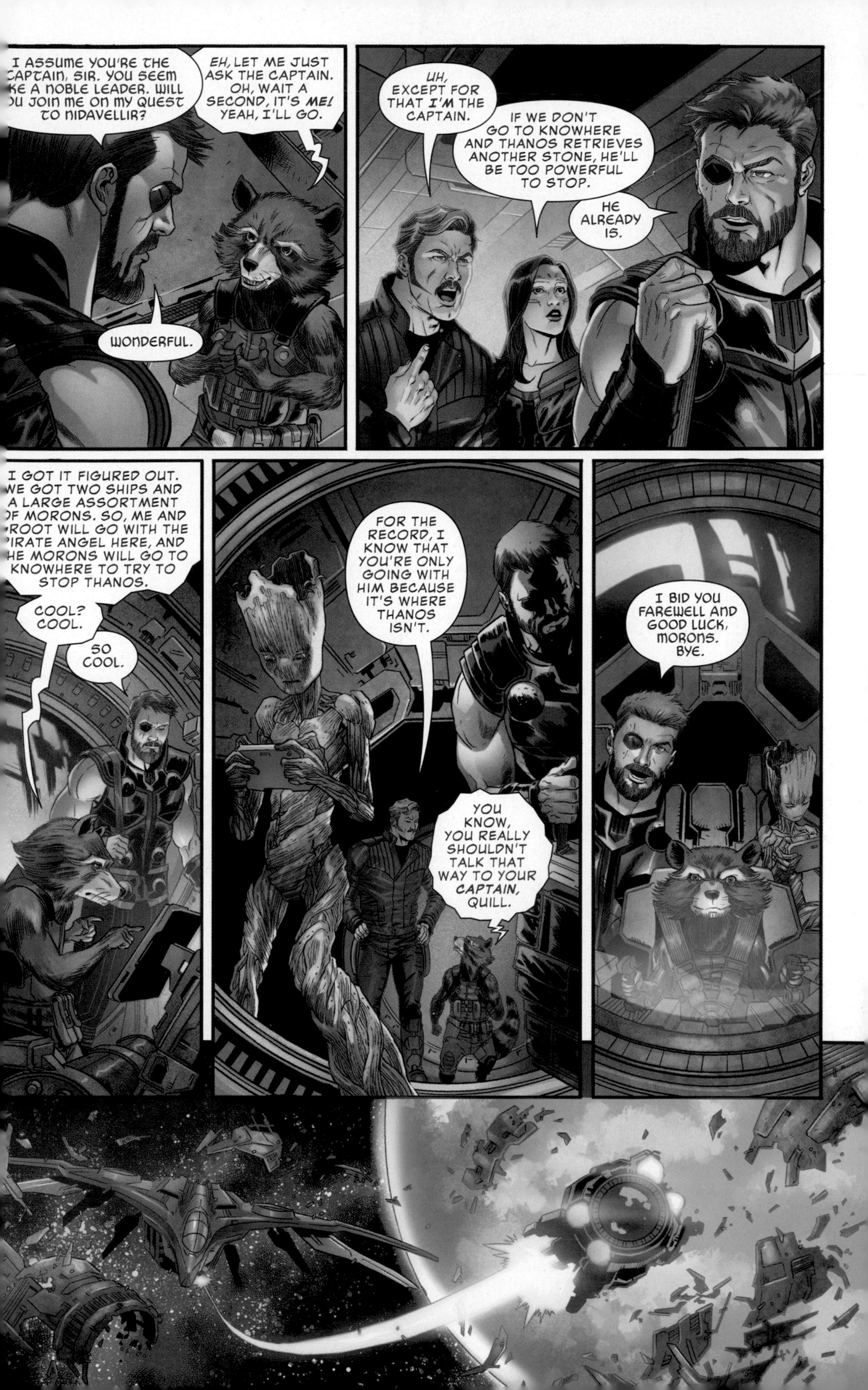
I ASSUME YOU'RE THE CAPTAIN, SIR. YOU SEEM KE A NOBLE LEADER. WILL OU JOIN ME ON MY QUEST TO NIDAVELLIR?
EH, LET ME JUST ASK THE CAPTAIN. OH, WAIT A SECOND, IT'S ME! YEAH, I'LL GO.
WONDERFUL.
UH, EXCEPT FOR THAT I'M THE CAPTAIN.
IF WE DON'T GO TO KNOWHERE AND THANOS RETRIEVES ANOTHER STONE, HE'LL BE TOO POWERFUL TO STOP.
HE ALREADY IS.
I GOT IT FIGURED OUT. WE GOT TWO SHIPS AND A LARGE ASSORTMENT OF MORONS. SO, ME AND ROOT WILL GO WITH THE IRATE ANGEL HERE, AND HE MORONS WILL GO TO KNOWHERE TO TRY TO STOP THANOS.
COOL? COOL.
SO COOL.
FOR THE RECORD, I KNOW THAT YOU'RE ONLY GOING WITH HIM BECAUSE IT'S WHERE THANOS ISN'T.
YOU KNOW, YOU REALLY SHOULDN'T TALK THAT WAY TO YOUR CAPTAIN, QUILL.
I BID YOU FAREWELL AND GOOD LUCK, MORONS. BYE.

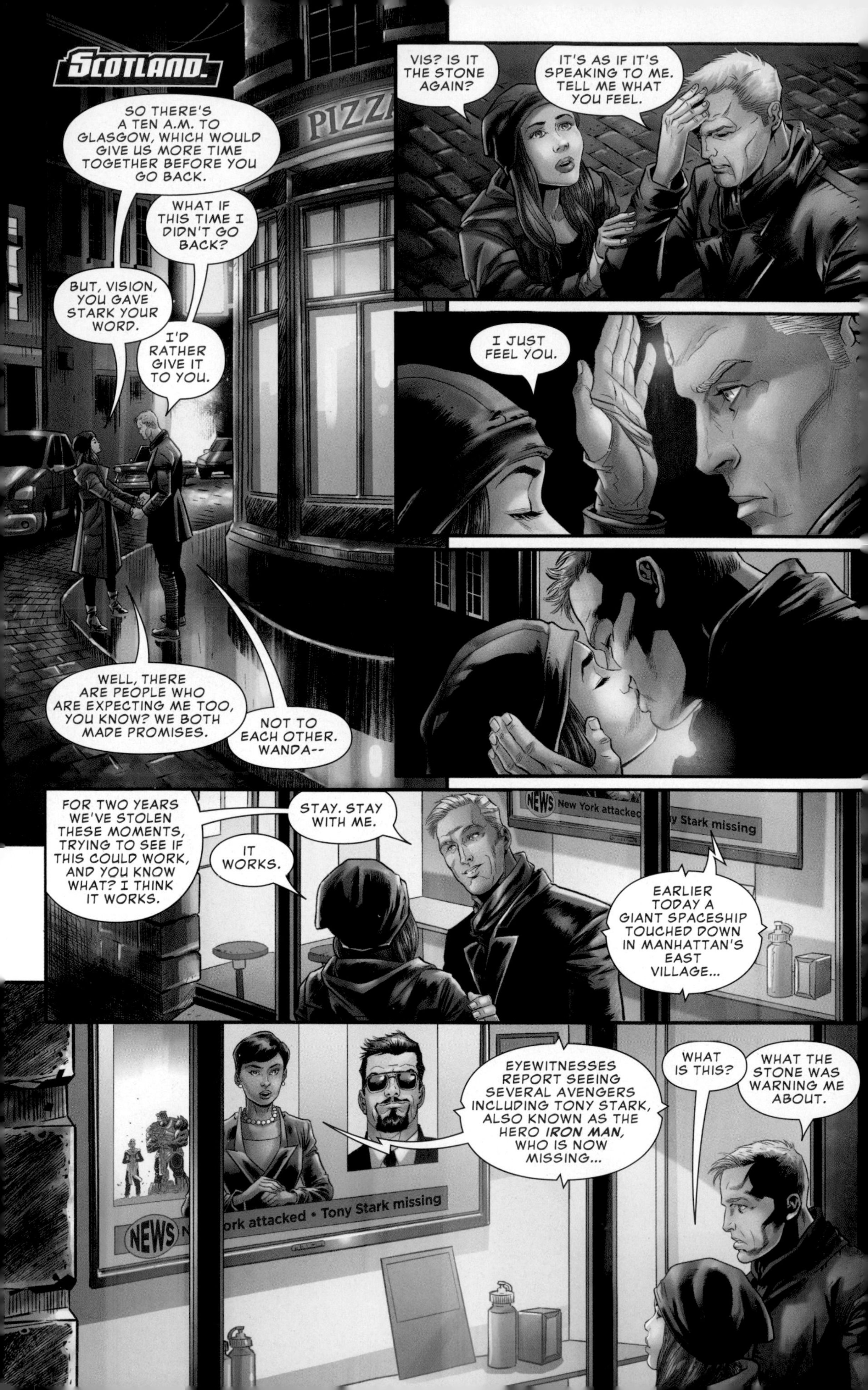
SCOTLAND.
SO THERE'S A TEN A.M. TO GLASGOW, WHICH WOULD GIVE US MORE TIME TOGETHER BEFORE YOU GO BACK.
WHAT IF THIS TIME I DIDN'T GO BACK?
BUT, VISION, YOU GAVE STARK YOUR WORD.
I'D RATHER GIVE IT TO YOU.
WELL, THERE ARE PEOPLE WHO ARE EXPECTING ME TOO, YOU KNOW? WE BOTH MADE PROMISES.
NOT TO EACH OTHER. WANDA--
VIS? IS IT THE STONE AGAIN?
IT'S AS IF IT'S SPEAKING TO ME. TELL ME WHAT YOU FEEL.
I JUST FEEL YOU.
FOR TWO YEARS WE'VE STOLEN THESE MOMENTS, TRYING TO SEE IF THIS COULD WORK, AND YOU KNOW WHAT? I THINK IT WORKS.
IT WORKS.
STAY. STAY WITH ME.
EARLIER TODAY A GIANT SPACESHIP TOUCHED DOWN IN MANHATTAN'S EAST VILLAGE...
EYEWITNESSES REPORT SEEING SEVERAL AVENGERS INCLUDING TONY STARK, ALSO KNOWN AS THE HERO IRON MAN, WHO IS NOW MISSING...
WHAT IS THIS?
WHAT THE STONE WAS WARNING ME ABOUT.

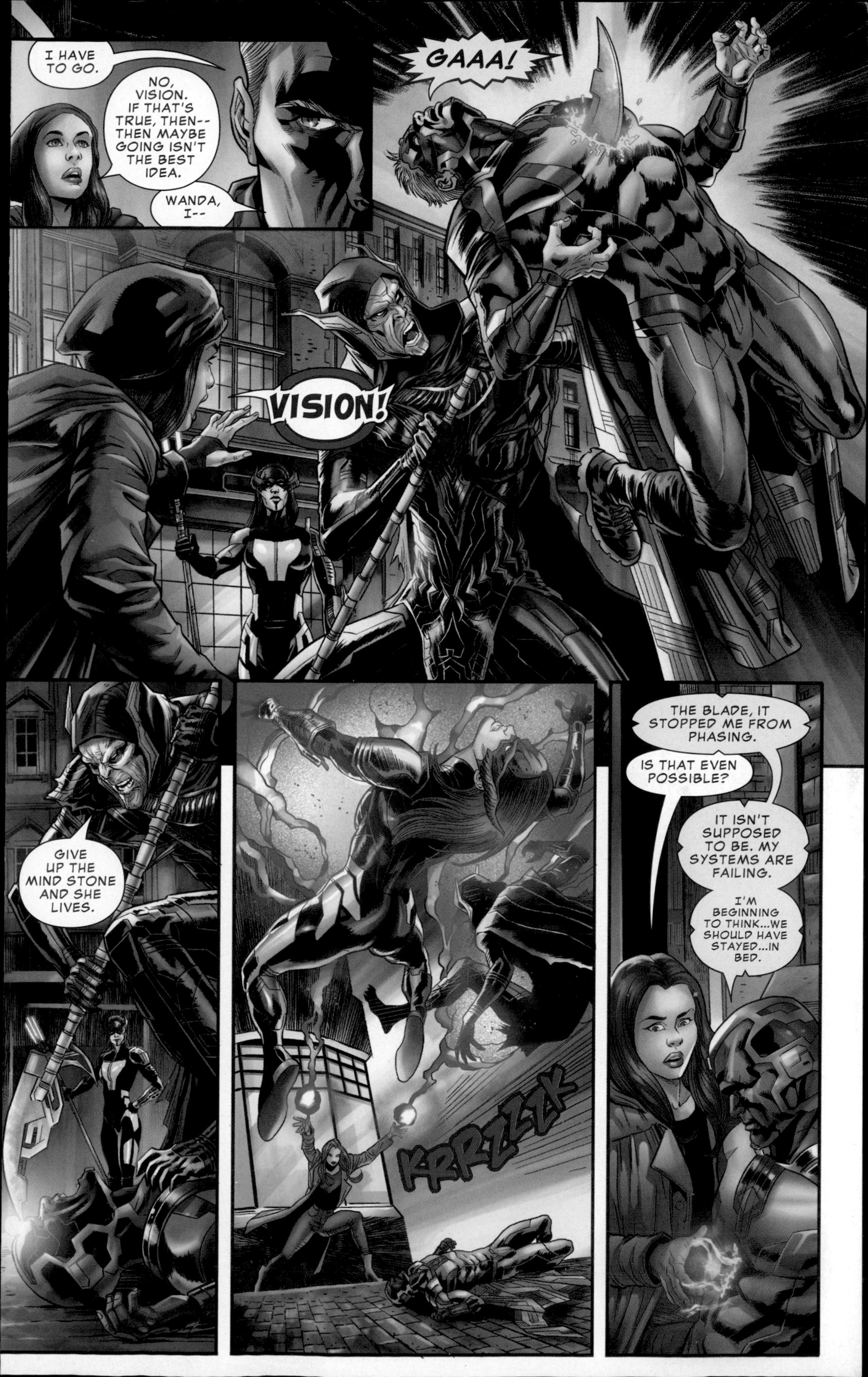
I HAVE TO GO.
NO, VISION. IF THAT'S TRUE, THEN-- THEN MAYBE GOING ISN'T THE BEST IDEA.
WANDA, I--
GAAA!
VISION!
GIVE UP THE MIND STONE AND SHE LIVES.
KRRZZZK
THE BLADE, IT STOPPED ME FROM PHASING.
IS THAT EVEN POSSIBLE?
IT ISN'T SUPPOSED TO BE. MY SYSTEMS ARE FAILING.
I'M BEGINNING TO THINK...WE SHOULD HAVE STAYED...IN BED.

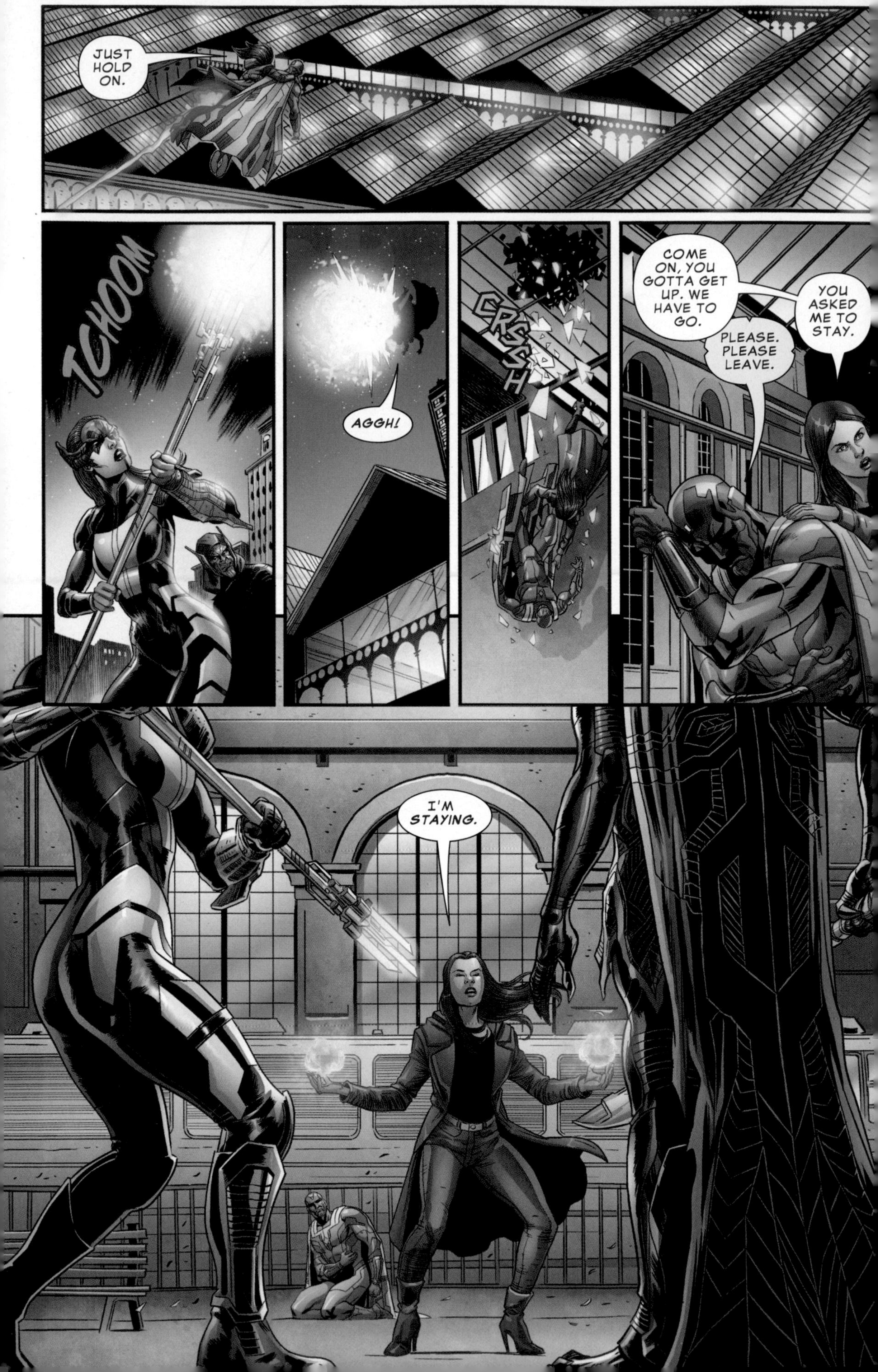
JUST HOLD ON.
TCHOOM
AGGH!
CRSSH
COME ON, YOU GOTTA GET UP. WE HAVE TO GO.
YOU ASKED ME TO STAY.
PLEASE. PLEASE LEAVE.
I'M STAYING.

MARVEL'S AVENGERS: ENDGAME
PRELUDE #2

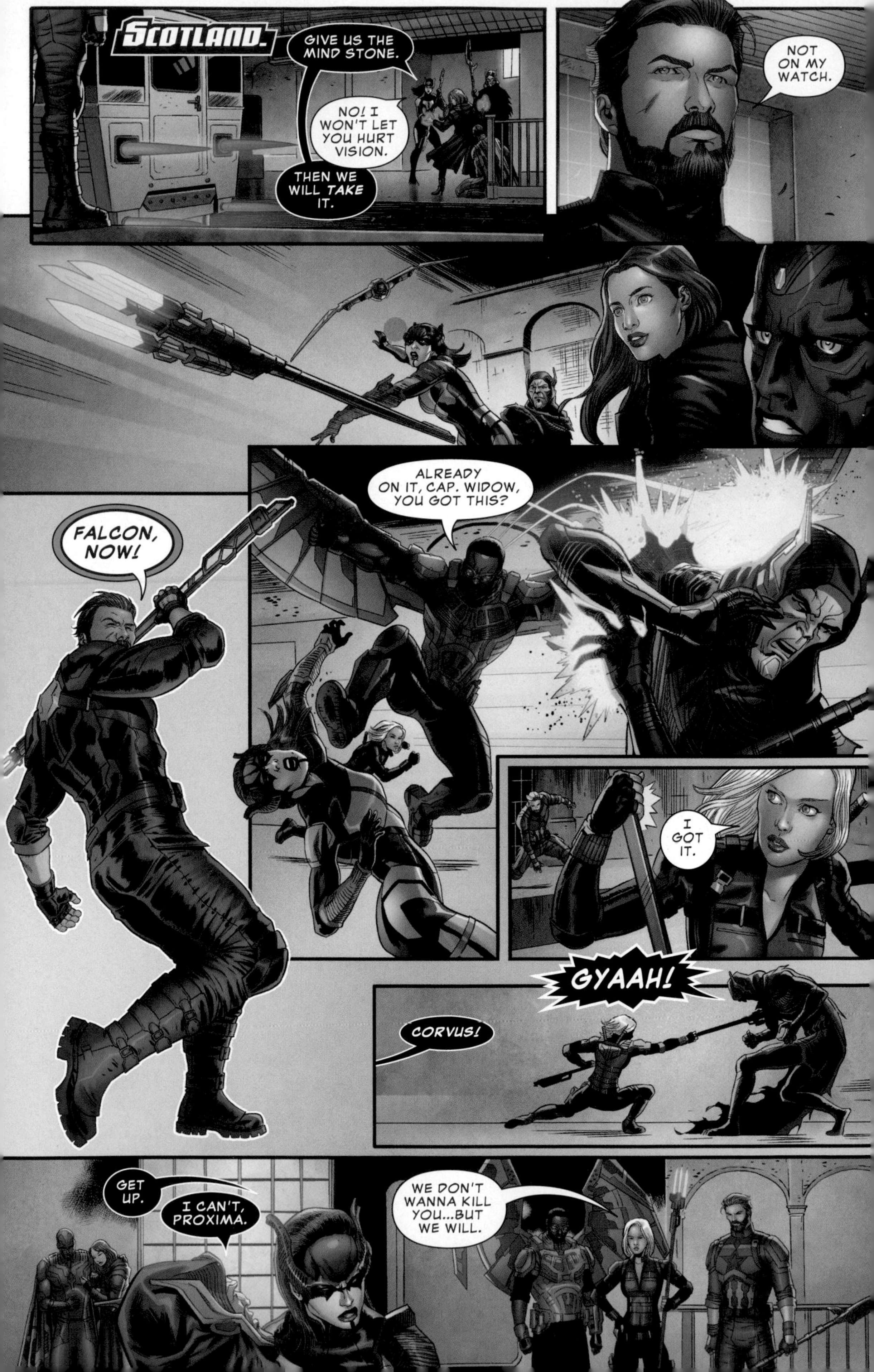
SCOTLAND.
GIVE US THE MIND STONE.
NO! I WON'T LET YOU HURT VISION.
THEN WE WILL TAKE IT.
NOT ON MY WATCH.
FALCON, NOW!
ALREADY ON IT, CAP. WIDOW, YOU GOT THIS?
I GOT IT.
GYAAH!
CORVUS!
GET UP.
I CAN'T, PROXIMA.
WE DON'T WANNA KILL YOU...BUT WE WILL.

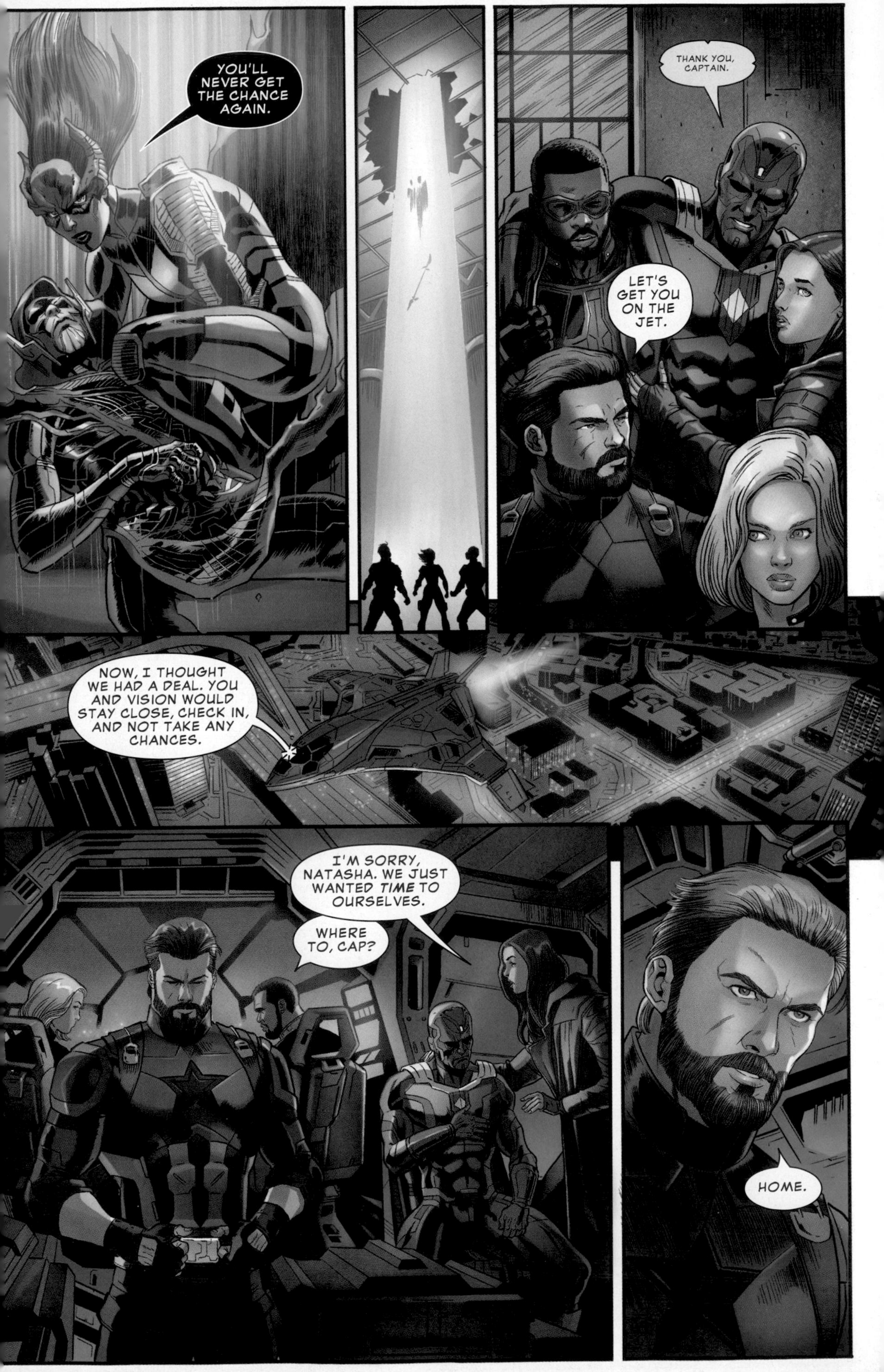
YOU'LL NEVER GET THE CHANCE AGAIN.
THANK YOU, CAPTAIN.
LET'S GET YOU ON THE JET.
NOW, I THOUGHT WE HAD A DEAL. YOU AND VISION WOULD STAY CLOSE, CHECK IN, AND NOT TAKE ANY CHANCES.
I'M SORRY, NATASHA. WE JUST WANTED *TIME* TO OURSELVES.
WHERE TO, CAP?
HOME.

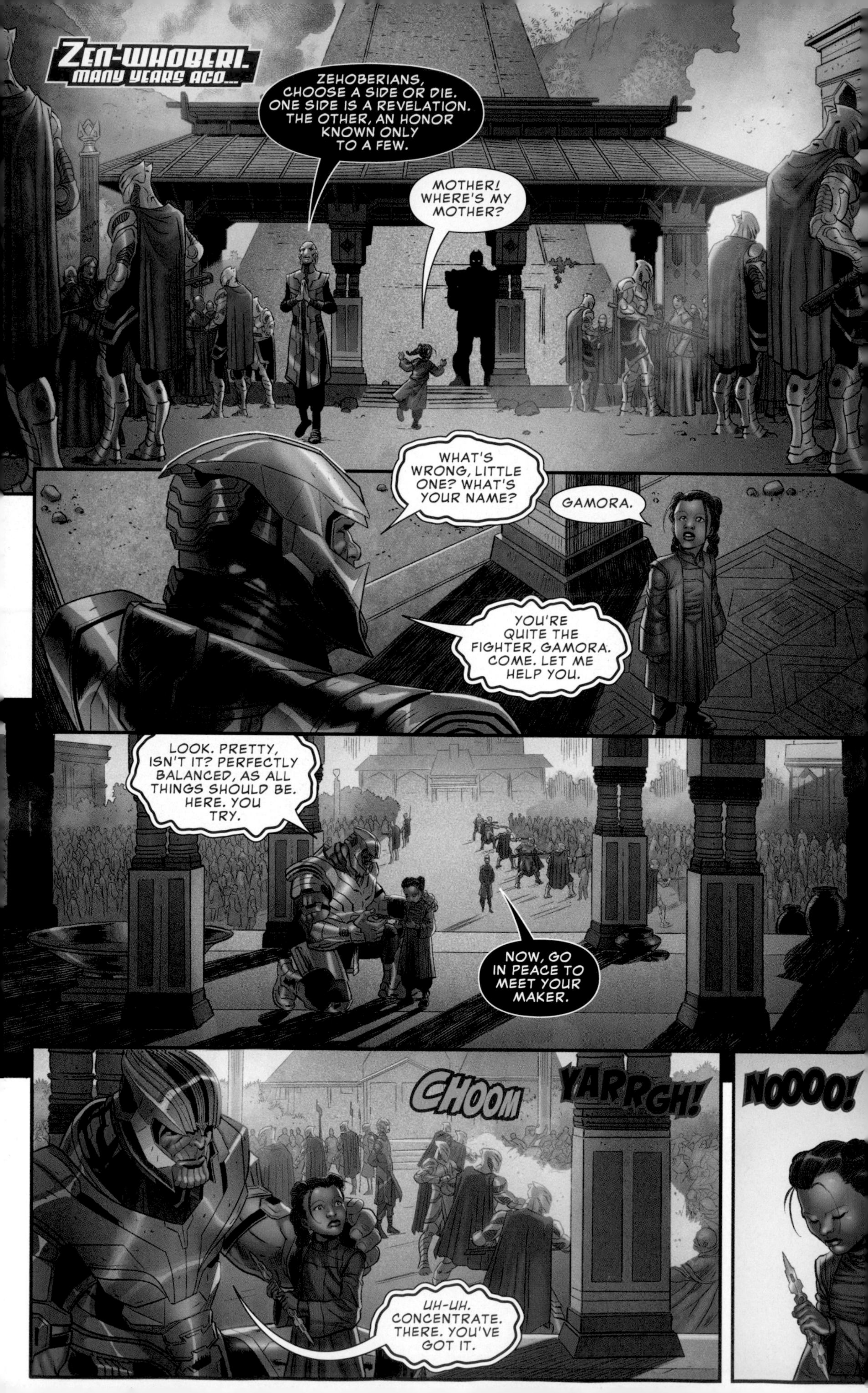
ZEN-WHOBERI. MANY YEARS AGO...
ZEHOBERIANS, CHOOSE A SIDE OR DIE. ONE SIDE IS A REVELATION. THE OTHER, AN HONOR KNOWN ONLY TO A FEW.
MOTHER! WHERE'S MY MOTHER?
WHAT'S WRONG, LITTLE ONE? WHAT'S YOUR NAME?
GAMORA.
YOU'RE QUITE THE FIGHTER, GAMORA. COME. LET ME HELP YOU.
LOOK. PRETTY, ISN'T IT? PERFECTLY BALANCED, AS ALL THINGS SHOULD BE. HERE. YOU TRY.
NOW, GO IN PEACE TO MEET YOUR MAKER.
CHOOM
YARRGH!
NOOOO!
UH-UH. CONCENTRATE. THERE. YOU'VE GOT IT.

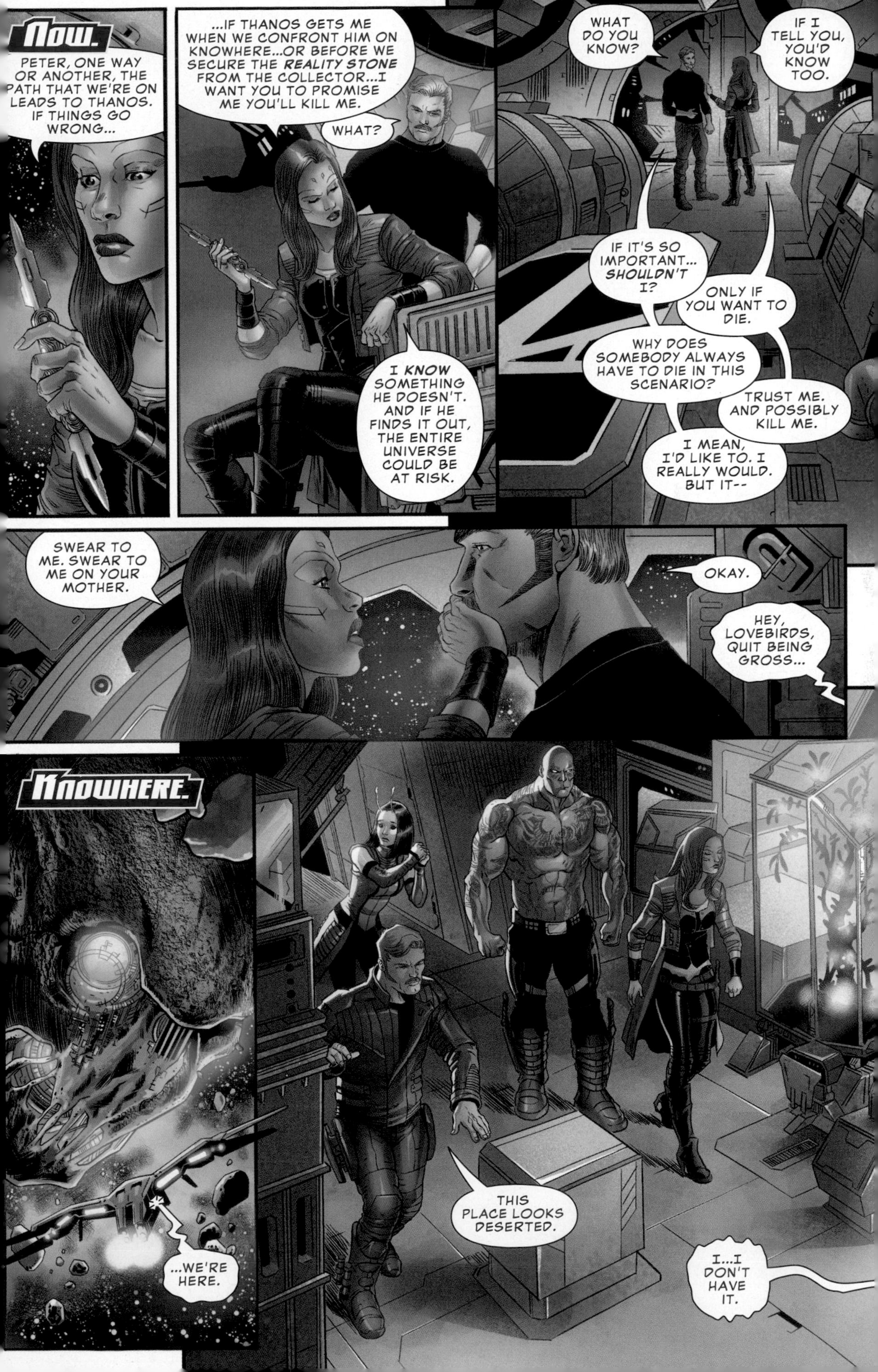
NOW.
PETER, ONE WAY OR ANOTHER, THE PATH THAT WE'RE ON LEADS TO THANOS. IF THINGS GO WRONG...
...IF THANOS GETS ME WHEN WE CONFRONT HIM ON KNOWHERE...OR BEFORE WE SECURE THE REALITY STONE FROM THE COLLECTOR...I WANT YOU TO PROMISE ME YOU'LL KILL ME.
WHAT?
I KNOW SOMETHING HE DOESN'T. AND IF HE FINDS IT OUT, THE ENTIRE UNIVERSE COULD BE AT RISK.
WHAT DO YOU KNOW?
IF I TELL YOU, YOU'D KNOW TOO.
IF IT'S SO IMPORTANT... SHOULDN'T I?
ONLY IF YOU WANT TO DIE.
WHY DOES SOMEBODY ALWAYS HAVE TO DIE IN THIS SCENARIO?
TRUST ME. AND POSSIBLY KILL ME.
I MEAN, I'D LIKE TO. I REALLY WOULD. BUT IT--
SWEAR TO ME. SWEAR TO ME ON YOUR MOTHER.
OKAY.
HEY, LOVEBIRDS, QUIT BEING GROSS...
KNOWHERE.
...WE'RE HERE.
THIS PLACE LOOKS DESERTED.
I...I DON'T HAVE IT.

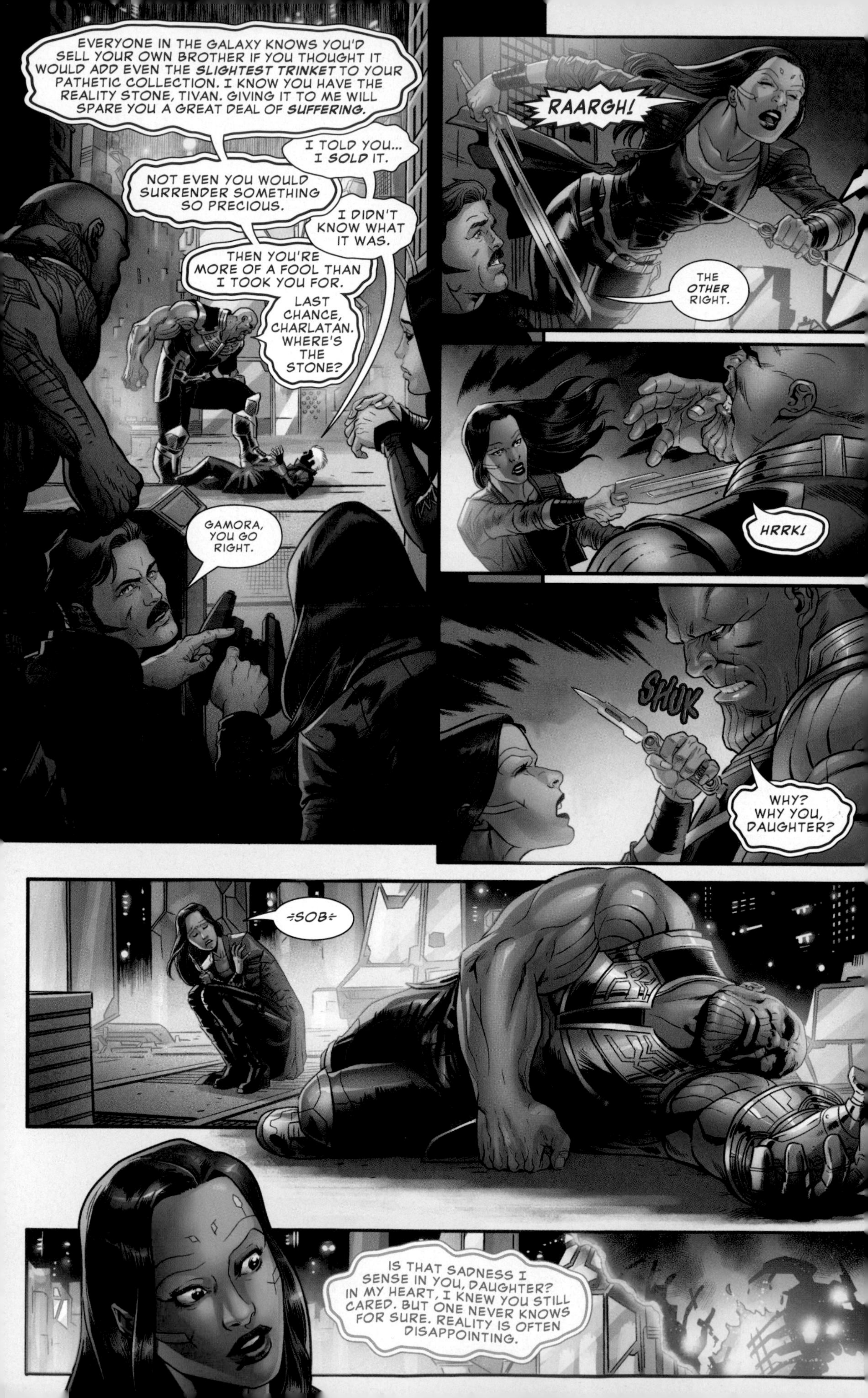
EVERYONE IN THE GALAXY KNOWS YOU'D SELL YOUR OWN BROTHER IF YOU THOUGHT IT WOULD ADD EVEN THE SLIGHTEST TRINKET TO YOUR PATHETIC COLLECTION. I KNOW YOU HAVE THE REALITY STONE, TIVAN. GIVING IT TO ME WILL SPARE YOU A GREAT DEAL OF SUFFERING.
I TOLD YOU... I SOLD IT.
NOT EVEN YOU WOULD SURRENDER SOMETHING SO PRECIOUS.
I DIDN'T KNOW WHAT IT WAS.
THEN YOU'RE MORE OF A FOOL THAN I TOOK YOU FOR.
LAST CHANCE, CHARLATAN. WHERE'S THE STONE?
GAMORA, YOU GO RIGHT.
RAARGH!
THE OTHER RIGHT.
HRRK!
SHUK
WHY? WHY YOU, DAUGHTER?
SOB
IS THAT SADNESS I SENSE IN YOU, DAUGHTER? IN MY HEART, I KNEW YOU STILL CARED. BUT ONE NEVER KNOWS FOR SURE. REALITY IS OFTEN DISAPPOINTING.

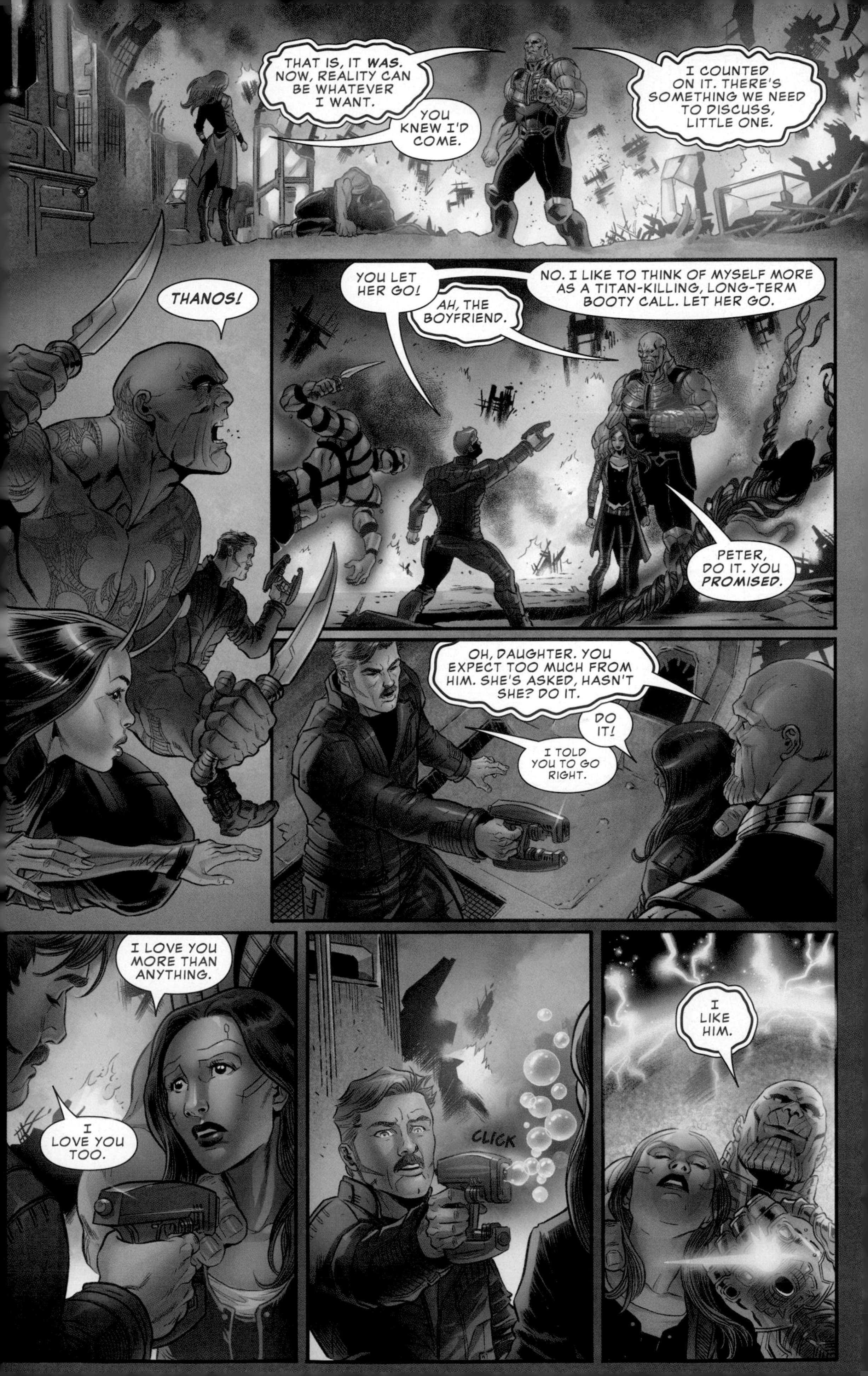
THAT IS, IT WAS. NOW, REALITY CAN BE WHATEVER I WANT.
YOU KNEW I'D COME.
I COUNTED ON IT. THERE'S SOMETHING WE NEED TO DISCUSS, LITTLE ONE.
THANOS!
YOU LET HER GO!
AH, THE BOYFRIEND.
NO. I LIKE TO THINK OF MYSELF MORE AS A TITAN-KILLING, LONG-TERM BOOTY CALL. LET HER GO.
PETER, DO IT. YOU PROMISED.
OH, DAUGHTER. YOU EXPECT TOO MUCH FROM HIM. SHE'S ASKED, HASN'T SHE? DO IT.
DO IT!
I TOLD YOU TO GO RIGHT.
I LOVE YOU MORE THAN ANYTHING.
I LOVE YOU TOO.
CLICK
I LIKE HIM.

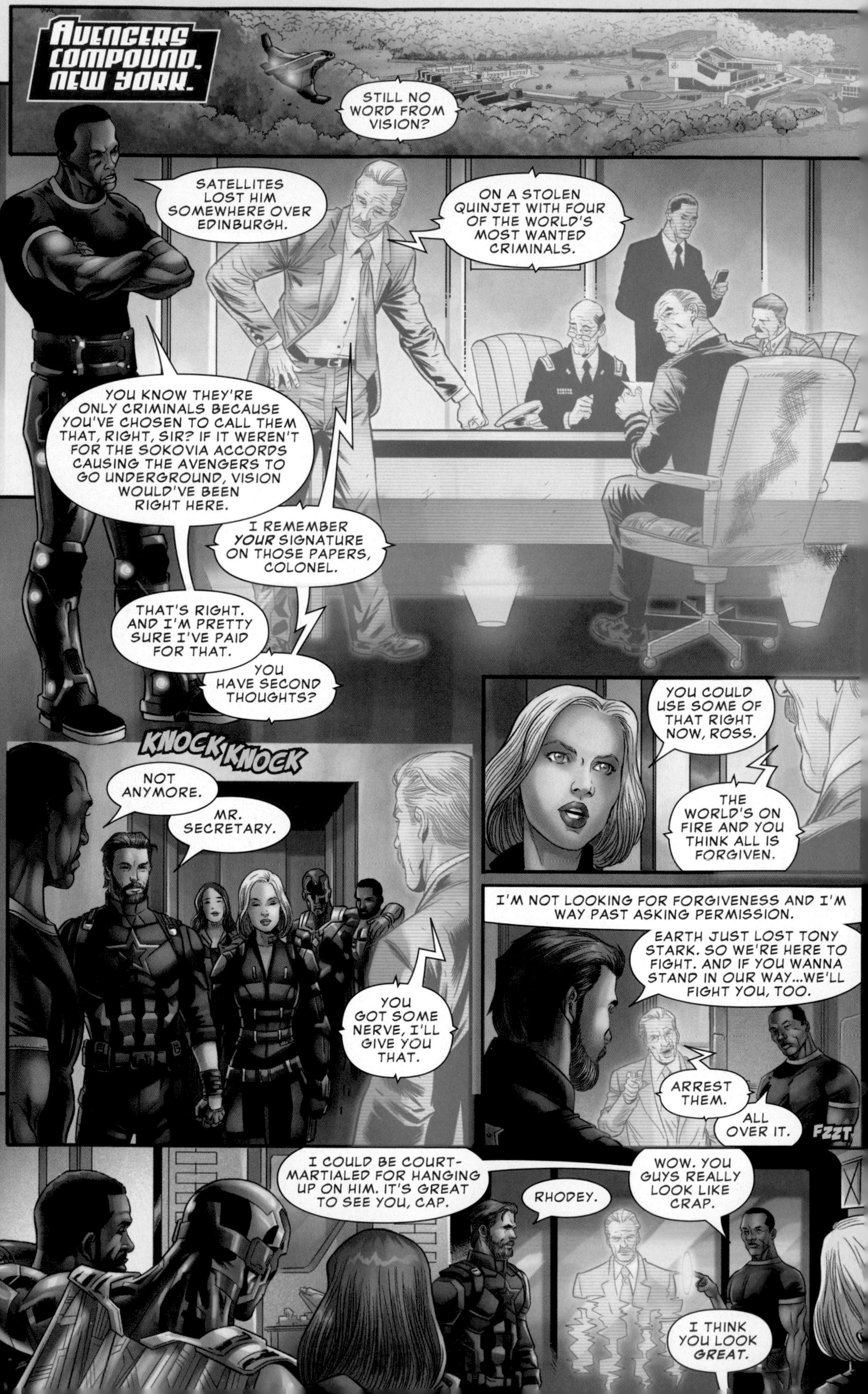
AVENGERS COMPOUND, NEW YORK.
STILL NO WORD FROM VISION?
SATELLITES LOST HIM SOMEWHERE OVER EDINBURGH.
ON A STOLEN QUINJET WITH FOUR OF THE WORLD'S MOST WANTED CRIMINALS.
YOU KNOW THEY'RE ONLY CRIMINALS BECAUSE YOU'VE CHOSEN TO CALL THEM THAT, RIGHT, SIR? IF IT WEREN'T FOR THE SOKOVIA ACCORDS CAUSING THE AVENGERS TO GO UNDERGROUND, VISION WOULD'VE BEEN RIGHT HERE.
I REMEMBER *YOUR* SIGNATURE ON THOSE PAPERS, COLONEL.
THAT'S RIGHT. AND I'M PRETTY SURE I'VE PAID FOR THAT.
YOU HAVE SECOND THOUGHTS?
KNOCK KNOCK
NOT ANYMORE.
MR. SECRETARY.
YOU GOT SOME NERVE, I'LL GIVE YOU THAT.
YOU COULD USE SOME OF THAT RIGHT NOW, ROSS.
THE WORLD'S ON FIRE AND YOU THINK ALL IS FORGIVEN.
I'M NOT LOOKING FOR FORGIVENESS AND I'M WAY PAST ASKING PERMISSION.
EARTH JUST LOST TONY STARK. SO WE'RE HERE TO FIGHT. AND IF YOU WANNA STAND IN OUR WAY...WE'LL FIGHT YOU, TOO.
ARREST THEM.
ALL OVER IT.
FZZT
I COULD BE COURT-MARTIALED FOR HANGING UP ON HIM. IT'S GREAT TO SEE YOU, CAP.
RHODEY.
WOW. YOU GUYS REALLY LOOK LIKE CRAP.
I THINK YOU LOOK *GREAT.*

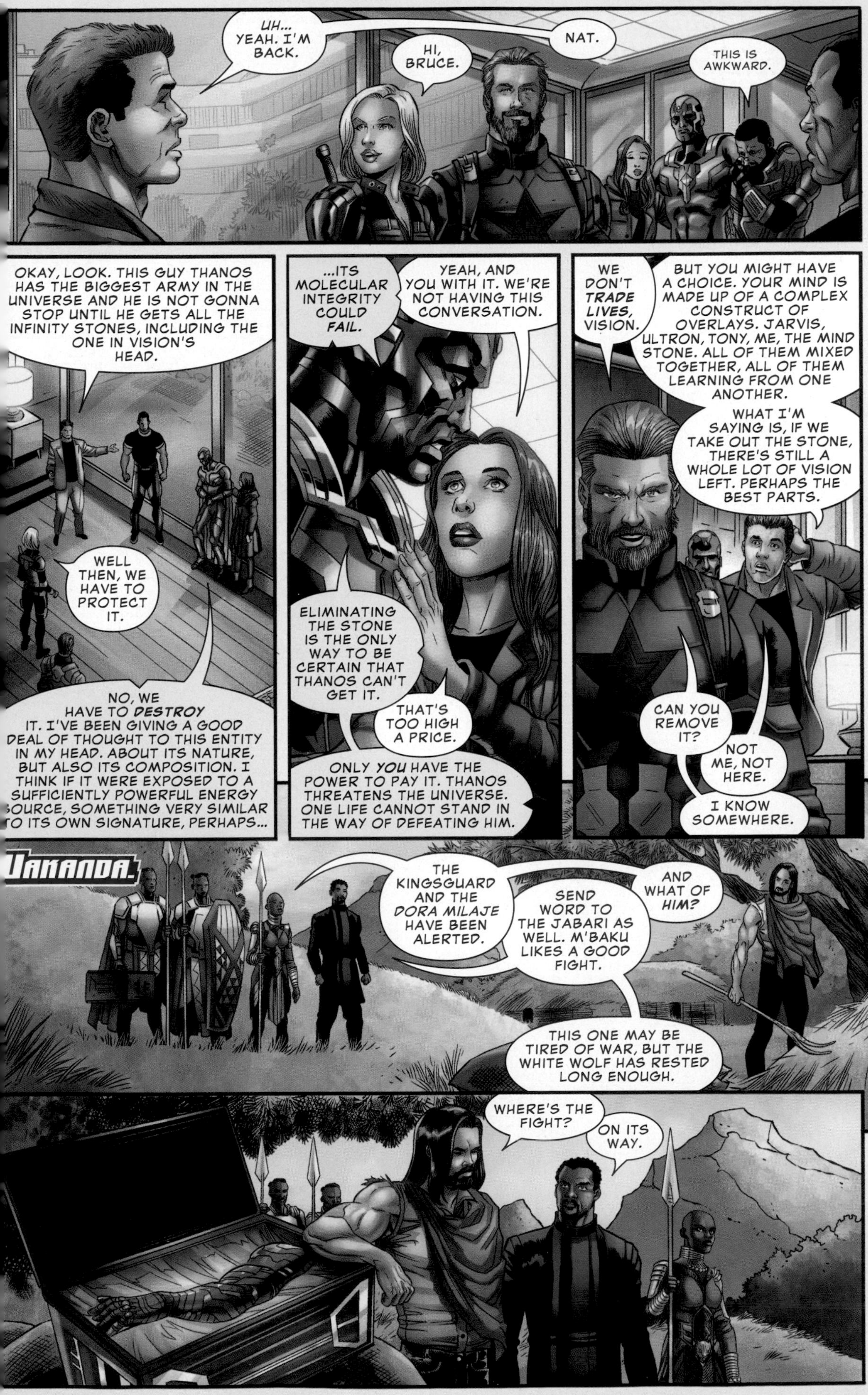
UH... YEAH. I'M BACK.
HI, BRUCE.
NAT.
THIS IS AWKWARD.
OKAY, LOOK. THIS GUY THANOS HAS THE BIGGEST ARMY IN THE UNIVERSE AND HE IS NOT GONNA STOP UNTIL HE GETS ALL THE INFINITY STONES, INCLUDING THE ONE IN VISION'S HEAD.
WELL THEN, WE HAVE TO PROTECT IT.
NO, WE HAVE TO *DESTROY* IT. I'VE BEEN GIVING A GOOD DEAL OF THOUGHT TO THIS ENTITY IN MY HEAD. ABOUT ITS NATURE, BUT ALSO ITS COMPOSITION. I THINK IF IT WERE EXPOSED TO A SUFFICIENTLY POWERFUL ENERGY SOURCE, SOMETHING VERY SIMILAR TO ITS OWN SIGNATURE, PERHAPS...
...ITS MOLECULAR INTEGRITY COULD *FAIL.*
YEAH, AND YOU WITH IT. WE'RE NOT HAVING THIS CONVERSATION.
ELIMINATING THE STONE IS THE ONLY WAY TO BE CERTAIN THAT THANOS CAN'T GET IT.
THAT'S TOO HIGH A PRICE.
ONLY *YOU* HAVE THE POWER TO PAY IT. THANOS THREATENS THE UNIVERSE. ONE LIFE CANNOT STAND IN THE WAY OF DEFEATING HIM.
WE DON'T *TRADE LIVES,* VISION.
BUT YOU MIGHT HAVE A CHOICE. YOUR MIND IS MADE UP OF A COMPLEX CONSTRUCT OF OVERLAYS. JARVIS, ULTRON, TONY, ME, THE MIND STONE. ALL OF THEM MIXED TOGETHER, ALL OF THEM LEARNING FROM ONE ANOTHER.
WHAT I'M SAYING IS, IF WE TAKE OUT THE STONE, THERE'S STILL A WHOLE LOT OF VISION LEFT. PERHAPS THE BEST PARTS.
CAN YOU REMOVE IT?
NOT ME, NOT HERE.
I KNOW SOMEWHERE.
WAKANDA.
THE KINGSGUARD AND THE *DORA MILAJE* HAVE BEEN ALERTED.
SEND WORD TO THE JABARI AS WELL. M'BAKU LIKES A GOOD FIGHT.
AND WHAT OF *HIM?*
THIS ONE MAY BE TIRED OF WAR, BUT THE WHITE WOLF HAS RESTED LONG ENOUGH.
WHERE'S THE FIGHT?
ON ITS WAY.

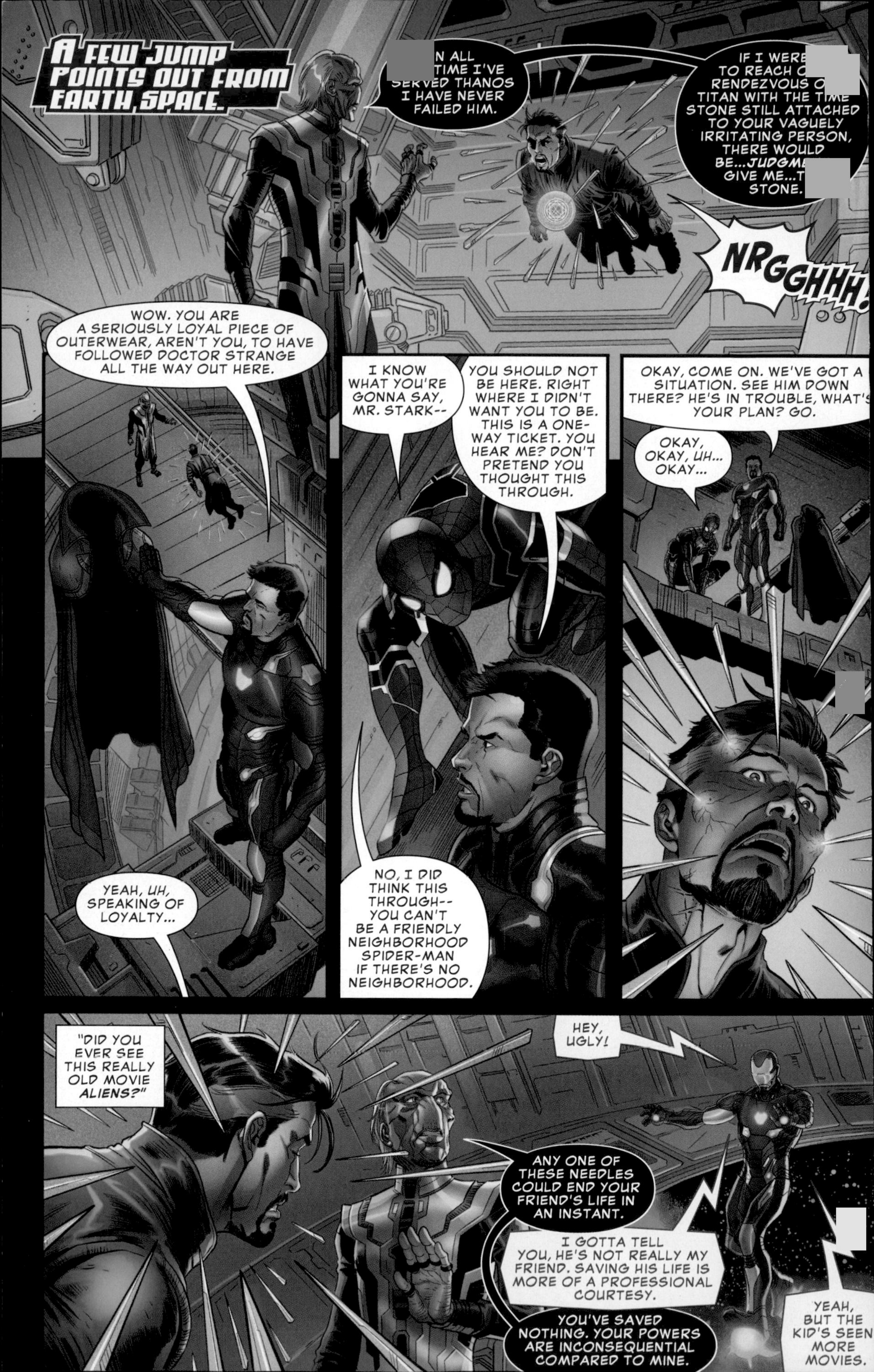
A FEW JUMP POINTS OUT FROM EARTH, SPACE.
ALL TIME I'VE SERVED THANOS I HAVE NEVER FAILED HIM.
IF I WERE TO REACH RENDEZVOUS TITAN WITH THE TIME STONE STILL ATTACHED TO YOUR VAGUELY IRRITATING PERSON, THERE WOULD BE... GIVE ME... STONE.
NRGGHHH!
WOW. YOU ARE A SERIOUSLY LOYAL PIECE OF OUTERWEAR, AREN'T YOU, TO HAVE FOLLOWED DOCTOR STRANGE ALL THE WAY OUT HERE.
YEAH, UH, SPEAKING OF LOYALTY...
I KNOW WHAT YOU'RE GONNA SAY, MR. STARK--
YOU SHOULD NOT BE HERE. RIGHT WHERE I DIDN'T WANT YOU TO BE. THIS IS A ONE-WAY TICKET. YOU HEAR ME? DON'T PRETEND YOU THOUGHT THIS THROUGH.
NO, I DID THINK THIS THROUGH--YOU CAN'T BE A FRIENDLY NEIGHBORHOOD SPIDER-MAN IF THERE'S NO NEIGHBORHOOD.
OKAY, COME ON. WE'VE GOT A SITUATION. SEE HIM DOWN THERE? HE'S IN TROUBLE, WHAT'S YOUR PLAN? GO.
OKAY, OKAY, UH... OKAY...
"DID YOU EVER SEE THIS REALLY OLD MOVIE *ALIENS?*"
HEY, UGLY!
ANY ONE OF THESE NEEDLES COULD END YOUR FRIEND'S LIFE IN AN INSTANT.
I GOTTA TELL YOU, HE'S NOT REALLY MY FRIEND. SAVING HIS LIFE IS MORE OF A PROFESSIONAL COURTESY.
YOU'VE SAVED NOTHING. YOUR POWERS ARE INCONSEQUENTIAL COMPARED TO MINE.
YEAH, BUT THE KID'S SEEN MORE MOVIES.

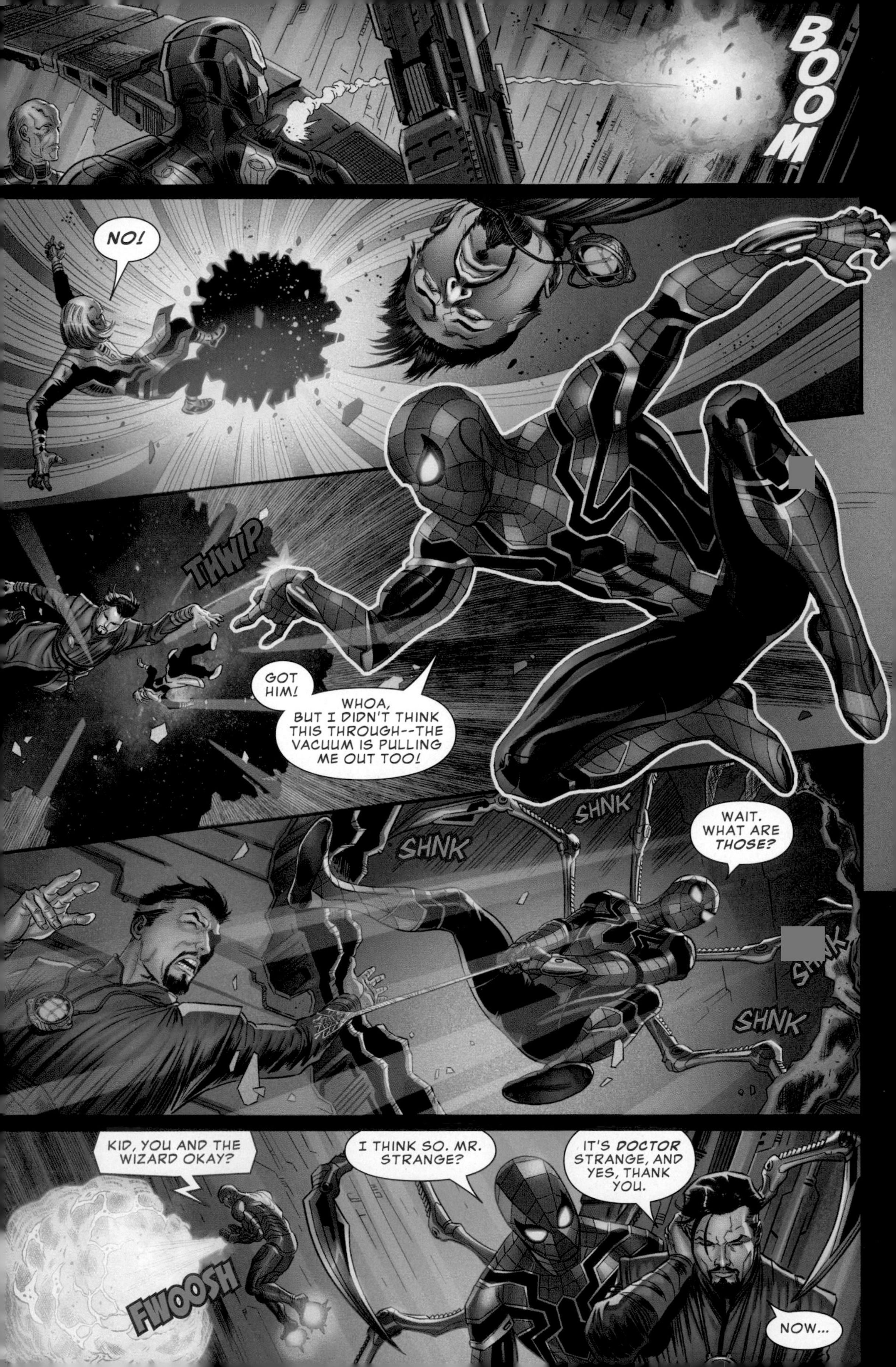
BOOM
NO!
THWIP
GOT HIM!
WHOA, BUT I DIDN'T THINK THIS THROUGH--THE VACUUM IS PULLING ME OUT TOO!
SHNK
SHNK
WAIT. WHAT ARE *THOSE?*
SHNK
KID, YOU AND THE WIZARD OKAY?
I THINK SO. MR. STRANGE?
IT'S *DOCTOR* STRANGE, AND YES, THANK YOU.
FWOOSH
NOW...

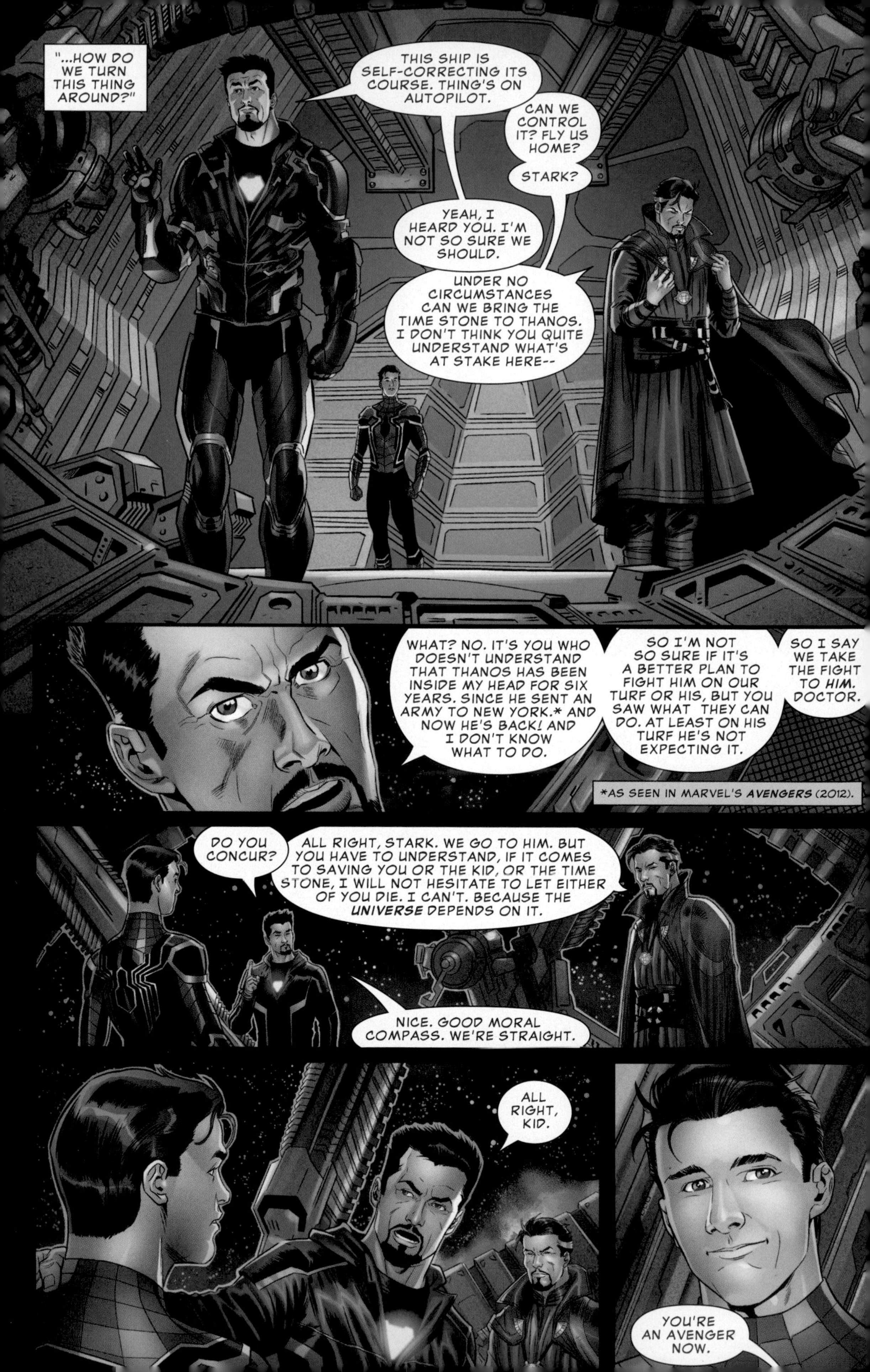

"...HOW DO WE TURN THIS THING AROUND?"
THIS SHIP IS SELF-CORRECTING ITS COURSE. THING'S ON AUTOPILOT.
CAN WE CONTROL IT? FLY US HOME?
STARK?
YEAH, I HEARD YOU. I'M NOT SO SURE WE SHOULD.
UNDER NO CIRCUMSTANCES CAN WE BRING THE TIME STONE TO THANOS. I DON'T THINK YOU QUITE UNDERSTAND WHAT'S AT STAKE HERE--
WHAT? NO. IT'S YOU WHO DOESN'T UNDERSTAND THAT THANOS HAS BEEN INSIDE MY HEAD FOR SIX YEARS. SINCE HE SENT AN ARMY TO NEW YORK.* AND NOW HE'S BACK! AND I DON'T KNOW WHAT TO DO.
SO I'M NOT SO SURE IF IT'S A BETTER PLAN TO FIGHT HIM ON OUR TURF OR HIS, BUT YOU SAW WHAT THEY CAN DO. AT LEAST ON HIS TURF HE'S NOT EXPECTING IT.
SO I SAY WE TAKE THE FIGHT TO *HIM*. DOCTOR.
*AS SEEN IN MARVEL'S *AVENGERS* (2012).
DO YOU CONCUR?
ALL RIGHT, STARK. WE GO TO HIM. BUT YOU HAVE TO UNDERSTAND, IF IT COMES TO SAVING YOU OR THE KID, OR THE TIME STONE, I WILL NOT HESITATE TO LET EITHER OF YOU DIE. I CAN'T. BECAUSE THE *UNIVERSE* DEPENDS ON IT.
NICE. GOOD MORAL COMPASS. WE'RE STRAIGHT.
ALL RIGHT, KID.
YOU'RE AN AVENGER NOW.

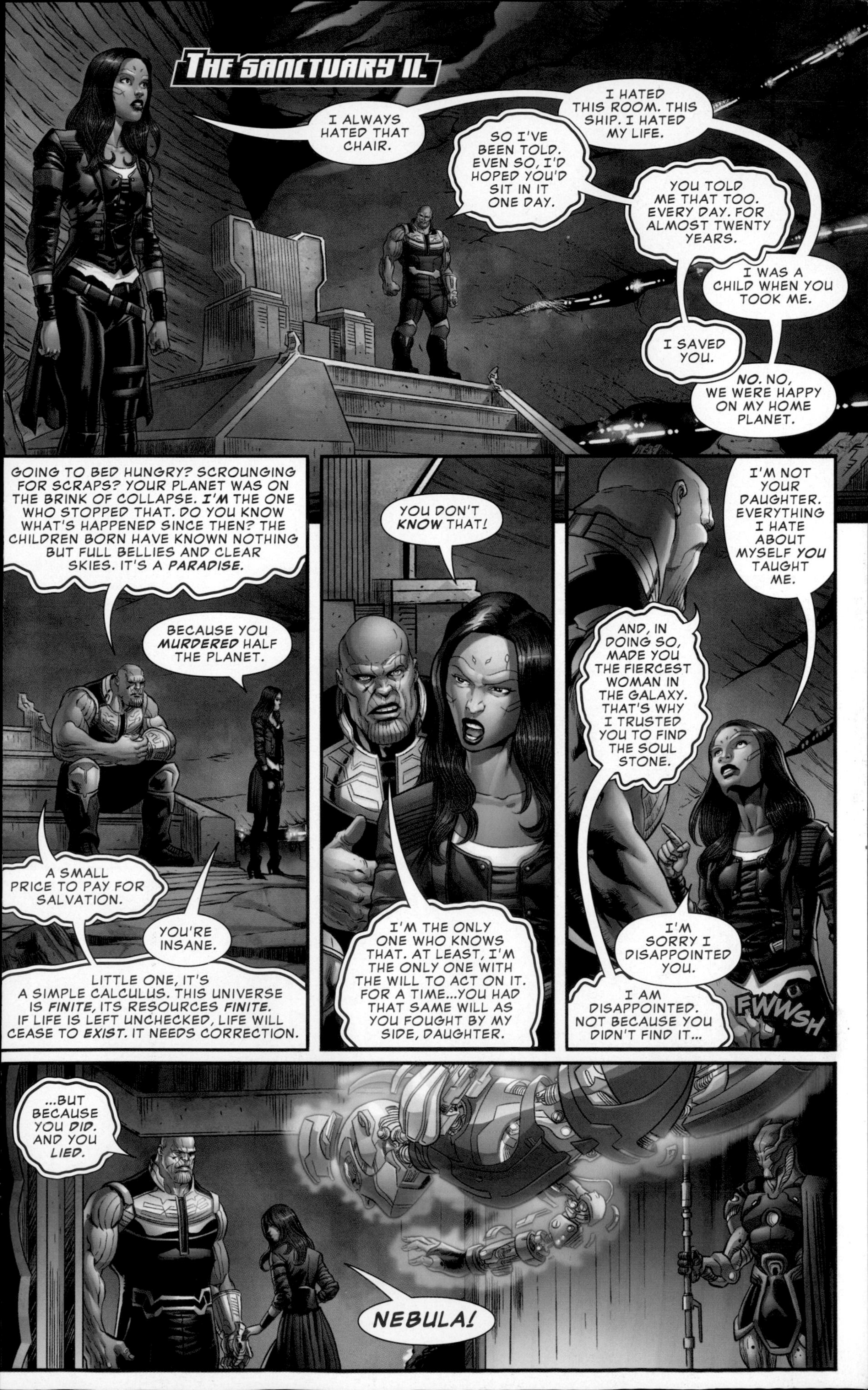
THE SANCTUARY II.
I ALWAYS HATED THAT CHAIR.
I HATED THIS ROOM. THIS SHIP. I HATED MY LIFE.
SO I'VE BEEN TOLD. EVEN SO, I'D HOPED YOU'D SIT IN IT ONE DAY.
YOU TOLD ME THAT TOO. EVERY DAY. FOR ALMOST TWENTY YEARS.
I WAS A CHILD WHEN YOU TOOK ME.
I SAVED YOU.
NO. NO, WE WERE HAPPY ON MY HOME PLANET.
GOING TO BED HUNGRY? SCROUNGING FOR SCRAPS? YOUR PLANET WAS ON THE BRINK OF COLLAPSE. I'M THE ONE WHO STOPPED THAT. DO YOU KNOW WHAT'S HAPPENED SINCE THEN? THE CHILDREN BORN HAVE KNOWN NOTHING BUT FULL BELLIES AND CLEAR SKIES. IT'S A PARADISE.
BECAUSE YOU MURDERED HALF THE PLANET.
A SMALL PRICE TO PAY FOR SALVATION.
YOU'RE INSANE.
LITTLE ONE, IT'S A SIMPLE CALCULUS. THIS UNIVERSE IS FINITE, ITS RESOURCES FINITE. IF LIFE IS LEFT UNCHECKED, LIFE WILL CEASE TO EXIST. IT NEEDS CORRECTION.
YOU DON'T KNOW THAT!
I'M THE ONLY ONE WHO KNOWS THAT. AT LEAST, I'M THE ONLY ONE WITH THE WILL TO ACT ON IT. FOR A TIME...YOU HAD THAT SAME WILL AS YOU FOUGHT BY MY SIDE, DAUGHTER.
I'M NOT YOUR DAUGHTER. EVERYTHING I HATE ABOUT MYSELF YOU TAUGHT ME.
AND, IN DOING SO, MADE YOU THE FIERCEST WOMAN IN THE GALAXY. THAT'S WHY I TRUSTED YOU TO FIND THE SOUL STONE.
I'M SORRY I DISAPPOINTED YOU.
I AM DISAPPOINTED. NOT BECAUSE YOU DIDN'T FIND IT...
FWWSH
...BUT BECAUSE YOU DID. AND YOU LIED.
NEBULA!

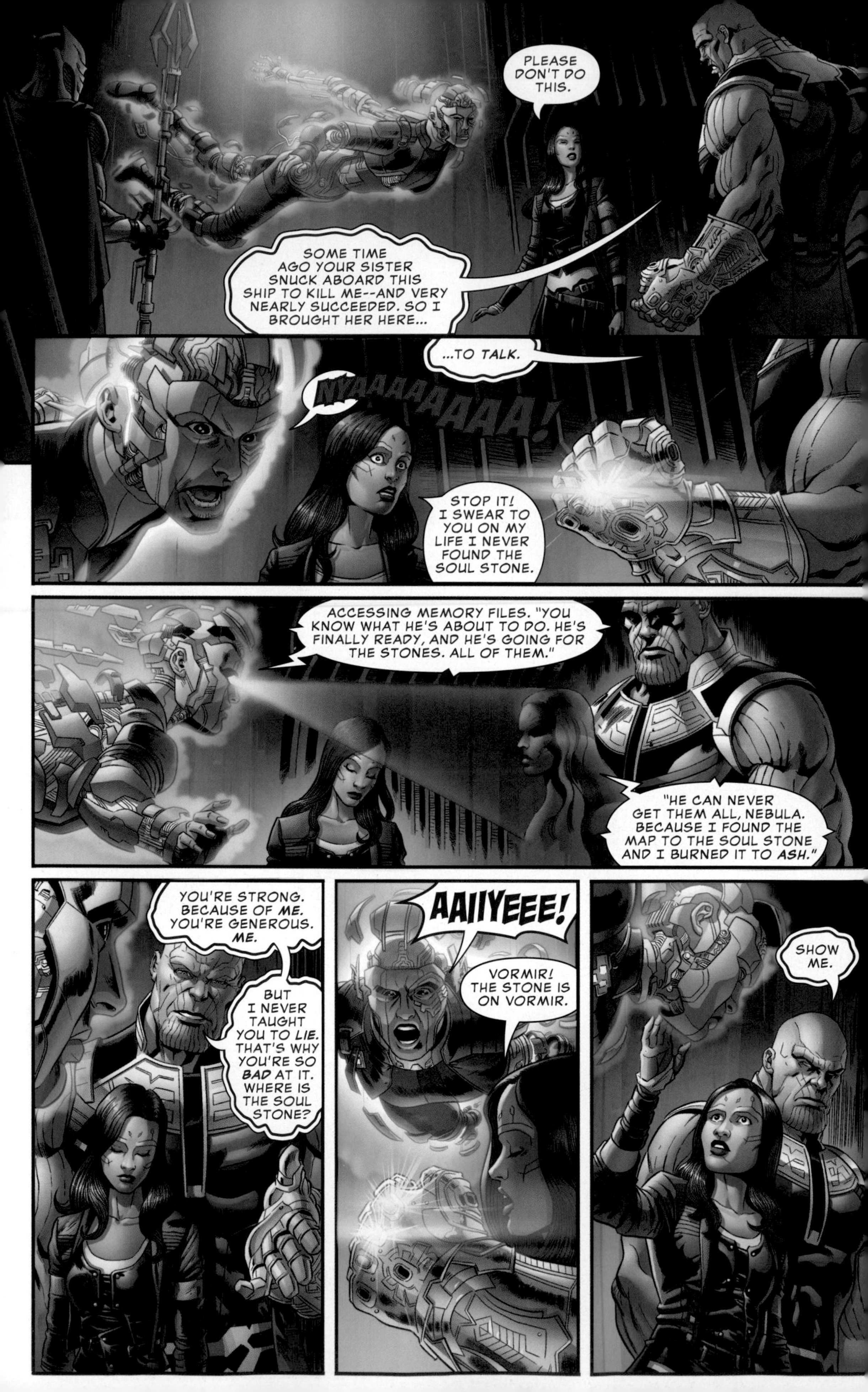
PLEASE DON'T DO THIS.
SOME TIME AGO YOUR SISTER SNUCK ABOARD THIS SHIP TO KILL ME--AND VERY NEARLY SUCCEEDED. SO I BROUGHT HER HERE...
...TO TALK.
NYAAAAAAAAA!
STOP IT! I SWEAR TO YOU ON MY LIFE I NEVER FOUND THE SOUL STONE.
ACCESSING MEMORY FILES. "YOU KNOW WHAT HE'S ABOUT TO DO. HE'S FINALLY READY, AND HE'S GOING FOR THE STONES. ALL OF THEM."
"HE CAN NEVER GET THEM ALL, NEBULA. BECAUSE I FOUND THE MAP TO THE SOUL STONE AND I BURNED IT TO ASH."
YOU'RE STRONG. BECAUSE OF ME. YOU'RE GENEROUS. ME.
BUT I NEVER TAUGHT YOU TO LIE. THAT'S WHY YOU'RE SO BAD AT IT. WHERE IS THE SOUL STONE?
AAIIYEEE!
VORMIR! THE STONE IS ON VORMIR.
SHOW ME.

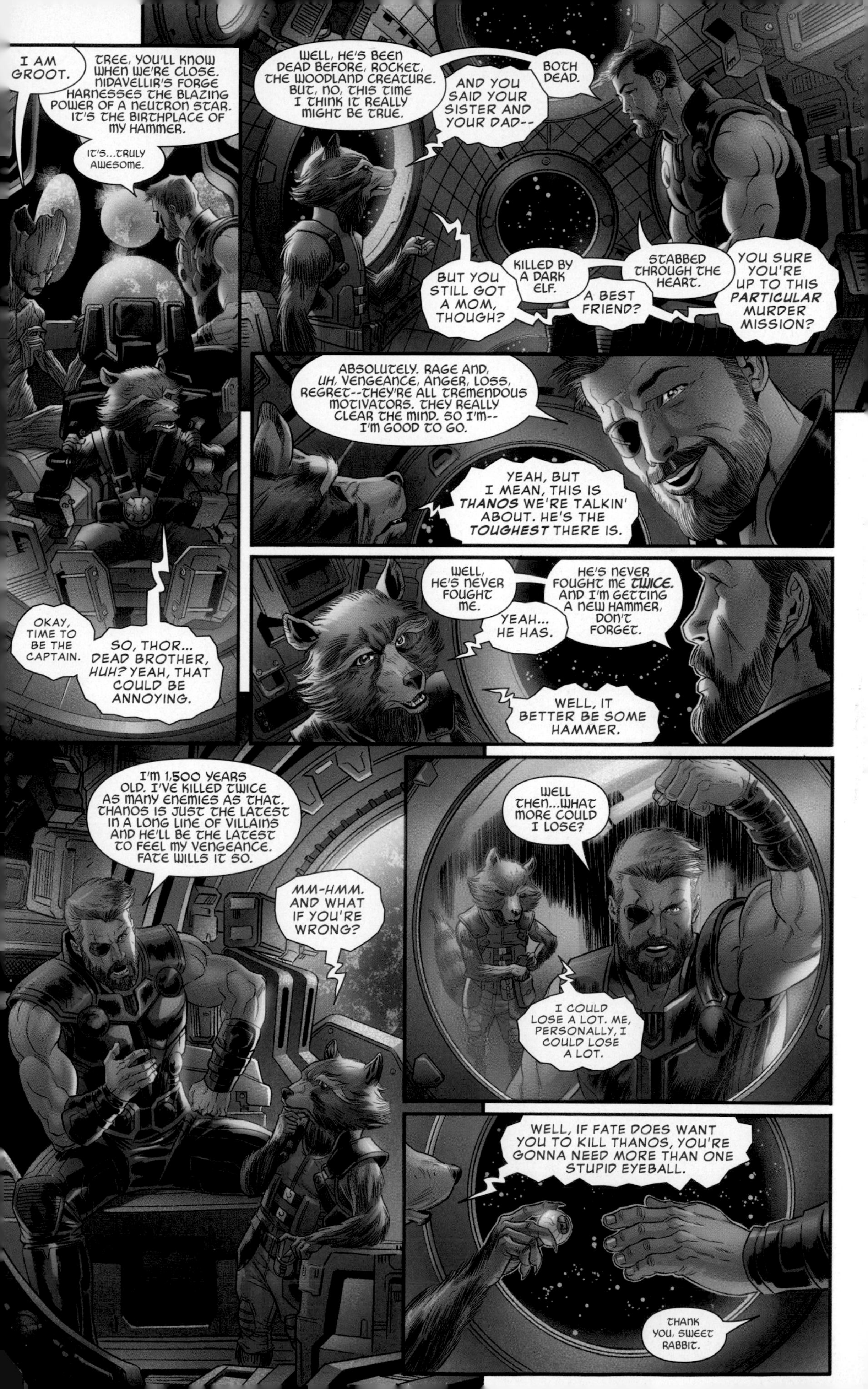
I AM GROOT.
TREE, YOU'LL KNOW WHEN WE'RE CLOSE. NIDAVELLIR'S FORGE HARNESSES THE BLAZING POWER OF A NEUTRON STAR. IT'S THE BIRTHPLACE OF MY HAMMER.
IT'S...TRULY AWESOME.
OKAY, TIME TO BE THE CAPTAIN.
SO, THOR... DEAD BROTHER, HUH? YEAH, THAT COULD BE ANNOYING.
WELL, HE'S BEEN DEAD BEFORE, ROCKET, THE WOODLAND CREATURE. BUT, NO, THIS TIME I THINK IT REALLY MIGHT BE TRUE.
AND YOU SAID YOUR SISTER AND YOUR DAD--
BOTH DEAD.
BUT YOU STILL GOT A MOM, THOUGH?
KILLED BY A DARK ELF.
A BEST FRIEND?
STABBED THROUGH THE HEART.
YOU SURE YOU'RE UP TO THIS PARTICULAR MURDER MISSION?
ABSOLUTELY. RAGE AND, UH, VENGEANCE, ANGER, LOSS, REGRET--THEY'RE ALL TREMENDOUS MOTIVATORS. THEY REALLY CLEAR THE MIND. SO I'M-- I'M GOOD TO GO.
YEAH, BUT I MEAN, THIS IS THANOS WE'RE TALKIN' ABOUT. HE'S THE TOUGHEST THERE IS.
WELL, HE'S NEVER FOUGHT ME.
YEAH... HE HAS.
HE'S NEVER FOUGHT ME TWICE. AND I'M GETTING A NEW HAMMER, DON'T FORGET.
WELL, IT BETTER BE SOME HAMMER.
I'M 1,500 YEARS OLD. I'VE KILLED TWICE AS MANY ENEMIES AS THAT. THANOS IS JUST THE LATEST IN A LONG LINE OF VILLAINS AND HE'LL BE THE LATEST TO FEEL MY VENGEANCE. FATE WILLS IT SO.
MM-HMM. AND WHAT IF YOU'RE WRONG?
WELL THEN...WHAT MORE COULD I LOSE?
I COULD LOSE A LOT. ME, PERSONALLY, I COULD LOSE A LOT.
WELL, IF FATE DOES WANT YOU TO KILL THANOS, YOU'RE GONNA NEED MORE THAN ONE STUPID EYEBALL.
THANK YOU, SWEET RABBIT.

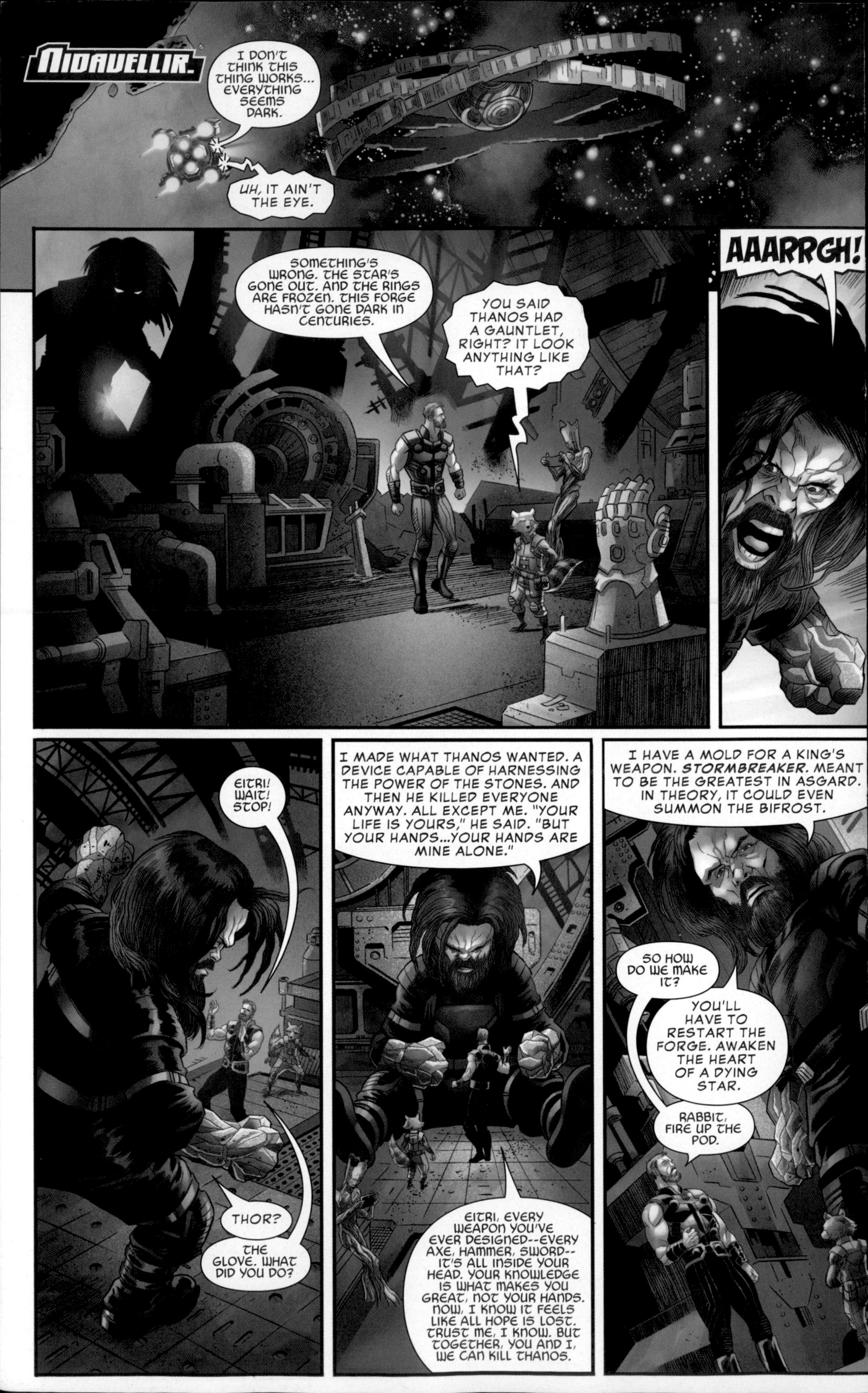
NIDAVELLIR.
I DON'T THINK THIS THING WORKS... EVERYTHING SEEMS DARK.
UH, IT AIN'T THE EYE.
SOMETHING'S WRONG. THE STAR'S GONE OUT. AND THE RINGS ARE FROZEN. THIS FORGE HASN'T GONE DARK IN CENTURIES.
YOU SAID THANOS HAD A GAUNTLET, RIGHT? IT LOOK ANYTHING LIKE THAT?
AAARRGH!
EITRI! WAIT! STOP!
THOR?
THE GLOVE. WHAT DID YOU DO?
I MADE WHAT THANOS WANTED. A DEVICE CAPABLE OF HARNESSING THE POWER OF THE STONES. AND THEN HE KILLED EVERYONE ANYWAY. ALL EXCEPT ME. "YOUR LIFE IS YOURS," HE SAID. "BUT YOUR HANDS...YOUR HANDS ARE MINE ALONE."
EITRI, EVERY WEAPON YOU'VE EVER DESIGNED--EVERY AXE, HAMMER, SWORD--IT'S ALL INSIDE YOUR HEAD. YOUR KNOWLEDGE IS WHAT MAKES YOU GREAT, NOT YOUR HANDS. NOW, I KNOW IT FEELS LIKE ALL HOPE IS LOST. TRUST ME, I KNOW. BUT TOGETHER, YOU AND I, WE CAN KILL THANOS.
I HAVE A MOLD FOR A KING'S WEAPON. STORMBREAKER. MEANT TO BE THE GREATEST IN ASGARD. IN THEORY, IT COULD EVEN SUMMON THE BIFROST.
SO HOW DO WE MAKE IT?
YOU'LL HAVE TO RESTART THE FORGE. AWAKEN THE HEART OF A DYING STAR.
RABBIT, FIRE UP THE POD.

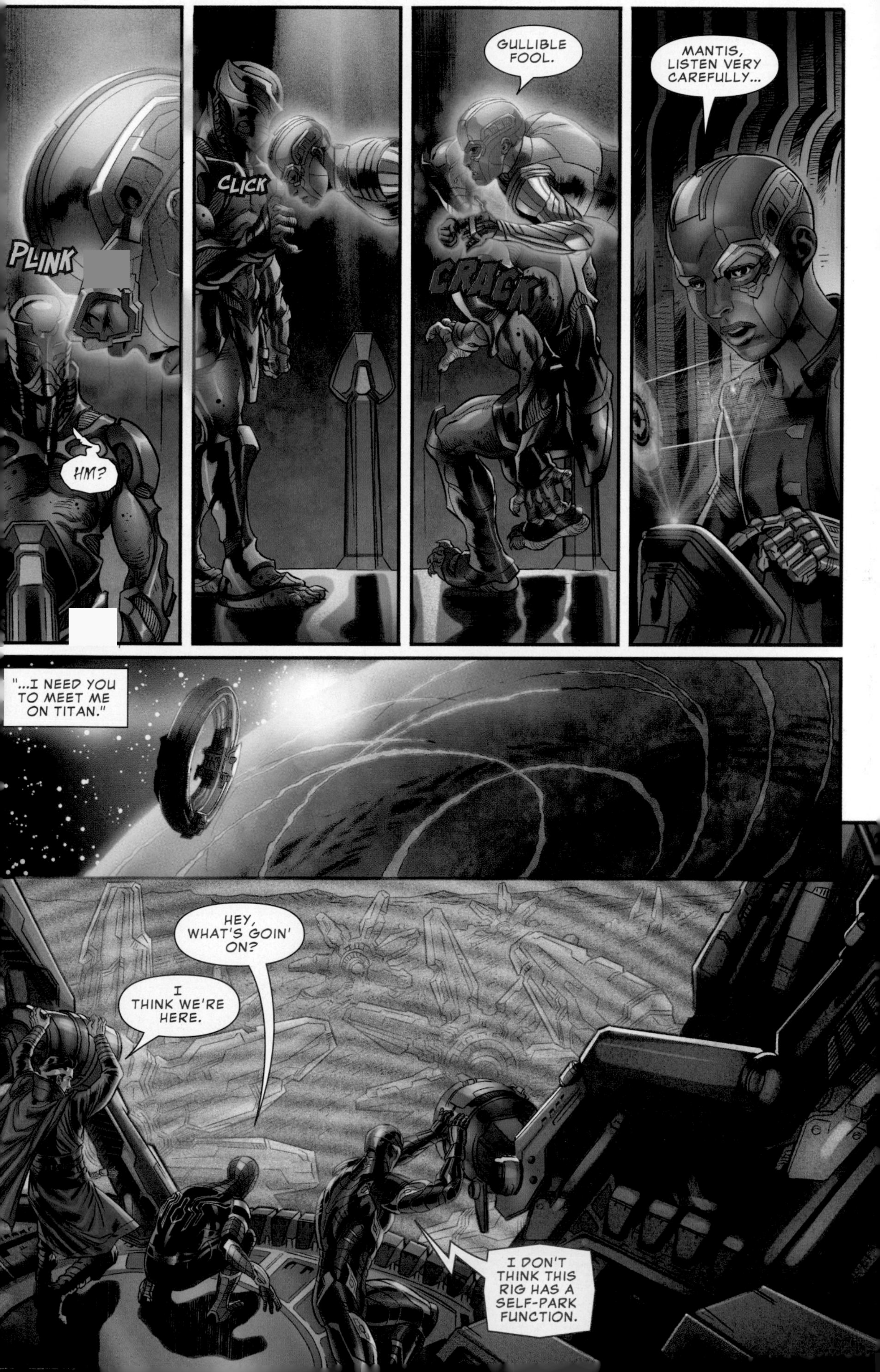
PLINK
HM?
CLICK
GULLIBLE FOOL.
CRACK
MANTIS, LISTEN VERY CAREFULLY...
"...I NEED YOU TO MEET ME ON TITAN."
HEY, WHAT'S GOIN' ON?
I THINK WE'RE HERE.
I DON'T THINK THIS RIG HAS A SELF-PARK FUNCTION.

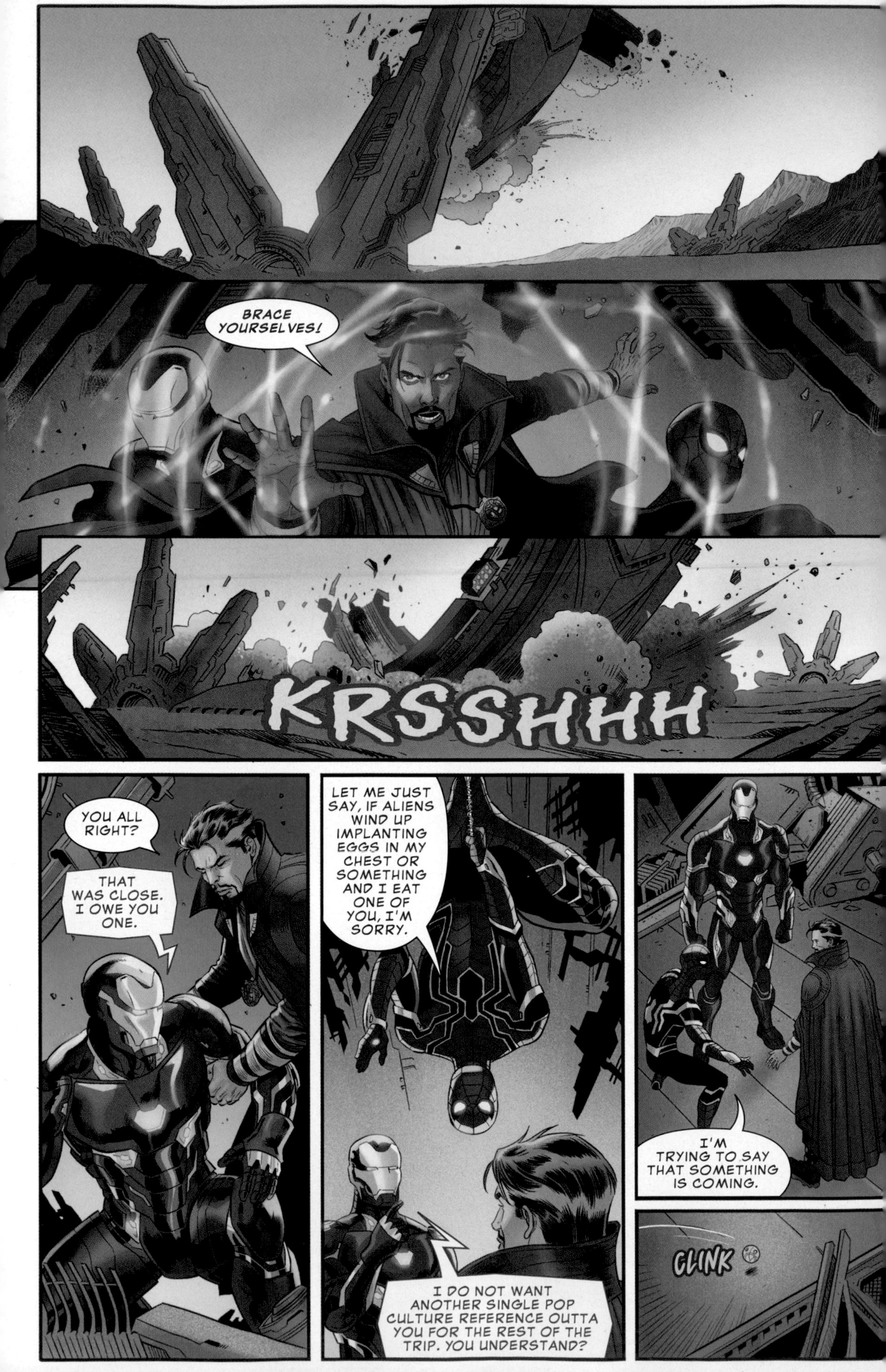
BRACE YOURSELVES!
KRSSHHH
YOU ALL RIGHT?
THAT WAS CLOSE. I OWE YOU ONE.
LET ME JUST SAY, IF ALIENS WIND UP IMPLANTING EGGS IN MY CHEST OR SOMETHING AND I EAT ONE OF YOU, I'M SORRY.
I DO NOT WANT ANOTHER SINGLE POP CULTURE REFERENCE OUTTA YOU FOR THE REST OF THE TRIP. YOU UNDERSTAND?
I'M TRYING TO SAY THAT SOMETHING IS COMING.
CLINK

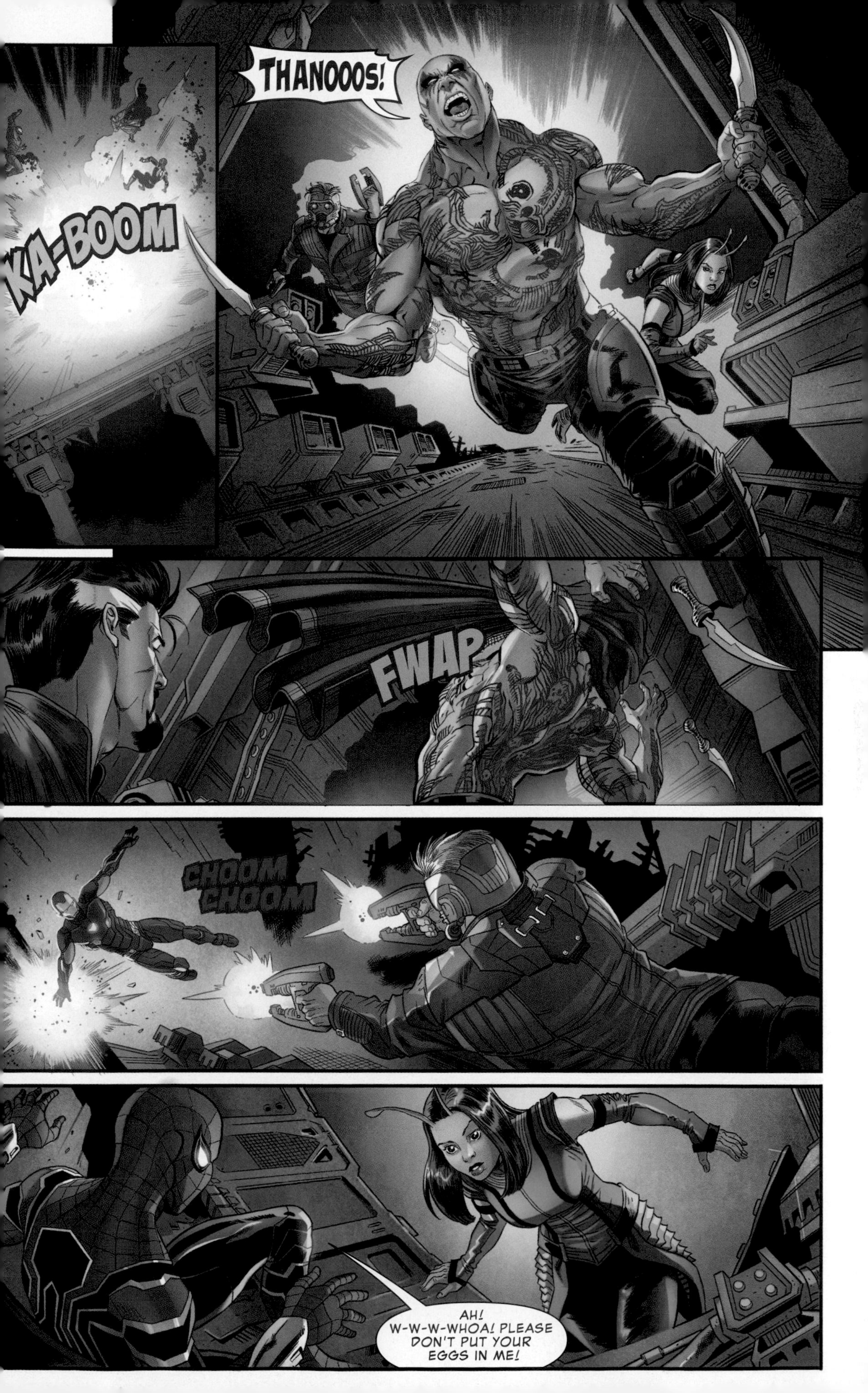
KA-BOOM
THANOOOS!
FWAP
CHOOM
CHOOM
AH! W-W-W-WHOA! PLEASE DON'T PUT YOUR EGGS IN ME!

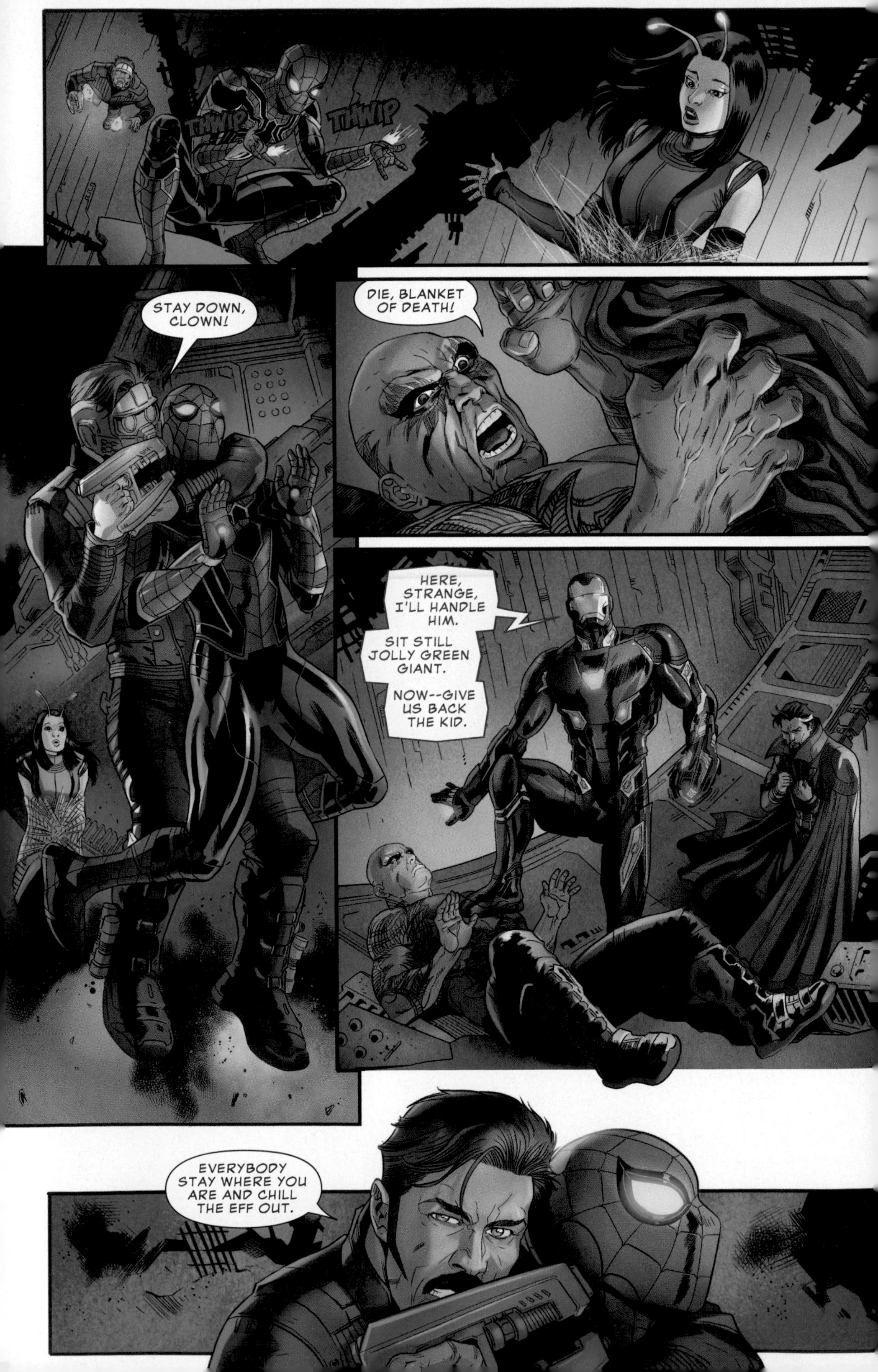
THWIP
THWIP
STAY DOWN, CLOWN!
DIE, BLANKET OF DEATH!
HERE, STRANGE, I'LL HANDLE HIM.
SIT STILL JOLLY GREEN GIANT.
NOW--GIVE US BACK THE KID.
EVERYBODY STAY WHERE YOU ARE AND CHILL THE EFF OUT.

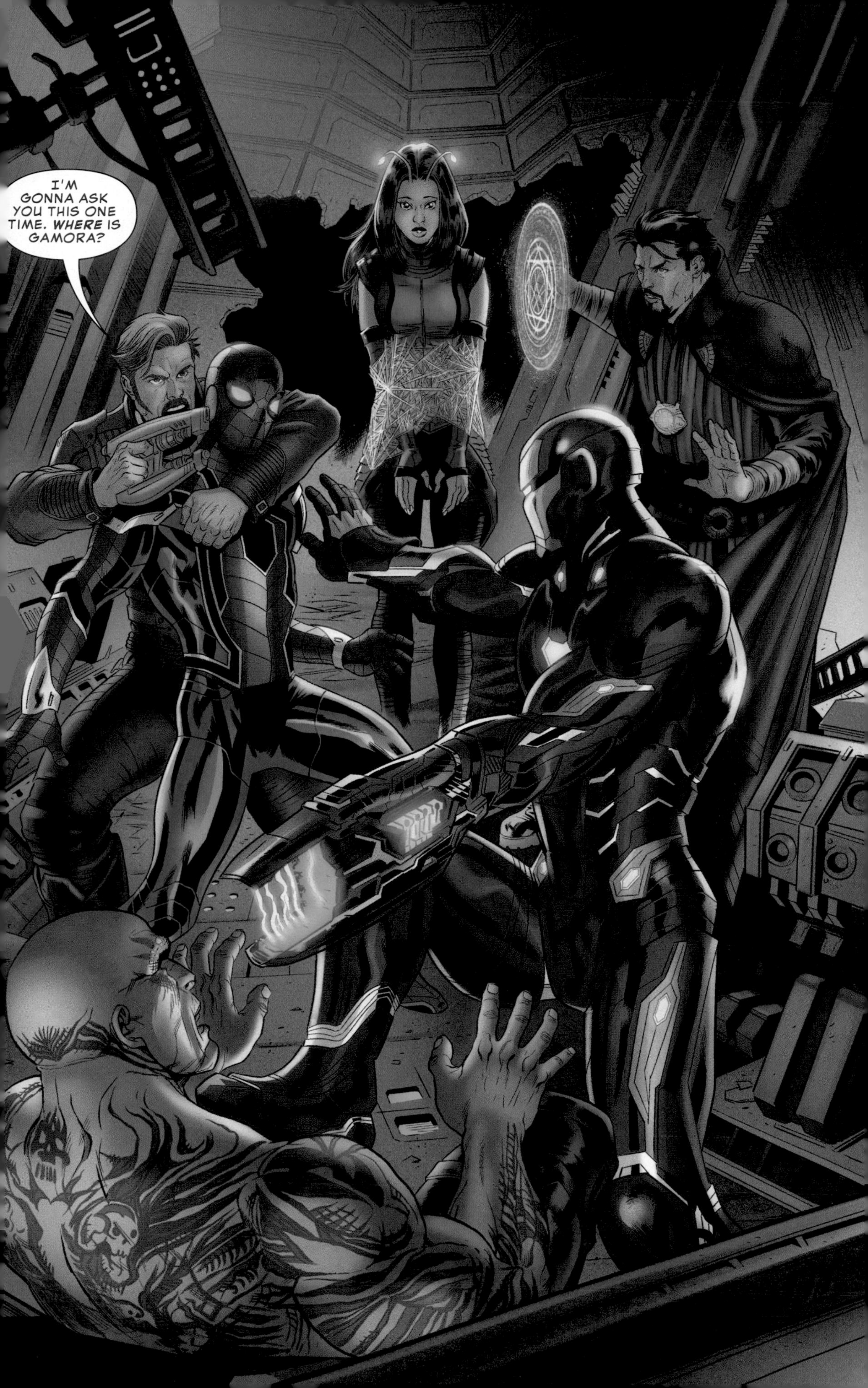
I'M GONNA ASK YOU THIS ONE TIME. WHERE IS GAMORA?

MARVEL'S AVENGERS: ENDGAME
PRELUDE #3

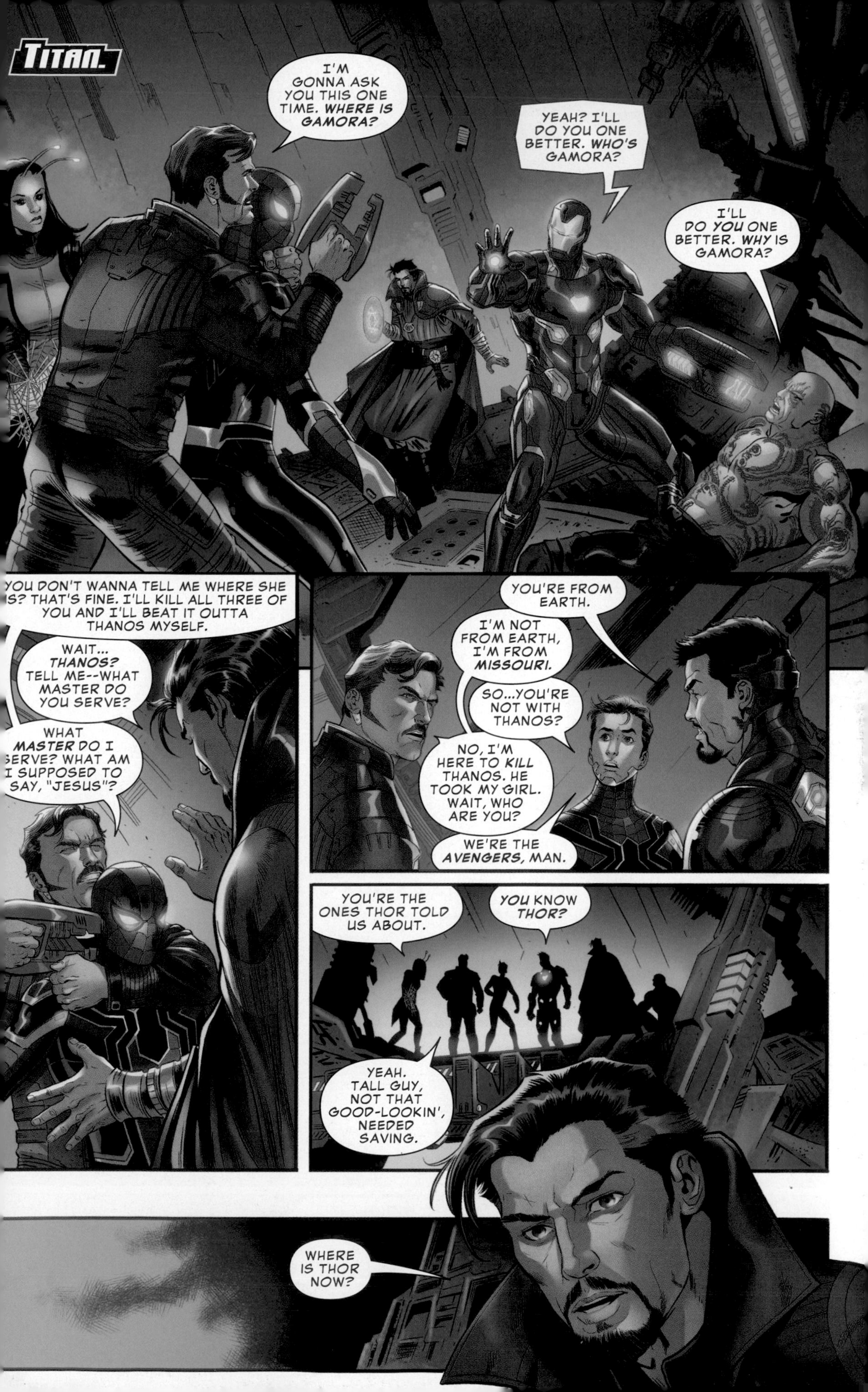
TITAN.
I'M GONNA ASK YOU THIS ONE TIME. WHERE IS GAMORA?
YEAH? I'LL DO YOU ONE BETTER. WHO'S GAMORA?
I'LL DO YOU ONE BETTER. WHY IS GAMORA?
YOU DON'T WANNA TELL ME WHERE SHE IS? THAT'S FINE. I'LL KILL ALL THREE OF YOU AND I'LL BEAT IT OUTTA THANOS MYSELF.
WAIT... THANOS? TELL ME--WHAT MASTER DO YOU SERVE?
WHAT MASTER DO I SERVE? WHAT AM I SUPPOSED TO SAY, "JESUS"?
YOU'RE FROM EARTH.
I'M NOT FROM EARTH, I'M FROM MISSOURI.
SO...YOU'RE NOT WITH THANOS?
NO, I'M HERE TO KILL THANOS. HE TOOK MY GIRL. WAIT, WHO ARE YOU?
WE'RE THE AVENGERS, MAN.
YOU'RE THE ONES THOR TOLD US ABOUT.
YOU KNOW THOR?
YEAH. TALL GUY, NOT THAT GOOD-LOOKIN', NEEDED SAVING.
WHERE IS THOR NOW?

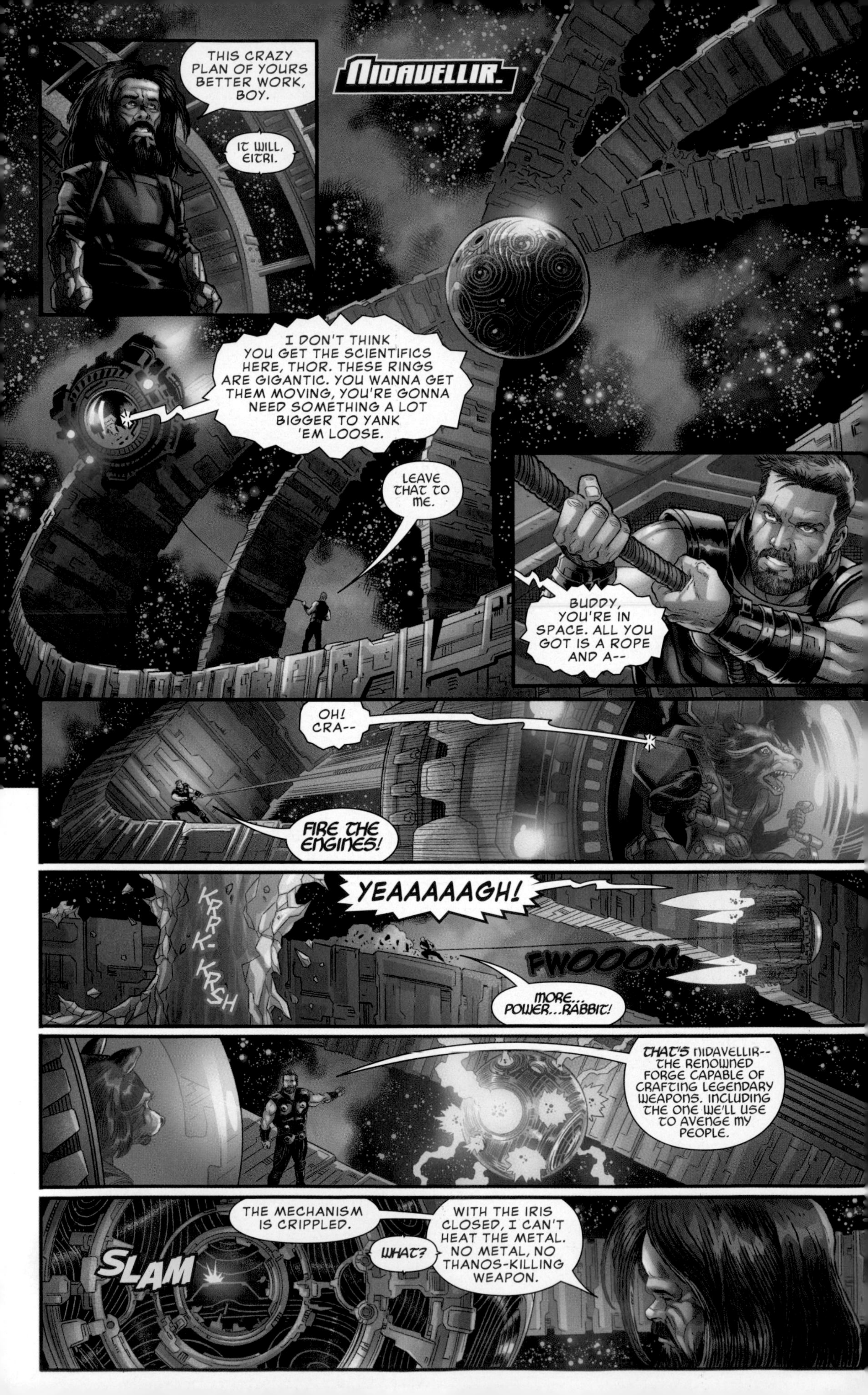
NIDAVELLIR.
THIS CRAZY PLAN OF YOURS BETTER WORK, BOY.
IT WILL, EITRI.
I DON'T THINK YOU GET THE SCIENTIFICS HERE, THOR. THESE RINGS ARE GIGANTIC. YOU WANNA GET THEM MOVING, YOU'RE GONNA NEED SOMETHING A LOT BIGGER TO YANK 'EM LOOSE.
LEAVE THAT TO ME.
BUDDY, YOU'RE IN SPACE. ALL YOU GOT IS A ROPE AND A--
OH! CRA--
FIRE THE ENGINES!
YEAAAAAGH!
KRRK-KRSH
FWOOOM
MORE... POWER...RABBIT!
THAT'S NIDAVELLIR-- THE RENOWNED FORGE CAPABLE OF CRAFTING LEGENDARY WEAPONS. INCLUDING THE ONE WE'LL USE TO AVENGE MY PEOPLE.
SLAM
THE MECHANISM IS CRIPPLED.
WHAT?
WITH THE IRIS CLOSED, I CAN'T HEAT THE METAL. NO METAL, NO THANOS-KILLING WEAPON.

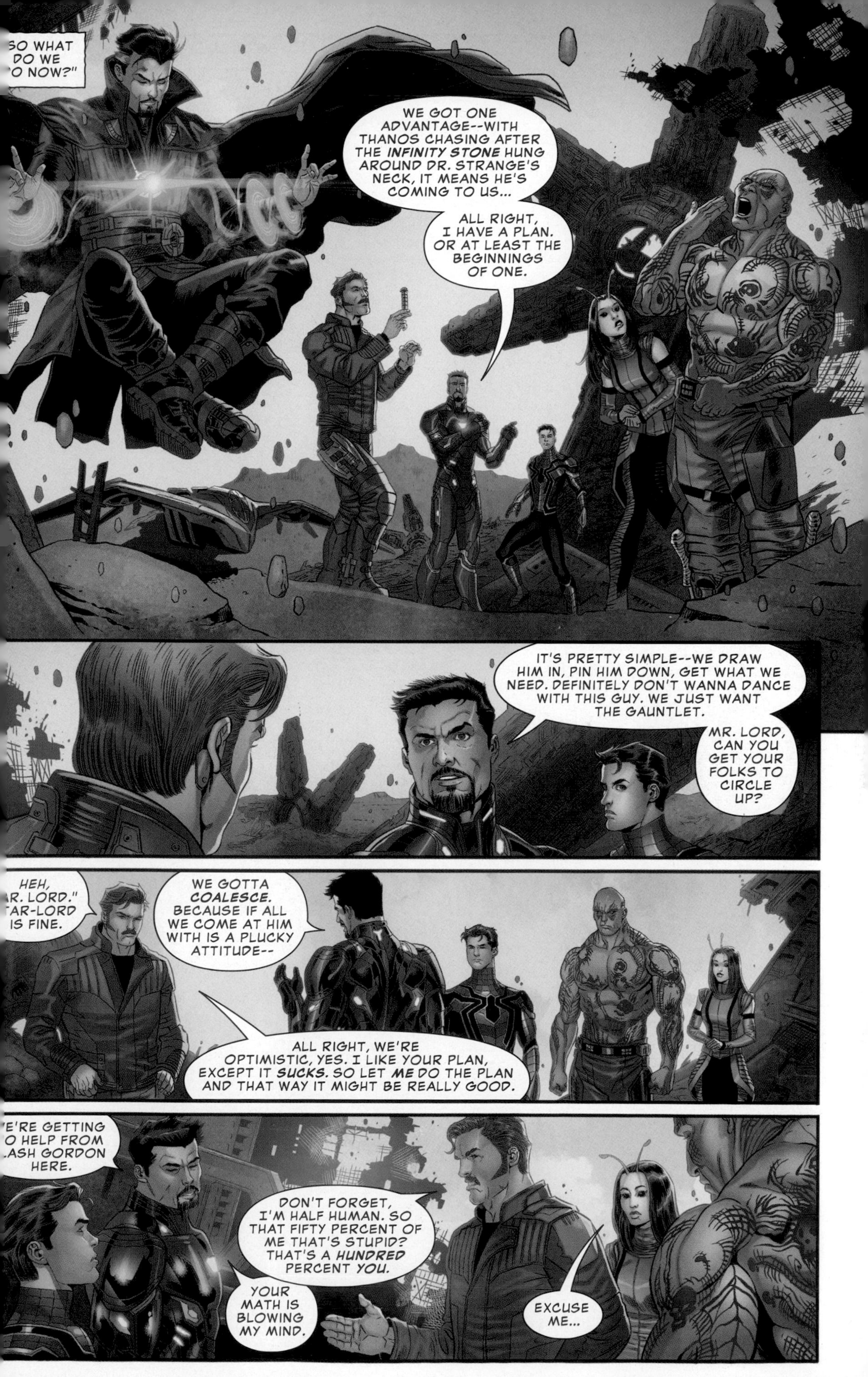

SO WHAT DO WE 'O NOW?"
WE GOT ONE ADVANTAGE--WITH THANOS CHASING AFTER THE *INFINITY STONE* HUNG AROUND DR. STRANGE'S NECK, IT MEANS HE'S COMING TO US...
ALL RIGHT, I HAVE A PLAN. OR AT LEAST THE BEGINNINGS OF ONE.
IT'S PRETTY SIMPLE--WE DRAW HIM IN, PIN HIM DOWN, GET WHAT WE NEED. DEFINITELY DON'T WANNA DANCE WITH THIS GUY. WE JUST WANT THE GAUNTLET.
MR. LORD, CAN YOU GET YOUR FOLKS TO CIRCLE UP?
HEH, R. LORD." TAR-LORD IS FINE.
WE GOTTA *COALESCE.* BECAUSE IF ALL WE COME AT HIM WITH IS A PLUCKY ATTITUDE--
ALL RIGHT, WE'RE OPTIMISTIC, YES. I LIKE YOUR PLAN, EXCEPT IT *SUCKS.* SO LET *ME* DO THE PLAN AND THAT WAY IT MIGHT BE REALLY GOOD.
E'RE GETTING O HELP FROM LASH GORDON HERE.
DON'T FORGET, I'M HALF HUMAN. SO THAT FIFTY PERCENT OF ME THAT'S STUPID? THAT'S A *HUNDRED* PERCENT *YOU.*
YOUR MATH IS BLOWING MY MIND.
EXCUSE ME...

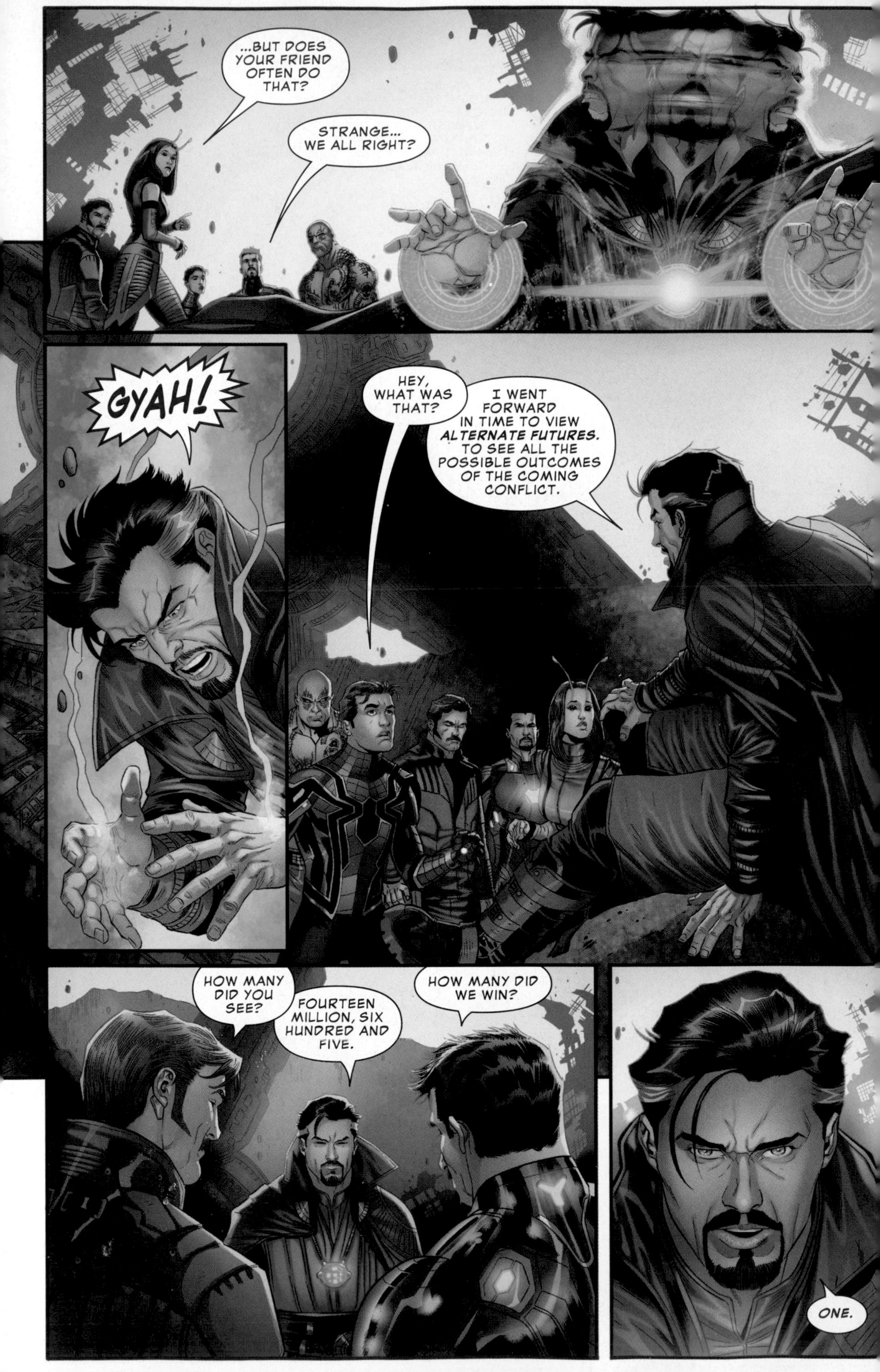
...BUT DOES YOUR FRIEND OFTEN DO THAT?
STRANGE... WE ALL RIGHT?
GYAH!
HEY, WHAT WAS THAT?
I WENT FORWARD IN TIME TO VIEW *ALTERNATE FUTURES.* TO SEE ALL THE POSSIBLE OUTCOMES OF THE COMING CONFLICT.
HOW MANY DID YOU SEE?
FOURTEEN MILLION, SIX HUNDRED AND FIVE.
HOW MANY DID WE WIN?
ONE.

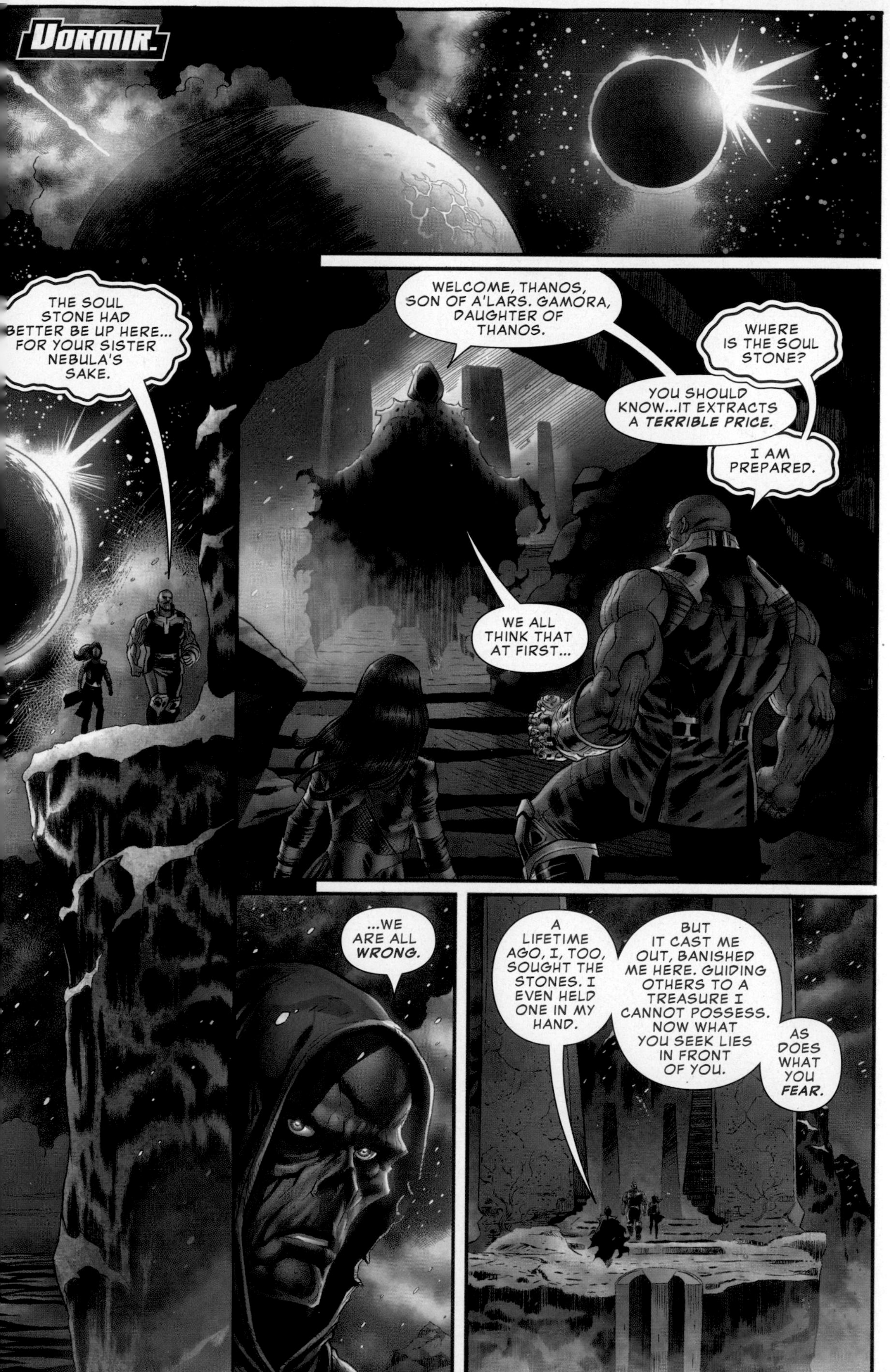
VORMIR.
THE SOUL STONE HAD BETTER BE UP HERE... FOR YOUR SISTER NEBULA'S SAKE.
WELCOME, THANOS, SON OF A'LARS. GAMORA, DAUGHTER OF THANOS.
WHERE IS THE SOUL STONE?
YOU SHOULD KNOW...IT EXTRACTS A TERRIBLE PRICE.
I AM PREPARED.
WE ALL THINK THAT AT FIRST...
...WE ARE ALL WRONG.
A LIFETIME AGO, I, TOO, SOUGHT THE STONES. I EVEN HELD ONE IN MY HAND.
BUT IT CAST ME OUT, BANISHED ME HERE. GUIDING OTHERS TO A TREASURE I CANNOT POSSESS. NOW WHAT YOU SEEK LIES IN FRONT OF YOU.
AS DOES WHAT YOU FEAR.

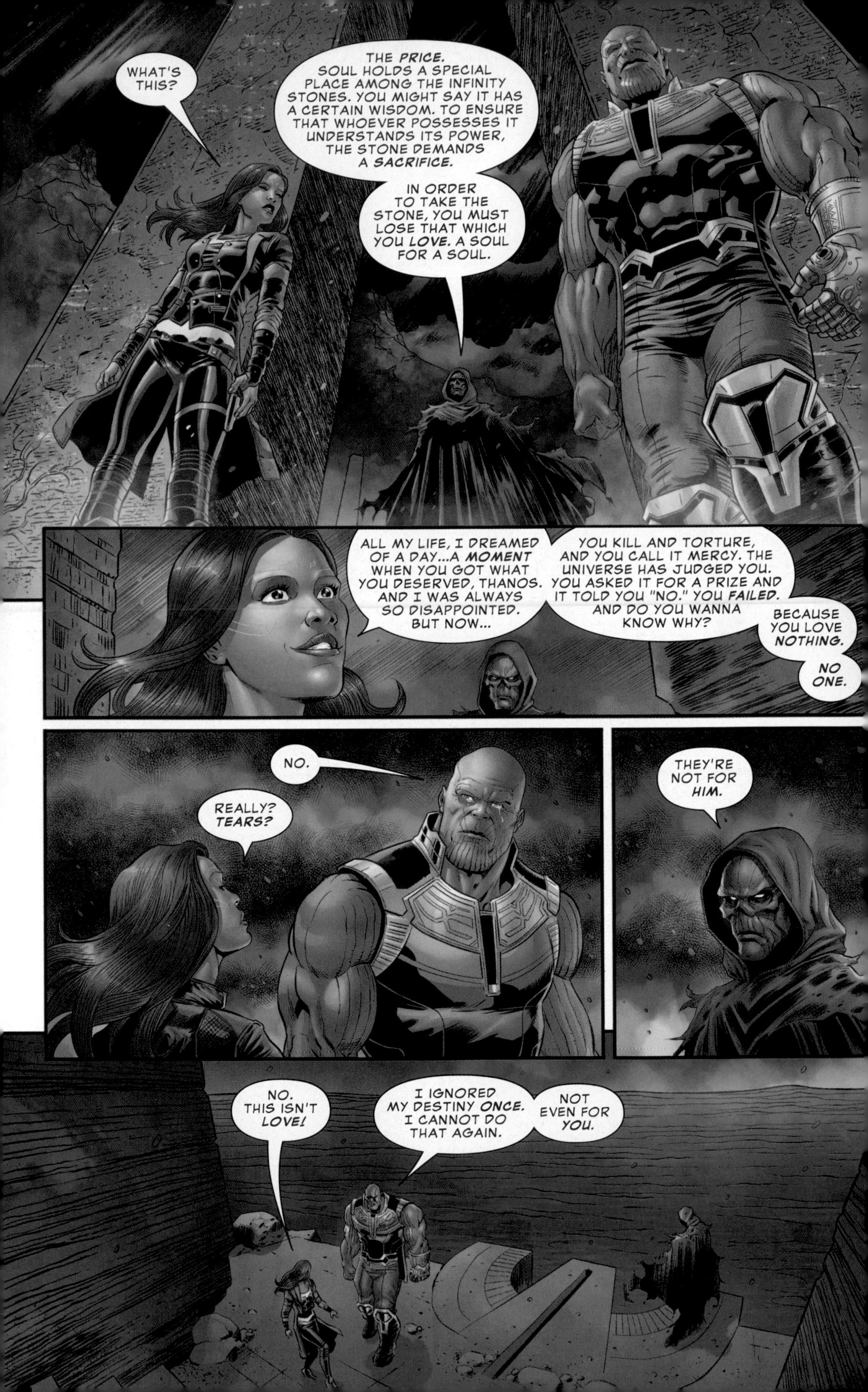
WHAT'S THIS?
THE PRICE. SOUL HOLDS A SPECIAL PLACE AMONG THE INFINITY STONES. YOU MIGHT SAY IT HAS A CERTAIN WISDOM. TO ENSURE THAT WHOEVER POSSESSES IT UNDERSTANDS ITS POWER, THE STONE DEMANDS A SACRIFICE.
IN ORDER TO TAKE THE STONE, YOU MUST LOSE THAT WHICH YOU LOVE. A SOUL FOR A SOUL.
ALL MY LIFE, I DREAMED OF A DAY...A MOMENT WHEN YOU GOT WHAT YOU DESERVED, THANOS. AND I WAS ALWAYS SO DISAPPOINTED. BUT NOW...
YOU KILL AND TORTURE, AND YOU CALL IT MERCY. THE UNIVERSE HAS JUDGED YOU. YOU ASKED IT FOR A PRIZE AND IT TOLD YOU "NO." YOU FAILED. AND DO YOU WANNA KNOW WHY?
BECAUSE YOU LOVE NOTHING.
NO ONE.
NO.
REALLY? TEARS?
THEY'RE NOT FOR HIM.
NO. THIS ISN'T LOVE!
I IGNORED MY DESTINY ONCE. I CANNOT DO THAT AGAIN.
NOT EVEN FOR YOU.

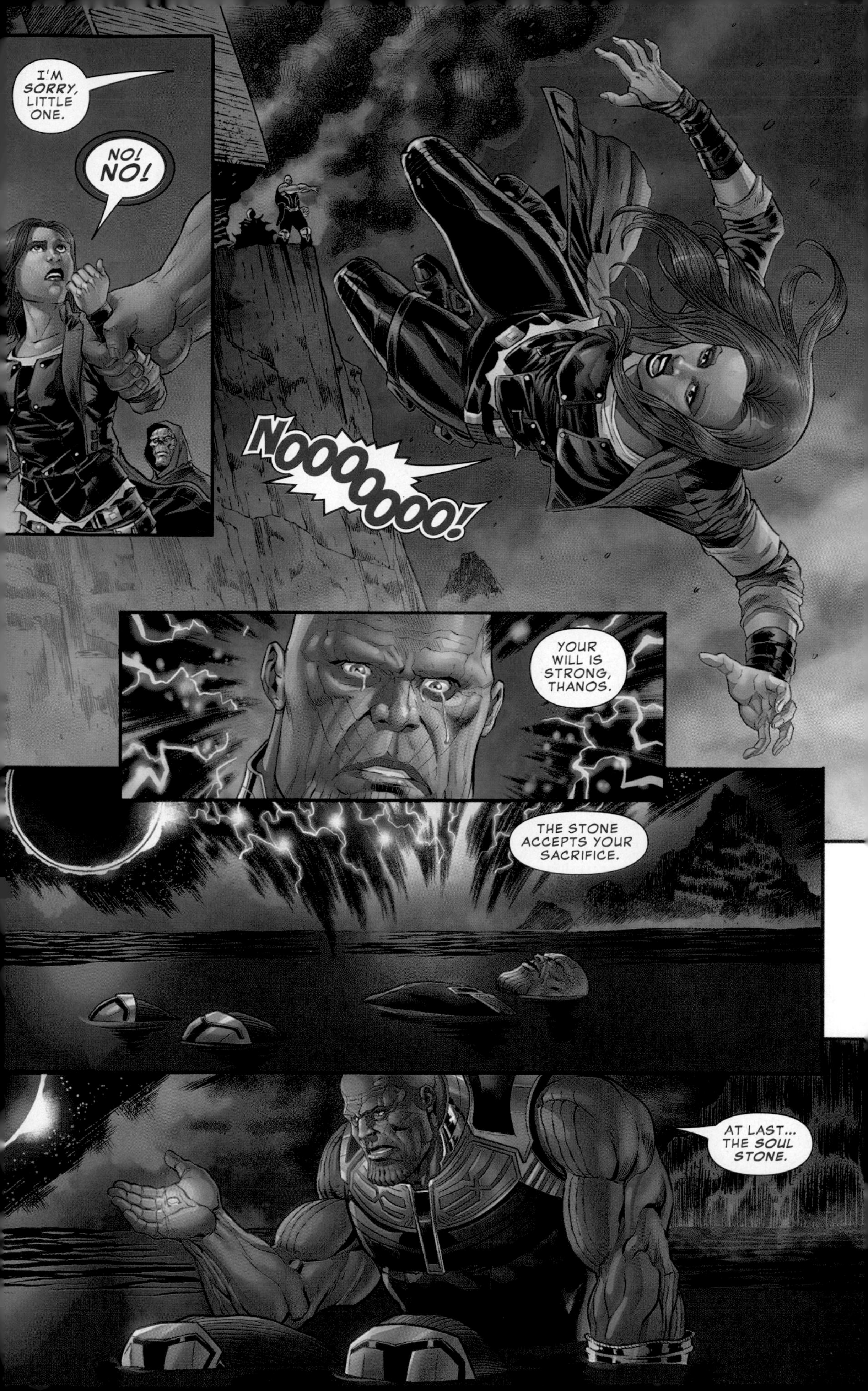

I'M SORRY, LITTLE ONE.
NO! NO!
NOOOOOOOO!
YOUR WILL IS STRONG, THANOS.
THE STONE ACCEPTS YOUR SACRIFICE.
AT LAST... THE SOUL STONE.

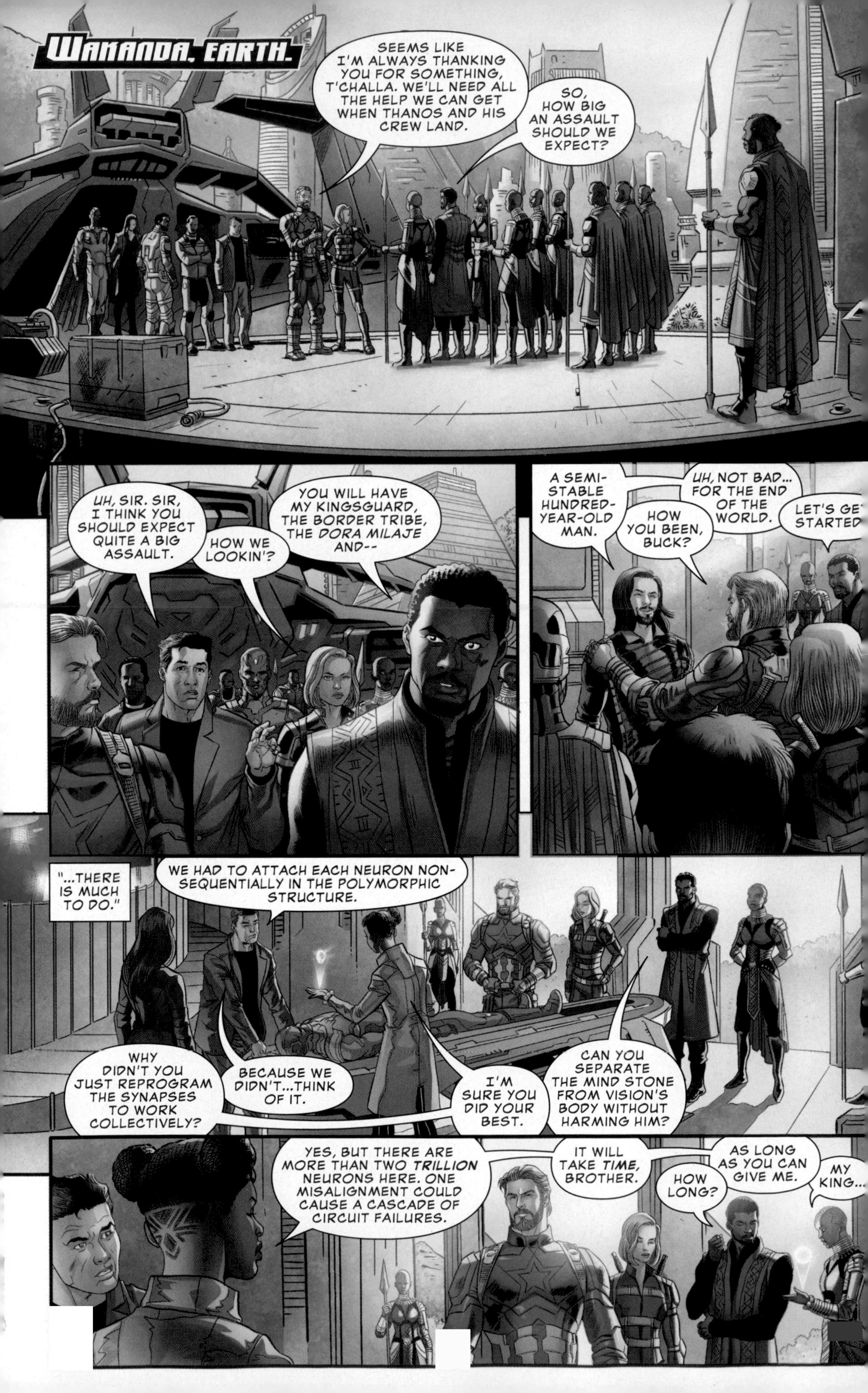
WAKANDA, EARTH.
SEEMS LIKE I'M ALWAYS THANKING YOU FOR SOMETHING, T'CHALLA. WE'LL NEED ALL THE HELP WE CAN GET WHEN THANOS AND HIS CREW LAND.
SO, HOW BIG AN ASSAULT SHOULD WE EXPECT?
UH, SIR. SIR, I THINK YOU SHOULD EXPECT QUITE A BIG ASSAULT.
HOW WE LOOKIN'?
YOU WILL HAVE MY KINGSGUARD, THE BORDER TRIBE, THE DORA MILAJE AND--
HOW YOU BEEN, BUCK?
A SEMI-STABLE HUNDRED-YEAR-OLD MAN.
UH, NOT BAD... FOR THE END OF THE WORLD.
LET'S GET STARTED
"...THERE IS MUCH TO DO."
WE HAD TO ATTACH EACH NEURON NON-SEQUENTIALLY IN THE POLYMORPHIC STRUCTURE.
WHY DIDN'T YOU JUST REPROGRAM THE SYNAPSES TO WORK COLLECTIVELY?
BECAUSE WE DIDN'T...THINK OF IT.
I'M SURE YOU DID YOUR BEST.
CAN YOU SEPARATE THE MIND STONE FROM VISION'S BODY WITHOUT HARMING HIM?
YES, BUT THERE ARE MORE THAN TWO TRILLION NEURONS HERE. ONE MISALIGNMENT COULD CAUSE A CASCADE OF CIRCUIT FAILURES.
HOW LONG?
IT WILL TAKE TIME, BROTHER.
AS LONG AS YOU CAN GIVE ME.
MY KING...

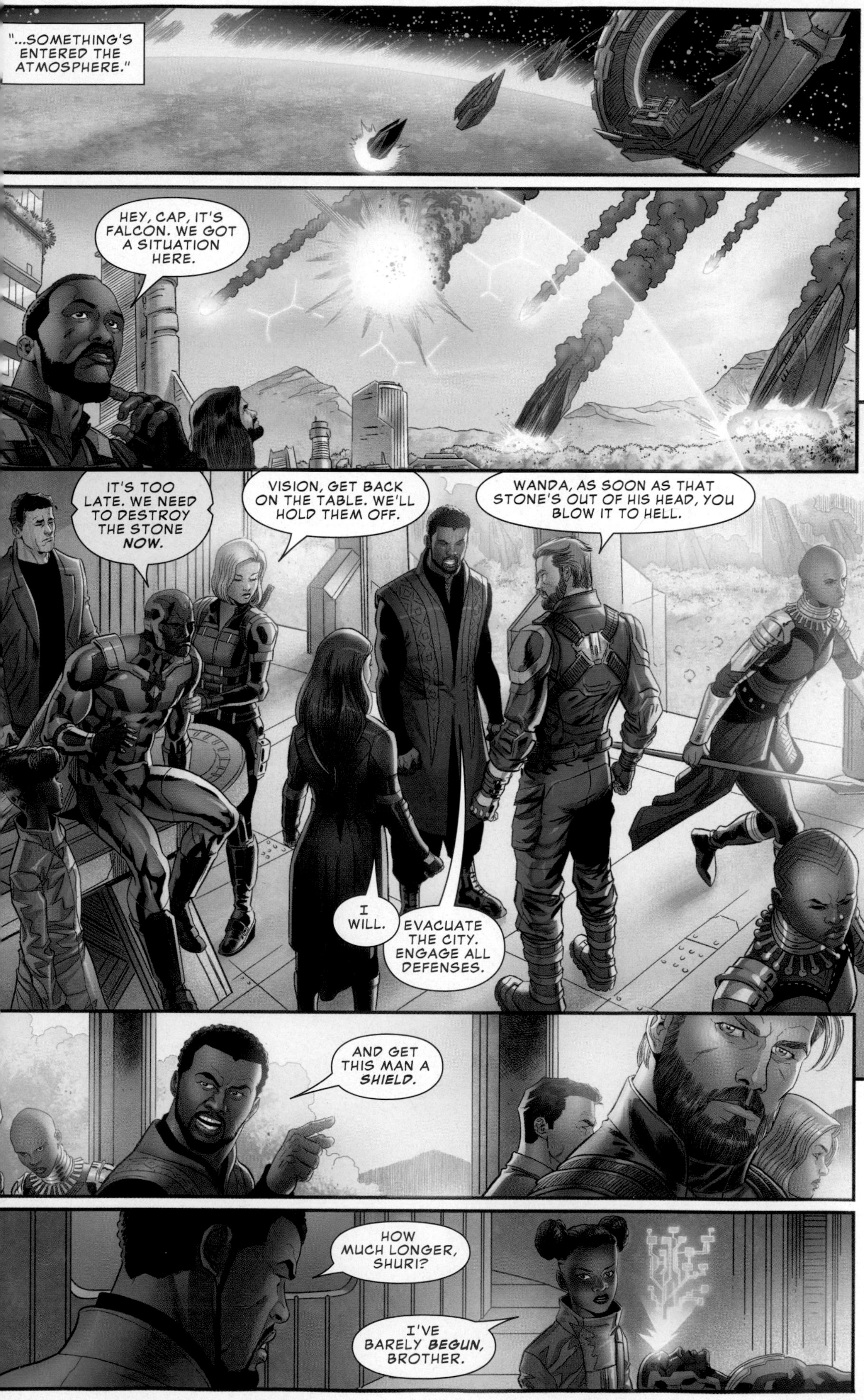
"...SOMETHING'S ENTERED THE ATMOSPHERE."
HEY, CAP, IT'S FALCON. WE GOT A SITUATION HERE.
IT'S TOO LATE. WE NEED TO DESTROY THE STONE NOW.
VISION, GET BACK ON THE TABLE. WE'LL HOLD THEM OFF.
WANDA, AS SOON AS THAT STONE'S OUT OF HIS HEAD, YOU BLOW IT TO HELL.
I WILL.
EVACUATE THE CITY. ENGAGE ALL DEFENSES.
AND GET THIS MAN A SHIELD.
HOW MUCH LONGER, SHURI?
I'VE BARELY BEGUN, BROTHER.

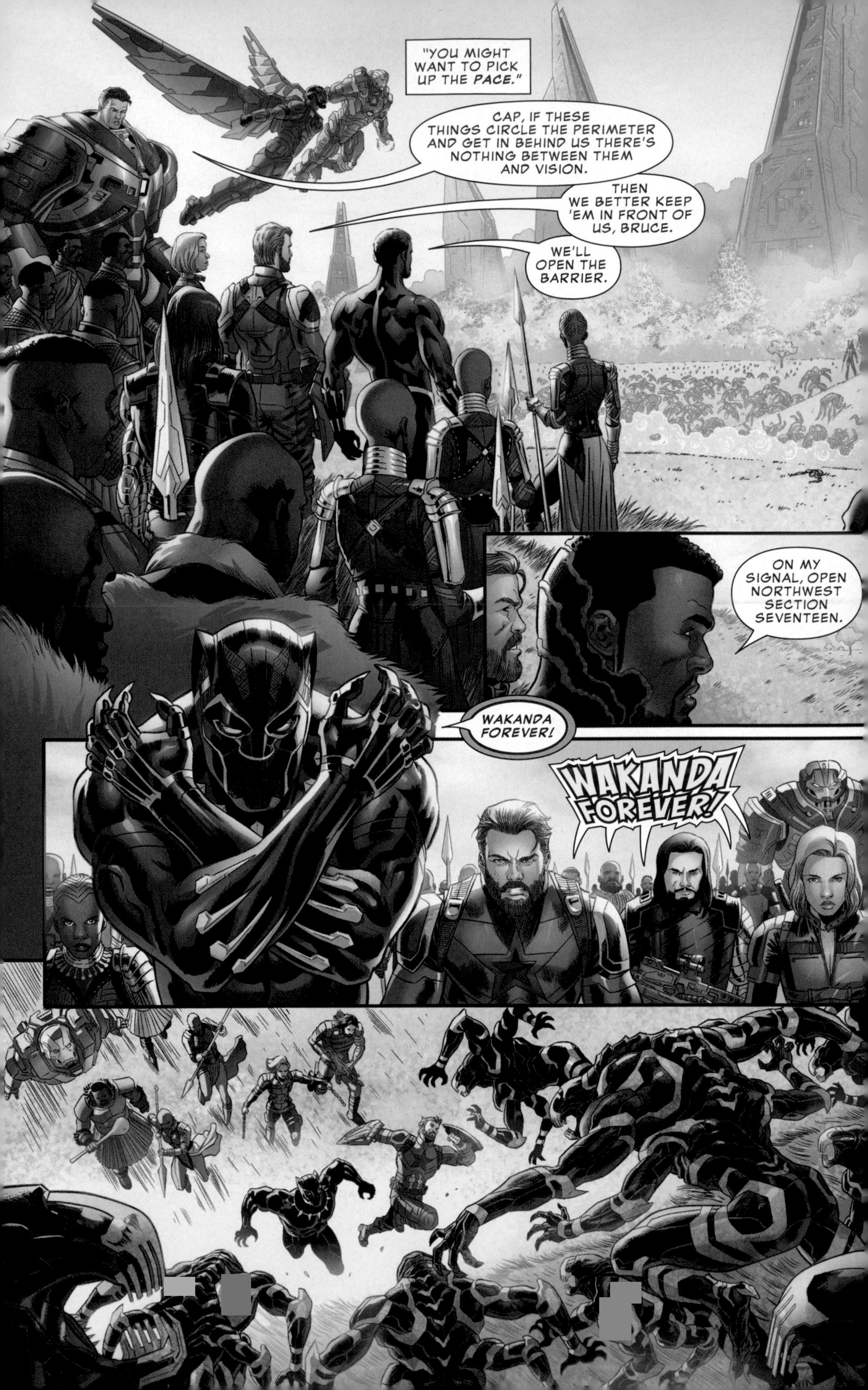

"YOU MIGHT WANT TO PICK UP THE *PACE.*"
CAP, IF THESE THINGS CIRCLE THE PERIMETER AND GET IN BEHIND US THERE'S NOTHING BETWEEN THEM AND VISION.
THEN WE BETTER KEEP 'EM IN FRONT OF US, BRUCE.
WE'LL OPEN THE BARRIER.
ON MY SIGNAL, OPEN NORTHWEST SECTION SEVENTEEN.
WAKANDA FOREVER!
WAKANDA FOREVER!

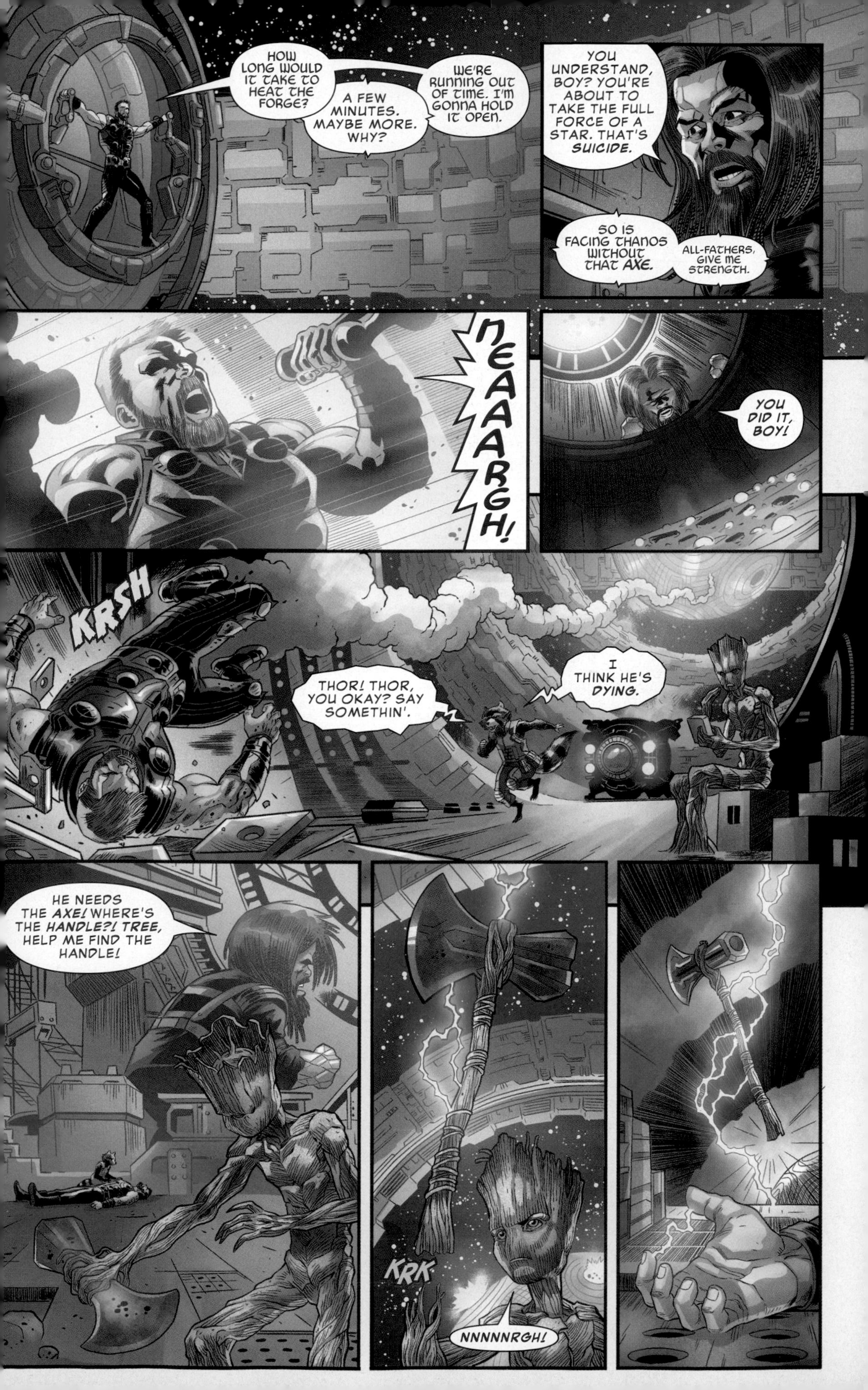
HOW LONG WOULD IT TAKE TO HEAT THE FORGE?
A FEW MINUTES. MAYBE MORE. WHY?
WE'RE RUNNING OUT OF TIME. I'M GONNA HOLD IT OPEN.
YOU UNDERSTAND, BOY? YOU'RE ABOUT TO TAKE THE FULL FORCE OF A STAR. THAT'S SUICIDE.
SO IS FACING THANOS WITHOUT THAT AXE.
ALL-FATHERS, GIVE ME STRENGTH.
NEAAAARGH!
YOU DID IT, BOY!
KRSH
THOR! THOR, YOU OKAY? SAY SOMETHIN'.
I THINK HE'S DYING.
HE NEEDS THE AXE! WHERE'S THE HANDLE?! TREE, HELP ME FIND THE HANDLE!
KRK
NNNNNRGH!

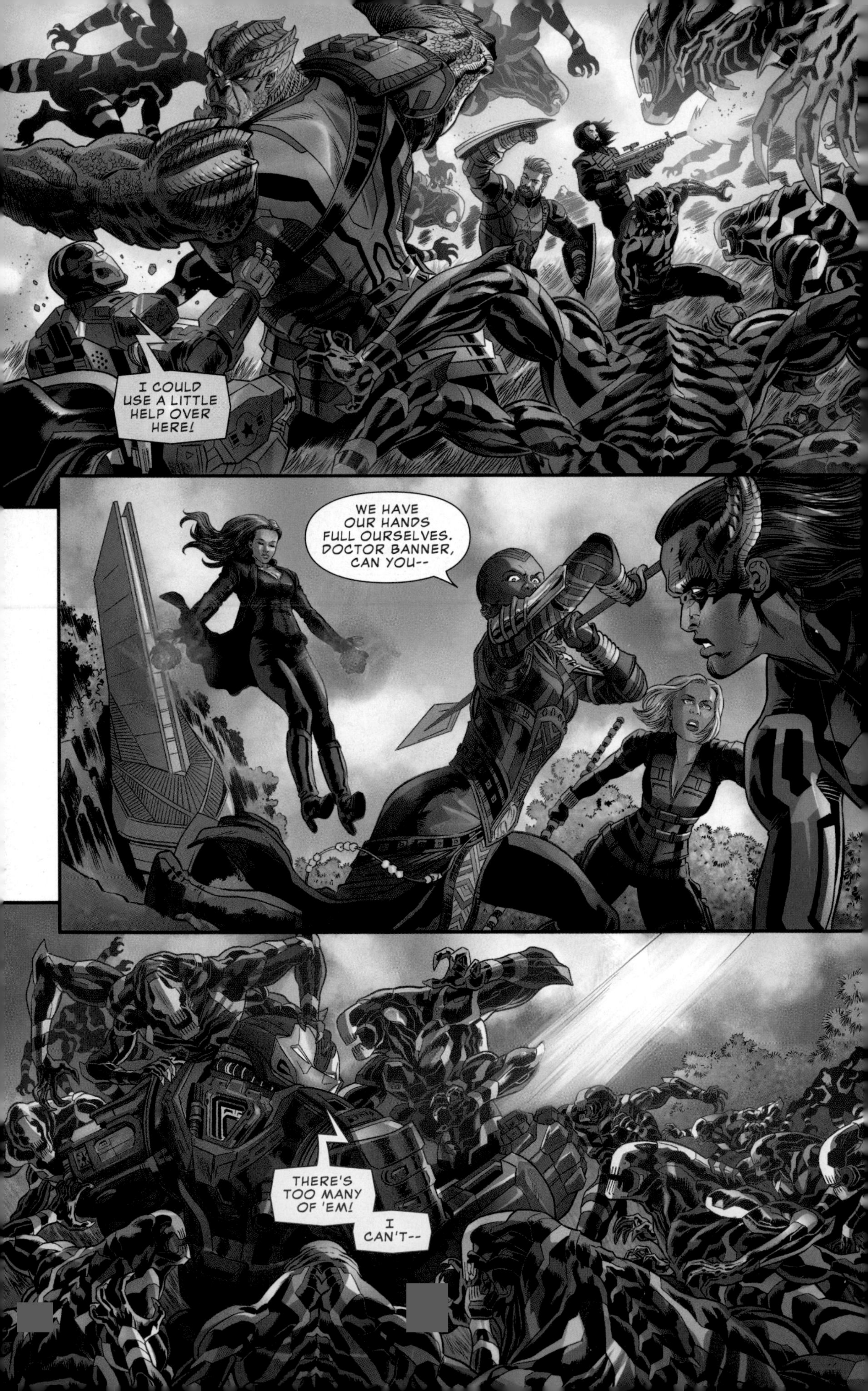
I COULD USE A LITTLE HELP OVER HERE!
WE HAVE OUR HANDS FULL OURSELVES. DOCTOR BANNER, CAN YOU--
THERE'S TOO MANY OF 'EM!
I CAN'T--

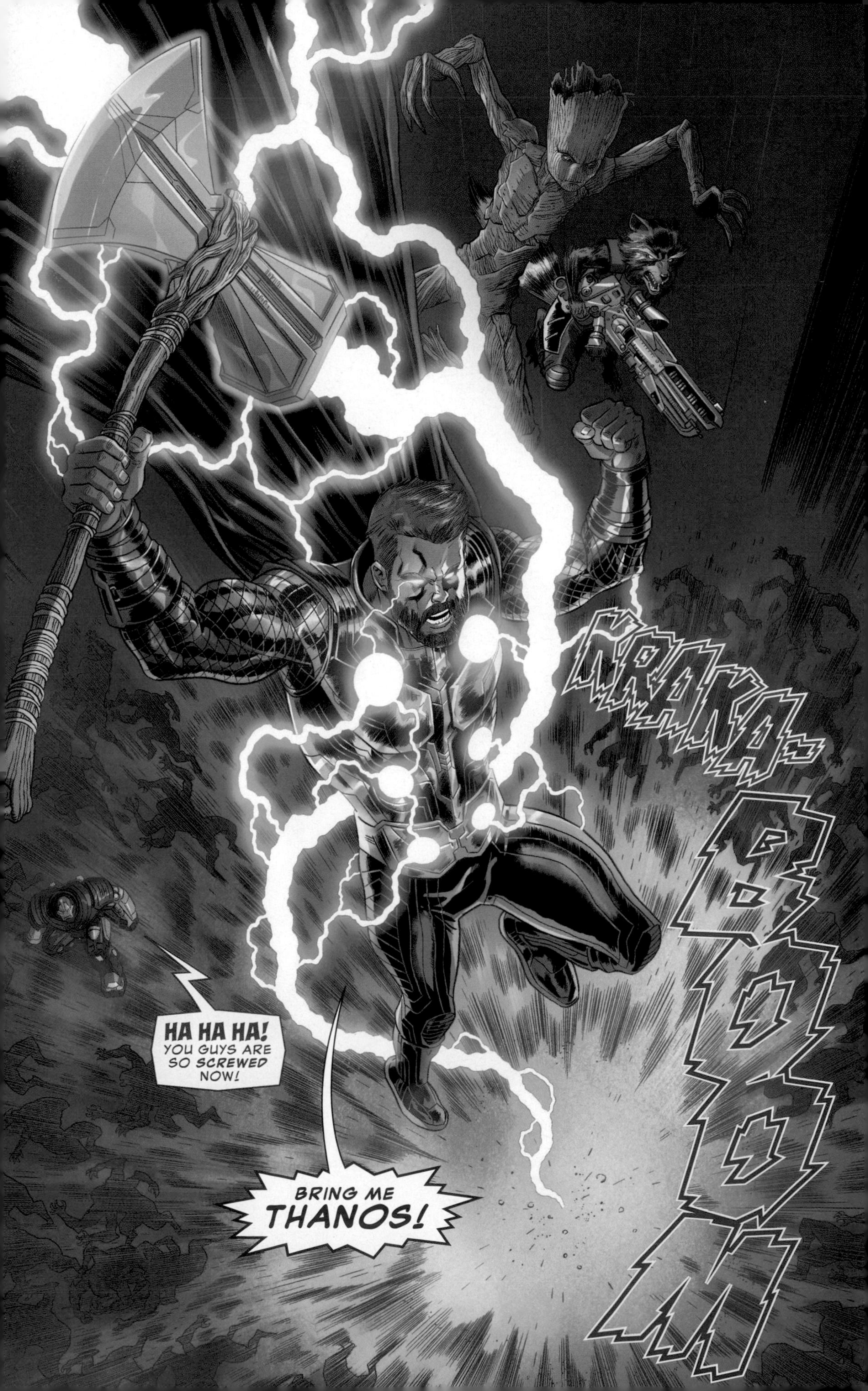
KRAKA-BOOM
HA HA HA! YOU GUYS ARE SO SCREWED NOW!
BRING ME THANOS!

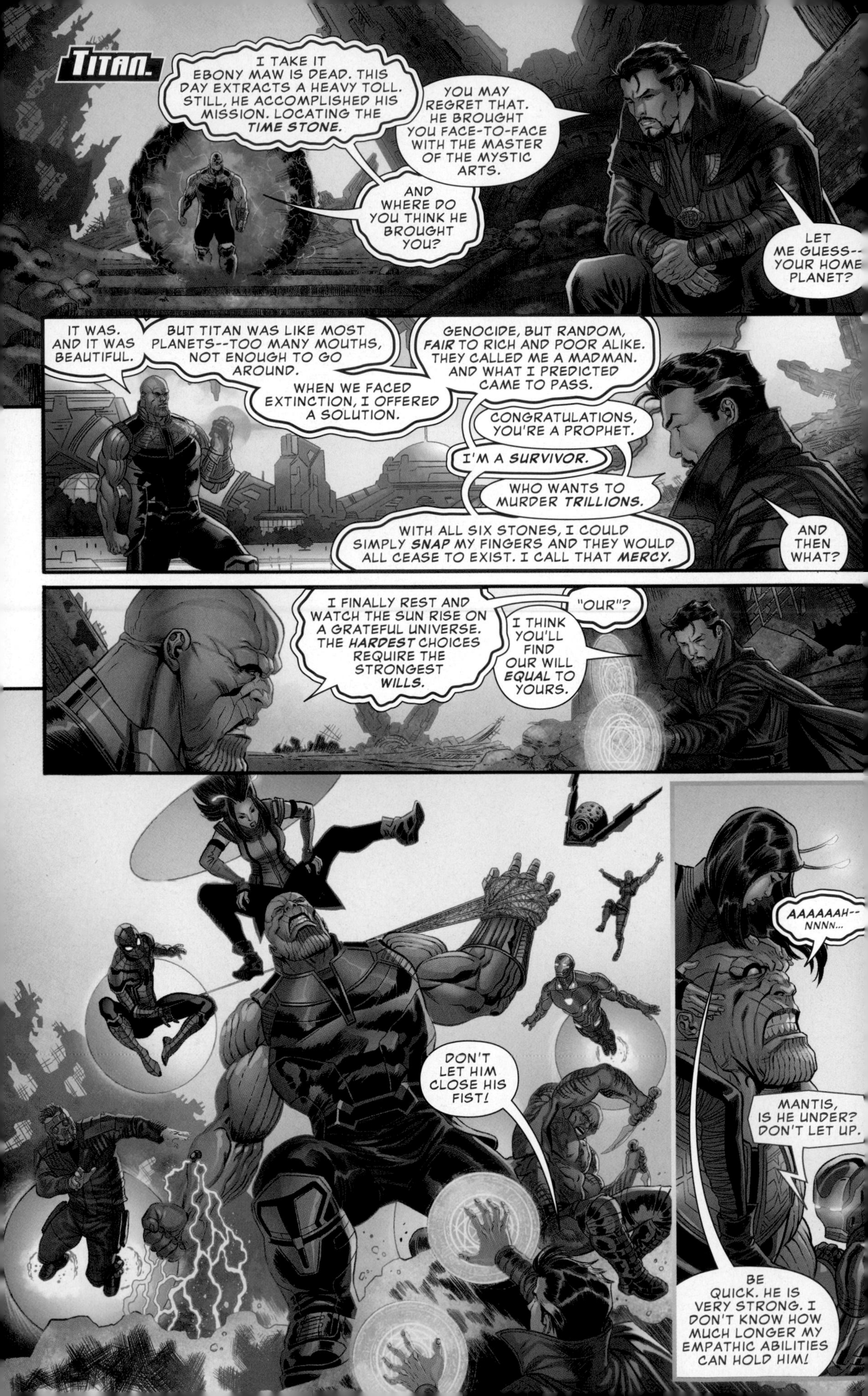
TITAN.
I TAKE IT EBONY MAW IS DEAD. THIS DAY EXTRACTS A HEAVY TOLL. STILL, HE ACCOMPLISHED HIS MISSION. LOCATING THE TIME STONE.
YOU MAY REGRET THAT. HE BROUGHT YOU FACE-TO-FACE WITH THE MASTER OF THE MYSTIC ARTS.
AND WHERE DO YOU THINK HE BROUGHT YOU?
LET ME GUESS-- YOUR HOME PLANET?
IT WAS. AND IT WAS BEAUTIFUL.
BUT TITAN WAS LIKE MOST PLANETS--TOO MANY MOUTHS, NOT ENOUGH TO GO AROUND.
WHEN WE FACED EXTINCTION, I OFFERED A SOLUTION.
GENOCIDE, BUT RANDOM, FAIR TO RICH AND POOR ALIKE. THEY CALLED ME A MADMAN. AND WHAT I PREDICTED CAME TO PASS.
CONGRATULATIONS, YOU'RE A PROPHET.
I'M A SURVIVOR.
WHO WANTS TO MURDER TRILLIONS.
WITH ALL SIX STONES, I COULD SIMPLY SNAP MY FINGERS AND THEY WOULD ALL CEASE TO EXIST. I CALL THAT MERCY.
AND THEN WHAT?
I FINALLY REST AND WATCH THE SUN RISE ON A GRATEFUL UNIVERSE. THE HARDEST CHOICES REQUIRE THE STRONGEST WILLS.
"OUR"?
I THINK YOU'LL FIND OUR WILL EQUAL TO YOURS.
DON'T LET HIM CLOSE HIS FIST!
AAAAAAH-- NNNN...
MANTIS, IS HE UNDER? DON'T LET UP.
BE QUICK. HE IS VERY STRONG. I DON'T KNOW HOW MUCH LONGER MY EMPATHIC ABILITIES CAN HOLD HIM!

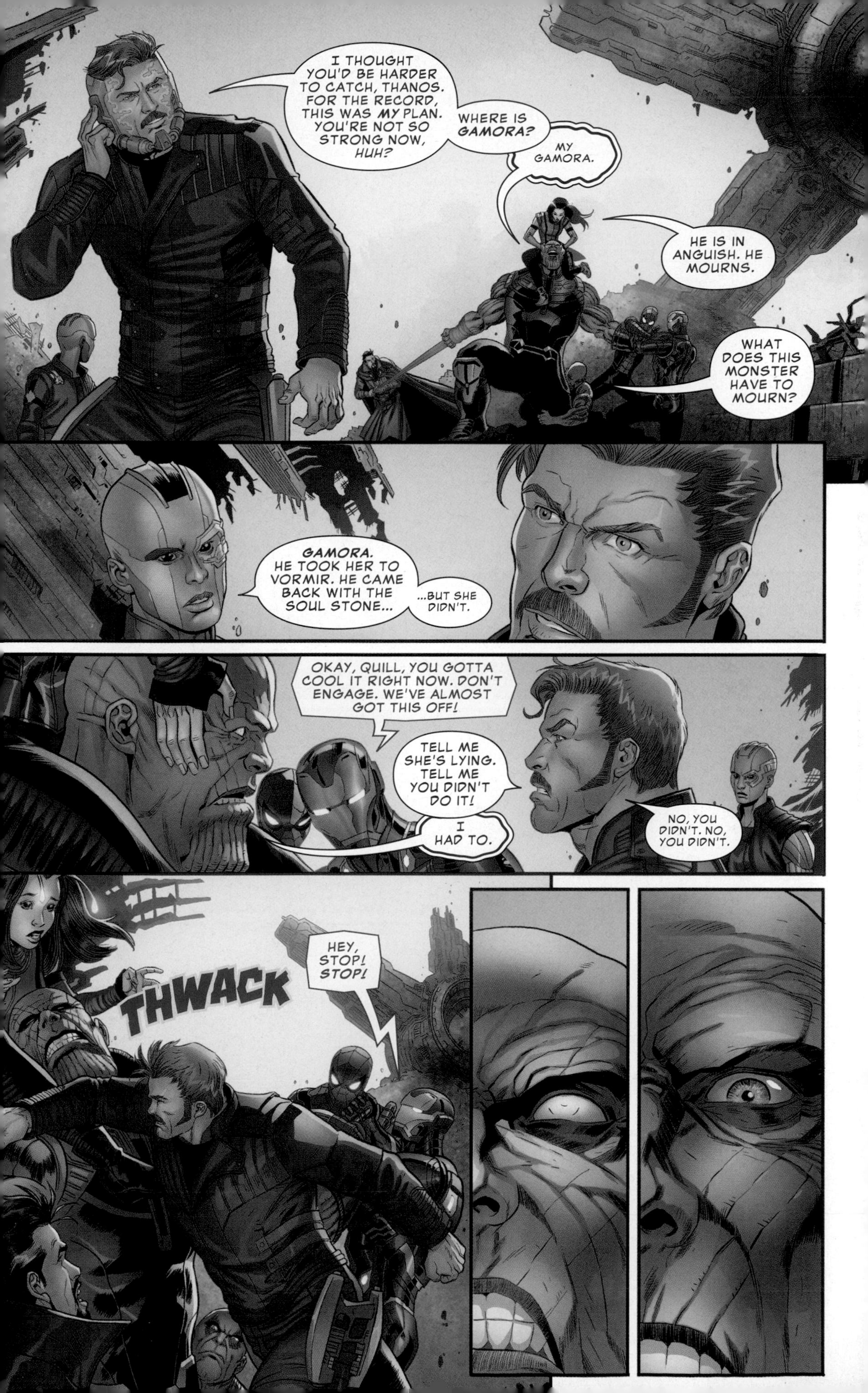
I THOUGHT YOU'D BE HARDER TO CATCH, THANOS. FOR THE RECORD, THIS WAS MY PLAN. YOU'RE NOT SO STRONG NOW, HUH?
WHERE IS GAMORA?
MY GAMORA.
HE IS IN ANGUISH. HE MOURNS.
WHAT DOES THIS MONSTER HAVE TO MOURN?
GAMORA. HE TOOK HER TO VORMIR. HE CAME BACK WITH THE SOUL STONE...
...BUT SHE DIDN'T.
OKAY, QUILL, YOU GOTTA COOL IT RIGHT NOW. DON'T ENGAGE. WE'VE ALMOST GOT THIS OFF!
TELL ME SHE'S LYING. TELL ME YOU DIDN'T DO IT!
I HAD TO.
NO, YOU DIDN'T. NO, YOU DIDN'T.
THWACK
HEY, STOP! STOP!

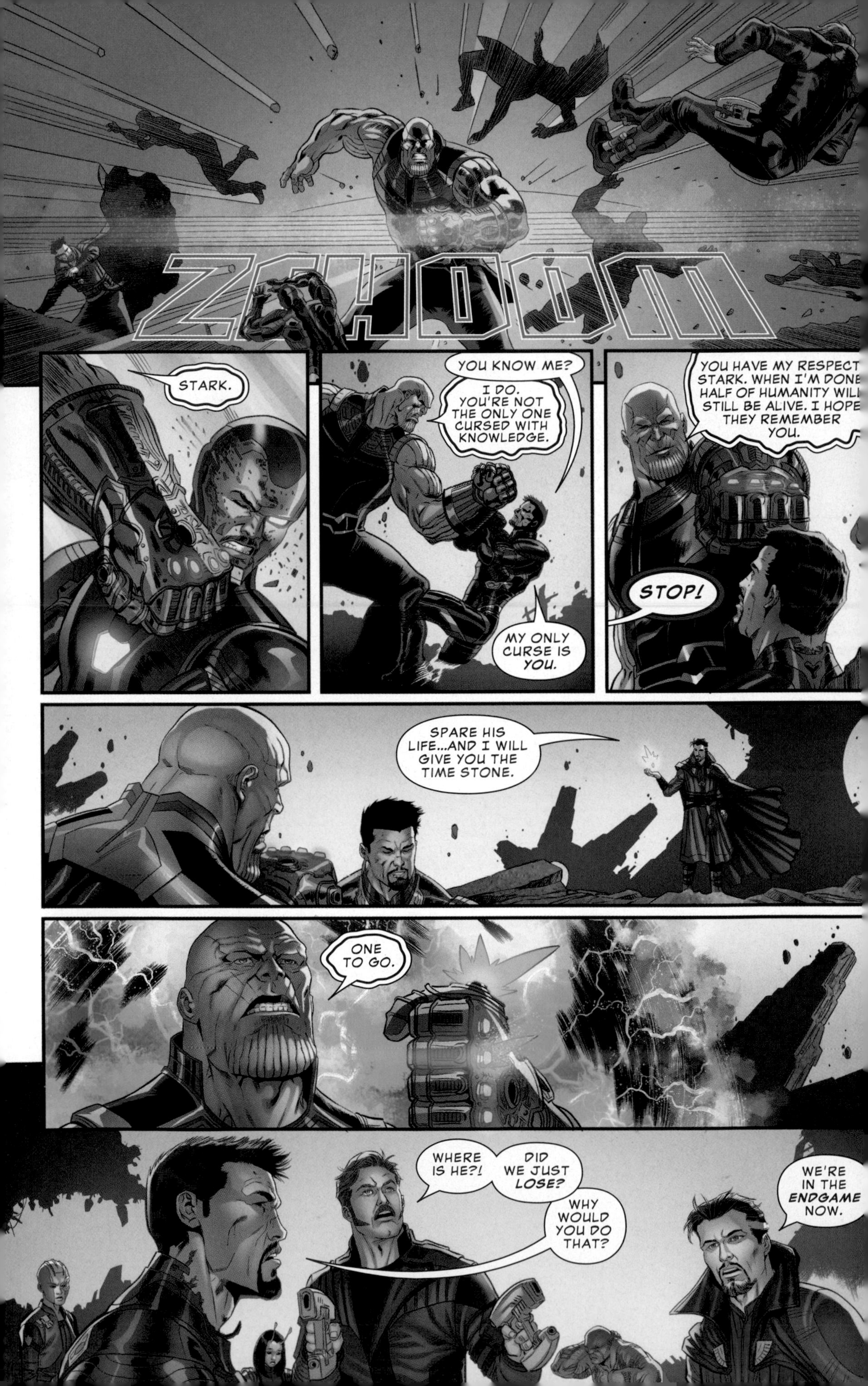
ZCHOOM
STARK.
YOU KNOW ME?
I DO. YOU'RE NOT THE ONLY ONE CURSED WITH KNOWLEDGE.
MY ONLY CURSE IS *YOU.*
YOU HAVE MY RESPECT STARK. WHEN I'M DONE HALF OF HUMANITY WILL STILL BE ALIVE. I HOPE THEY REMEMBER YOU.
STOP!
SPARE HIS LIFE...AND I WILL GIVE YOU THE TIME STONE.
ONE TO GO.
WHERE IS HE?!
DID WE JUST *LOSE?*
WHY WOULD YOU DO THAT?
WE'RE IN THE *ENDGAME* NOW.

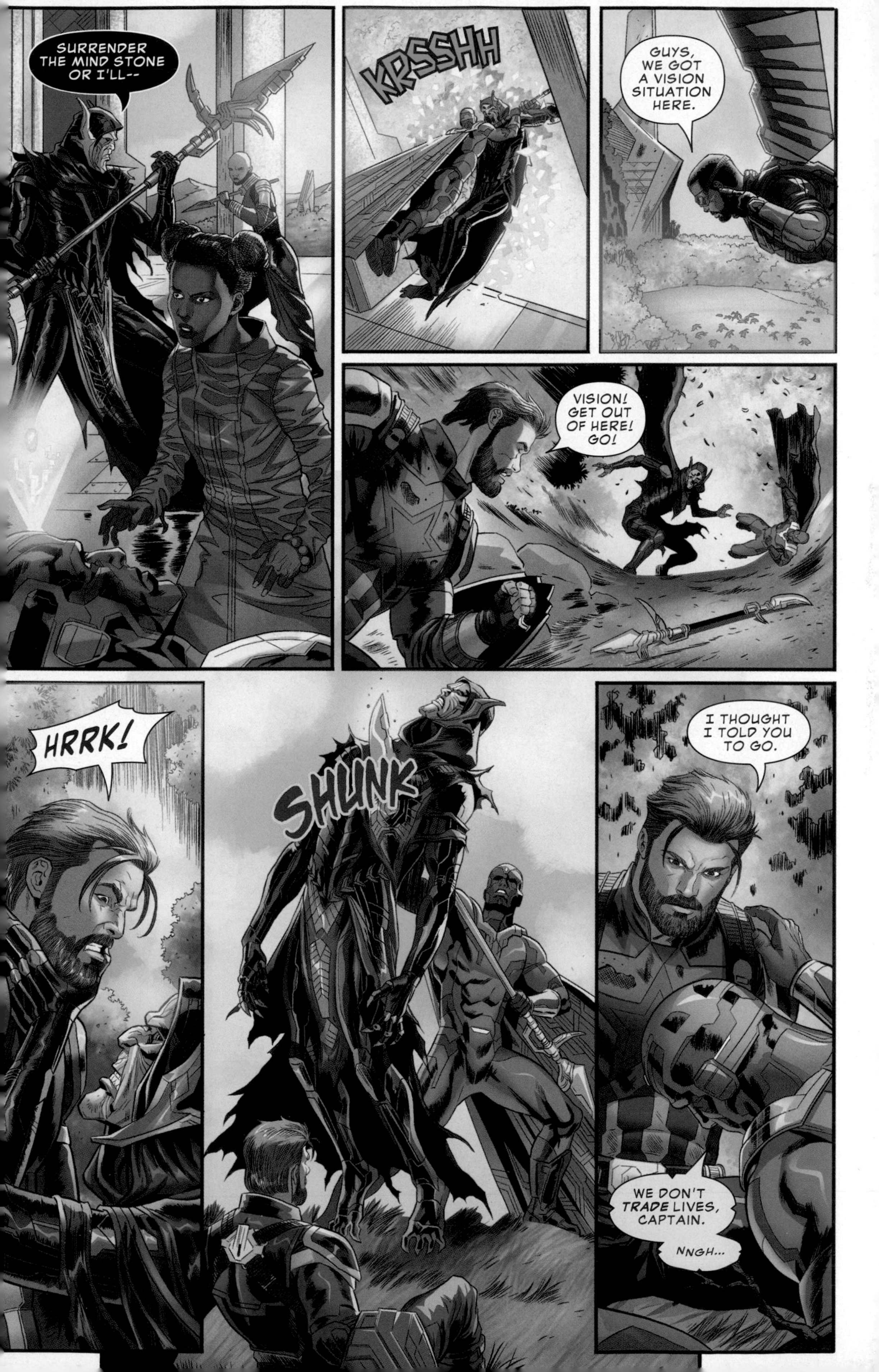
SURRENDER THE MIND STONE OR I'LL--
KRSSHH
GUYS, WE GOT A VISION SITUATION HERE.
VISION! GET OUT OF HERE! GO!
HRRK!
SHUNK
I THOUGHT I TOLD YOU TO GO.
WE DON'T TRADE LIVES, CAPTAIN.
NNGH...

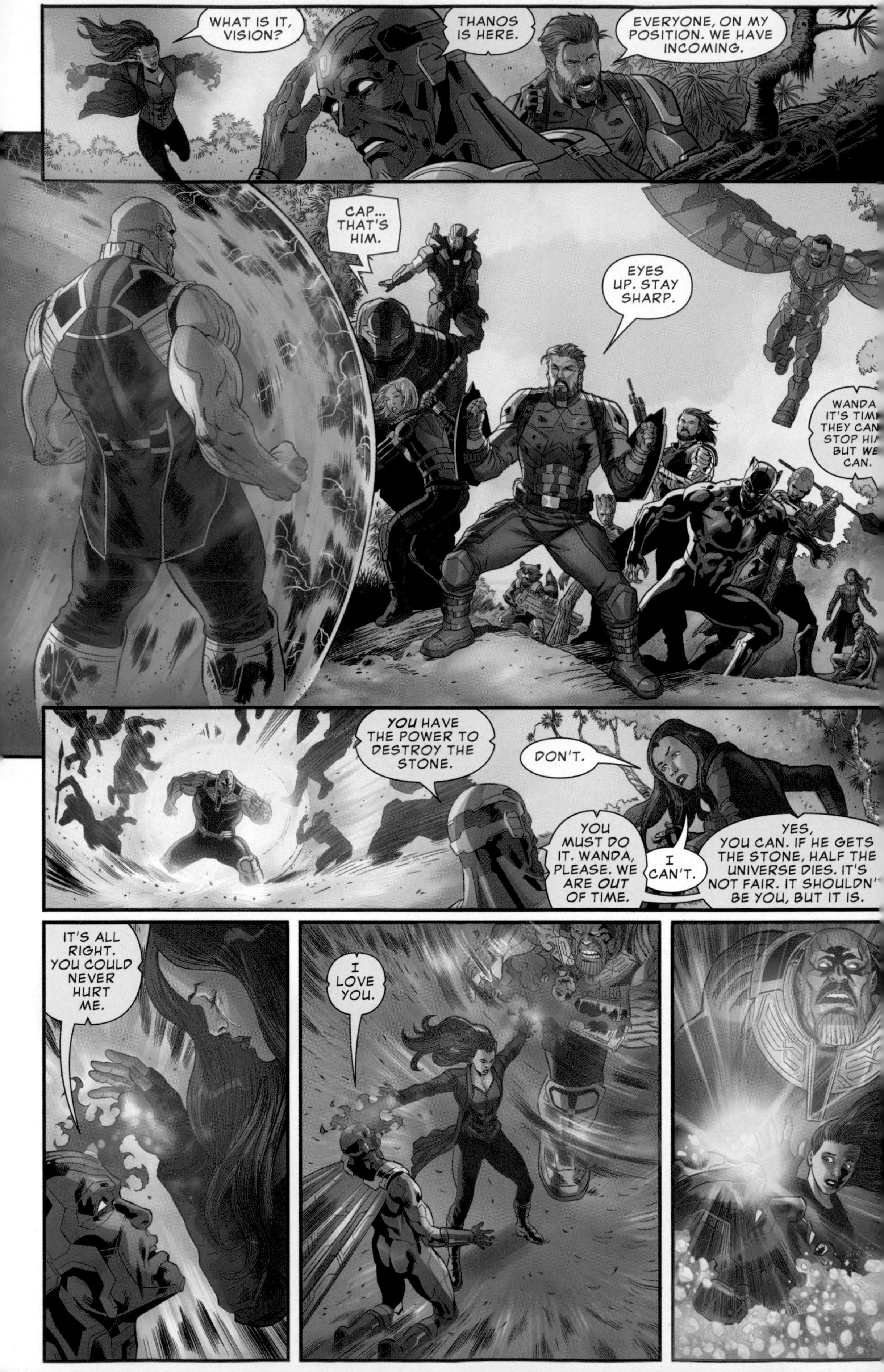

WHAT IS IT, VISION?
THANOS IS HERE.
EVERYONE, ON MY POSITION. WE HAVE INCOMING.
CAP... THAT'S HIM.
EYES UP. STAY SHARP.
WANDA IT'S TIM THEY CAN STOP HI BUT WE CAN.
YOU HAVE THE POWER TO DESTROY THE STONE.
DON'T.
YOU MUST DO IT. WANDA, PLEASE. WE ARE OUT OF TIME.
I CAN'T.
YES, YOU CAN. IF HE GETS THE STONE, HALF THE UNIVERSE DIES. IT'S NOT FAIR. IT SHOULDN' BE YOU, BUT IT IS.
IT'S ALL RIGHT. YOU COULD NEVER HURT ME.
I LOVE YOU.

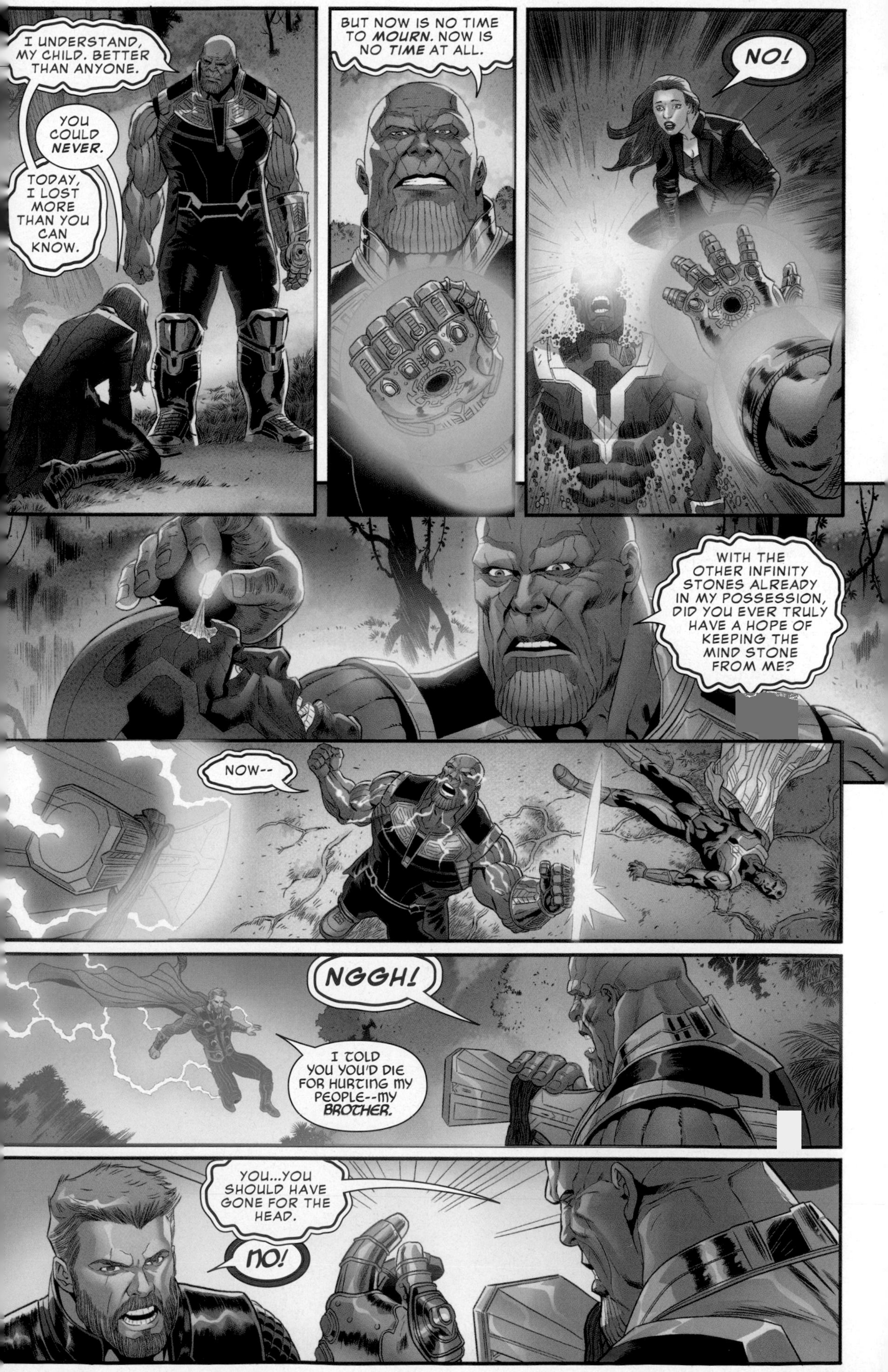
I UNDERSTAND, MY CHILD. BETTER THAN ANYONE.
YOU COULD NEVER.
TODAY, I LOST MORE THAN YOU CAN KNOW.
BUT NOW IS NO TIME TO MOURN. NOW IS NO TIME AT ALL.
NO!
WITH THE OTHER INFINITY STONES ALREADY IN MY POSSESSION, DID YOU EVER TRULY HAVE A HOPE OF KEEPING THE MIND STONE FROM ME?
NOW--
NGGH!
I TOLD YOU YOU'D DIE FOR HURTING MY PEOPLE--MY BROTHER.
YOU...YOU SHOULD HAVE GONE FOR THE HEAD.
NO!

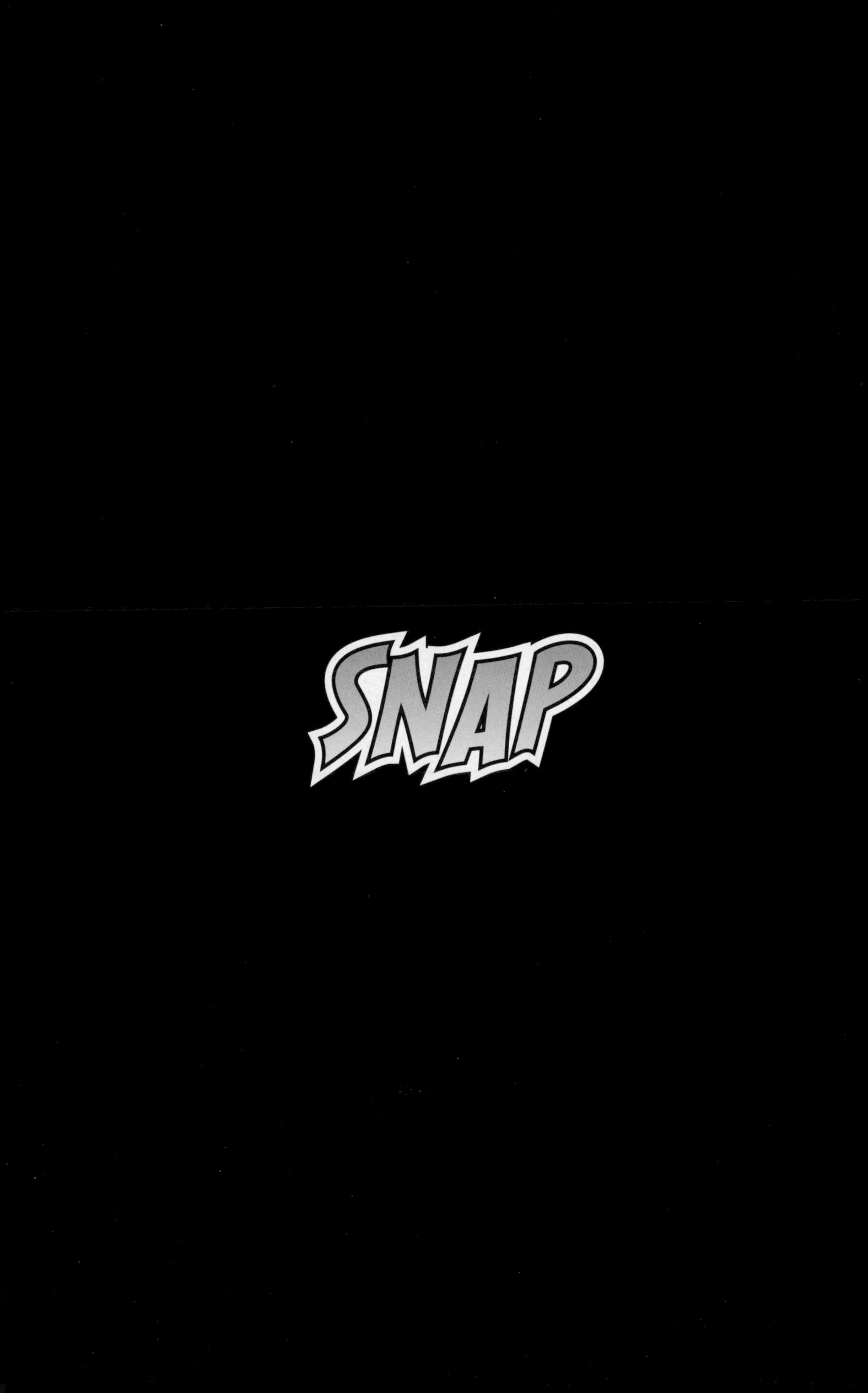
SNAP

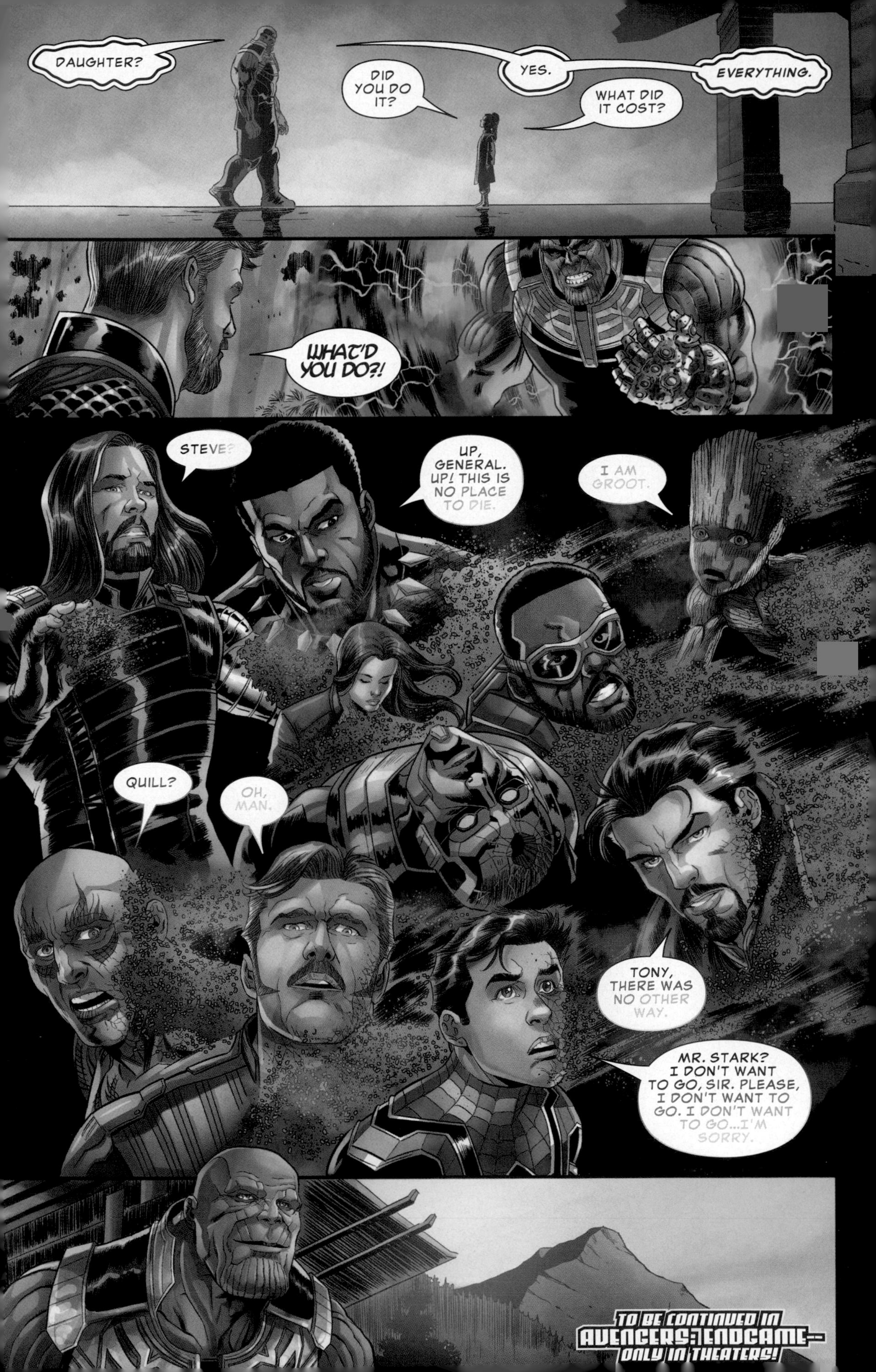
DAUGHTER?
DID YOU DO IT?
YES.
WHAT DID IT COST?
EVERYTHING.
WHAT'D YOU DO?!
STEVE?
UP, GENERAL. UP! THIS IS NO PLACE TO DIE.
I AM GROOT.
QUILL?
OH, MAN.
TONY, THERE WAS NO OTHER WAY.
MR. STARK? I DON'T WANT TO GO, SIR. PLEASE, I DON'T WANT TO GO. I DON'T WANT TO GO...I'M SORRY.
TO BE CONTINUED IN AVENGERS: ENDGAME-- ONLY IN THEATERS!

WITH ALL THE INFINITY GEMS COLLECTED, THANOS SEEKS TO HONOR MISTRESS DEATH WITH THE ULTIMATE TRIBUTE IN THE FIRST CHAPTER OF JIM STARLIN'S *INFINITY GAUNTLET.*

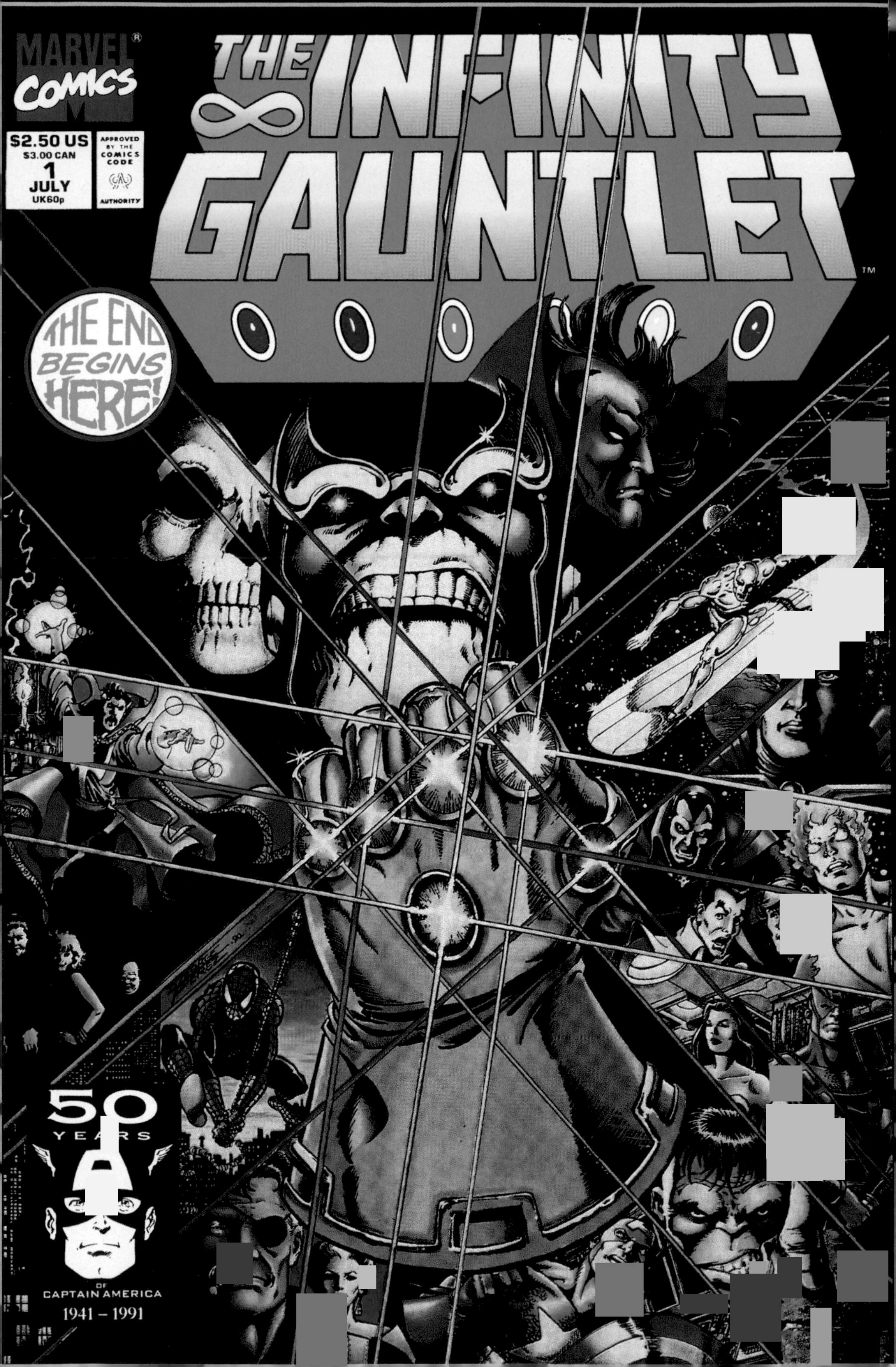
MARVEL COMICS
THE INFINITY GAUNTLET
$2.50 US
$3.00 CAN
1
JULY
UK60p
APPROVED BY THE COMICS CODE AUTHORITY
THE END BEGINS HERE!
50 YEARS OF CAPTAIN AMERICA
1941 – 1991

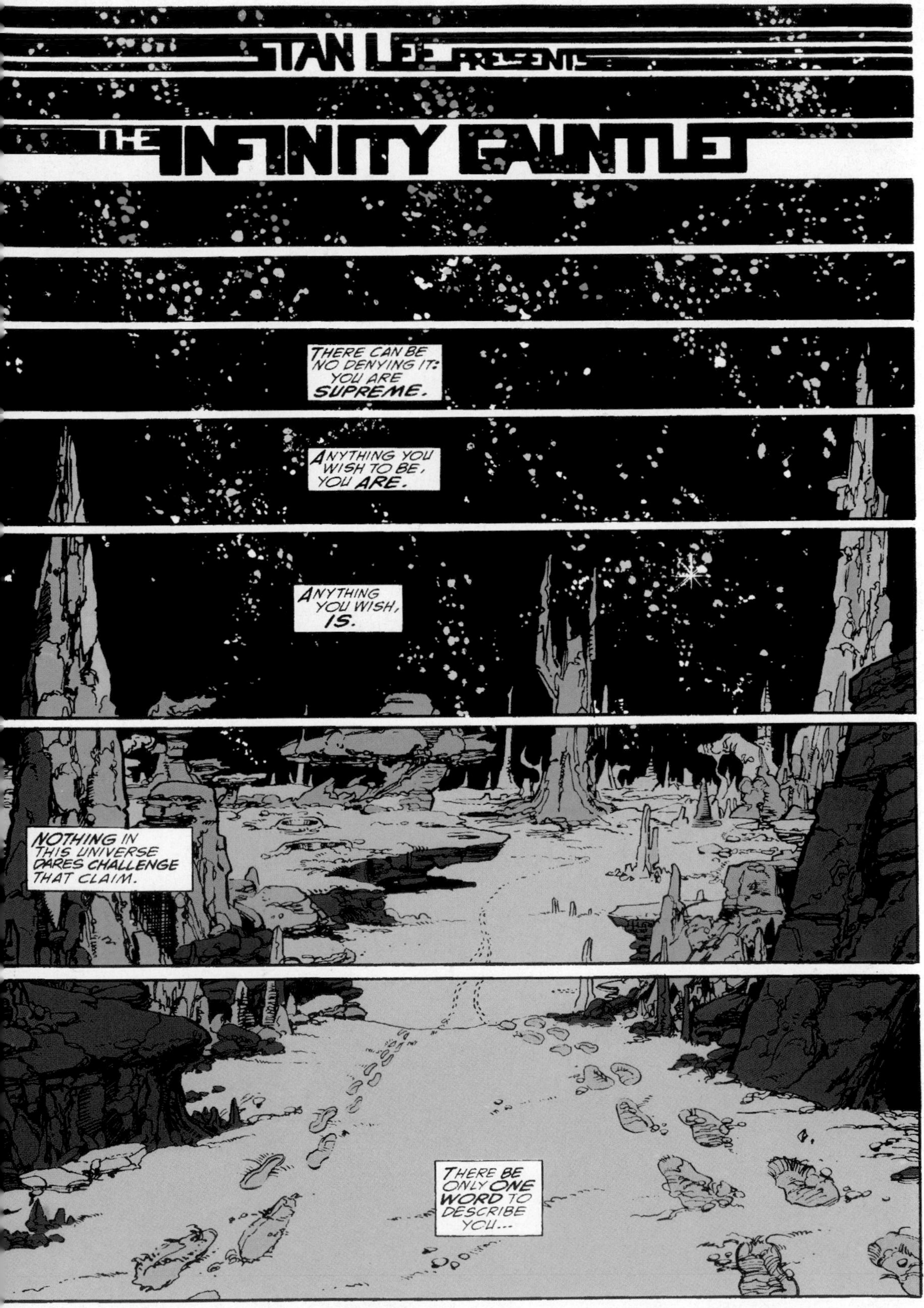
STAN LEE PRESENTS
THE INFINITY GAUNTLET
THERE CAN BE NO DENYING IT: YOU ARE SUPREME.
ANYTHING YOU WISH TO BE, YOU ARE.
ANYTHING YOU WISH, IS.
NOTHING IN THIS UNIVERSE DARES CHALLENGE THAT CLAIM.
THERE BE ONLY ONE WORD TO DESCRIBE YOU...

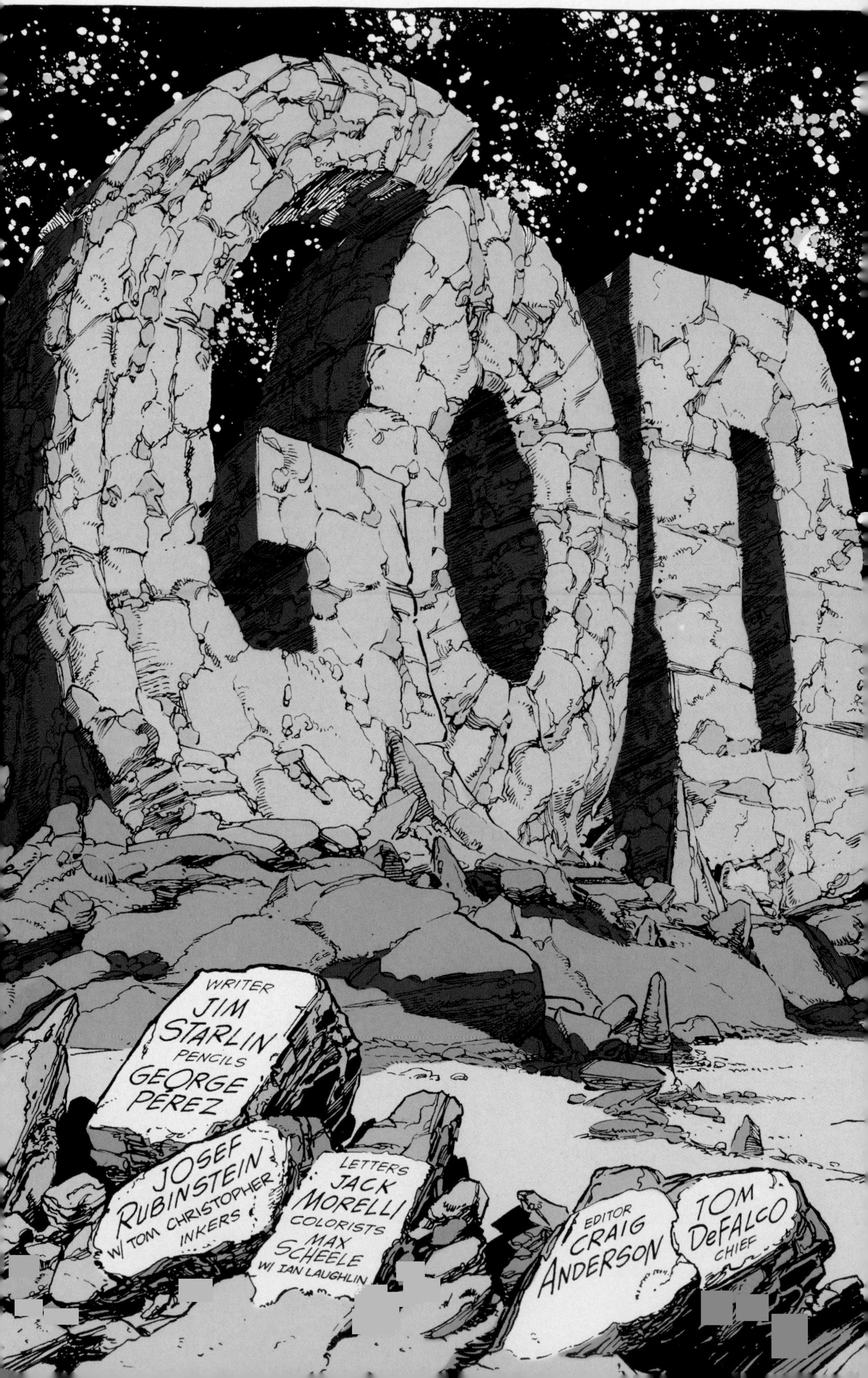
GOD
WRITER
JIM STARLIN
PENCILS
GEORGE PEREZ
JOSEF RUBINSTEIN
W/ TOM CHRISTOPHER
INKERS
LETTERS
JACK MORELLI
COLORISTS
MAX SCHEELE
W/ IAN LAUGHLIN
EDITOR
CRAIG ANDERSON
TOM DeFALCO
CHIEF

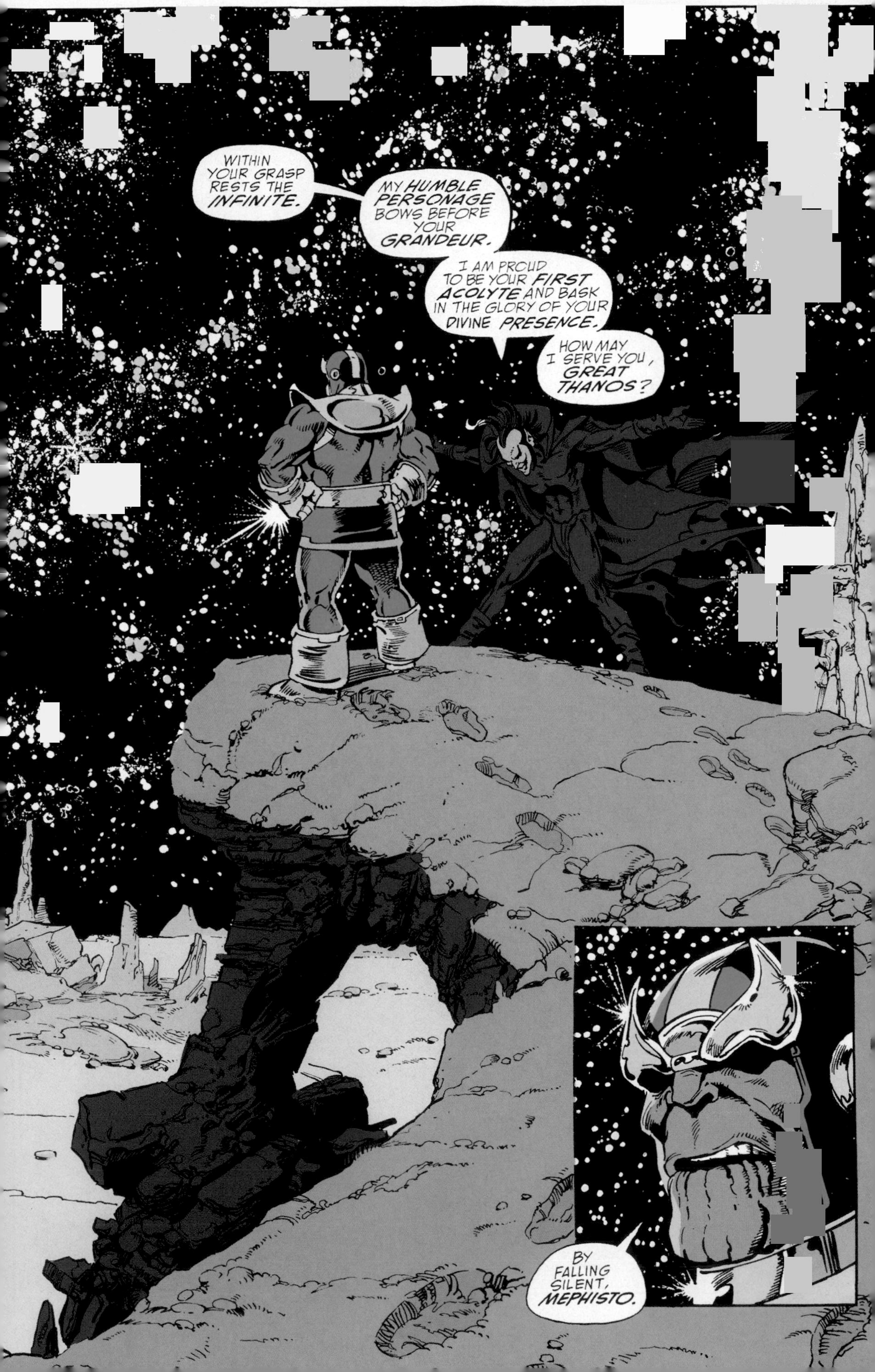
WITHIN YOUR GRASP RESTS THE INFINITE.
MY HUMBLE PERSONAGE BOWS BEFORE YOUR GRANDEUR.
I AM PROUD TO BE YOUR FIRST ACOLYTE AND BASK IN THE GLORY OF YOUR DIVINE PRESENCE.
HOW MAY I SERVE YOU, GREAT THANOS?
BY FALLING SILENT, MEPHISTO.

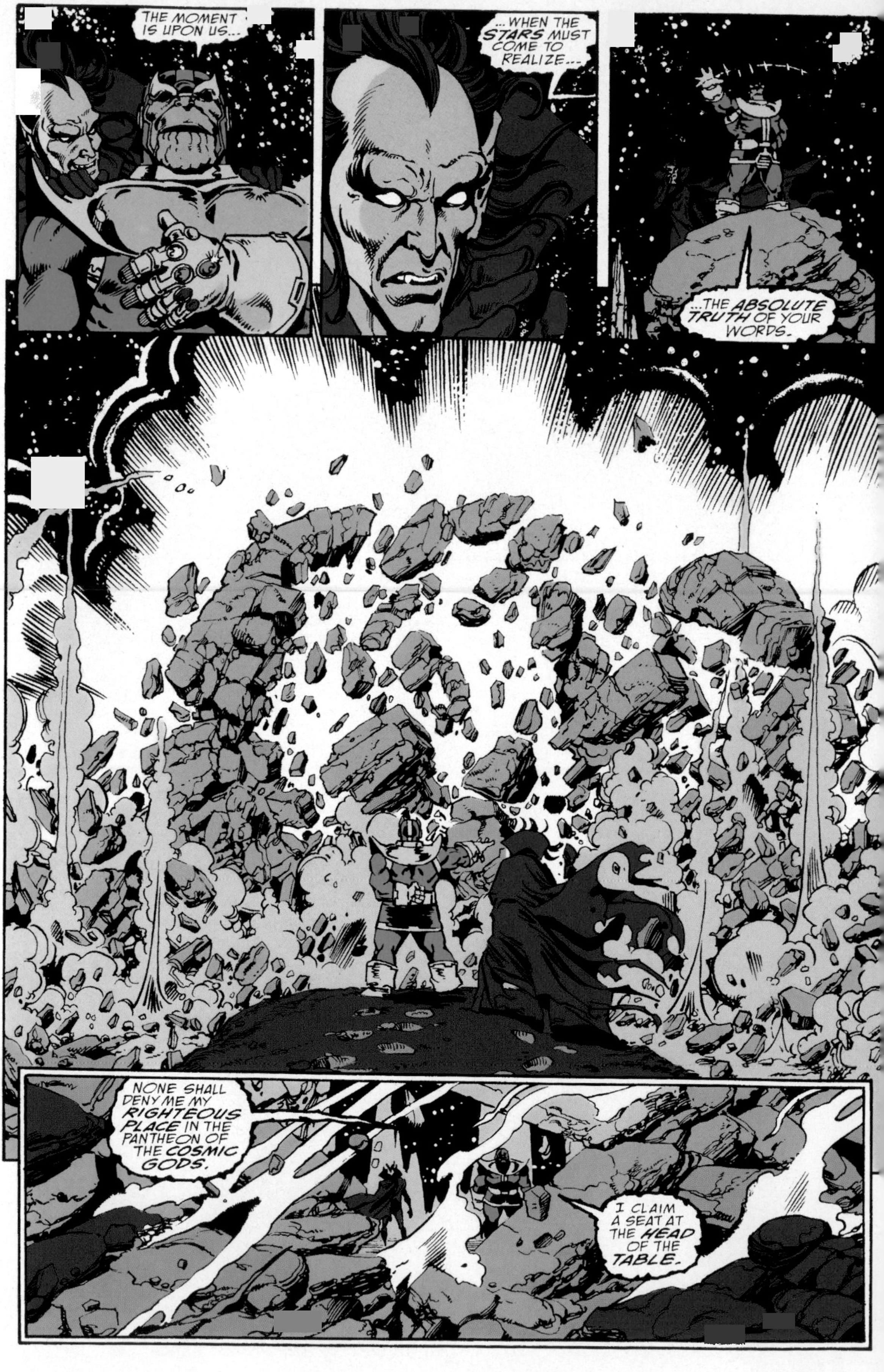
THE MOMENT IS UPON US...
...WHEN THE STARS MUST COME TO REALIZE...
...THE ABSOLUTE TRUTH OF YOUR WORDS.
NONE SHALL DENY ME MY RIGHTEOUS PLACE IN THE PANTHEON OF THE COSMIC GODS.
I CLAIM A SEAT AT THE HEAD OF THE TABLE.

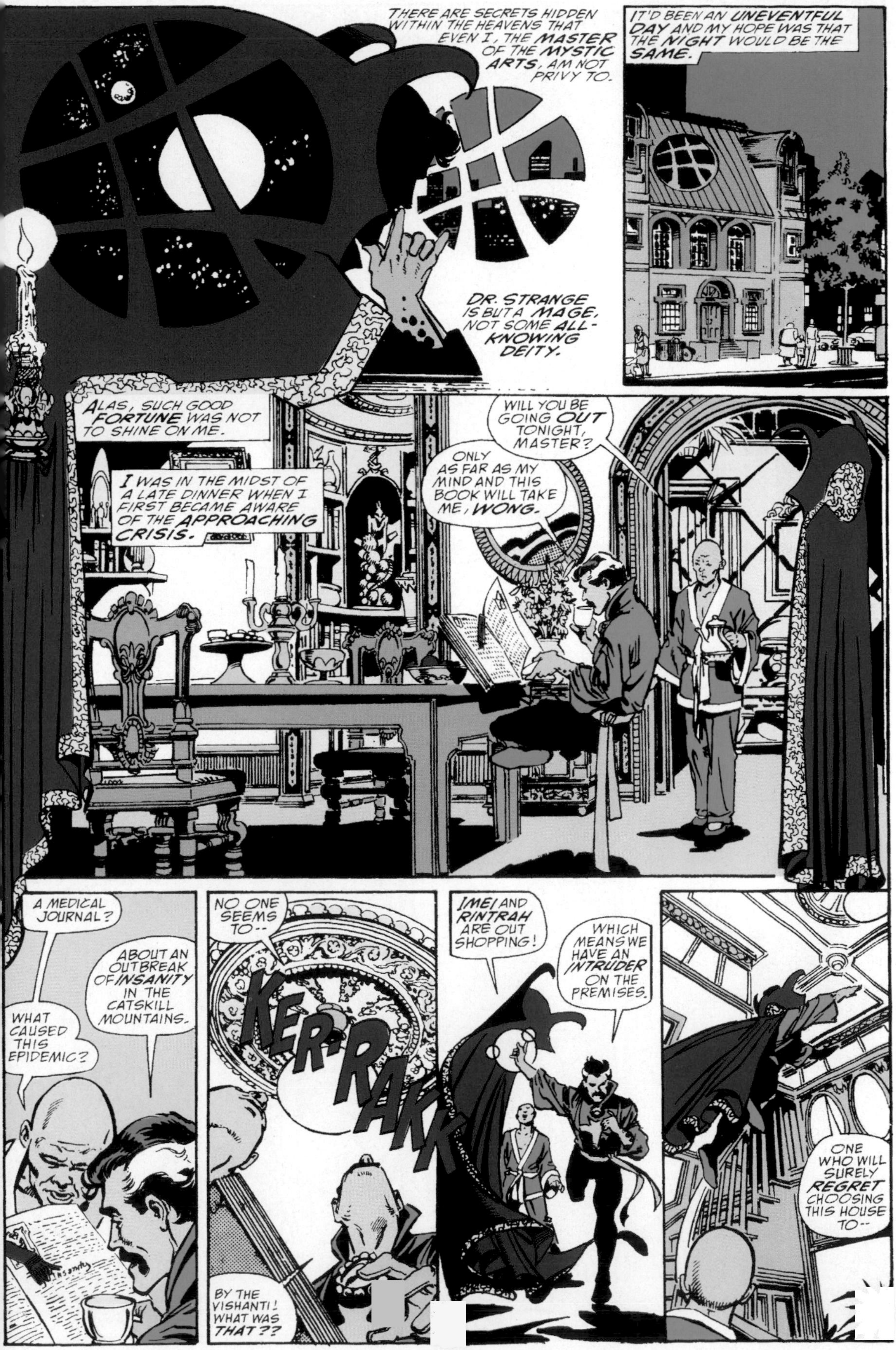

THERE ARE SECRETS HIDDEN WITHIN THE HEAVENS THAT EVEN I, THE MASTER OF THE MYSTIC ARTS, AM NOT PRIVY TO.
IT'D BEEN AN UNEVENTFUL DAY AND MY HOPE WAS THAT THE NIGHT WOULD BE THE SAME.
DR. STRANGE IS BUT A MAGE, NOT SOME ALL-KNOWING DEITY.
ALAS, SUCH GOOD FORTUNE WAS NOT TO SHINE ON ME.
I WAS IN THE MIDST OF A LATE DINNER WHEN I FIRST BECAME AWARE OF THE APPROACHING CRISIS.
WILL YOU BE GOING OUT TONIGHT, MASTER?
ONLY AS FAR AS MY MIND AND THIS BOOK WILL TAKE ME, WONG.
A MEDICAL JOURNAL?
ABOUT AN OUTBREAK OF INSANITY IN THE CATSKILL MOUNTAINS.
WHAT CAUSED THIS EPIDEMIC?
NO ONE SEEMS TO--
KER-RAKK
BY THE VISHANTI! WHAT WAS THAT??
IMEI AND RINTRAH ARE OUT SHOPPING!
WHICH MEANS WE HAVE AN INTRUDER ON THE PREMISES.
ONE WHO WILL SURELY REGRET CHOOSING THIS HOUSE TO--

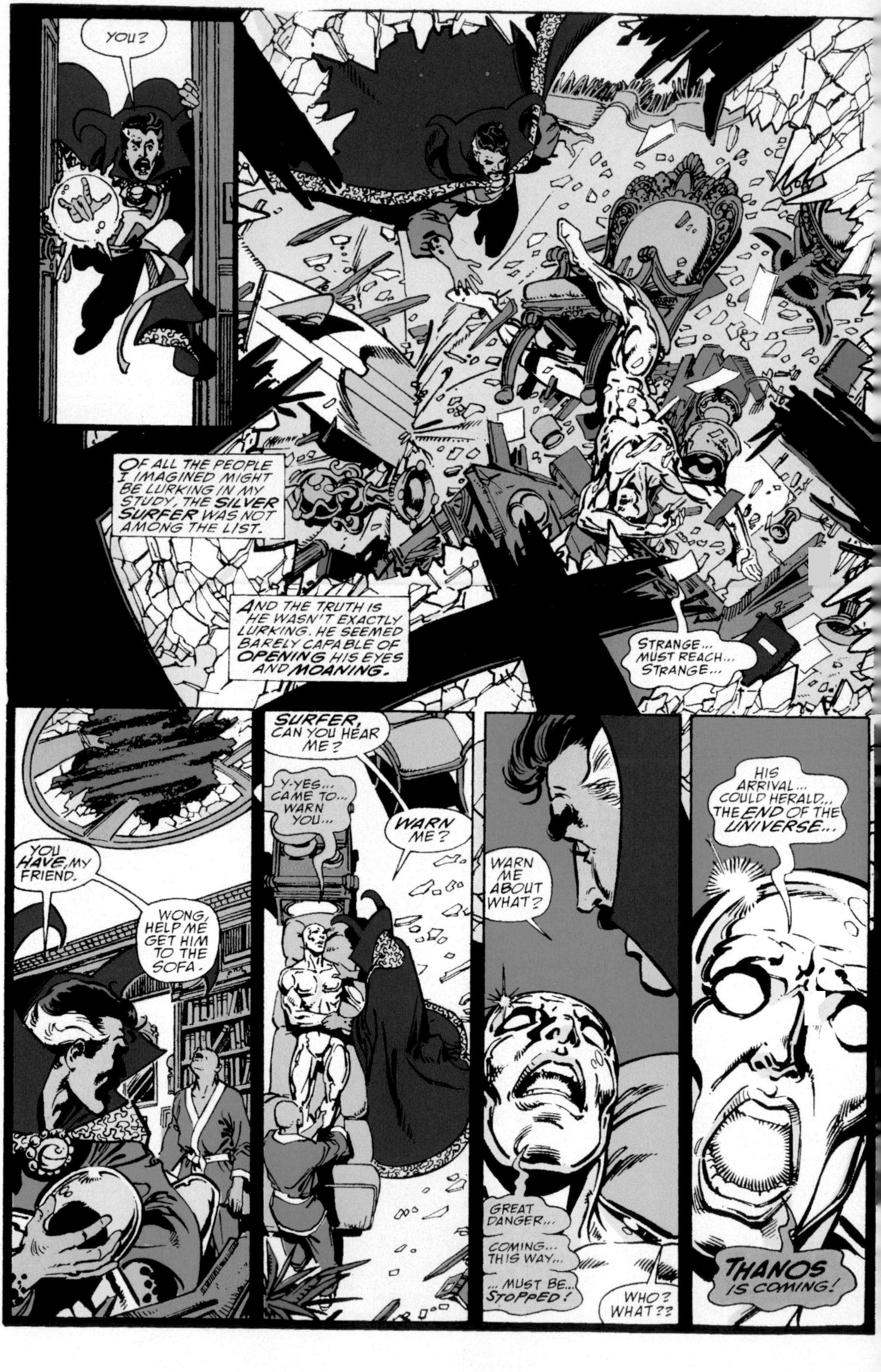
YOU?
OF ALL THE PEOPLE I IMAGINED MIGHT BE LURKING IN MY STUDY, THE SILVER SURFER WAS NOT AMONG THE LIST.
AND THE TRUTH IS HE WASN'T EXACTLY LURKING. HE SEEMED BARELY CAPABLE OF OPENING HIS EYES AND MOANING.
STRANGE... MUST REACH... STRANGE...
YOU HAVE, MY FRIEND.
WONG, HELP ME GET HIM TO THE SOFA.
SURFER, CAN YOU HEAR ME?
Y-YES... CAME TO... WARN YOU...
WARN ME?
WARN ME ABOUT WHAT?
GREAT DANGER...
COMING... THIS WAY...
... MUST BE... STOPPED!
WHO? WHAT??
HIS ARRIVAL... COULD HERALD... THE END OF THE UNIVERSE...
THANOS IS COMING!

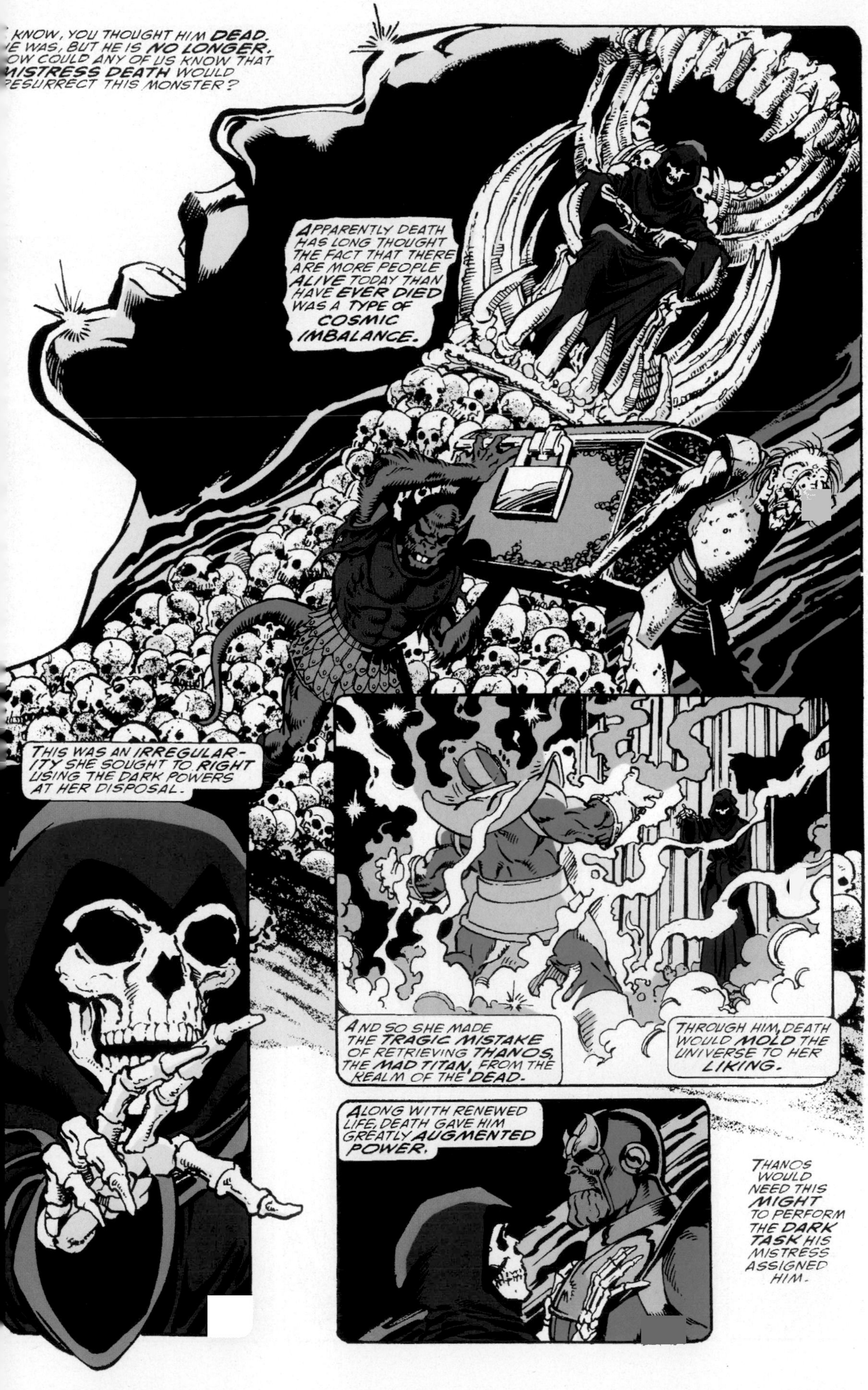

KNOW, YOU THOUGHT HIM DEAD.
E WAS, BUT HE IS NO LONGER.
OW COULD ANY OF US KNOW THAT
MISTRESS DEATH WOULD
ESURRECT THIS MONSTER?
APPARENTLY DEATH HAS LONG THOUGHT THE FACT THAT THERE ARE MORE PEOPLE ALIVE TODAY THAN HAVE EVER DIED WAS A TYPE OF COSMIC IMBALANCE.
THIS WAS AN IRREGULARITY SHE SOUGHT TO RIGHT USING THE DARK POWERS AT HER DISPOSAL.
AND SO SHE MADE THE TRAGIC MISTAKE OF RETRIEVING THANOS, THE MAD TITAN, FROM THE REALM OF THE DEAD.
THROUGH HIM, DEATH WOULD MOLD THE UNIVERSE TO HER LIKING.
ALONG WITH RENEWED LIFE, DEATH GAVE HIM GREATLY AUGMENTED POWER.
THANOS WOULD NEED THIS MIGHT TO PERFORM THE DARK TASK HIS MISTRESS ASSIGNED HIM.

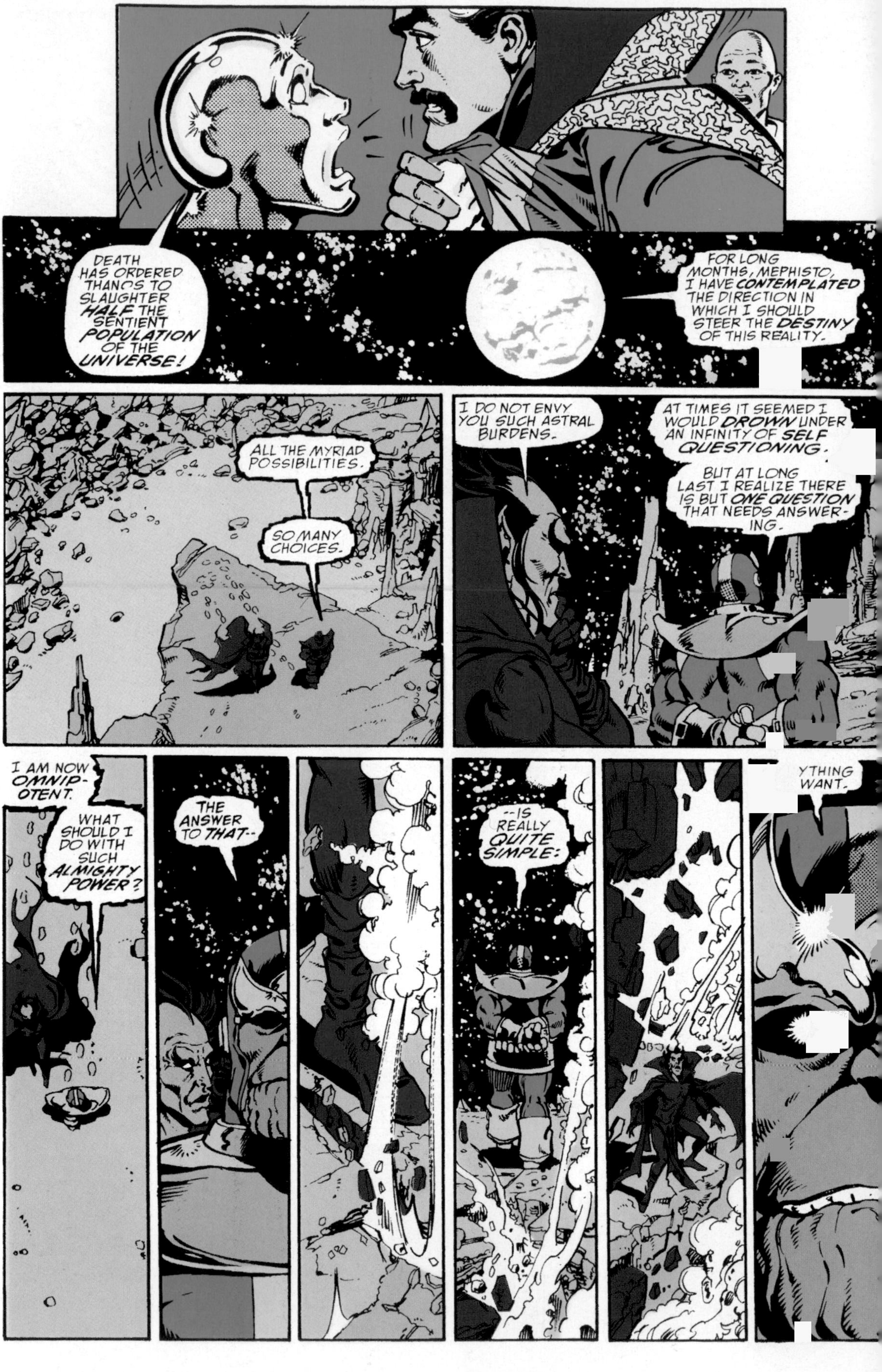
DEATH HAS ORDERED THANOS TO SLAUGHTER HALF THE SENTIENT POPULATION OF THE UNIVERSE!
FOR LONG MONTHS, MEPHISTO, I HAVE CONTEMPLATED THE DIRECTION IN WHICH I SHOULD STEER THE DESTINY OF THIS REALITY.
ALL THE MYRIAD POSSIBILITIES.
SO MANY CHOICES.
I DO NOT ENVY YOU SUCH ASTRAL BURDENS.
AT TIMES IT SEEMED I WOULD DROWN UNDER AN INFINITY OF SELF QUESTIONING.
BUT AT LONG LAST I REALIZE THERE IS BUT ONE QUESTION THAT NEEDS ANSWERING.
I AM NOW OMNIPOTENT.
WHAT SHOULD I DO WITH SUCH ALMIGHTY POWER?
THE ANSWER TO THAT--
--IS REALLY QUITE SIMPLE:
YTHING WANT.

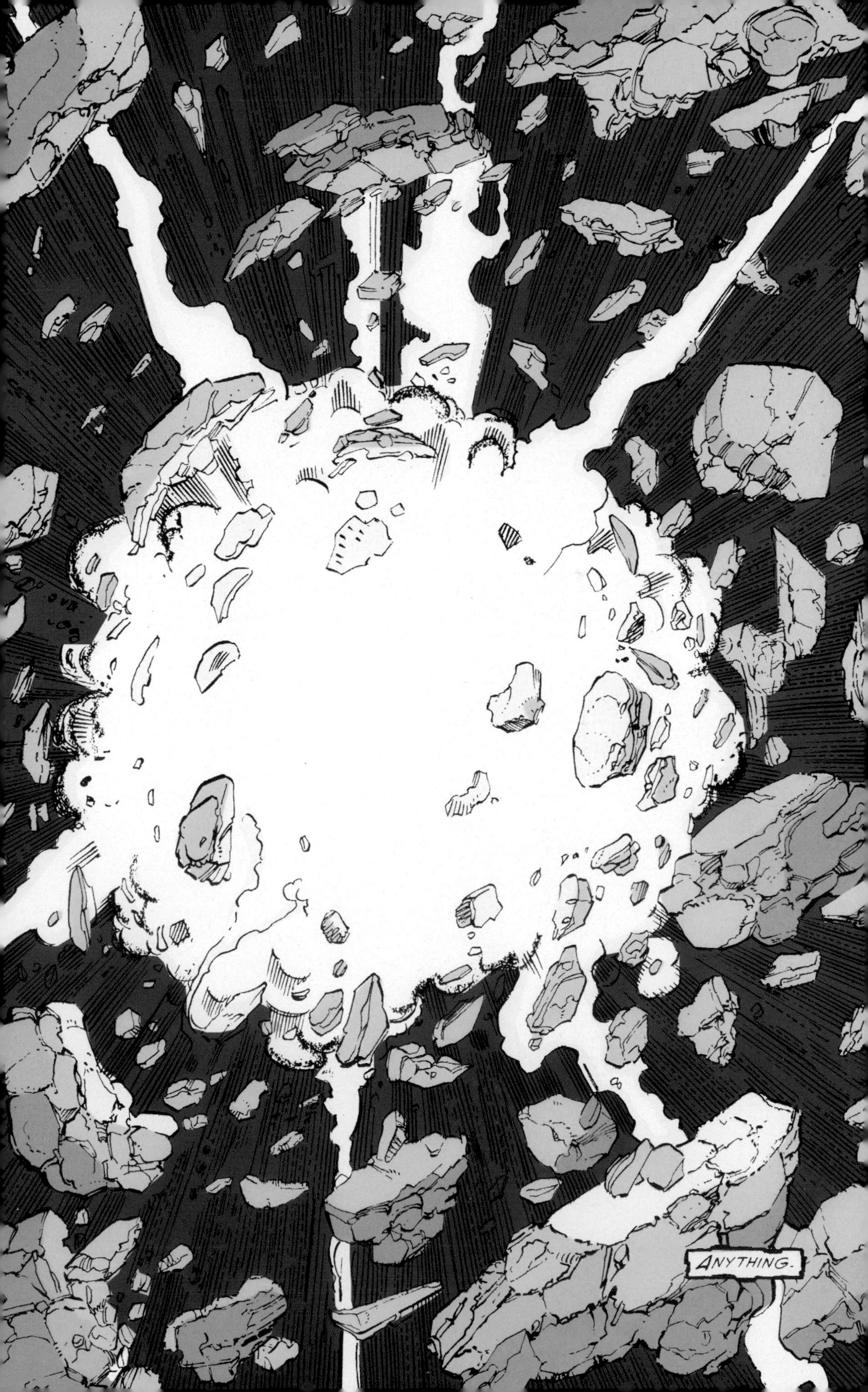
ANYTHING.

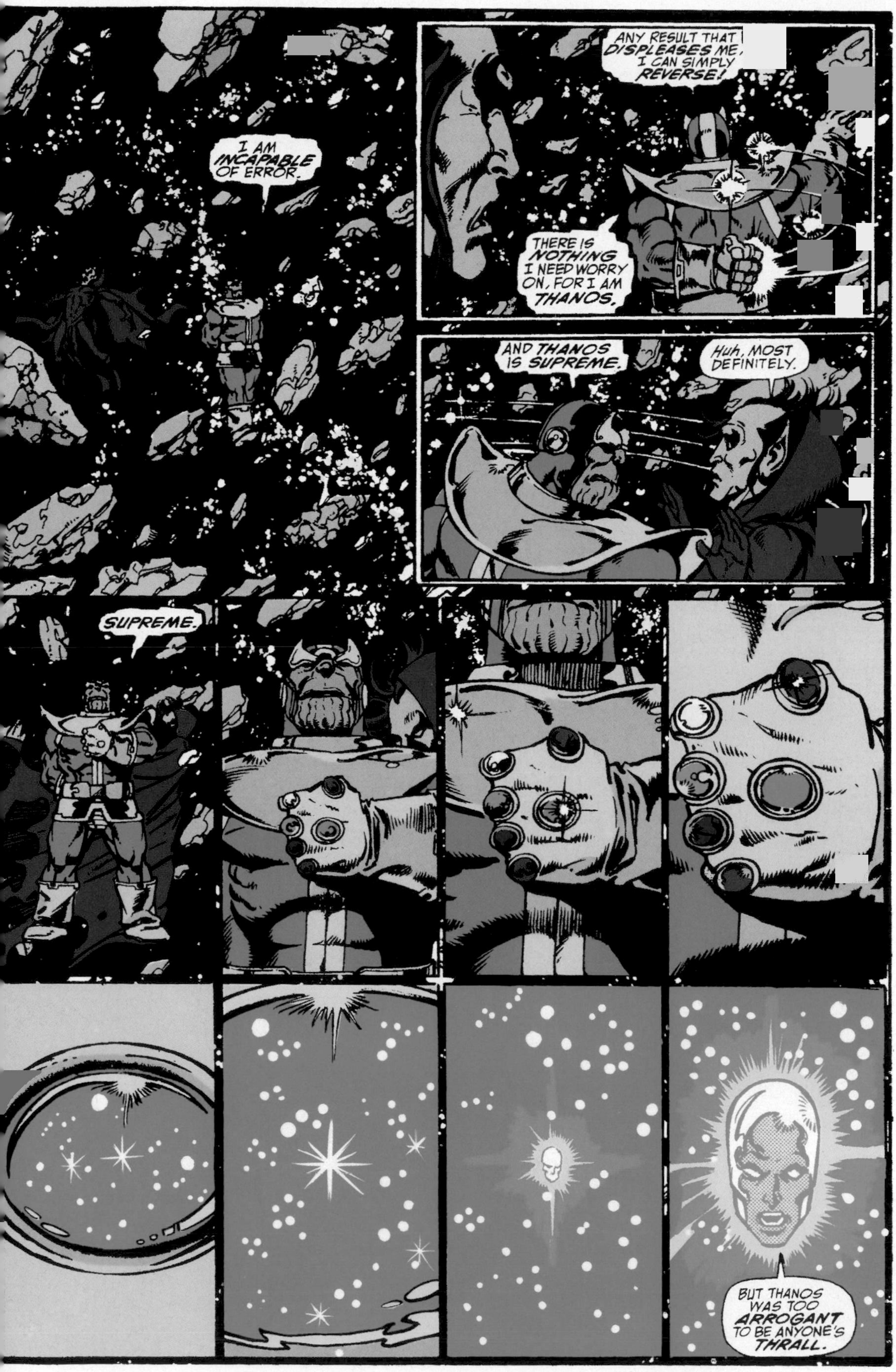
I AM INCAPABLE OF ERROR.
ANY RESULT THAT DISPLEASES ME, I CAN SIMPLY REVERSE!
THERE IS NOTHING I NEED WORRY ON, FOR I AM THANOS.
AND THANOS IS SUPREME.
Huh, MOST DEFINITELY.
SUPREME.
BUT THANOS WAS TOO ARROGANT TO BE ANYONE'S THRALL.

HIS *SINISTER SCHEME* WAS CONCEIVED WHILE GAZING INTO THE DEPTHS OF DEATH'S *INFINITY WELL.*

*N*OT EVEN DEATH REALIZED WHAT *LIMITLESS MIGHT* THE MAD TITAN WAS STRIVING FOR. THROUGH *CUNNING, SHEER STRENGTH, AND MURDER,* THANOS WRESTED THE *INFINITY GEMS* FROM THOSE THAT POSSESSED THEM AND WITH EACH ACQUISITION HE GAINED *MASTERY* OVER...

THE SOUL

THE MIND

POWER

TIME

REALITY

SPACE

*T*HERE HE LEARNT OF THE *SOUL* OR *INFINITY GEMS'* TRUE *POWER* AND CONVINCED HIS *DARK MISTRESS* THAT THE TASK ASSIGNED HIM COULD NOT BE CARRIED TO FRUITION *WITHOUT THEM.*

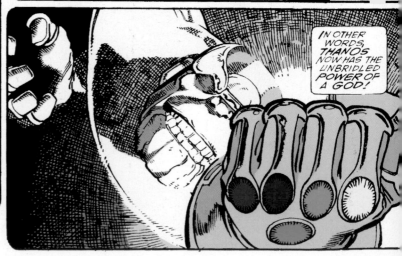

IN OTHER WORDS, *THANOS* NOW HAS THE *UNBRIDLED POWER* OF A *GOD!*

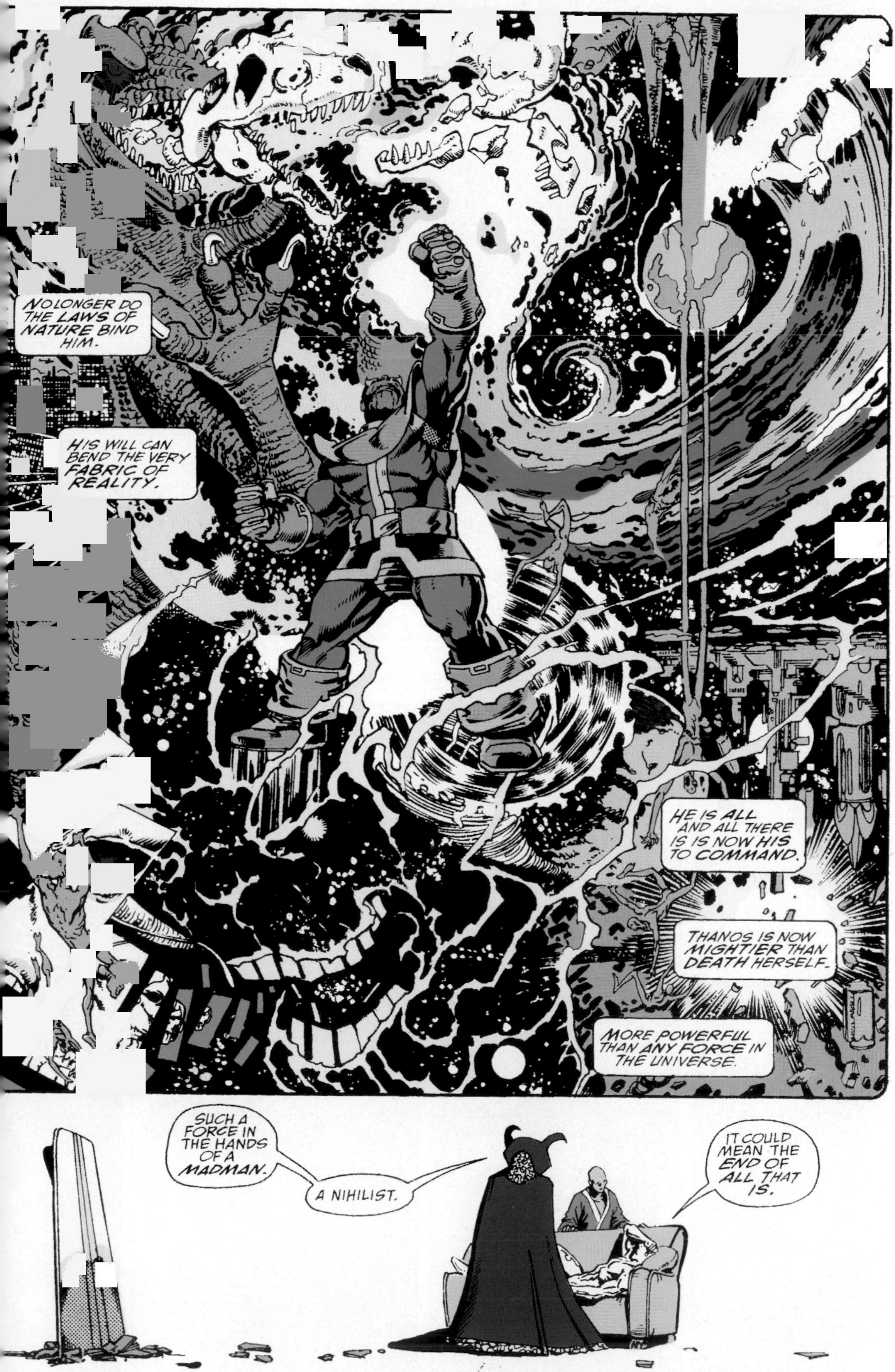
NO LONGER DO THE LAWS OF NATURE BIND HIM.
HIS WILL CAN BEND THE VERY FABRIC OF REALITY.
HE IS ALL AND ALL THERE IS IS NOW HIS TO COMMAND.
THANOS IS NOW MIGHTIER THAN DEATH HERSELF.
MORE POWERFUL THAN ANY FORCE IN THE UNIVERSE.
SUCH A FORCE IN THE HANDS OF A MADMAN.
A NIHILIST.
IT COULD MEAN THE END OF ALL THAT IS.

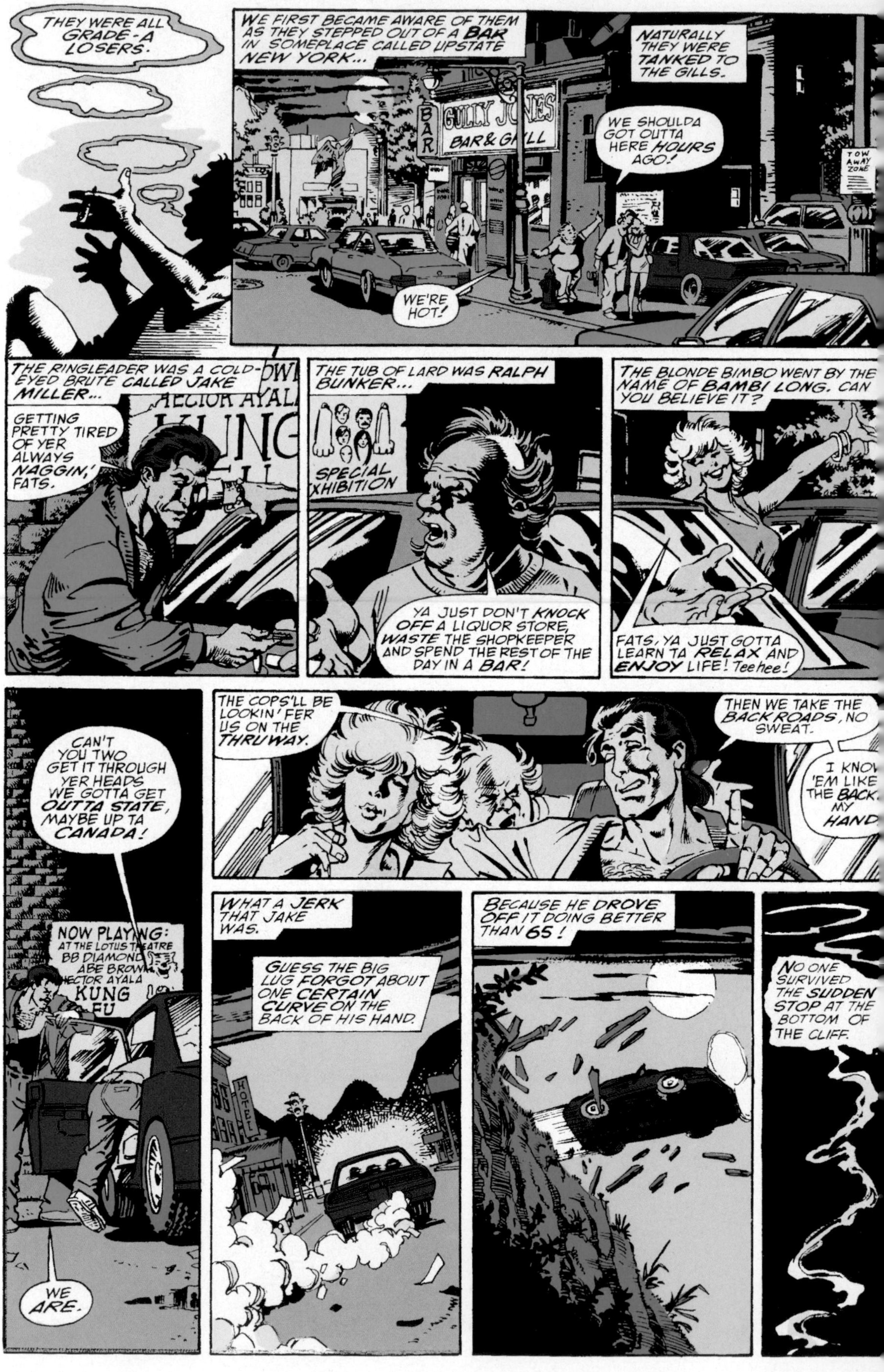

THEY WERE ALL GRADE-A LOSERS.
WE FIRST BECAME AWARE OF THEM AS THEY STEPPED OUT OF A BAR IN SOMEPLACE CALLED UPSTATE NEW YORK...
NATURALLY THEY WERE TANKED TO THE GILLS.
BAR
GULLY JONES
BAR & GRILL
TOW AWAY ZONE
WE SHOULDA GOT OUTTA HERE HOURS AGO!
WE'RE HOT!
THE RINGLEADER WAS A COLD-EYED BRUTE CALLED JAKE MILLER...
GETTING PRETTY TIRED OF YER ALWAYS NAGGIN,' FATS.
THE TUB OF LARD WAS RALPH BUNKER...
SPECIAL EXHIBITION
YA JUST DON'T KNOCK OFF A LIQUOR STORE, WASTE THE SHOPKEEPER AND SPEND THE REST OF THE DAY IN A BAR!
THE BLONDE BIMBO WENT BY THE NAME OF BAMBI LONG. CAN YOU BELIEVE IT?
FATS, YA JUST GOTTA LEARN TA RELAX AND ENJOY LIFE! Tee hee!
CAN'T YOU TWO GET IT THROUGH YER HEADS WE GOTTA GET OUTTA STATE, MAYBE UP TA CANADA!
NOW PLAYING: AT THE LOTUS THEATRE BB DIAMOND ABE BROWN HECTOR AYALA KUNG FU
WE ARE.
THE COPS'LL BE LOOKIN' FER US ON THE THRUWAY.
THEN WE TAKE THE BACK ROADS, NO SWEAT.
I KNOW 'EM LIKE THE BACK MY HAND
WHAT A JERK THAT JAKE WAS.
GUESS THE BIG LUG FORGOT ABOUT ONE CERTAIN CURVE ON THE BACK OF HIS HAND.
HOTEL
BECAUSE HE DROVE OFF IT DOING BETTER THAN 65!
NO ONE SURVIVED THE SUDDEN STOP AT THE BOTTOM OF THE CLIFF.

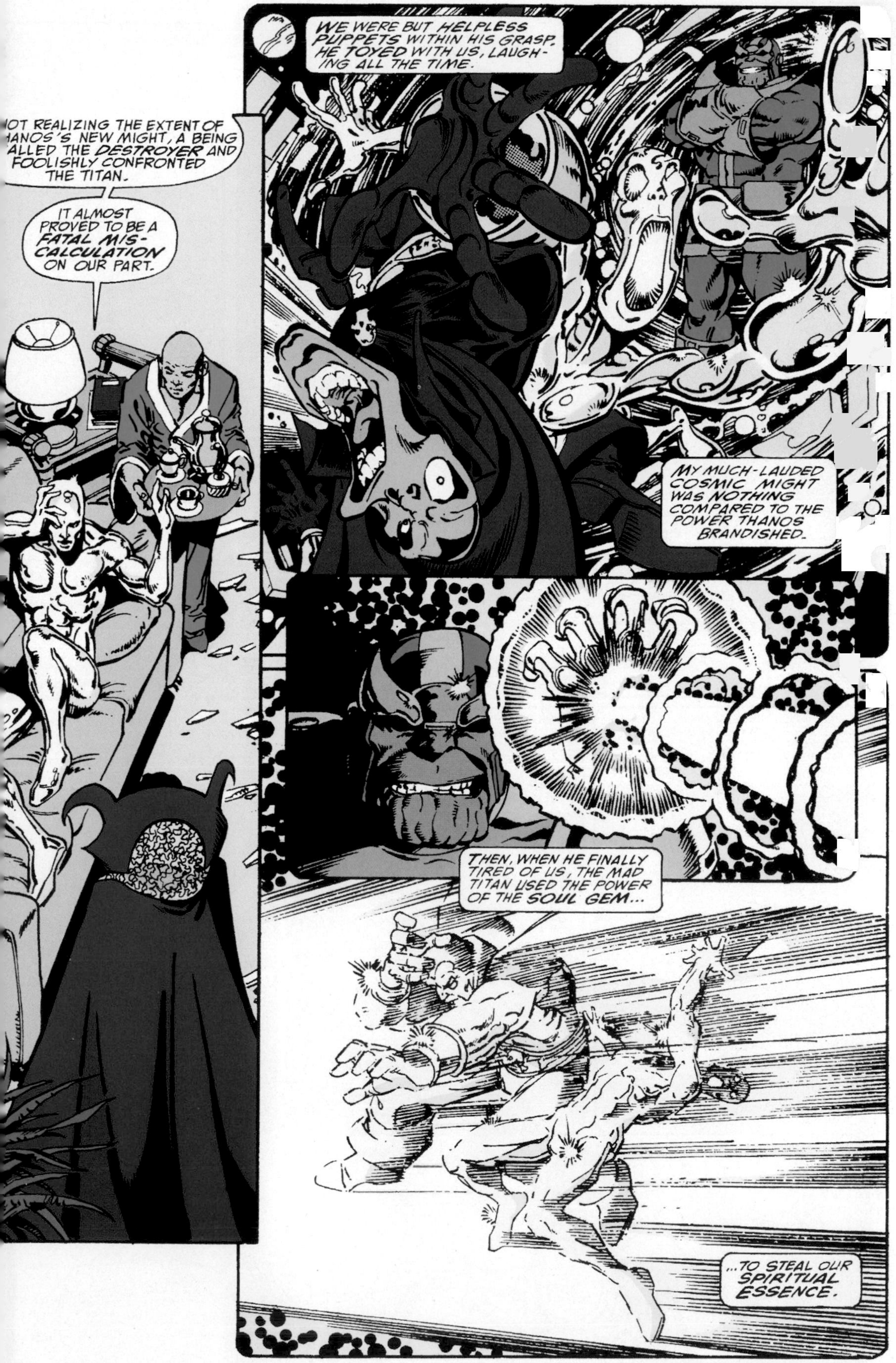
OT REALIZING THE EXTENT OF HANOS'S NEW MIGHT, A BEING ALLED THE DESTROYER AND FOOLISHLY CONFRONTED THE TITAN.
IT ALMOST PROVED TO BE A FATAL MIS-CALCULATION ON OUR PART.
WE WERE BUT HELPLESS PUPPETS WITHIN HIS GRASP. HE TOYED WITH US, LAUGHING ALL THE TIME.
MY MUCH-LAUDED COSMIC MIGHT WAS NOTHING COMPARED TO THE POWER THANOS BRANDISHED.
THEN, WHEN HE FINALLY TIRED OF US, THE MAD TITAN USED THE POWER OF THE SOUL GEM...
...TO STEAL OUR SPIRITUAL ESSENCE.

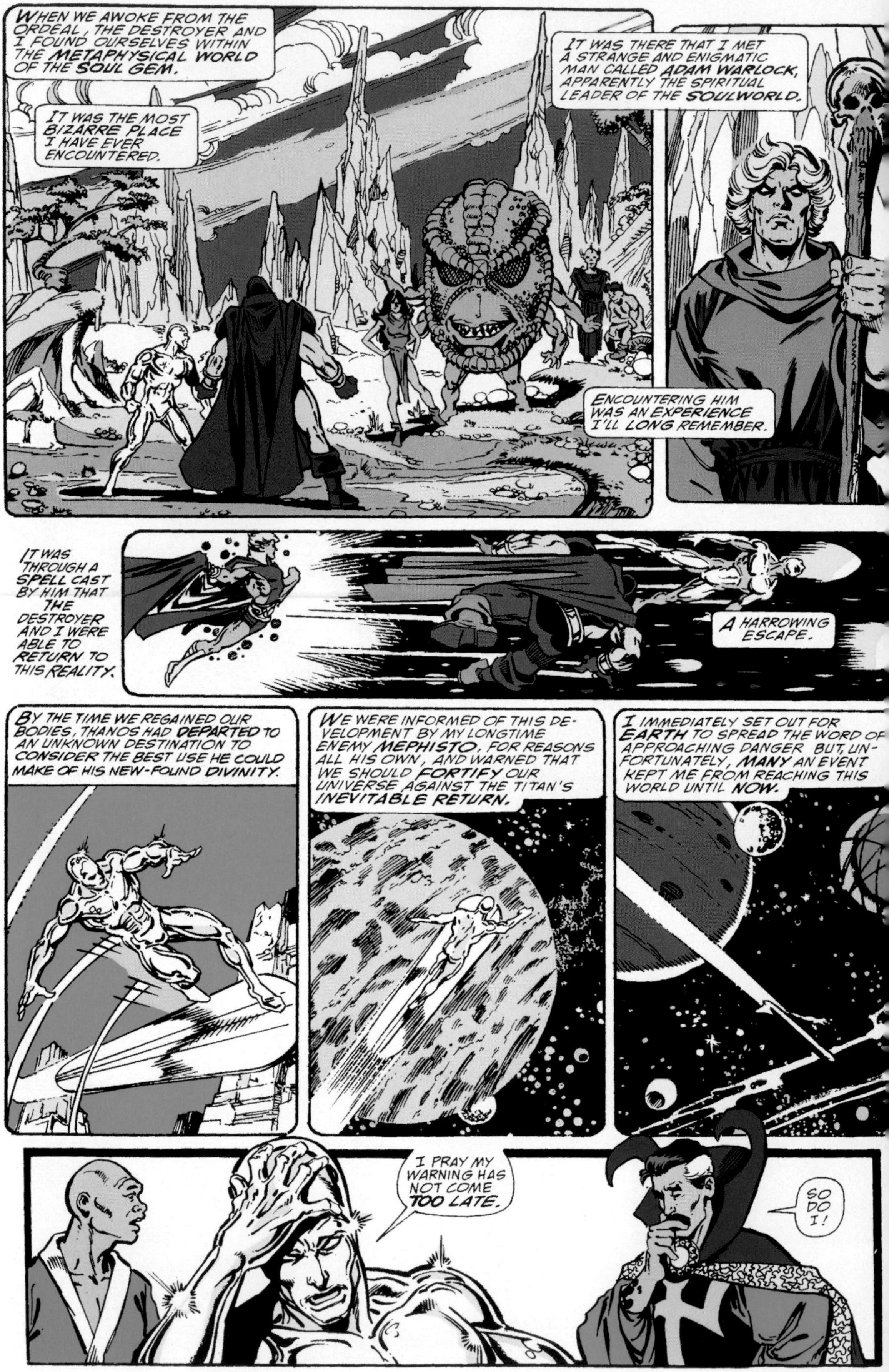

WHEN WE AWOKE FROM THE ORDEAL, THE DESTROYER AND I FOUND OURSELVES WITHIN THE METAPHYSICAL WORLD OF THE SOUL GEM.
IT WAS THE MOST BIZARRE PLACE I HAVE EVER ENCOUNTERED.
IT WAS THERE THAT I MET A STRANGE AND ENIGMATIC MAN CALLED ADAM WARLOCK, APPARENTLY THE SPIRITUAL LEADER OF THE SOULWORLD.
ENCOUNTERING HIM WAS AN EXPERIENCE I'LL LONG REMEMBER.
IT WAS THROUGH A SPELL CAST BY HIM THAT THE DESTROYER AND I WERE ABLE TO RETURN TO THIS REALITY.
A HARROWING ESCAPE.
BY THE TIME WE REGAINED OUR BODIES, THANOS HAD DEPARTED TO AN UNKNOWN DESTINATION TO CONSIDER THE BEST USE HE COULD MAKE OF HIS NEW-FOUND DIVINITY.
WE WERE INFORMED OF THIS DEVELOPMENT BY MY LONGTIME ENEMY MEPHISTO, FOR REASONS ALL HIS OWN, AND WARNED THAT WE SHOULD FORTIFY OUR UNIVERSE AGAINST THE TITAN'S INEVITABLE RETURN.
I IMMEDIATELY SET OUT FOR EARTH TO SPREAD THE WORD OF APPROACHING DANGER BUT, UNFORTUNATELY, MANY AN EVENT KEPT ME FROM REACHING THIS WORLD UNTIL NOW.
I PRAY MY WARNING HAS NOT COME TOO LATE.
SO DO I!

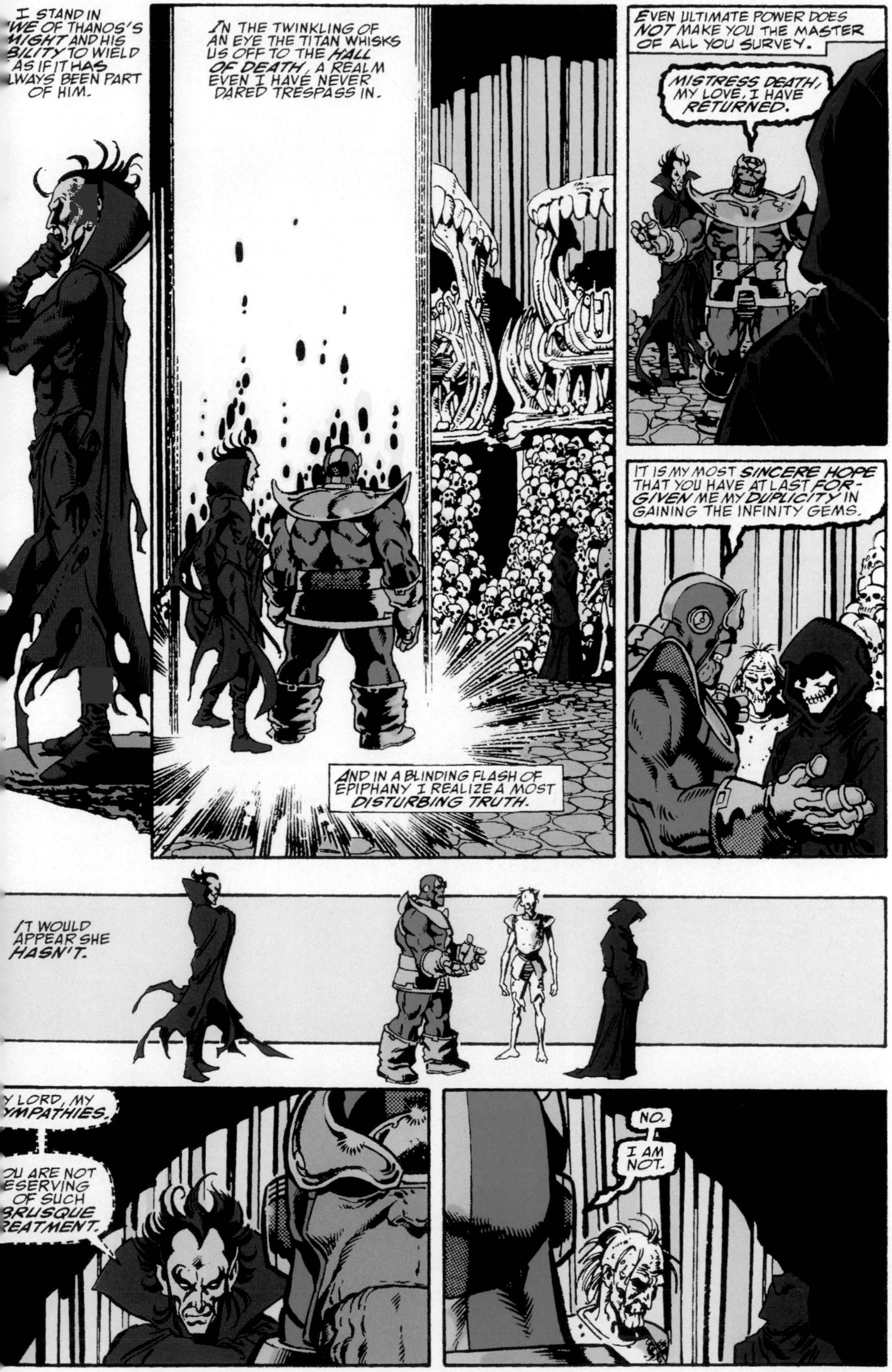
I STAND IN WE OF THANOS'S MIGHT AND HIS BILITY TO WIELD AS IF IT HAS LWAYS BEEN PART OF HIM.
IN THE TWINKLING OF AN EYE THE TITAN WHISKS US OFF TO THE HALL OF DEATH, A REALM EVEN I HAVE NEVER DARED TRESPASS IN.
AND IN A BLINDING FLASH OF EPIPHANY I REALIZE A MOST DISTURBING TRUTH.
EVEN ULTIMATE POWER DOES NOT MAKE YOU THE MASTER OF ALL YOU SURVEY.
MISTRESS DEATH, MY LOVE, I HAVE RETURNED.
IT IS MY MOST SINCERE HOPE THAT YOU HAVE AT LAST FOR-GIVEN ME MY DUPLICITY IN GAINING THE INFINITY GEMS.
IT WOULD APPEAR SHE HASN'T.
Y LORD, MY YMPATHIES.
OU ARE NOT ESERVING OF SUCH BRUSQUE REATMENT.
NO.
I AM NOT.

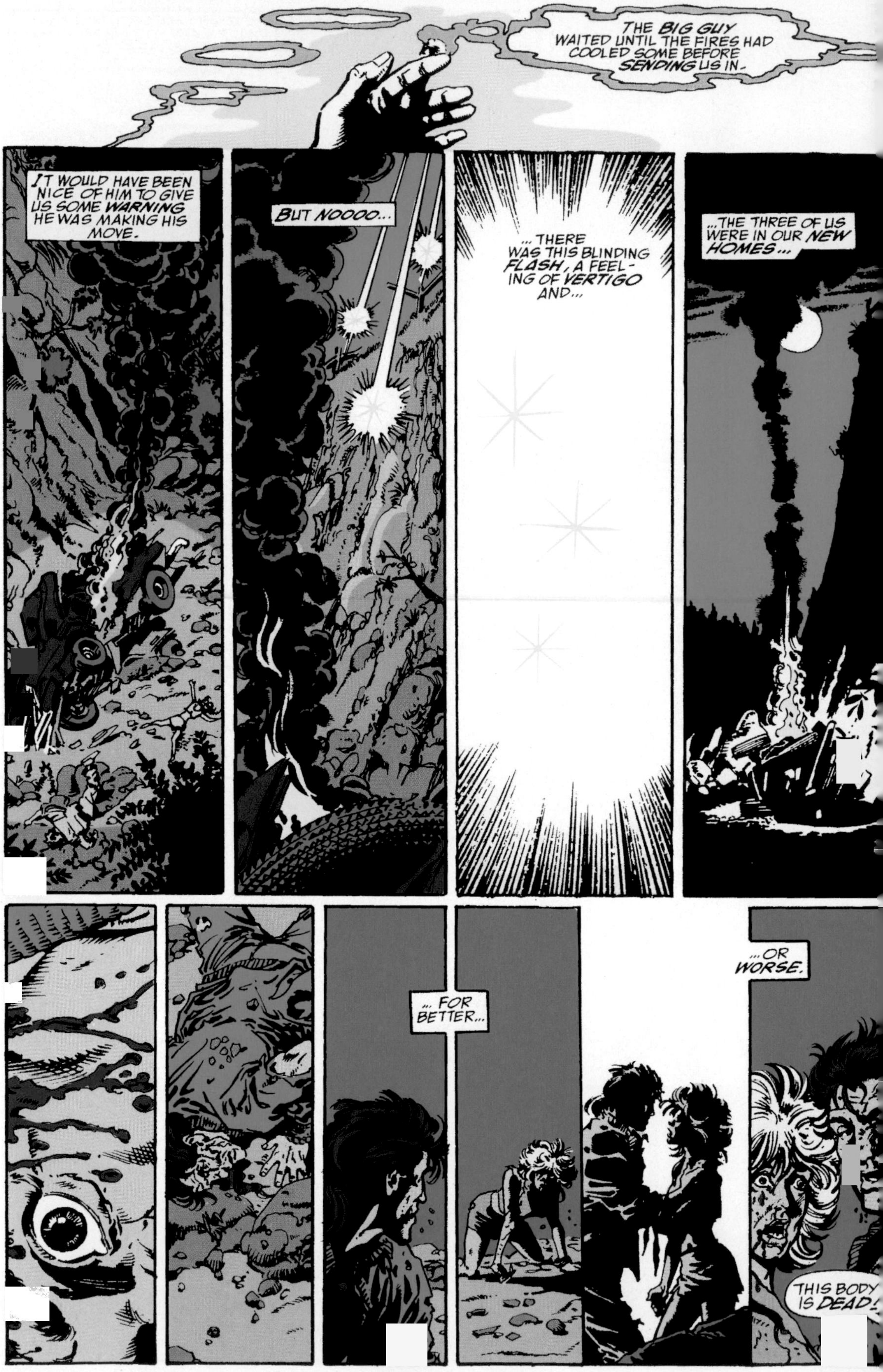

THE BIG GUY WAITED UNTIL THE FIRES HAD COOLED SOME BEFORE SENDING US IN.
IT WOULD HAVE BEEN NICE OF HIM TO GIVE US SOME WARNING HE WAS MAKING HIS MOVE.
BUT NOOOO...
...THERE WAS THIS BLINDING FLASH, A FEELING OF VERTIGO AND...
...THE THREE OF US WERE IN OUR NEW HOMES...
...FOR BETTER...
...OR WORSE.
THIS BODY IS DEAD!

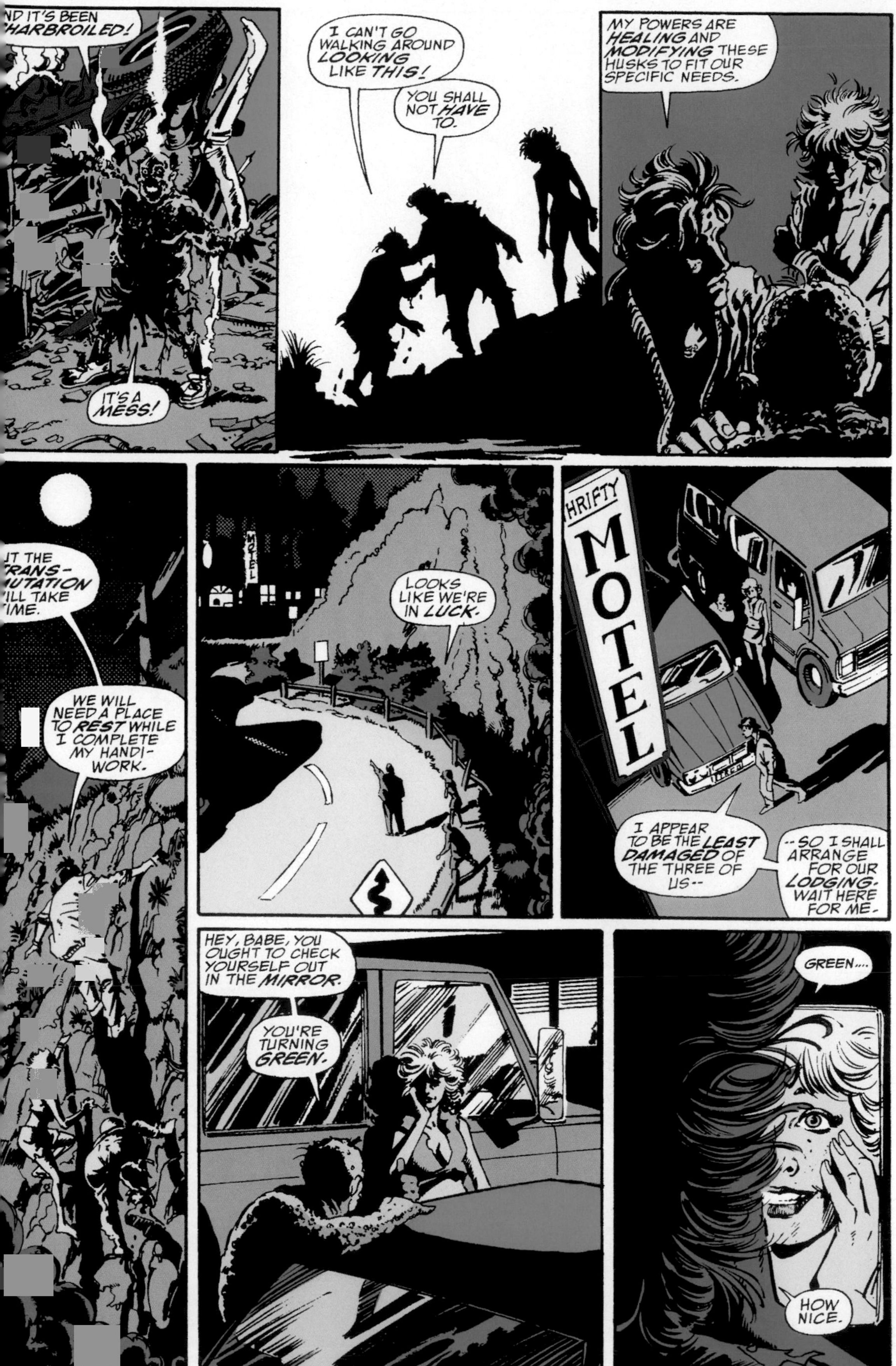
ND IT'S BEEN HARBROILED!
IT'S A MESS!
I CAN'T GO WALKING AROUND LOOKING LIKE THIS!
YOU SHALL NOT HAVE TO.
MY POWERS ARE HEALING AND MODIFYING THESE HUSKS TO FIT OUR SPECIFIC NEEDS.
UT THE TRANS-MUTATION ILL TAKE IME.
WE WILL NEED A PLACE TO REST WHILE I COMPLETE MY HANDI-WORK.
MOTEL
LOOKS LIKE WE'RE IN LUCK.
HRIFTY
MOTEL
I APPEAR TO BE THE LEAST DAMAGED OF THE THREE OF US--
--SO I SHALL ARRANGE FOR OUR LODGING. WAIT HERE FOR ME.
HEY, BABE, YOU OUGHT TO CHECK YOURSELF OUT IN THE MIRROR.
YOU'RE TURNING GREEN.
GREEN....
HOW NICE.

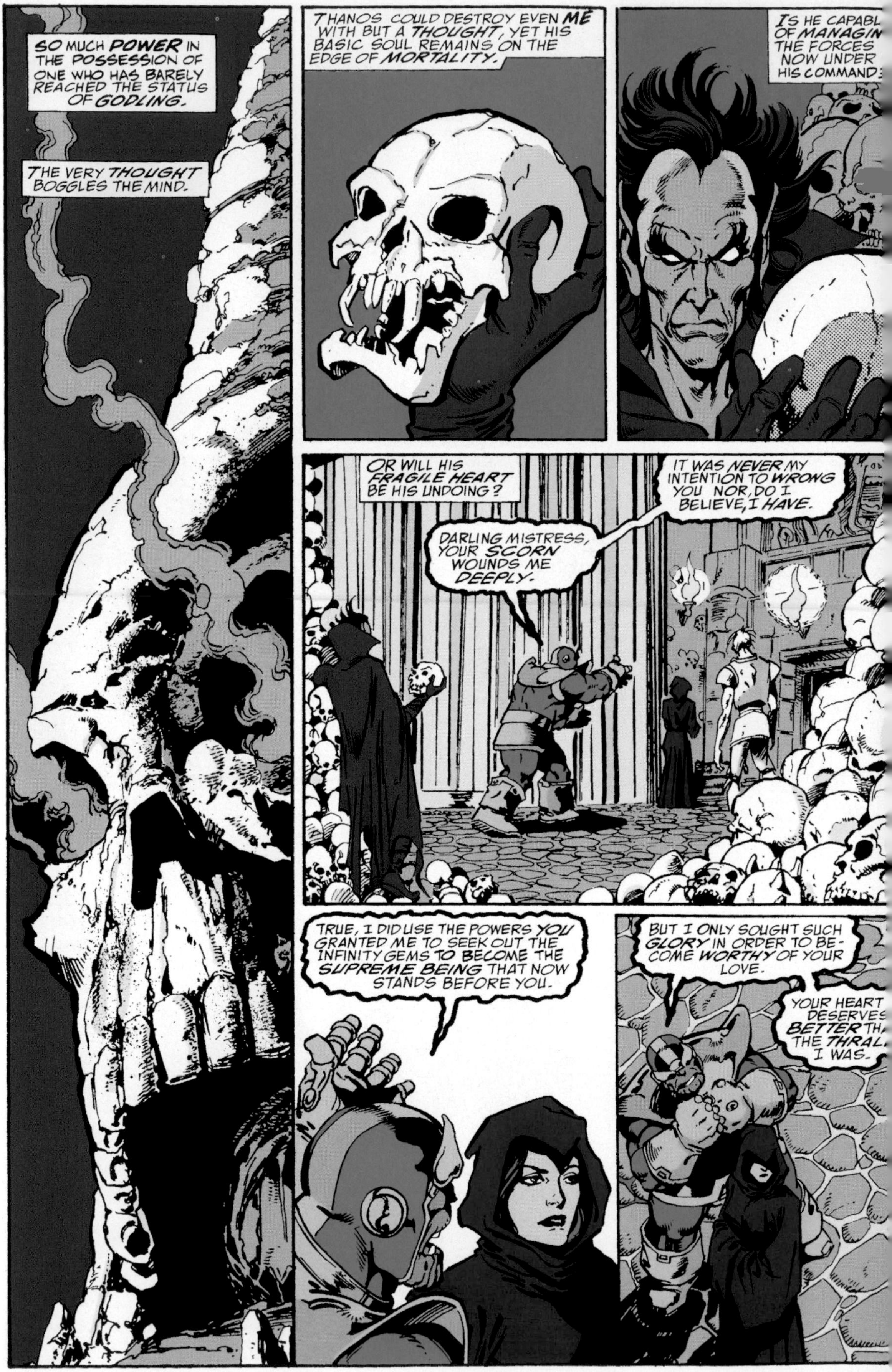
SO MUCH POWER IN THE POSSESSION OF ONE WHO HAS BARELY REACHED THE STATUS OF GODLING.
THE VERY THOUGHT BOGGLES THE MIND.
THANOS COULD DESTROY EVEN ME WITH BUT A THOUGHT, YET HIS BASIC SOUL REMAINS ON THE EDGE OF MORTALITY.
IS HE CAPABL OF MANAGIN THE FORCES NOW UNDER HIS COMMAND?
OR WILL HIS FRAGILE HEART BE HIS UNDOING?
DARLING MISTRESS, YOUR SCORN WOUNDS ME DEEPLY.
IT WAS NEVER MY INTENTION TO WRONG YOU NOR, DO I BELIEVE, I HAVE.
TRUE, I DID USE THE POWERS YOU GRANTED ME TO SEEK OUT THE INFINITY GEMS TO BECOME THE SUPREME BEING THAT NOW STANDS BEFORE YOU.
BUT I ONLY SOUGHT SUCH GLORY IN ORDER TO BECOME WORTHY OF YOUR LOVE.
YOUR HEART DESERVES BETTER THA THE THRAL I WAS.

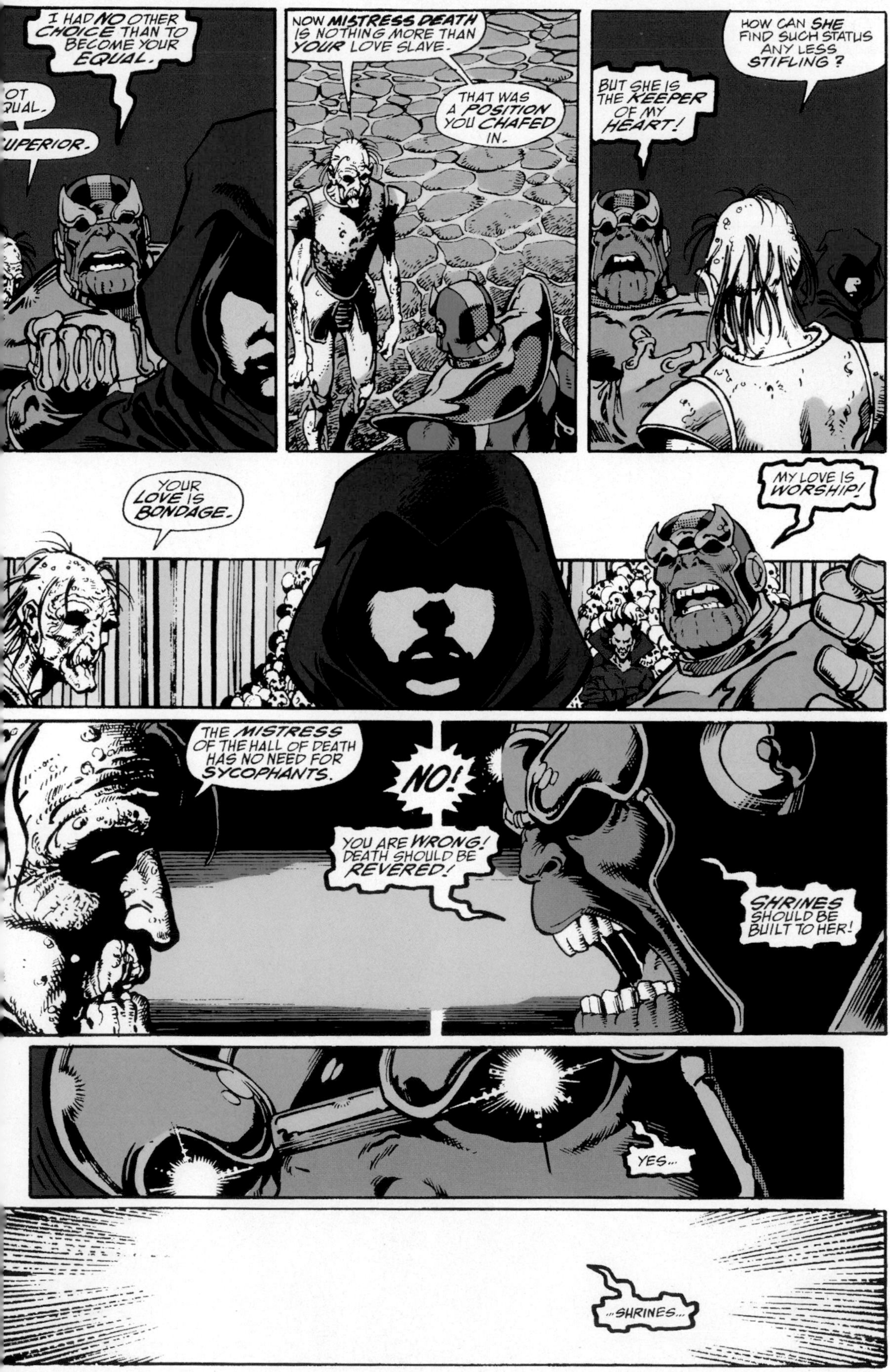
I HAD NO OTHER CHOICE THAN TO BECOME YOUR EQUAL.
OT QUAL.
UPERIOR.
NOW MISTRESS DEATH IS NOTHING MORE THAN YOUR LOVE SLAVE.
THAT WAS A POSITION YOU CHAFED IN.
HOW CAN SHE FIND SUCH STATUS ANY LESS STIFLING?
BUT SHE IS THE KEEPER OF MY HEART!
YOUR LOVE IS BONDAGE.
MY LOVE IS WORSHIP!
THE MISTRESS OF THE HALL OF DEATH HAS NO NEED FOR SYCOPHANTS.
NO!
YOU ARE WRONG! DEATH SHOULD BE REVERED!
SHRINES SHOULD BE BUILT TO HER!
YES...
...SHRINES...

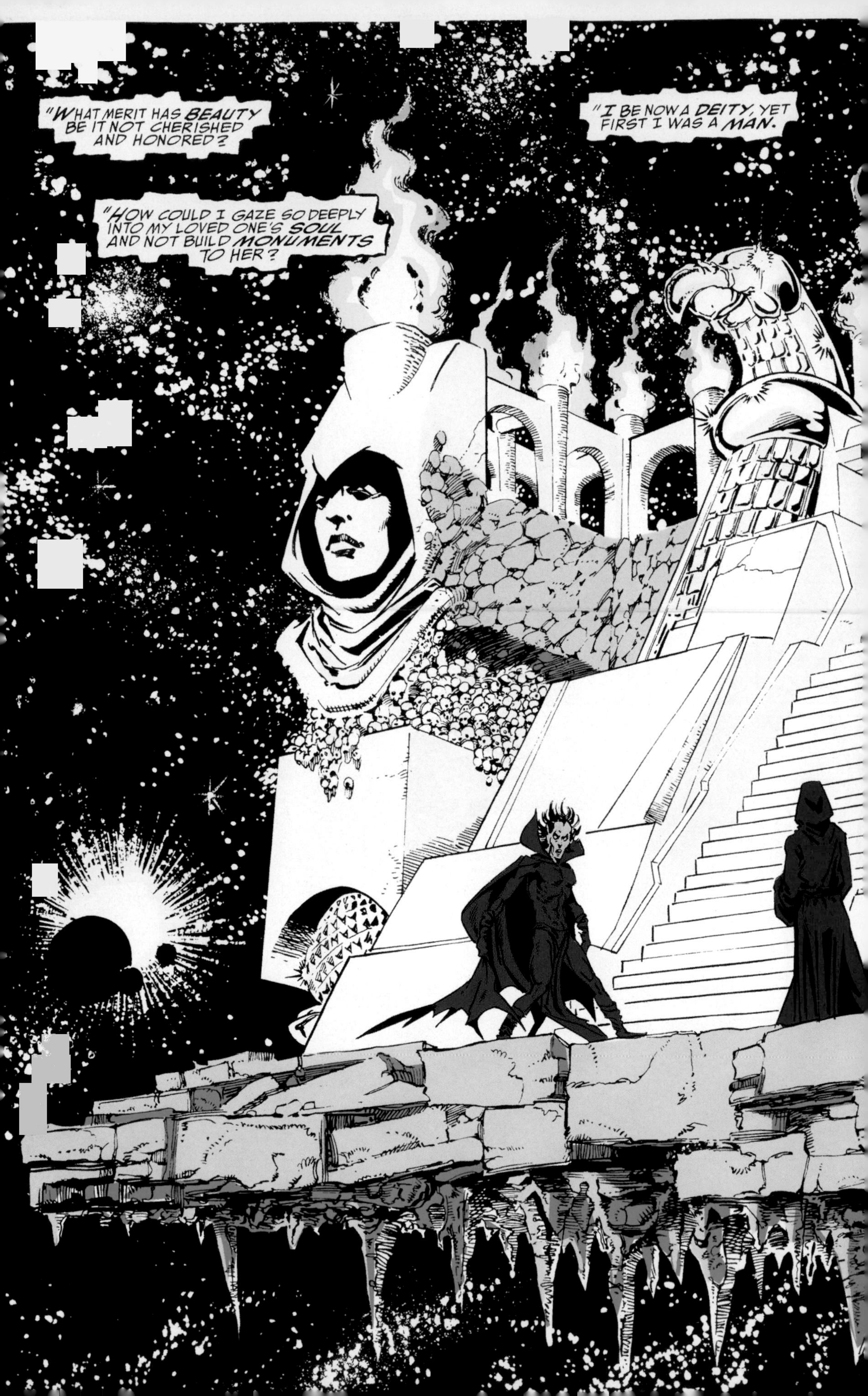
"WHAT MERIT HAS BEAUTY BE IT NOT CHERISHED AND HONORED?
"HOW COULD I GAZE SO DEEPLY INTO MY LOVED ONE'S SOUL AND NOT BUILD MONUMENTS TO HER?
"I BE NOW A DEITY, YET FIRST I WAS A MAN.

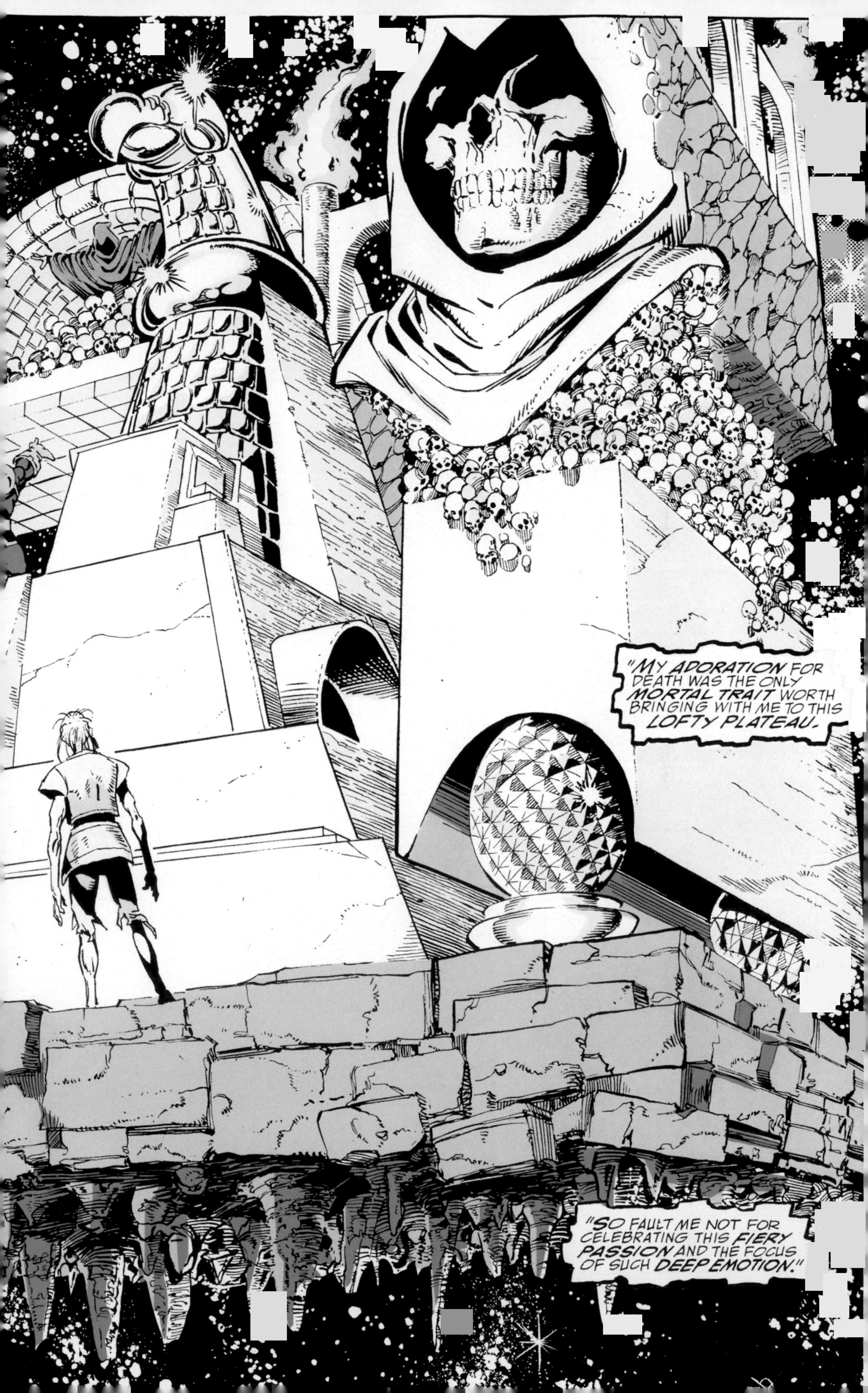
"MY ADORATION FOR DEATH WAS THE ONLY MORTAL TRAIT WORTH BRINGING WITH ME TO THIS LOFTY PLATEAU.
"SO FAULT ME NOT FOR CELEBRATING THIS FIERY PASSION AND THE FOCUS OF SUCH DEEP EMOTION."

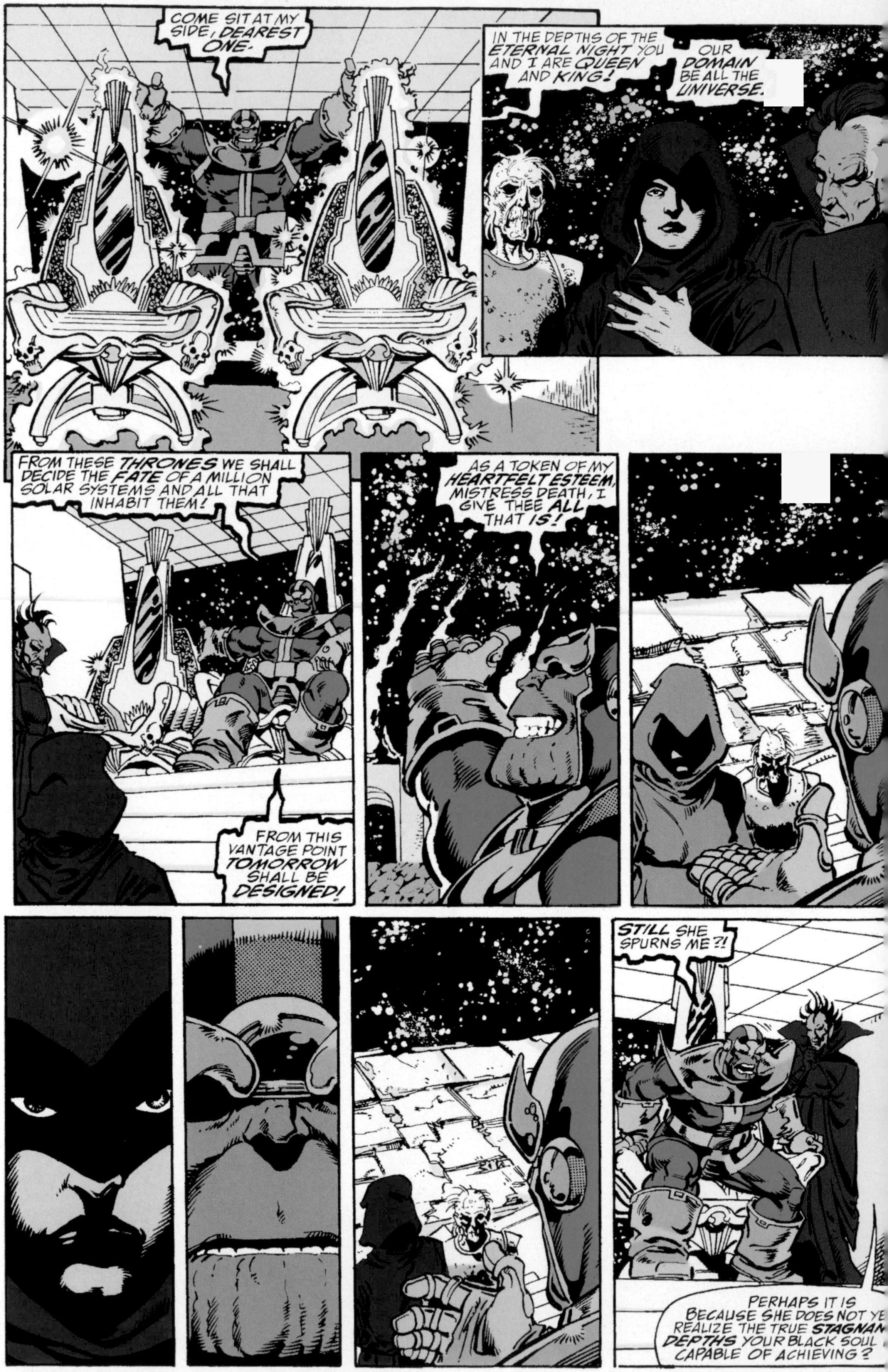
COME SIT AT MY SIDE, DEAREST ONE-
IN THE DEPTHS OF THE ETERNAL NIGHT YOU AND I ARE QUEEN AND KING!
OUR DOMAIN BE ALL THE UNIVERSE.
FROM THESE THRONES WE SHALL DECIDE THE FATE OF A MILLION SOLAR SYSTEMS AND ALL THAT INHABIT THEM!
FROM THIS VANTAGE POINT TOMORROW SHALL BE DESIGNED!
AS A TOKEN OF MY HEARTFELT ESTEEM, MISTRESS DEATH, I GIVE THEE ALL THAT IS!
STILL SHE SPURNS ME?!
PERHAPS IT IS BECAUSE SHE DOES NOT YE
REALIZE THE TRUE STAGNAN
DEPTHS YOUR BLACK SOUL
CAPABLE OF ACHIEVING?

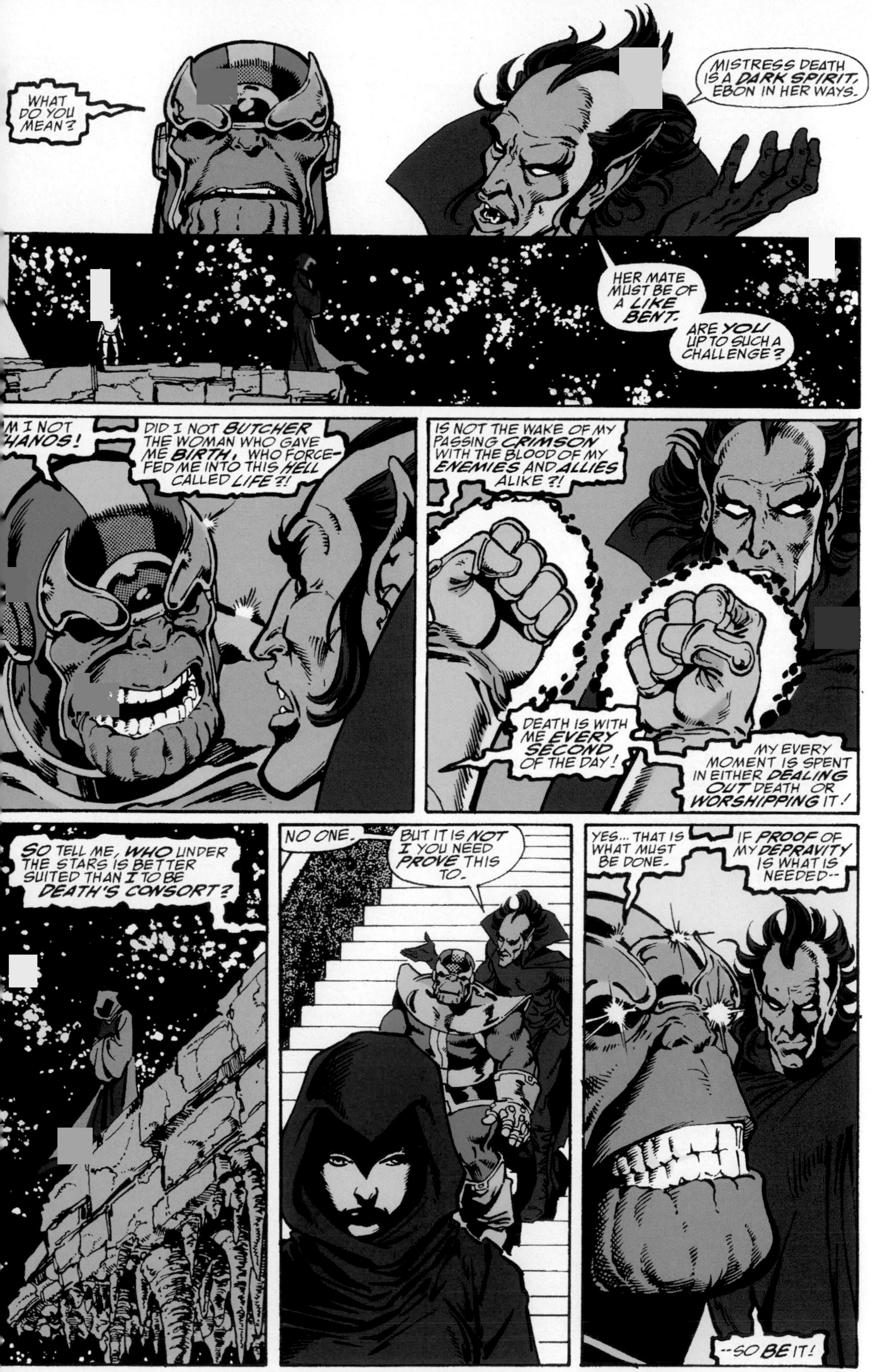
WHAT DO YOU MEAN?
MISTRESS DEATH IS A DARK SPIRIT, EBON IN HER WAYS.
HER MATE MUST BE OF A LIKE BENT.
ARE YOU UP TO SUCH A CHALLENGE?
M I NOT HANOS!
DID I NOT BUTCHER THE WOMAN WHO GAVE ME BIRTH, WHO FORCE-FED ME INTO THIS HELL CALLED LIFE?!
IS NOT THE WAKE OF MY PASSING CRIMSON WITH THE BLOOD OF MY ENEMIES AND ALLIES ALIKE?!
DEATH IS WITH ME EVERY SECOND OF THE DAY!
MY EVERY MOMENT IS SPENT IN EITHER DEALING OUT DEATH OR WORSHIPPING IT!
SO TELL ME, WHO UNDER THE STARS IS BETTER SUITED THAN I TO BE DEATH'S CONSORT?
NO ONE.
BUT IT IS NOT I YOU NEED PROVE THIS TO.
YES... THAT IS WHAT MUST BE DONE.
IF PROOF OF MY DEPRAVITY IS WHAT IS NEEDED--
--SO BE IT!

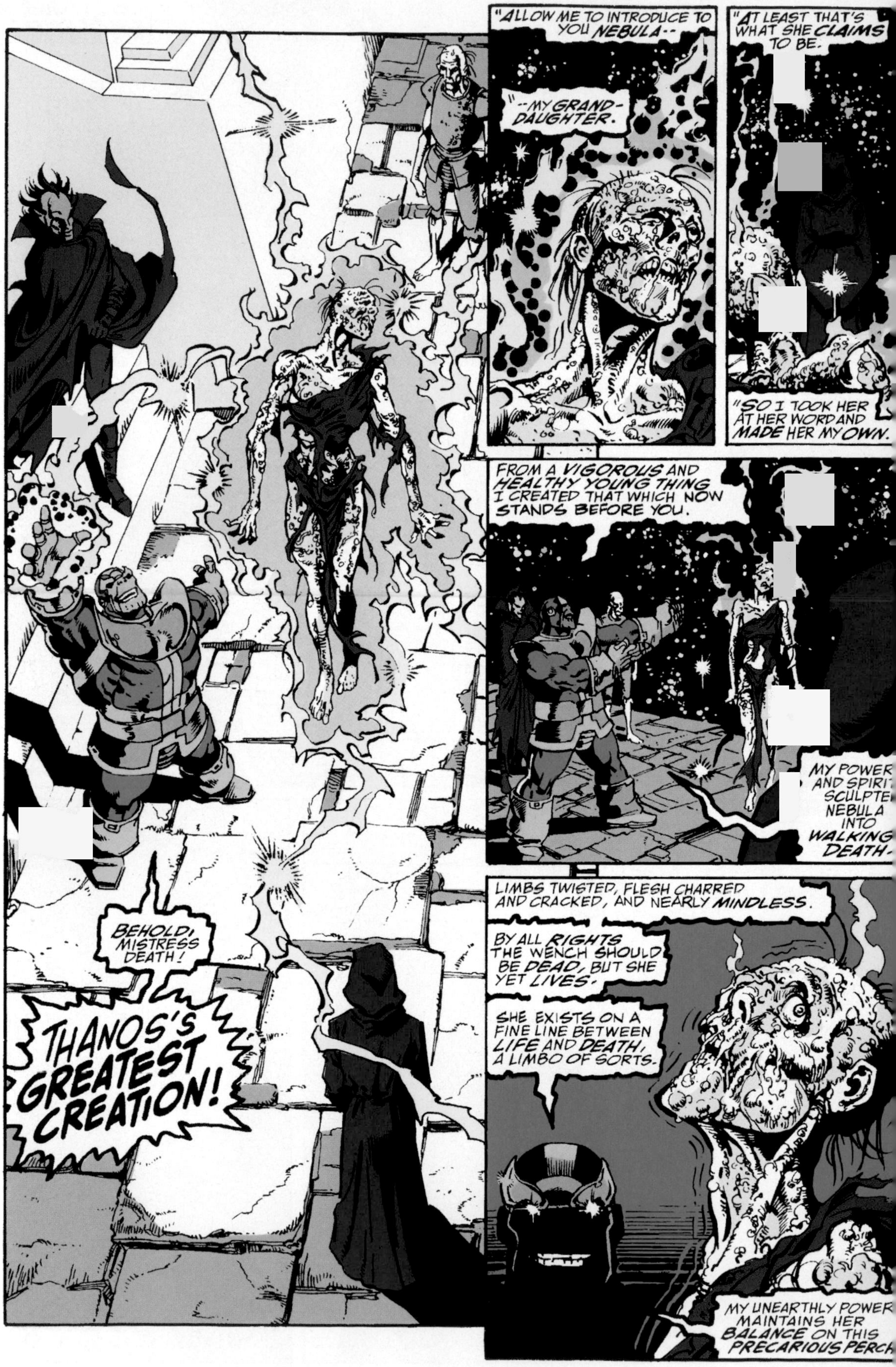
"ALLOW ME TO INTRODUCE TO YOU NEBULA--
"--MY GRAND-DAUGHTER.
"AT LEAST THAT'S WHAT SHE CLAIMS TO BE.
"SO I TOOK HER AT HER WORD AND MADE HER MY OWN.
BEHOLD, MISTRESS DEATH!
THANOS'S GREATEST CREATION!
FROM A VIGOROUS AND HEALTHY YOUNG THING I CREATED THAT WHICH NOW STANDS BEFORE YOU.
MY POWER AND SPIRIT SCULPTED NEBULA INTO WALKING DEATH-
LIMBS TWISTED, FLESH CHARRED AND CRACKED, AND NEARLY MINDLESS.
BY ALL RIGHTS THE WENCH SHOULD BE DEAD, BUT SHE YET LIVES.
SHE EXISTS ON A FINE LINE BETWEEN LIFE AND DEATH, A LIMBO OF SORTS.
MY UNEARTHLY POWER MAINTAINS HER BALANCE ON THIS PRECARIOUS PERCH

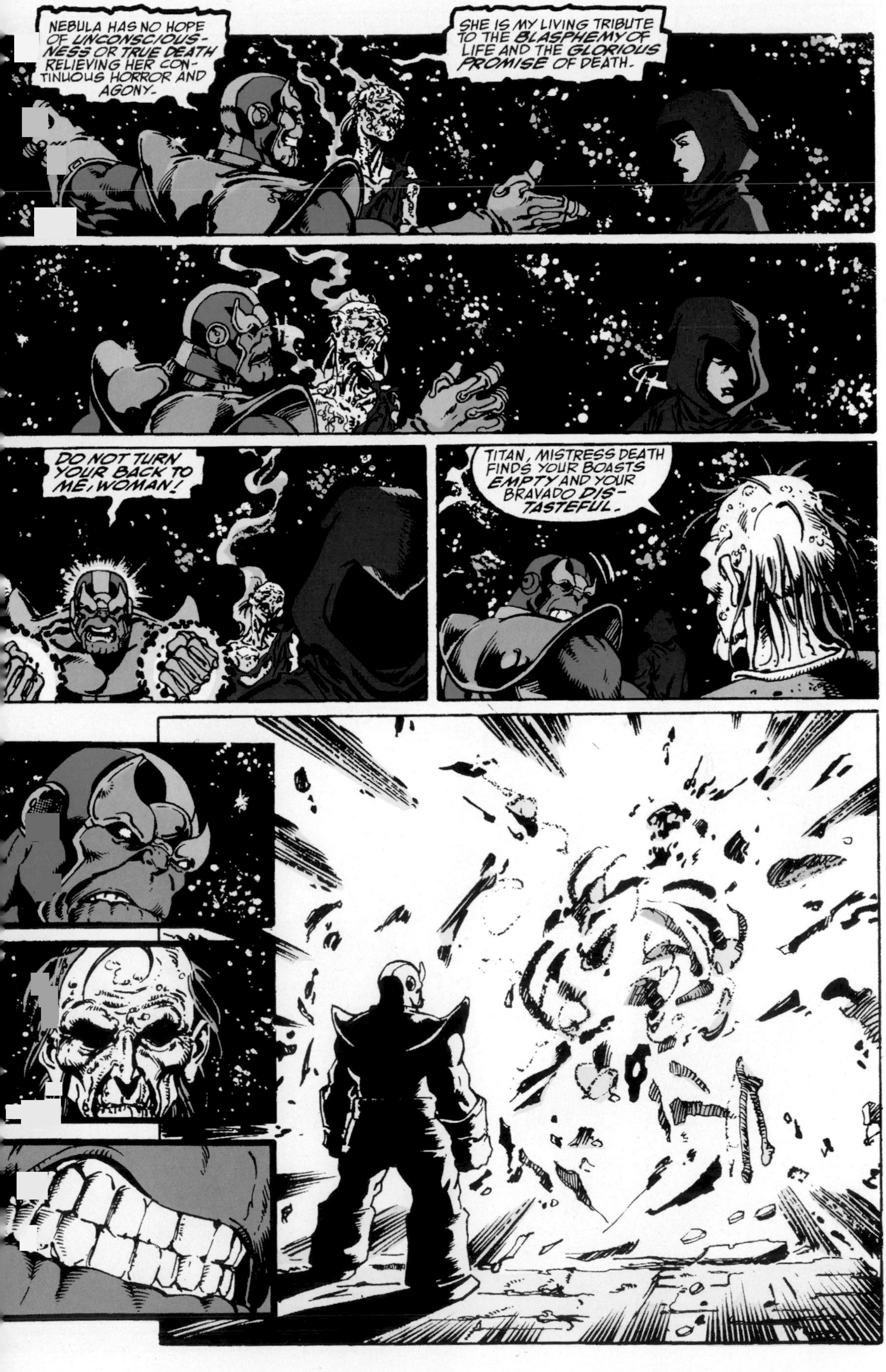
NEBULA HAS NO HOPE OF UNCONSCIOUSNESS OR TRUE DEATH RELIEVING HER CONTINUOUS HORROR AND AGONY.
SHE IS MY LIVING TRIBUTE TO THE BLASPHEMY OF LIFE AND THE GLORIOUS PROMISE OF DEATH.
DO NOT TURN YOUR BACK TO ME, WOMAN!
TITAN, MISTRESS DEATH FINDS YOUR BOASTS EMPTY AND YOUR BRAVADO DISTASTEFUL.

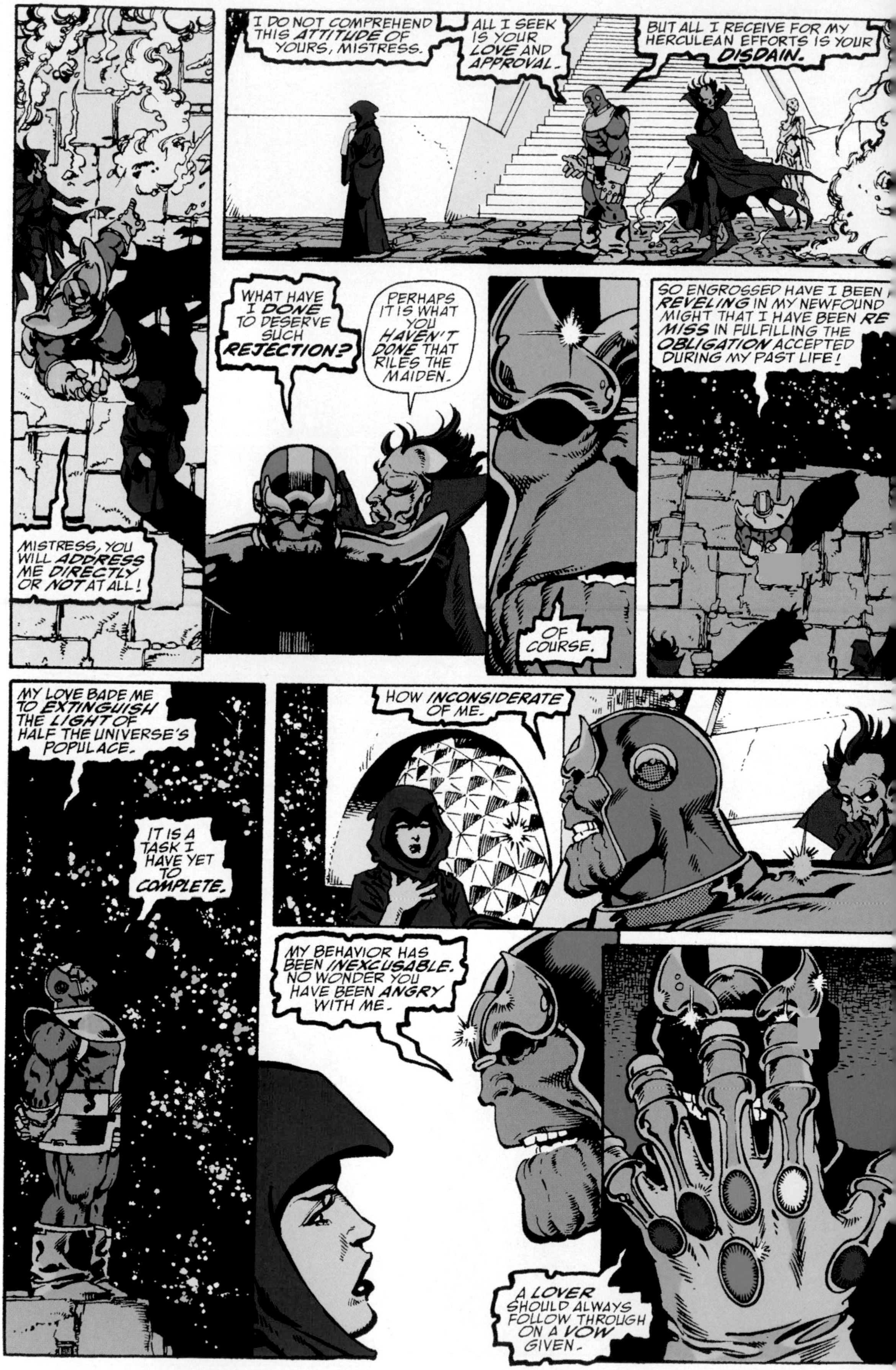

I DO NOT COMPREHEND THIS ATTITUDE OF YOURS, MISTRESS.
ALL I SEEK IS YOUR LOVE AND APPROVAL.
BUT ALL I RECEIVE FOR MY HERCULEAN EFFORTS IS YOUR DISDAIN.
MISTRESS, YOU WILL ADDRESS ME DIRECTLY OR NOT AT ALL!
WHAT HAVE I DONE TO DESERVE SUCH REJECTION?
PERHAPS IT IS WHAT YOU HAVEN'T DONE THAT RILES THE MAIDEN.
OF COURSE.
MY LOVE BADE ME TO EXTINGUISH THE LIGHT OF HALF THE UNIVERSE'S POPULACE.
IT IS A TASK I HAVE YET TO COMPLETE.
HOW INCONSIDERATE OF ME.
MY BEHAVIOR HAS BEEN INEXCUSABLE. NO WONDER YOU HAVE BEEN ANGRY WITH ME.
A LOVER SHOULD ALWAYS FOLLOW THROUGH ON A VOW GIVEN.

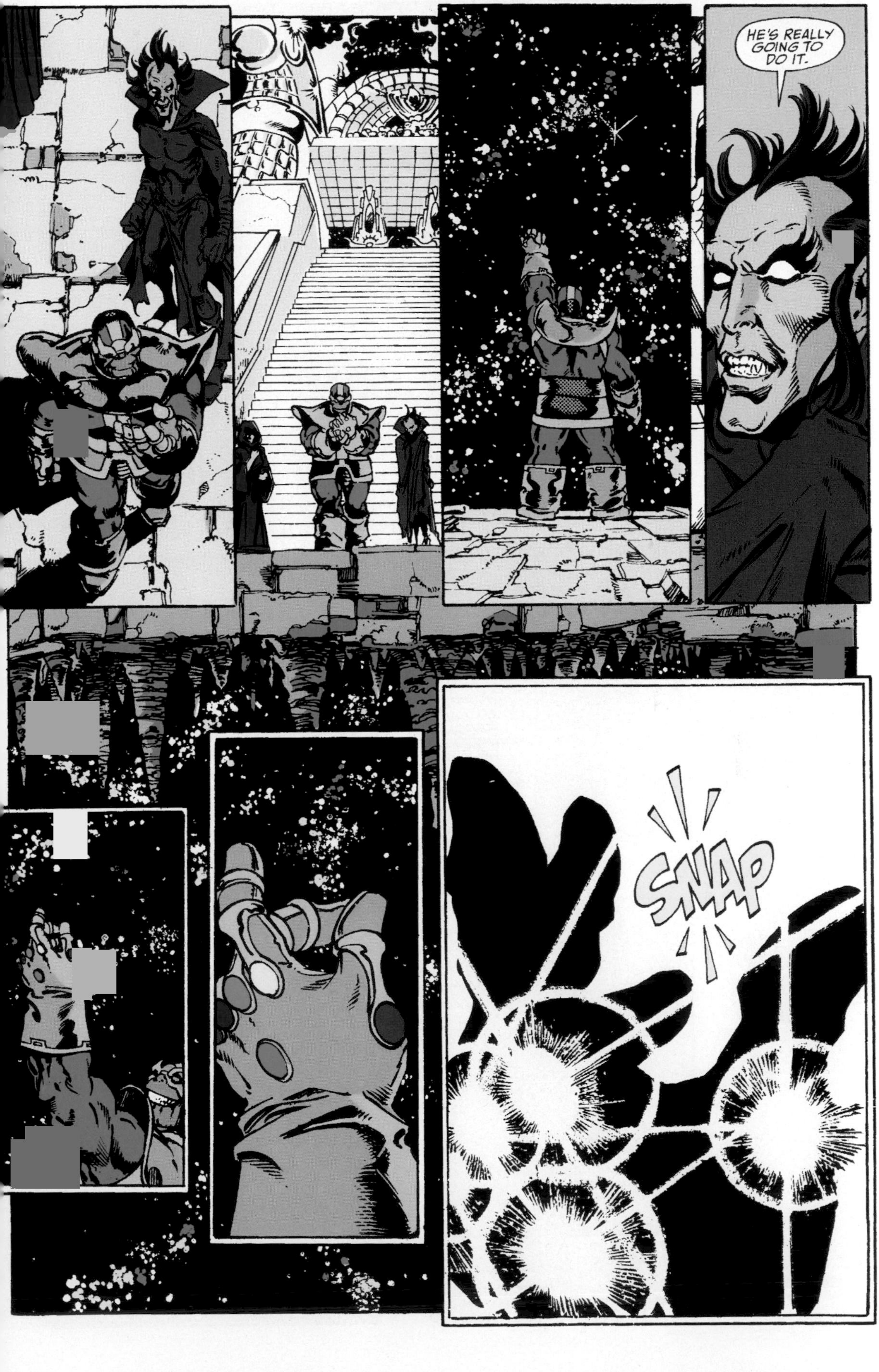
HE'S REALLY GOING TO DO IT.
SNAP

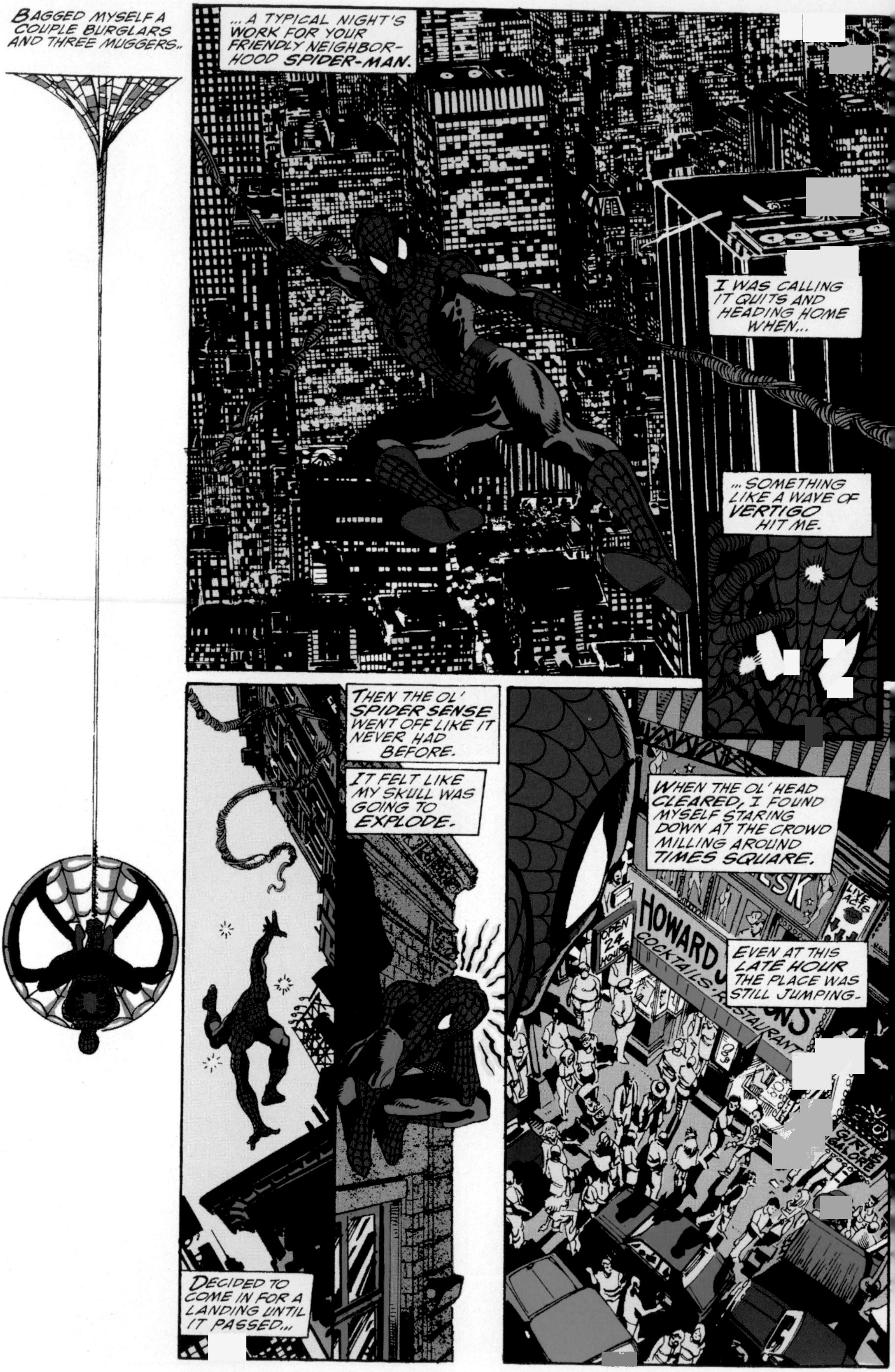
BAGGED MYSELF A COUPLE BURGLARS AND THREE MUGGERS...
...A TYPICAL NIGHT'S WORK FOR YOUR FRIENDLY NEIGHBOR-HOOD SPIDER-MAN.
I WAS CALLING IT QUITS AND HEADING HOME WHEN...
...SOMETHING LIKE A WAVE OF VERTIGO HIT ME.
THEN THE OL' SPIDER SENSE WENT OFF LIKE IT NEVER HAD BEFORE.
IT FELT LIKE MY SKULL WAS GOING TO EXPLODE.
DECIDED TO COME IN FOR A LANDING UNTIL IT PASSED...
WHEN THE OL' HEAD CLEARED, I FOUND MYSELF STARING DOWN AT THE CROWD MILLING AROUND TIMES SQUARE.
EVEN AT THIS LATE HOUR THE PLACE WAS STILL JUMPING.
HOWARD J
COCKTAILS
RESTAURANT
OPEN 24 HOURS
LIVE ACTS
GIRLS GALORE

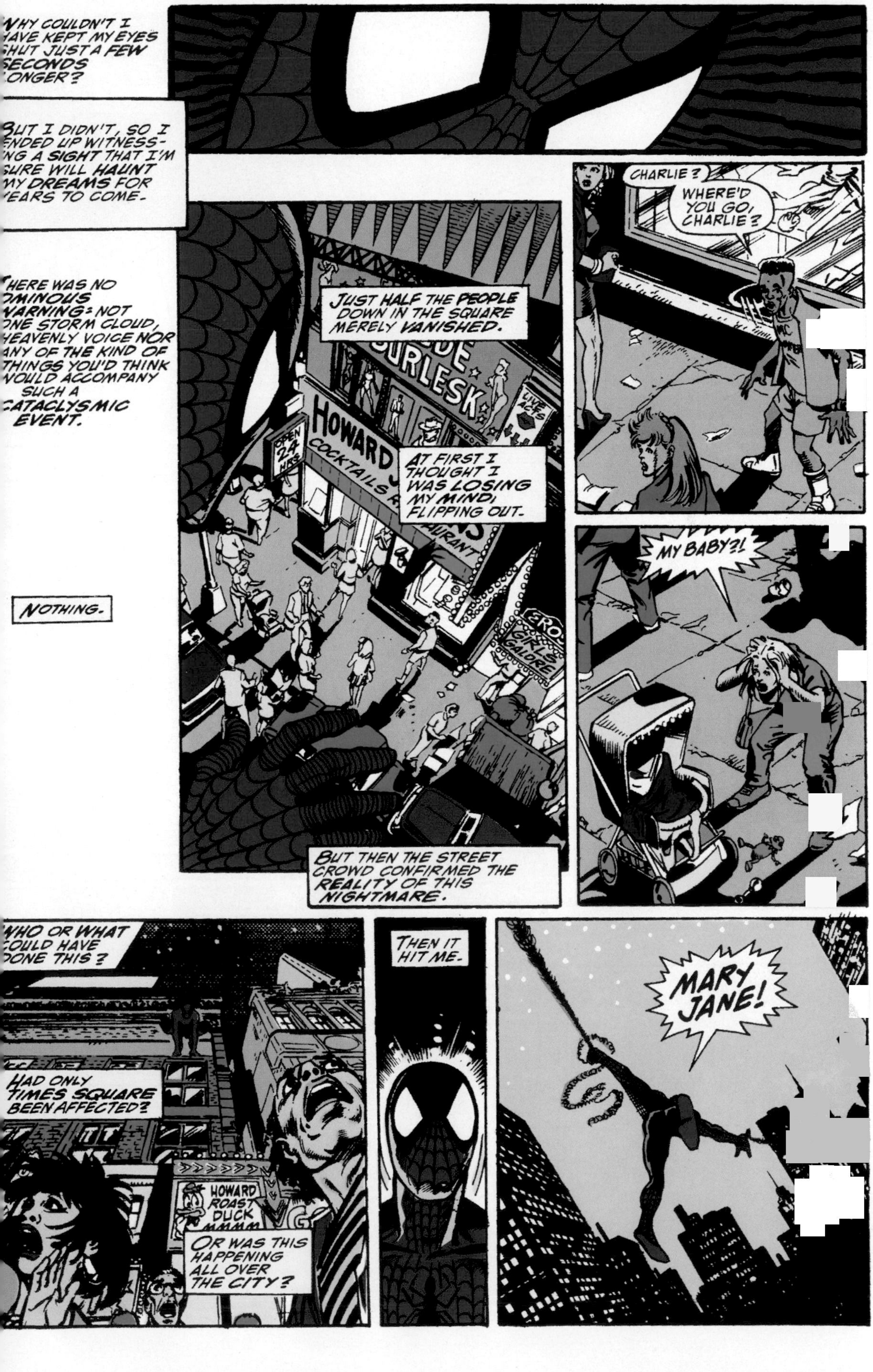
WHY COULDN'T I HAVE KEPT MY EYES SHUT JUST A FEW SECONDS LONGER?
BUT I DIDN'T, SO I ENDED UP WITNESSING A SIGHT THAT I'M SURE WILL HAUNT MY DREAMS FOR YEARS TO COME.
THERE WAS NO OMINOUS WARNING: NOT ONE STORM CLOUD, HEAVENLY VOICE NOR ANY OF THE KIND OF THINGS YOU'D THINK WOULD ACCOMPANY SUCH A CATACLYSMIC EVENT.
NOTHING.
JUST HALF THE PEOPLE DOWN IN THE SQUARE MERELY VANISHED.
BURLESK
HOWARD J
COCKTAILS
OPEN 24 HRS.
LIVE ACTS
AT FIRST I THOUGHT I WAS LOSING MY MIND, FLIPPING OUT.
GIRLS GALORE
BUT THEN THE STREET CROWD CONFIRMED THE REALITY OF THIS NIGHTMARE.
CHARLIE?
WHERE'D YOU GO, CHARLIE?
MY BABY?!
WHO OR WHAT COULD HAVE DONE THIS?
HAD ONLY TIMES SQUARE BEEN AFFECTED?
HOWARD ROAST DUCK MMMM
OR WAS THIS HAPPENING ALL OVER THE CITY?
THEN IT HIT ME.
MARY JANE!

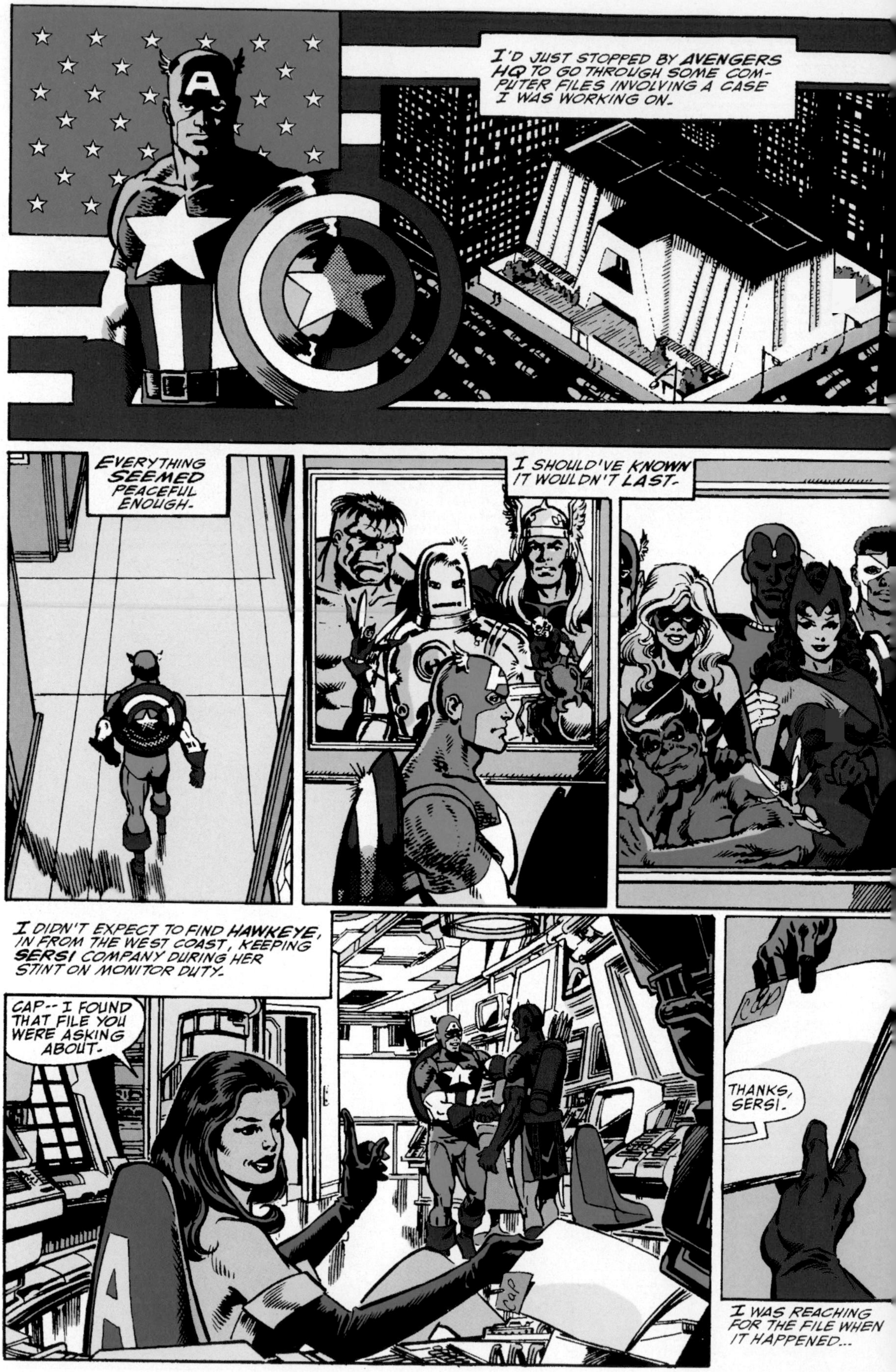

I'D JUST STOPPED BY AVENGERS HQ TO GO THROUGH SOME COMPUTER FILES INVOLVING A CASE I WAS WORKING ON.
EVERYTHING SEEMED PEACEFUL ENOUGH.
I SHOULD'VE KNOWN IT WOULDN'T LAST.
I DIDN'T EXPECT TO FIND HAWKEYE, IN FROM THE WEST COAST, KEEPING SERSI COMPANY DURING HER STINT ON MONITOR DUTY.
CAP-- I FOUND THAT FILE YOU WERE ASKING ABOUT.
THANKS, SERSI.
I WAS REACHING FOR THE FILE WHEN IT HAPPENED...

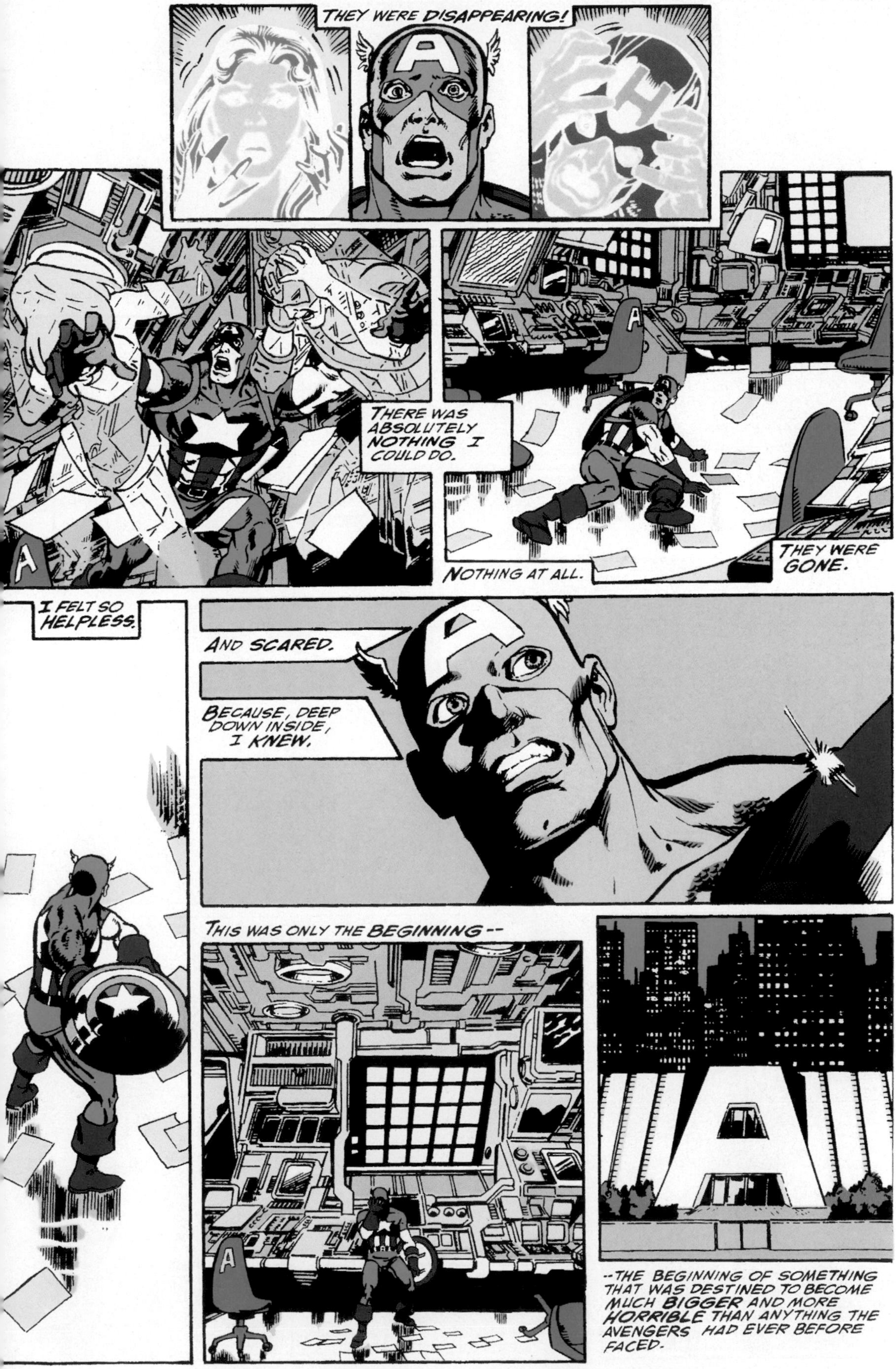
THEY WERE DISAPPEARING!
THERE WAS ABSOLUTELY NOTHING I COULD DO.
NOTHING AT ALL.
THEY WERE GONE.
I FELT SO HELPLESS.
AND SCARED.
BECAUSE, DEEP DOWN INSIDE, I KNEW.
THIS WAS ONLY THE BEGINNING--
--THE BEGINNING OF SOMETHING THAT WAS DESTINED TO BECOME MUCH BIGGER AND MORE HORRIBLE THAN ANYTHING THE AVENGERS HAD EVER BEFORE FACED.

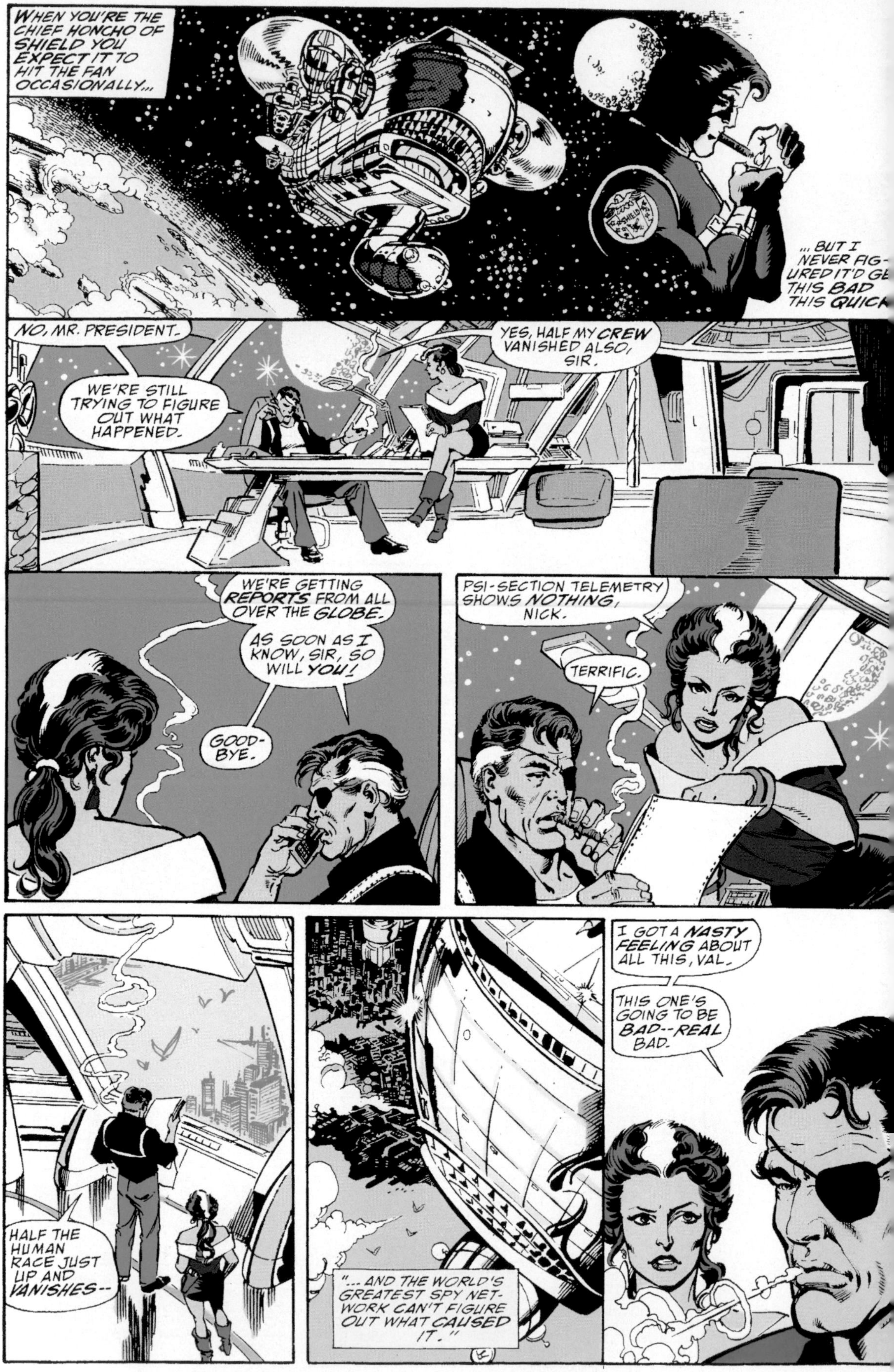

WHEN YOU'RE THE CHIEF HONCHO OF SHIELD YOU EXPECT IT TO HIT THE FAN OCCASIONALLY...
... BUT I NEVER FIGURED IT'D GE THIS BAD THIS QUICK
NO, MR. PRESIDENT.
WE'RE STILL TRYING TO FIGURE OUT WHAT HAPPENED.
YES, HALF MY CREW VANISHED ALSO, SIR.
WE'RE GETTING REPORTS FROM ALL OVER THE GLOBE.
AS SOON AS I KNOW, SIR, SO WILL YOU!
GOOD-BYE.
PSI-SECTION TELEMETRY SHOWS NOTHING, NICK.
TERRIFIC.
HALF THE HUMAN RACE JUST UP AND VANISHES--
"... AND THE WORLD'S GREATEST SPY NETWORK CAN'T FIGURE OUT WHAT CAUSED IT."
I GOT A NASTY FEELING ABOUT ALL THIS, VAL.
THIS ONE'S GOING TO BE BAD--REAL BAD.

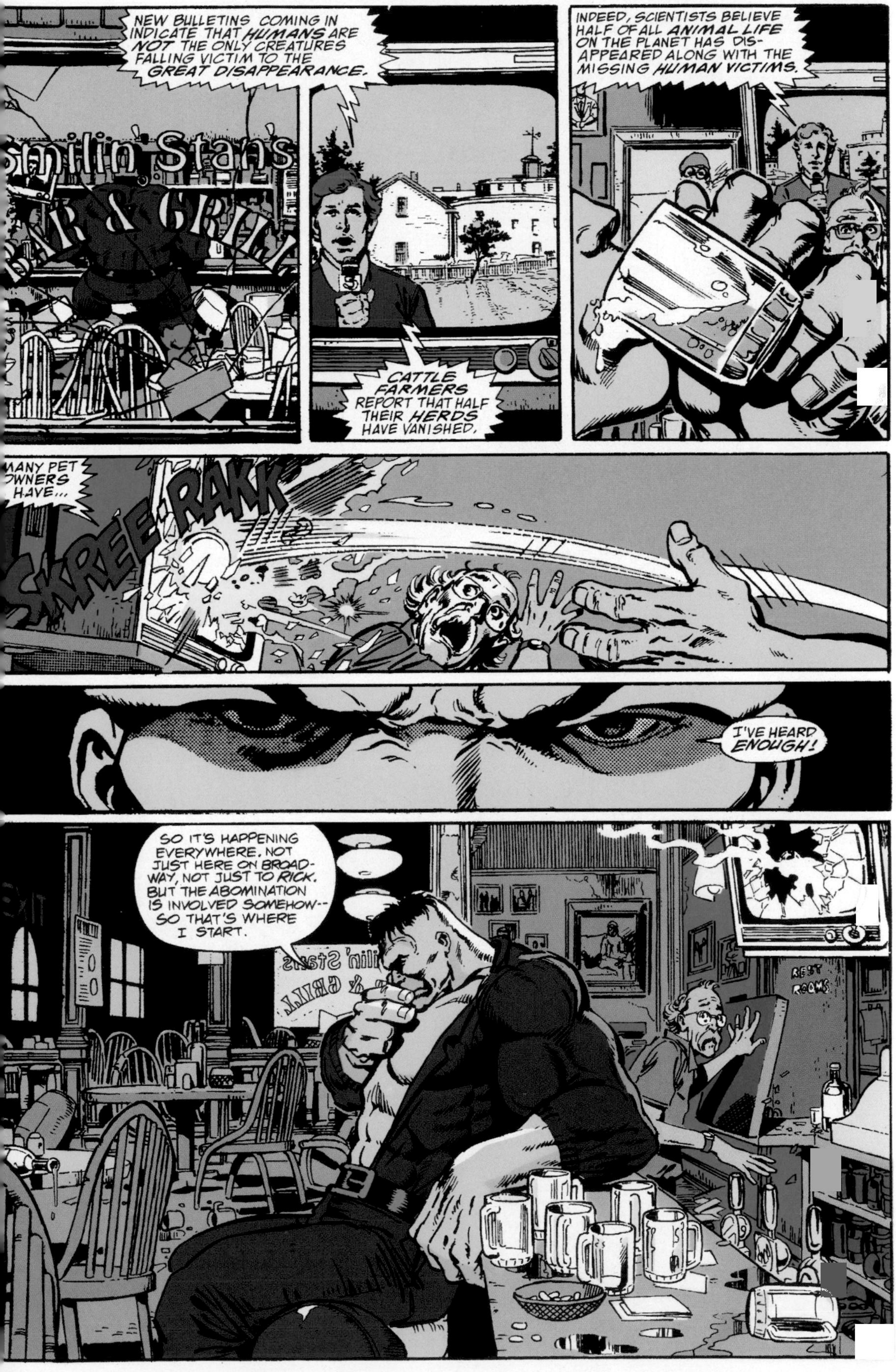
NEW BULLETINS COMING IN INDICATE THAT HUMANS ARE NOT THE ONLY CREATURES FALLING VICTIM TO THE GREAT DISAPPEARANCE.
Smilin' Stan's
CATTLE FARMERS REPORT THAT HALF THEIR HERDS HAVE VANISHED.
INDEED, SCIENTISTS BELIEVE HALF OF ALL ANIMAL LIFE ON THE PLANET HAS DISAPPEARED ALONG WITH THE MISSING HUMAN VICTIMS.
MANY PET OWNERS HAVE...
SKREE-RAKK
I'VE HEARD ENOUGH!
SO IT'S HAPPENING EVERYWHERE. NOT JUST HERE ON BROADWAY, NOT JUST TO RICK. BUT THE ABOMINATION IS INVOLVED SOMEHOW-- SO THAT'S WHERE I START.
REST ROOMS

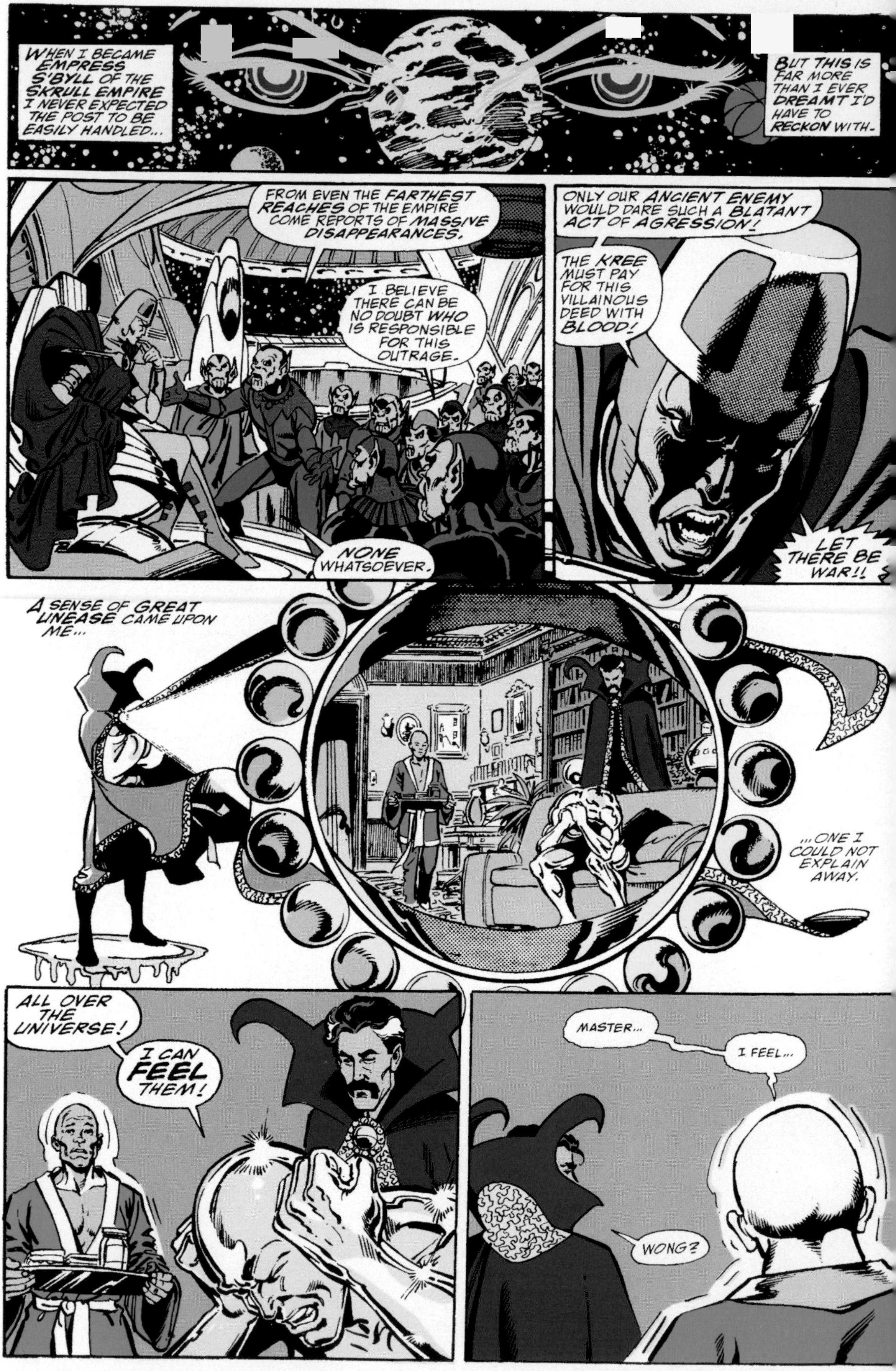

WHEN I BECAME EMPRESS S'BYLL OF THE SKRULL EMPIRE I NEVER EXPECTED THE POST TO BE EASILY HANDLED...
BUT THIS IS FAR MORE THAN I EVER DREAMT I'D HAVE TO RECKON WITH.
FROM EVEN THE FARTHEST REACHES OF THE EMPIRE COME REPORTS OF MASSIVE DISAPPEARANCES.
I BELIEVE THERE CAN BE NO DOUBT WHO IS RESPONSIBLE FOR THIS OUTRAGE.
NONE WHATSOEVER.
ONLY OUR ANCIENT ENEMY WOULD DARE SUCH A BLATANT ACT OF AGRESSION!
THE KREE MUST PAY FOR THIS VILLAINOUS DEED WITH BLOOD!
LET THERE BE WAR!!
A SENSE OF GREAT UNEASE CAME UPON ME...
...ONE I COULD NOT EXPLAIN AWAY.
ALL OVER THE UNIVERSE!
I CAN FEEL THEM!
MASTER...
I FEEL...
WONG?

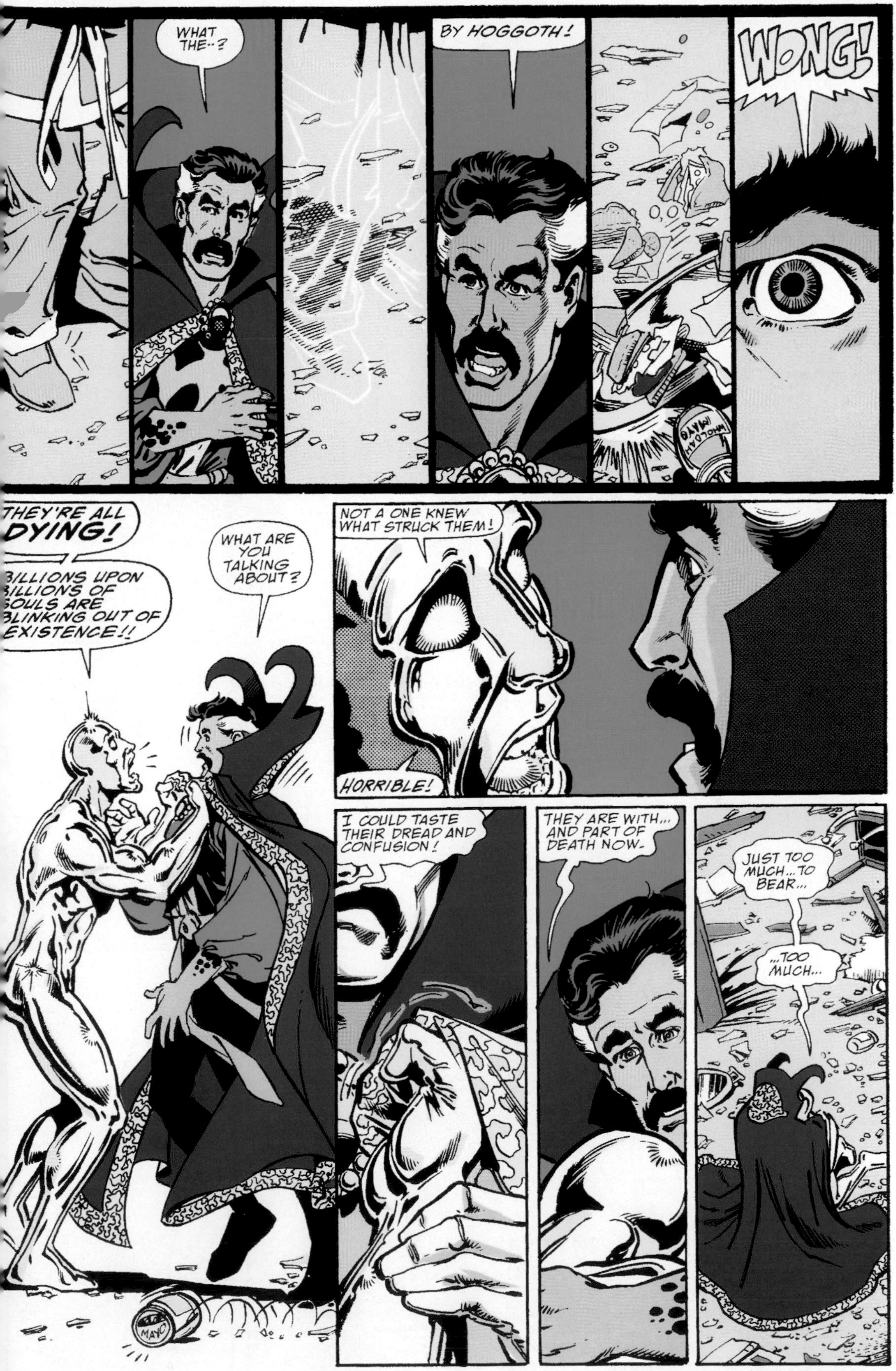
WHAT THE--?
BY HOGGOTH!
WONG!
WHOLDAH MAYO
THEY'RE ALL DYING!
BILLIONS UPON BILLIONS OF SOULS ARE BLINKING OUT OF EXISTENCE!!
WHAT ARE YOU TALKING ABOUT?
NOT A ONE KNEW WHAT STRUCK THEM!
HORRIBLE!
MAYO
I COULD TASTE THEIR DREAD AND CONFUSION!
THEY ARE WITH... AND PART OF DEATH NOW.
JUST TOO MUCH... TO BEAR...
...TOO MUCH...

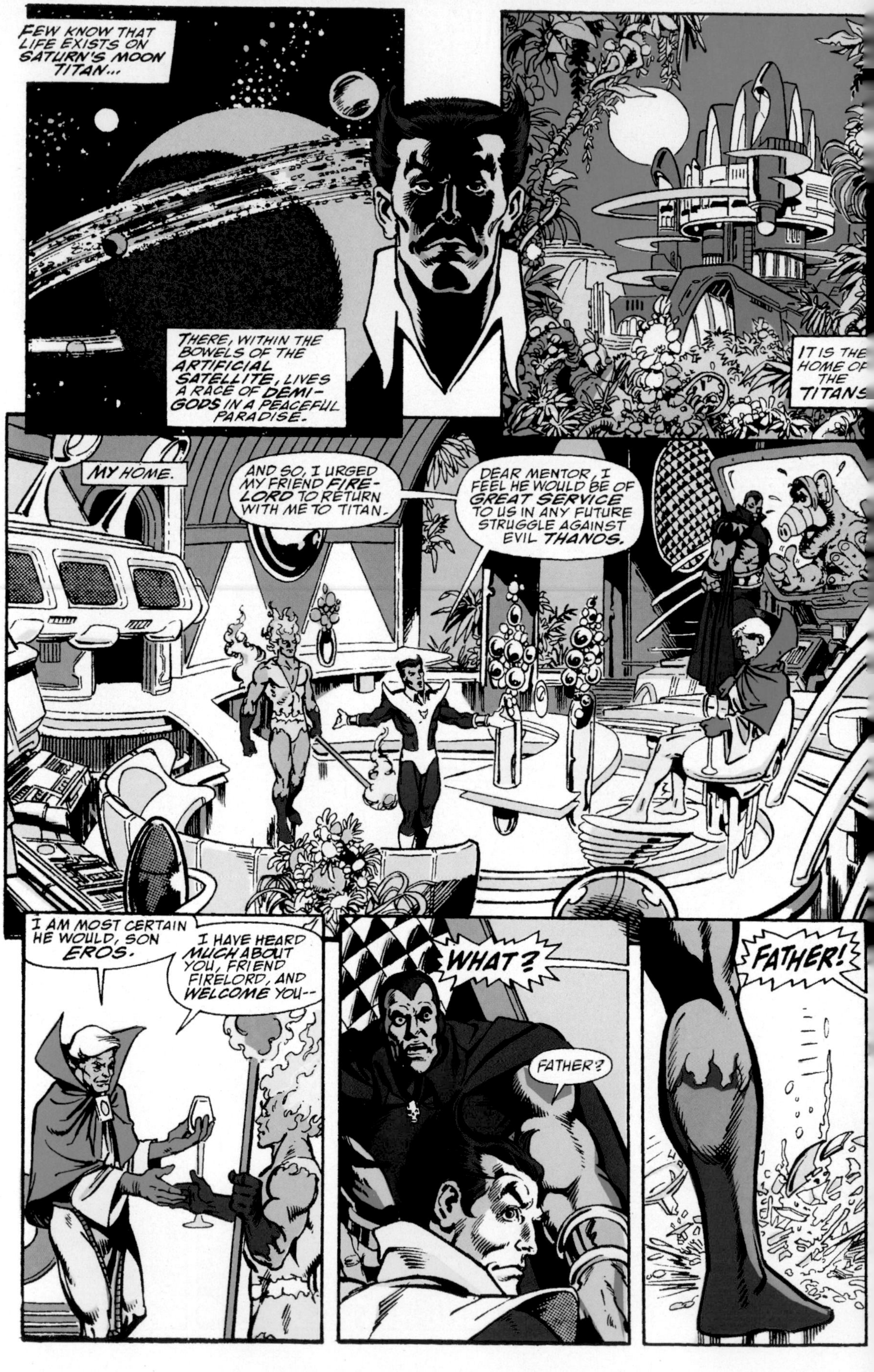
FEW KNOW THAT LIFE EXISTS ON SATURN'S MOON TITAN...
THERE, WITHIN THE BOWELS OF THE ARTIFICIAL SATELLITE, LIVES A RACE OF DEMI-GODS IN A PEACEFUL PARADISE.
IT IS THE HOME OF THE TITANS
MY HOME.
AND SO, I URGED MY FRIEND FIRE-LORD TO RETURN WITH ME TO TITAN.
DEAR MENTOR, I FEEL HE WOULD BE OF GREAT SERVICE TO US IN ANY FUTURE STRUGGLE AGAINST EVIL THANOS.
I AM MOST CERTAIN HE WOULD, SON EROS.
I HAVE HEARD MUCH ABOUT YOU, FRIEND FIRELORD, AND WELCOME YOU--
WHAT?
FATHER?
FATHER!

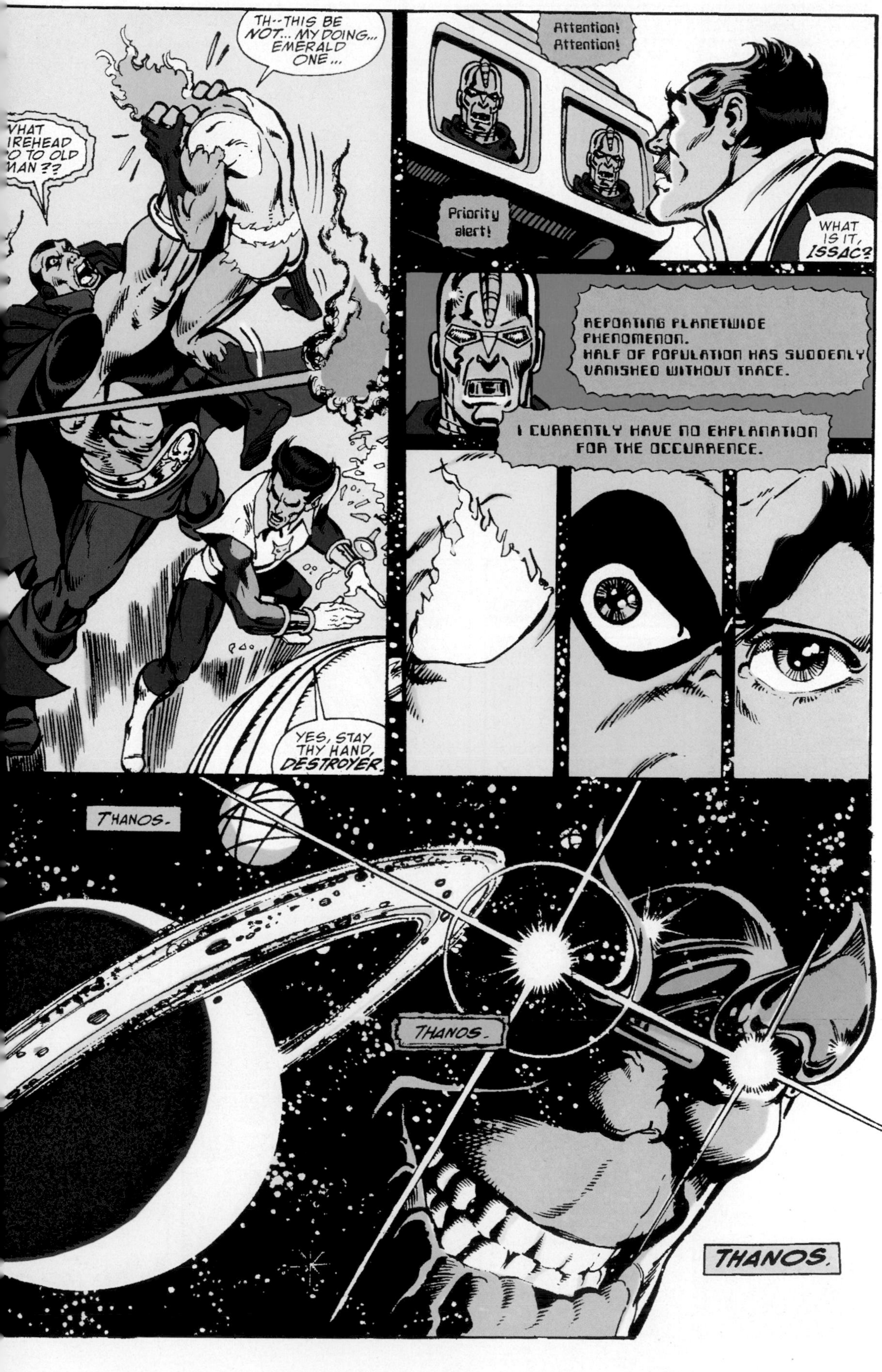
TH--THIS BE NOT... MY DOING... EMERALD ONE...
WHAT IREHEAD O TO OLD MAN??
YES, STAY THY HAND, DESTROYER.
Attention! Attention!
Priority alert!
WHAT IS IT, ISSAC?
REPORTING PLANETWIDE PHENOMENON. HALF OF POPULATION HAS SUDDENLY VANISHED WITHOUT TRACE.
I CURRENTLY HAVE NO EXPLANATION FOR THE OCCURRENCE.
THANOS.
THANOS.
THANOS.

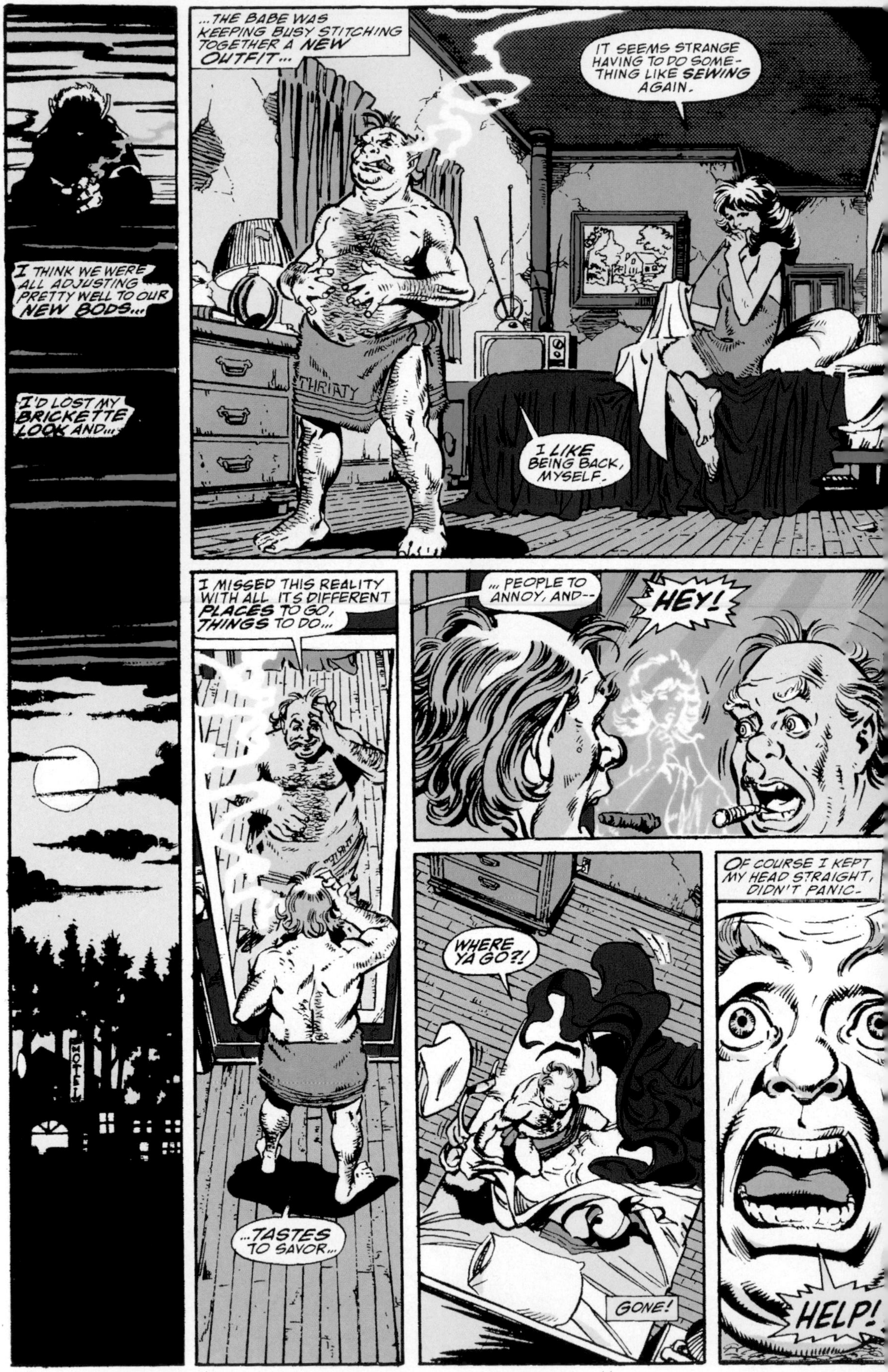
I THINK WE WERE ALL ADJUSTING PRETTY WELL TO OUR NEW BODS...
I'D LOST MY BRICKETTE LOOK AND...
...THE BABE WAS KEEPING BUSY STITCHING TOGETHER A NEW OUTFIT...
IT SEEMS STRANGE HAVING TO DO SOME-THING LIKE SEWING AGAIN.
THRIFTY
I LIKE BEING BACK, MYSELF.
I MISSED THIS REALITY WITH ALL ITS DIFFERENT PLACES TO GO, THINGS TO DO...
...TASTES TO SAVOR...
...PEOPLE TO ANNOY, AND--
HEY!
WHERE YA GO?!
GONE!
OF COURSE I KEPT MY HEAD STRAIGHT, DIDN'T PANIC-
HELP!
MOTEL

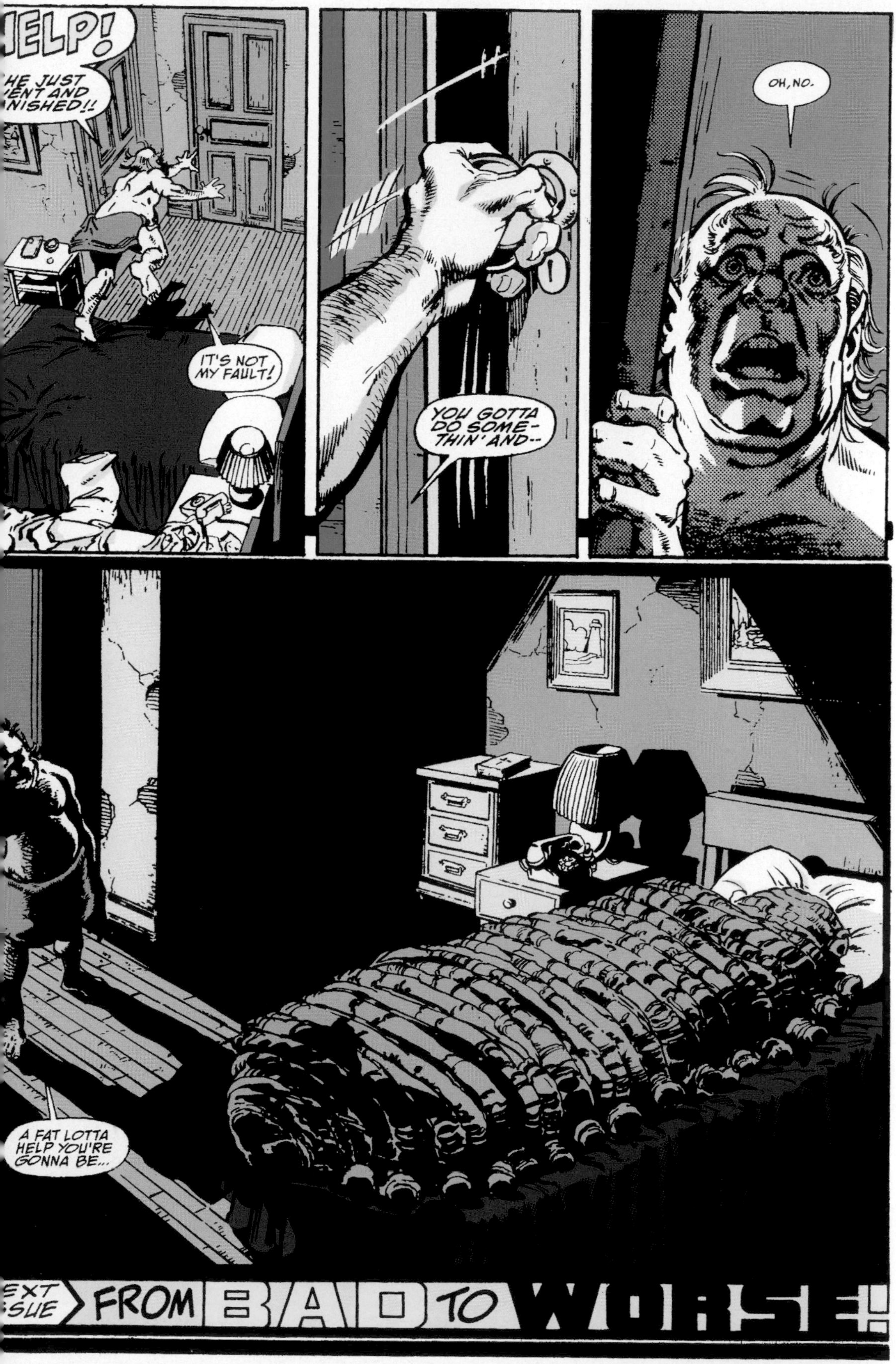

ELP!
HE JUST ENT AND NISHED!!
IT'S NOT MY FAULT!
YOU GOTTA DO SOME-THIN' AND--
OH, NO.
A FAT LOTTA HELP YOU'RE GONNA BE...
EXT SUE FROM BAD TO WORSE!

CONTINUED IN *INFINITY GAUNTLET TPB.*

HANOS HAS RETURNED TO EARTH. NOW THE GUARDIANS OF THE GALAXY AND THEIR ALLIES FACE THE MA
TITAN IN THE EPIC CONCLUSION TO BRIAN MICHAEL BENDIS' *GUARDIANS OF THE GALAXY* RUN!

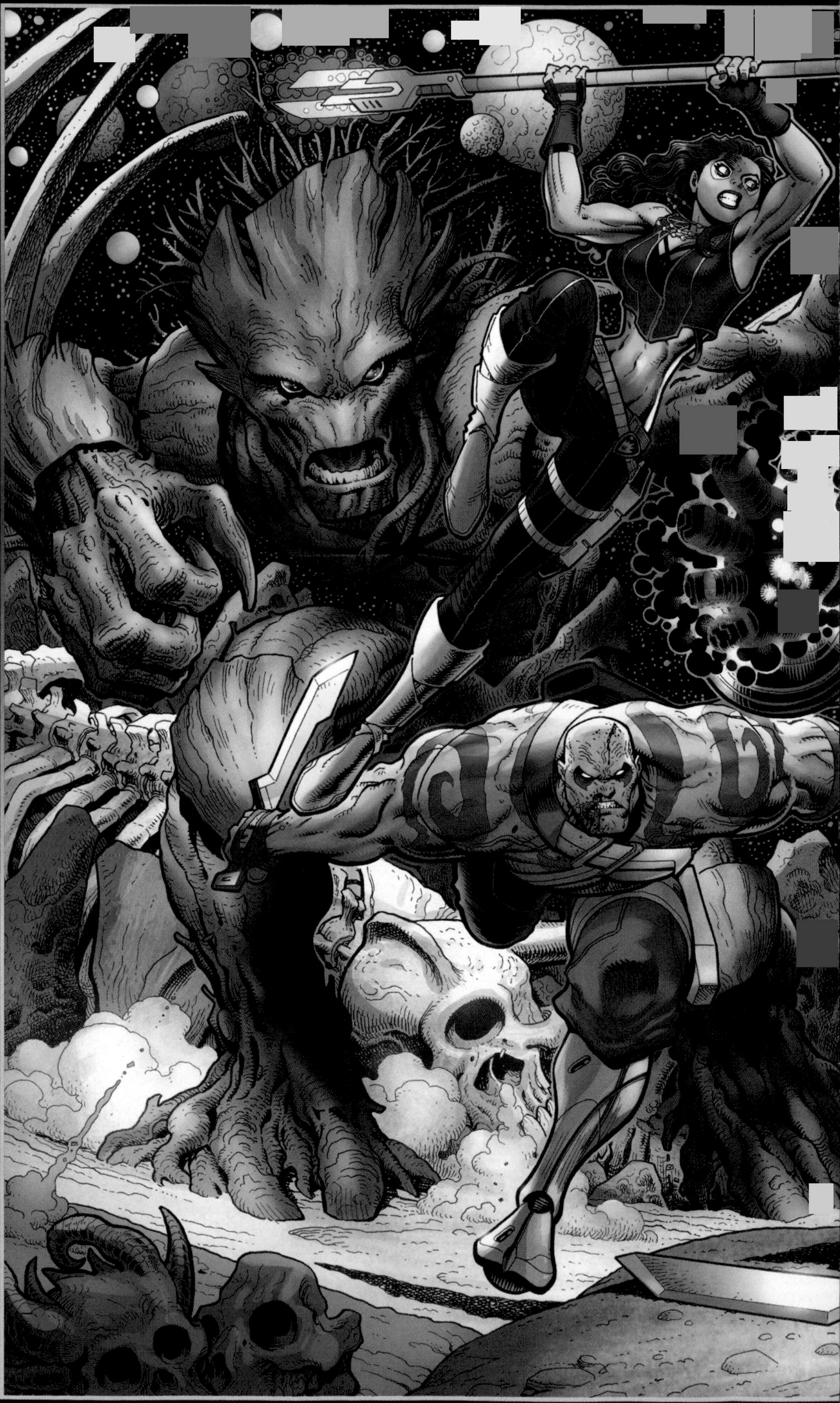

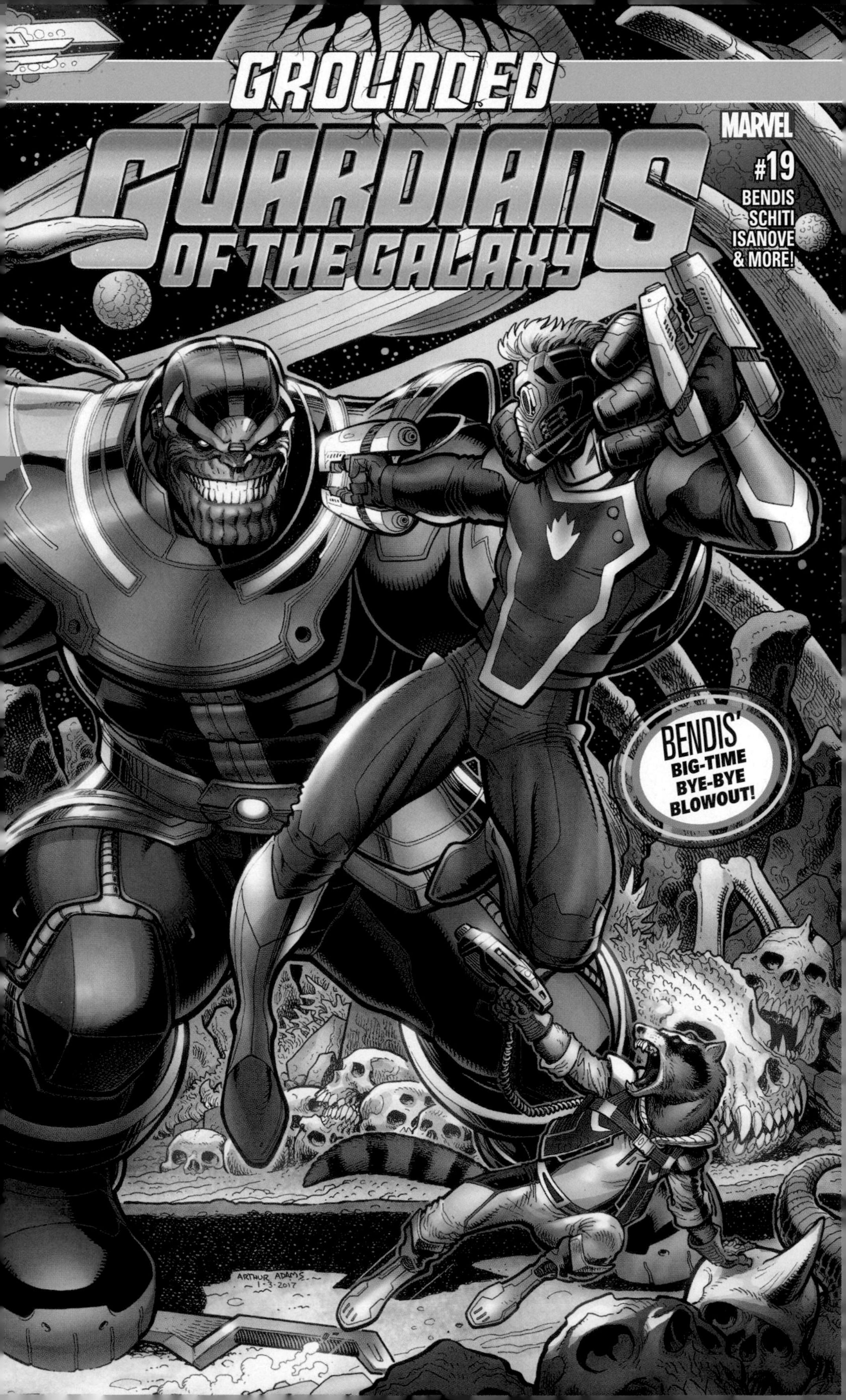
GROUNDED
GUARDIANS OF THE GALAXY
MARVEL
#19
BENDIS
SCHITI
ISANOVE
& MORE!
BENDIS' BIG-TIME BYE-BYE BLOWOUT!
ARTHUR ADAMS 1-3-2017

The entire galaxy is a mess. Warring empires and cosmic terrorists plague every corner. Someone has to rise above it all and fight for those who have no one to fight for them. A group of misfits — **Drax the Destroyer**, **Gamora**, **Rocket Raccoon**, and **Groot** — joined together under the leadership of **Peter Quill**, a.k.a. **Star-Lord**. With past and temporary team members **Ben Grimm**, a.k.a. **The Thing**, **Flash Thompson**, a.k.a. **Venom**, and **Angela Odinsdottir**, they serve a higher cause as the…

After a fierce battle on Earth — helping former teammate Captain Marvel in the super hero Civil War — the Guardians lost their ship. In the wreckage, they learned Peter Quill knew Thanos had been on Earth and kept it a secret from the others. Gamora left in a rage, clashing with S.H.I.E.L.D. and Captain Marvel before learning she was too late — Thanos was already off-planet. The others split up and tried to find a way back into space.

No one suspects that Thanos is coming back…

WRITER **BRIAN MICHAEL BENDIS**   ARTIST **VALERIO SCHITI**

COLOR ARTIST **RICHARD ISANOVE**

GUEST ARTISTS:

PHIL NOTO
PAGES 9-10 PENCILS & INKS

ANDREA SORRENTINO
PAGES 11-12 PENCILS, INKS, & COLORS

ED MCGUINNESS & MARK MORALES
PAGES 17-18 PENCILS & INKS

ARTHUR ADAMS
PAGES 23-24 PENCILS & INKS

KEVIN MAGUIRE
PAGES 25-26 PENCILS & INKS

MARK BAGLEY & ANDREW HENNESSEY
PAGES 27-28 PENCILS & INKS

SARA PICHELLI
PAGES 29-30 PENCILS & INKS

FILIPE ANDRADE
PAGES 31-32 PENCILS & INKS

LETTERER **VC'S CORY PETIT**   COVER BY **ARTHUR ADAMS & JASON KEITH**

ASSISTANT EDITOR **KATHLEEN WISNESKI**   ASSOCIATE EDITOR **DARREN SHAN**   EDITOR **JORDAN D. WHITE**

EDITOR IN CHIEF **AXEL ALONSO** CHIEF CREATIVE OFFICER **JOE QUESADA** PRESIDENT **DAN BUCKLEY** EXECUTIVE PRODUCER **ALAN FINE**

ANGELA COCREATED BY **TODD MCFARLANE** & **NEIL GAIMAN**

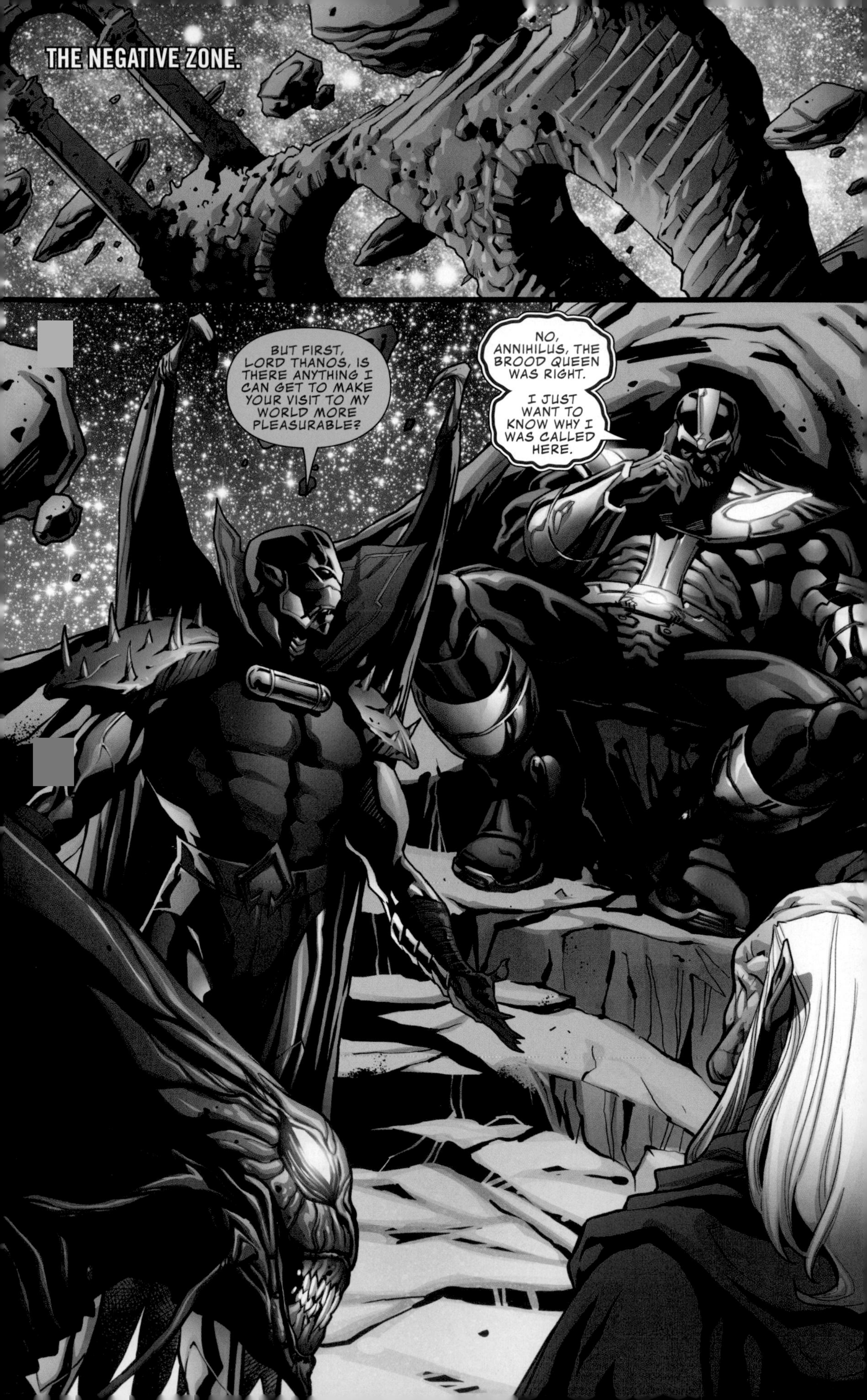
THE NEGATIVE ZONE.
BUT FIRST, LORD THANOS, IS THERE ANYTHING I CAN GET TO MAKE YOUR VISIT TO MY WORLD MORE PLEASURABLE?
NO, ANNIHILUS, THE BROOD QUEEN WAS RIGHT.
I JUST WANT TO KNOW WHY I WAS CALLED HERE.

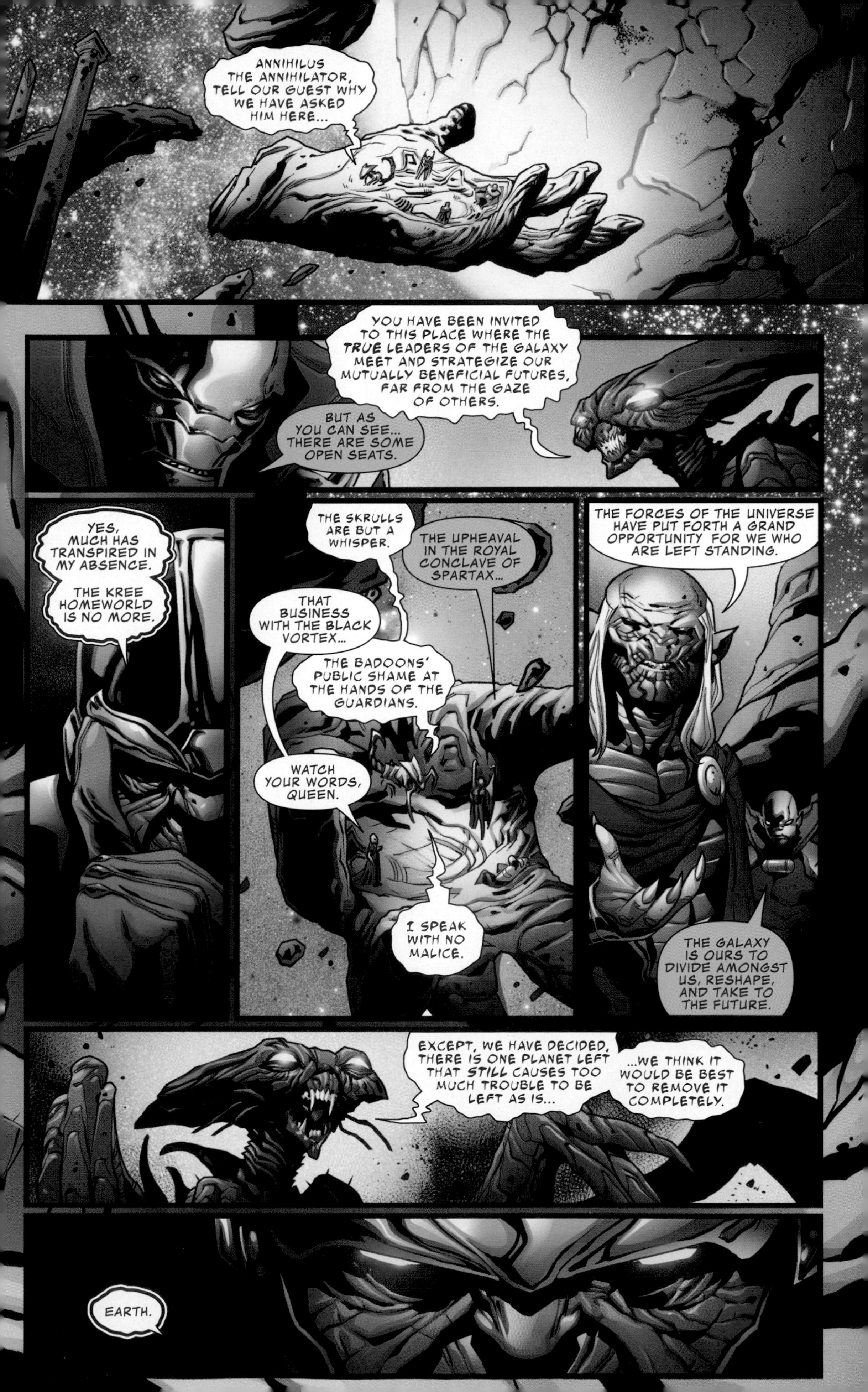
ANNIHILUS THE ANNIHILATOR, TELL OUR GUEST WHY WE HAVE ASKED HIM HERE...
YOU HAVE BEEN INVITED TO THIS PLACE WHERE THE TRUE LEADERS OF THE GALAXY MEET AND STRATEGIZE OUR MUTUALLY BENEFICIAL FUTURES, FAR FROM THE GAZE OF OTHERS.
BUT AS YOU CAN SEE... THERE ARE SOME OPEN SEATS.
YES, MUCH HAS TRANSPIRED IN MY ABSENCE.
THE KREE HOMEWORLD IS NO MORE.
THE SKRULLS ARE BUT A WHISPER.
THE UPHEAVAL IN THE ROYAL CONCLAVE OF SPARTAX...
THAT BUSINESS WITH THE BLACK VORTEX...
THE BADOONS' PUBLIC SHAME AT THE HANDS OF THE GUARDIANS.
WATCH YOUR WORDS, QUEEN.
I SPEAK WITH NO MALICE.
THE FORCES OF THE UNIVERSE HAVE PUT FORTH A GRAND OPPORTUNITY FOR WE WHO ARE LEFT STANDING.
THE GALAXY IS OURS TO DIVIDE AMONGST US, RESHAPE, AND TAKE TO THE FUTURE.
EXCEPT, WE HAVE DECIDED, THERE IS ONE PLANET LEFT THAT STILL CAUSES TOO MUCH TROUBLE TO BE LEFT AS IS...
...WE THINK IT WOULD BE BEST TO REMOVE IT COMPLETELY.
EARTH.

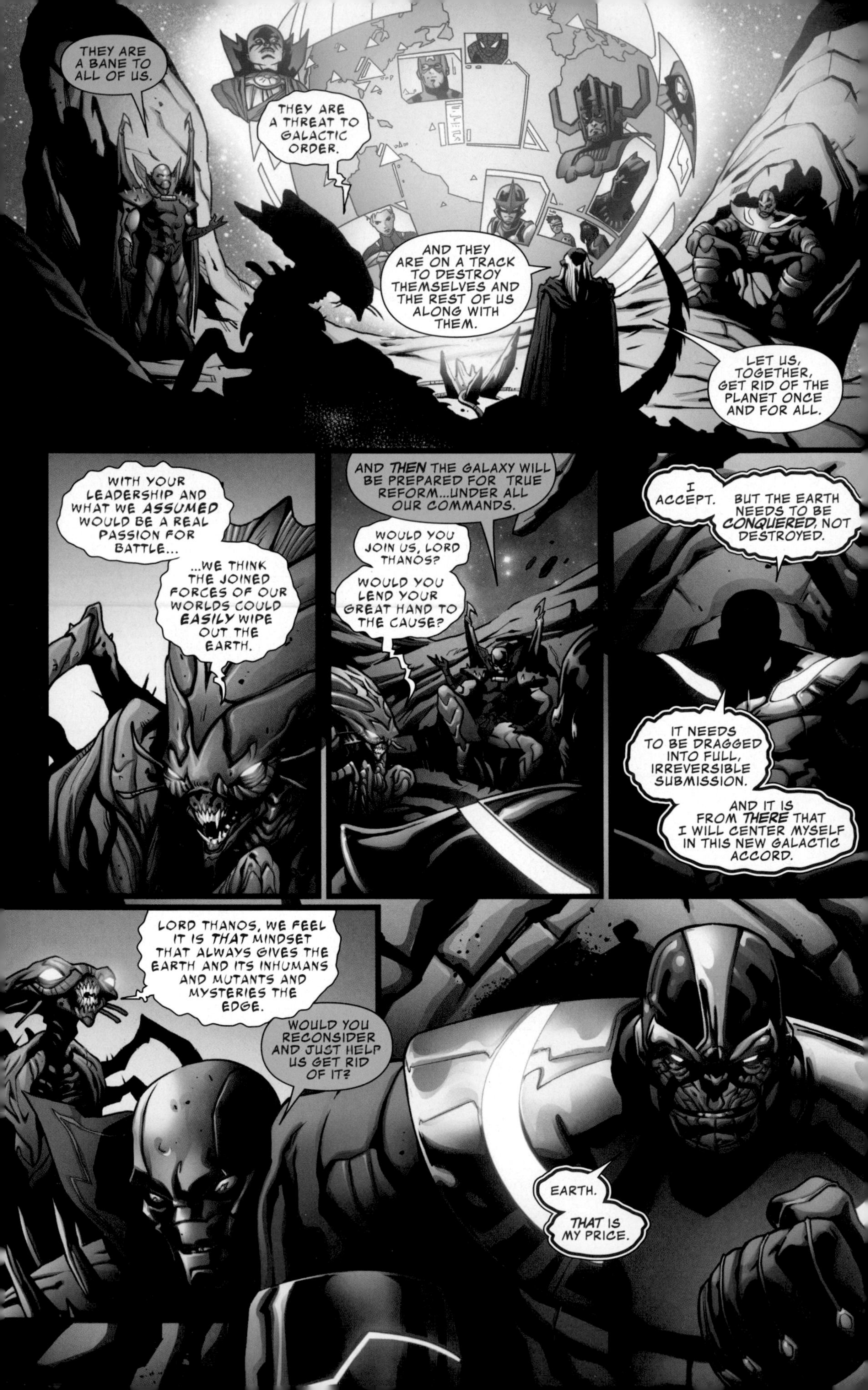
THEY ARE A BANE TO ALL OF US.
THEY ARE A THREAT TO GALACTIC ORDER.
AND THEY ARE ON A TRACK TO DESTROY THEMSELVES AND THE REST OF US ALONG WITH THEM.
LET US, TOGETHER, GET RID OF THE PLANET ONCE AND FOR ALL.
WITH YOUR LEADERSHIP AND WHAT WE ASSUMED WOULD BE A REAL PASSION FOR BATTLE...
...WE THINK THE JOINED FORCES OF OUR WORLDS COULD EASILY WIPE OUT THE EARTH.
AND THEN THE GALAXY WILL BE PREPARED FOR TRUE REFORM...UNDER ALL OUR COMMANDS.
WOULD YOU JOIN US, LORD THANOS?
WOULD YOU LEND YOUR GREAT HAND TO THE CAUSE?
I ACCEPT.
BUT THE EARTH NEEDS TO BE CONQUERED, NOT DESTROYED.
IT NEEDS TO BE DRAGGED INTO FULL, IRREVERSIBLE SUBMISSION.
AND IT IS FROM THERE THAT I WILL CENTER MYSELF IN THIS NEW GALACTIC ACCORD.
LORD THANOS, WE FEEL IT IS THAT MINDSET THAT ALWAYS GIVES THE EARTH AND ITS INHUMANS AND MUTANTS AND MYSTERIES THE EDGE.
WOULD YOU RECONSIDER AND JUST HELP US GET RID OF IT?
EARTH.
THAT IS MY PRICE.

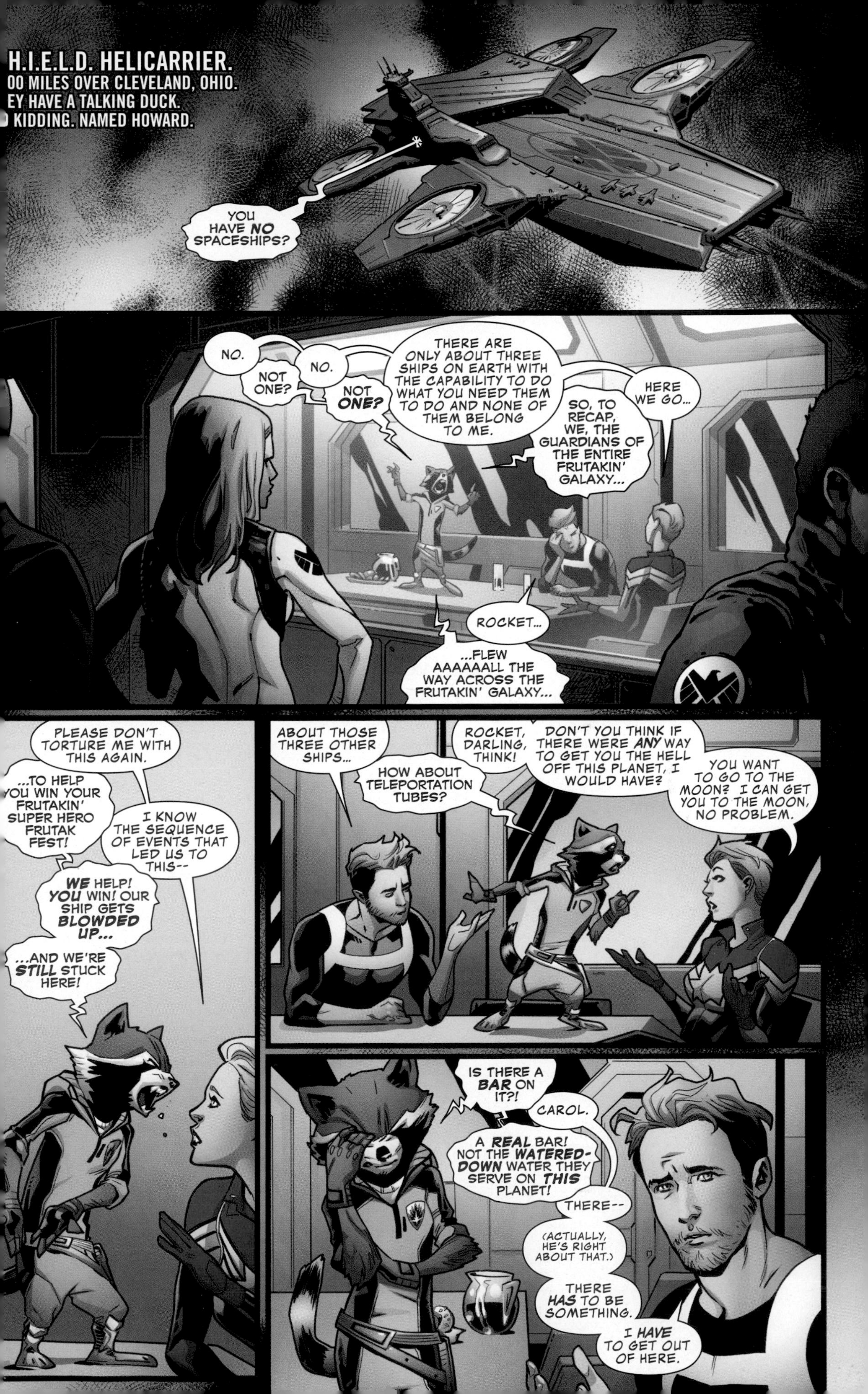
H.I.E.L.D. HELICARRIER.
00 MILES OVER CLEVELAND, OHIO.
EY HAVE A TALKING DUCK.
KIDDING. NAMED HOWARD.
YOU HAVE NO SPACESHIPS?
NO.
NOT ONE?
NO.
NOT ONE?
THERE ARE ONLY ABOUT THREE SHIPS ON EARTH WITH THE CAPABILITY TO DO WHAT YOU NEED THEM TO DO AND NONE OF THEM BELONG TO ME.
SO, TO RECAP, WE, THE GUARDIANS OF THE ENTIRE FRUTAKIN' GALAXY...
HERE WE GO...
ROCKET...
...FLEW AAAAAALL THE WAY ACROSS THE FRUTAKIN' GALAXY...
PLEASE DON'T TORTURE ME WITH THIS AGAIN.
...TO HELP YOU WIN YOUR FRUTAKIN' SUPER HERO FRUTAK FEST!
I KNOW THE SEQUENCE OF EVENTS THAT LED US TO THIS--
WE HELP! YOU WIN! OUR SHIP GETS BLOWDED UP...
...AND WE'RE STILL STUCK HERE!
ABOUT THOSE THREE OTHER SHIPS...
HOW ABOUT TELEPORTATION TUBES?
ROCKET, DARLING, THINK!
DON'T YOU THINK IF THERE WERE ANY WAY TO GET YOU THE HELL OFF THIS PLANET, I WOULD HAVE?
YOU WANT TO GO TO THE MOON? I CAN GET YOU TO THE MOON, NO PROBLEM.
IS THERE A BAR ON IT?!
CAROL.
A REAL BAR! NOT THE WATERED-DOWN WATER THEY SERVE ON THIS PLANET!
THERE--
(ACTUALLY, HE'S RIGHT ABOUT THAT.)
THERE HAS TO BE SOMETHING.
I HAVE TO GET OUT OF HERE.

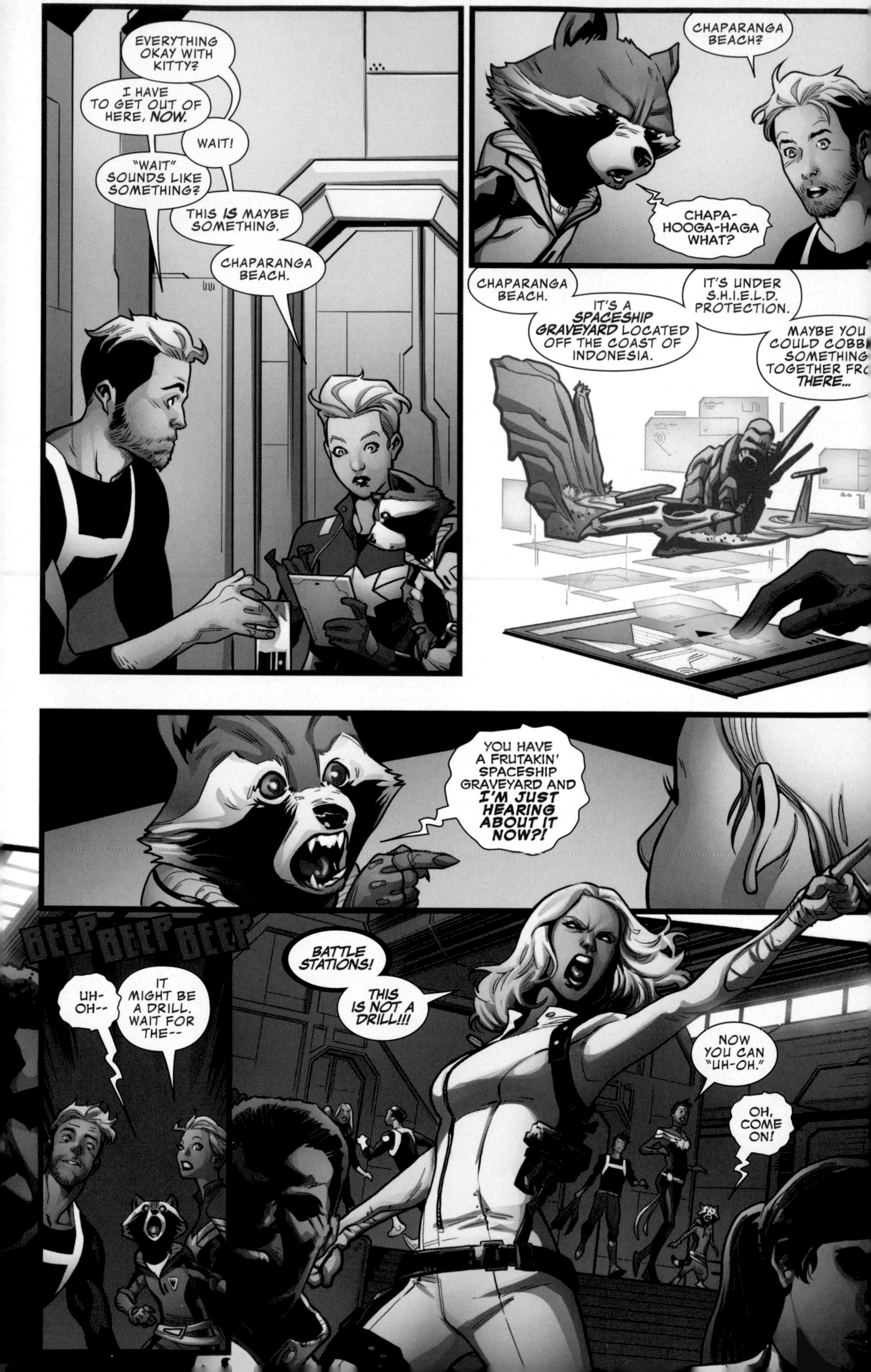
EVERYTHING OKAY WITH KITTY?
I HAVE TO GET OUT OF HERE, NOW.
WAIT!
"WAIT" SOUNDS LIKE SOMETHING?
THIS IS MAYBE SOMETHING.
CHAPARANGA BEACH.
CHAPARANGA BEACH?
CHAPA-HOOGA-HAGA WHAT?
CHAPARANGA BEACH.
IT'S A SPACESHIP GRAVEYARD LOCATED OFF THE COAST OF INDONESIA.
IT'S UNDER S.H.I.E.L.D. PROTECTION.
MAYBE YOU COULD COBB SOMETHING TOGETHER FR THERE...
YOU HAVE A FRUTAKIN' SPACESHIP GRAVEYARD AND I'M JUST HEARING ABOUT IT NOW?!
BEEP BEEP BEEP
UH-OH--
IT MIGHT BE A DRILL. WAIT FOR THE--
BATTLE STATIONS!
THIS IS NOT A DRILL!!!
NOW YOU CAN "UH-OH."
OH, COME ON!

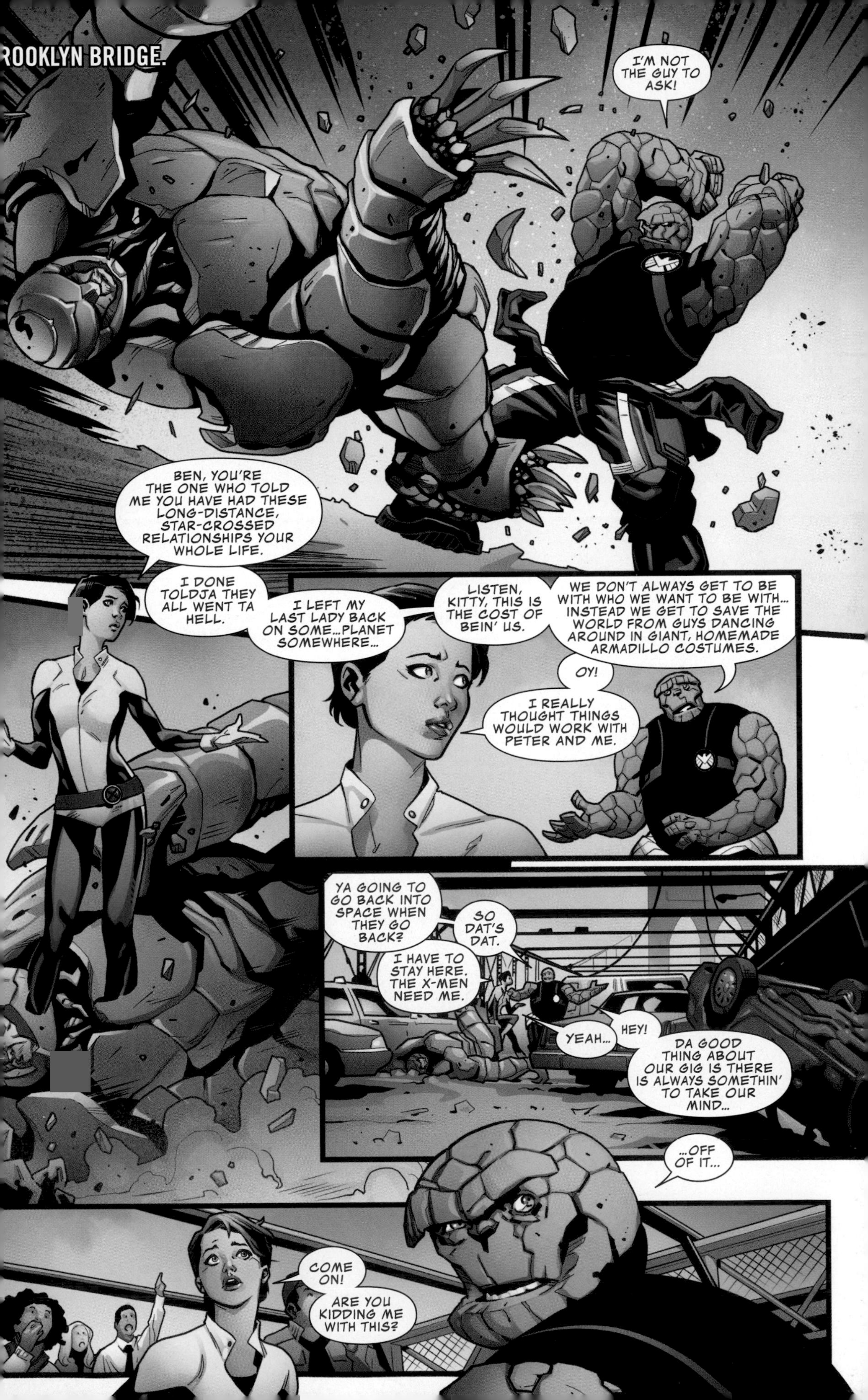
ROOKLYN BRIDGE.
I'M NOT THE GUY TO ASK!
BEN, YOU'RE THE ONE WHO TOLD ME YOU HAVE HAD THESE LONG-DISTANCE, STAR-CROSSED RELATIONSHIPS YOUR WHOLE LIFE.
I DONE TOLDJA THEY ALL WENT TA HELL.
I LEFT MY LAST LADY BACK ON SOME...PLANET SOMEWHERE...
LISTEN, KITTY, THIS IS THE COST OF BEIN' US.
WE DON'T ALWAYS GET TO BE WITH WHO WE WANT TO BE WITH... INSTEAD WE GET TO SAVE THE WORLD FROM GUYS DANCING AROUND IN GIANT, HOMEMADE ARMADILLO COSTUMES.
OY!
I REALLY THOUGHT THINGS WOULD WORK WITH PETER AND ME.
YA GOING TO GO BACK INTO SPACE WHEN THEY GO BACK?
SO DAT'S DAT.
I HAVE TO STAY HERE. THE X-MEN NEED ME.
YEAH...
HEY!
DA GOOD THING ABOUT OUR GIG IS THERE IS ALWAYS SOMETHIN' TO TAKE OUR MIND...
...OFF OF IT...
COME ON!
ARE YOU KIDDING ME WITH THIS?

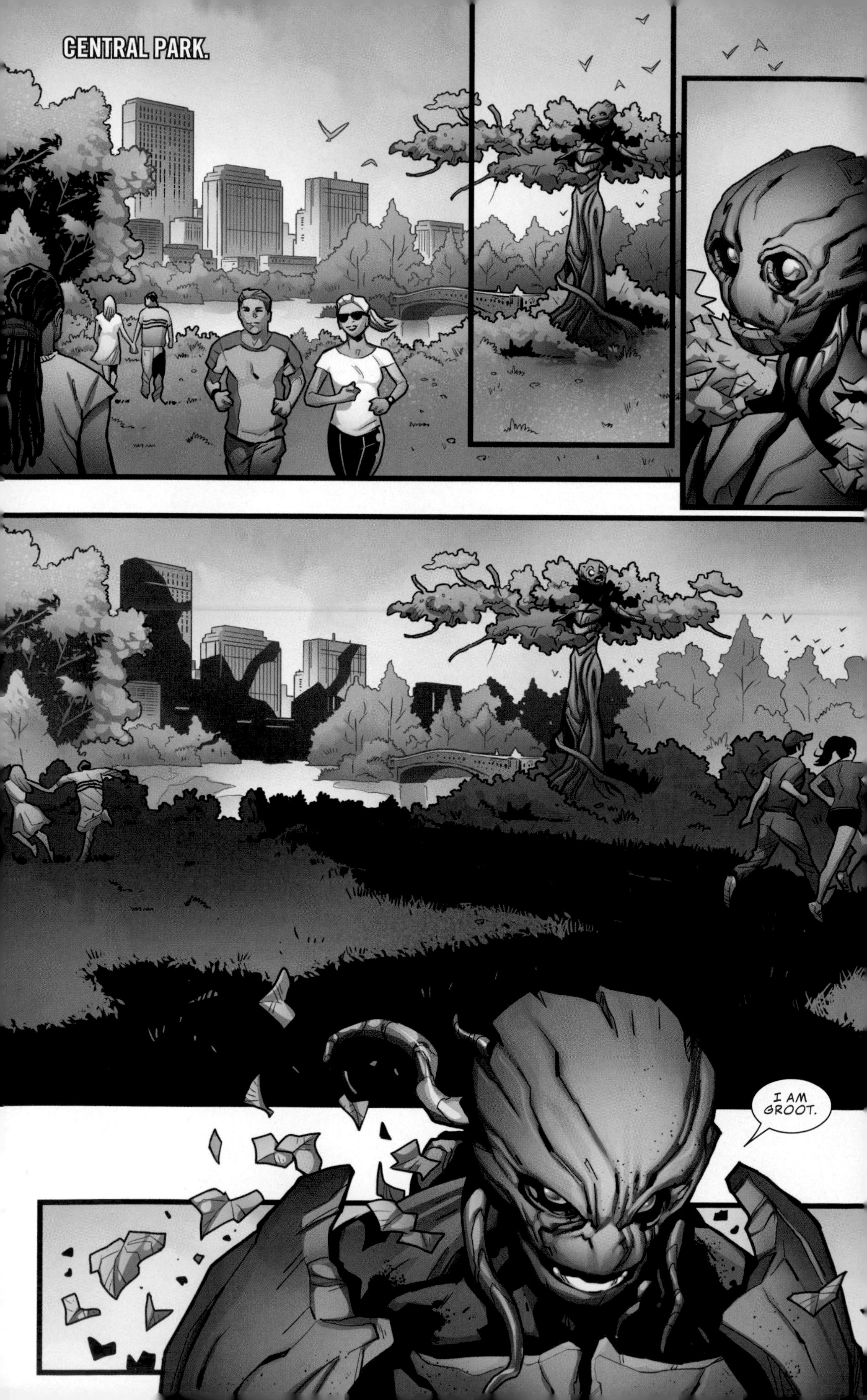
CENTRAL PARK.
I AM GROOT.

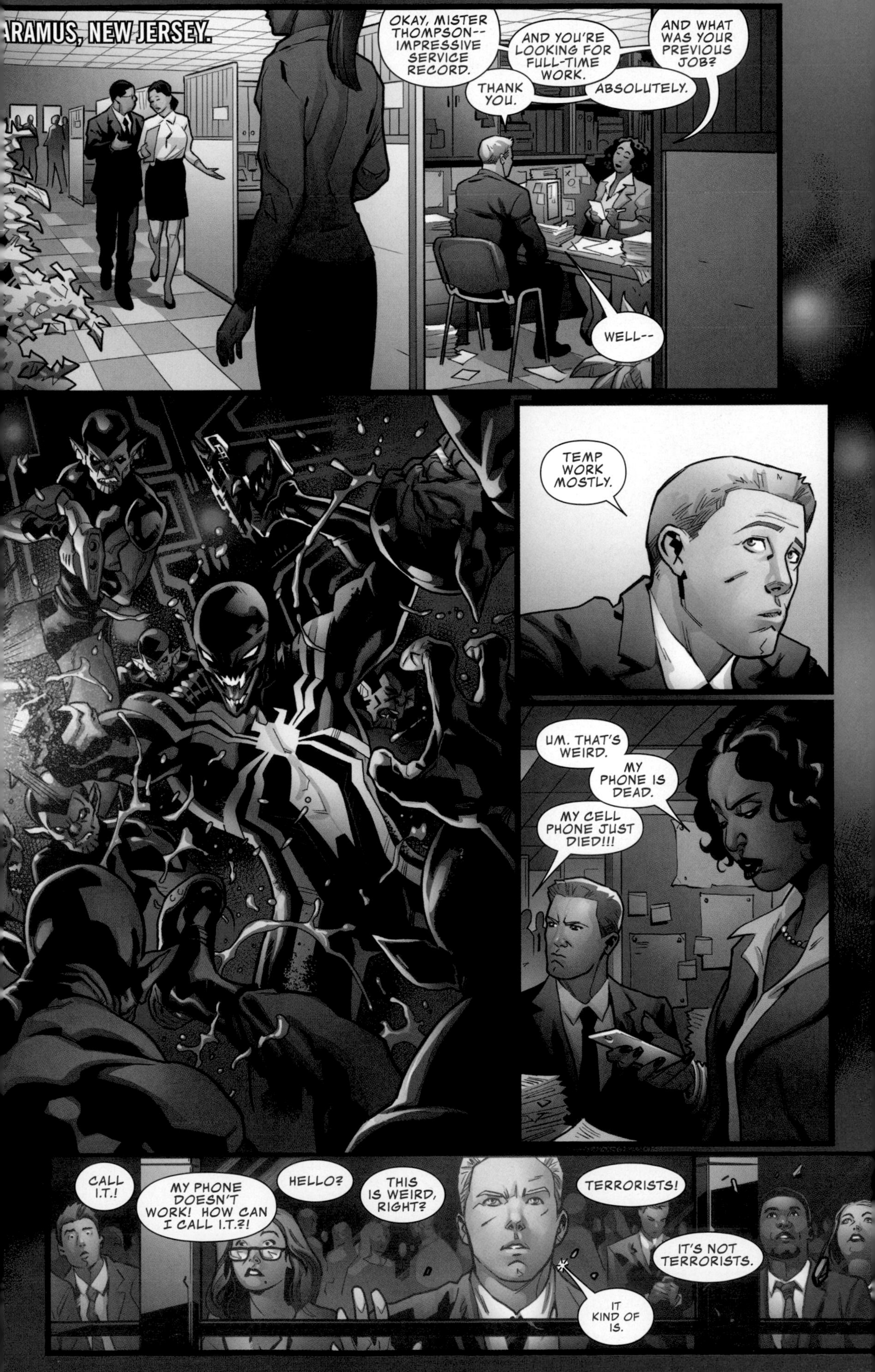
ARAMUS, NEW JERSEY.
OKAY, MISTER THOMPSON-- IMPRESSIVE SERVICE RECORD.
THANK YOU.
AND YOU'RE LOOKING FOR FULL-TIME WORK.
ABSOLUTELY.
AND WHAT WAS YOUR PREVIOUS JOB?
WELL--
TEMP WORK MOSTLY.
UM. THAT'S WEIRD.
MY PHONE IS DEAD.
MY CELL PHONE JUST DIED!!!
CALL I.T.!
MY PHONE DOESN'T WORK! HOW CAN I CALL I.T.?!
HELLO?
THIS IS WEIRD, RIGHT?
TERRORISTS!
IT'S NOT TERRORISTS.
IT KIND OF IS.

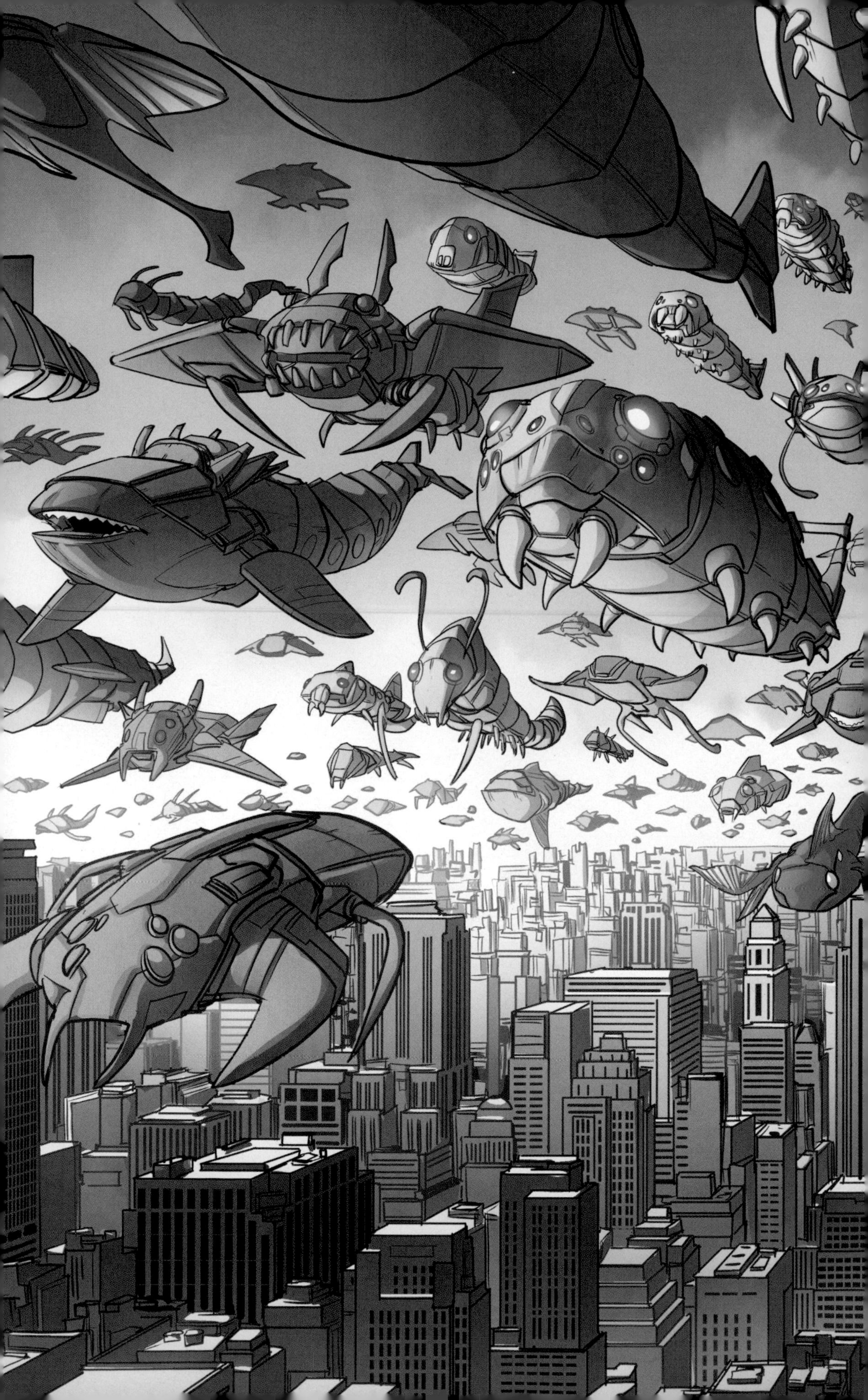

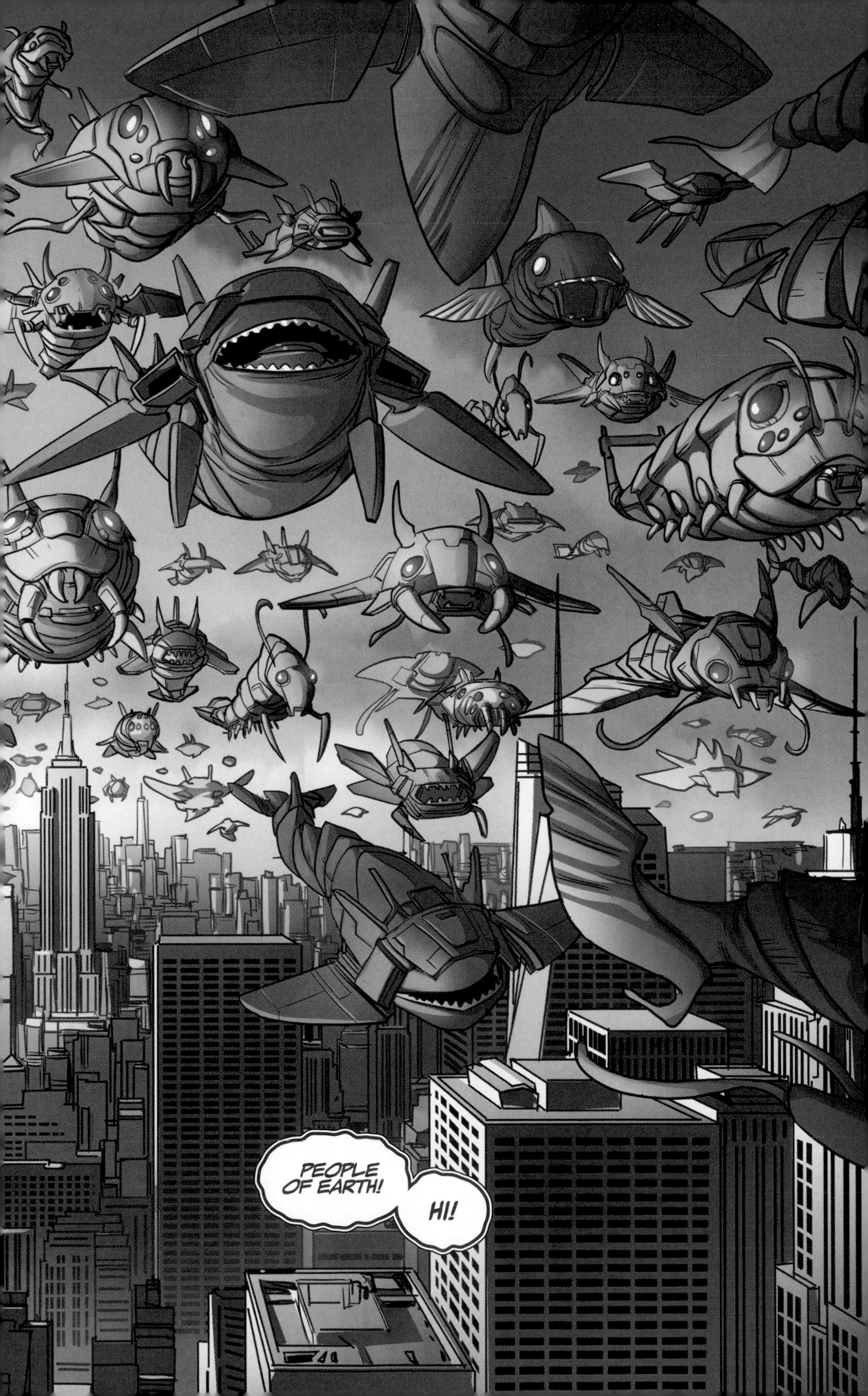
PEOPLE OF EARTH!
HI!

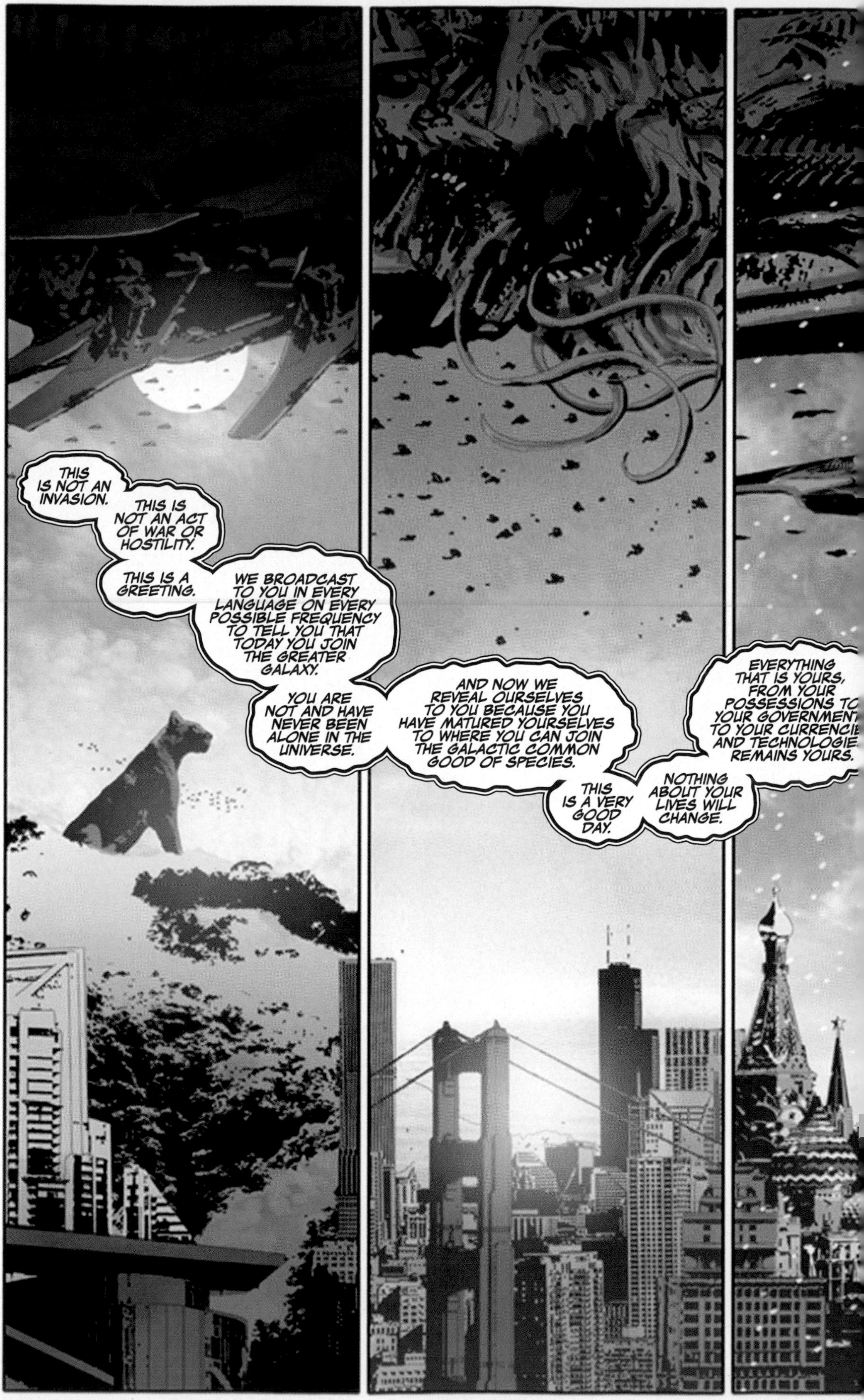

THIS IS NOT AN INVASION.
THIS IS NOT AN ACT OF WAR OR HOSTILITY.
THIS IS A GREETING.
WE BROADCAST TO YOU IN EVERY LANGUAGE ON EVERY POSSIBLE FREQUENCY TO TELL YOU THAT TODAY YOU JOIN THE GREATER GALAXY.
YOU ARE NOT AND HAVE NEVER BEEN ALONE IN THE UNIVERSE.
AND NOW WE REVEAL OURSELVES TO YOU BECAUSE YOU HAVE MATURED YOURSELVES TO WHERE YOU CAN JOIN THE GALACTIC COMMON GOOD OF SPECIES.
THIS IS A VERY GOOD DAY.
NOTHING ABOUT YOUR LIVES WILL CHANGE.
EVERYTHING THAT IS YOURS, FROM YOUR POSSESSIONS TO YOUR GOVERNMENT TO YOUR CURRENCIE AND TECHNOLOGIE REMAINS YOURS.

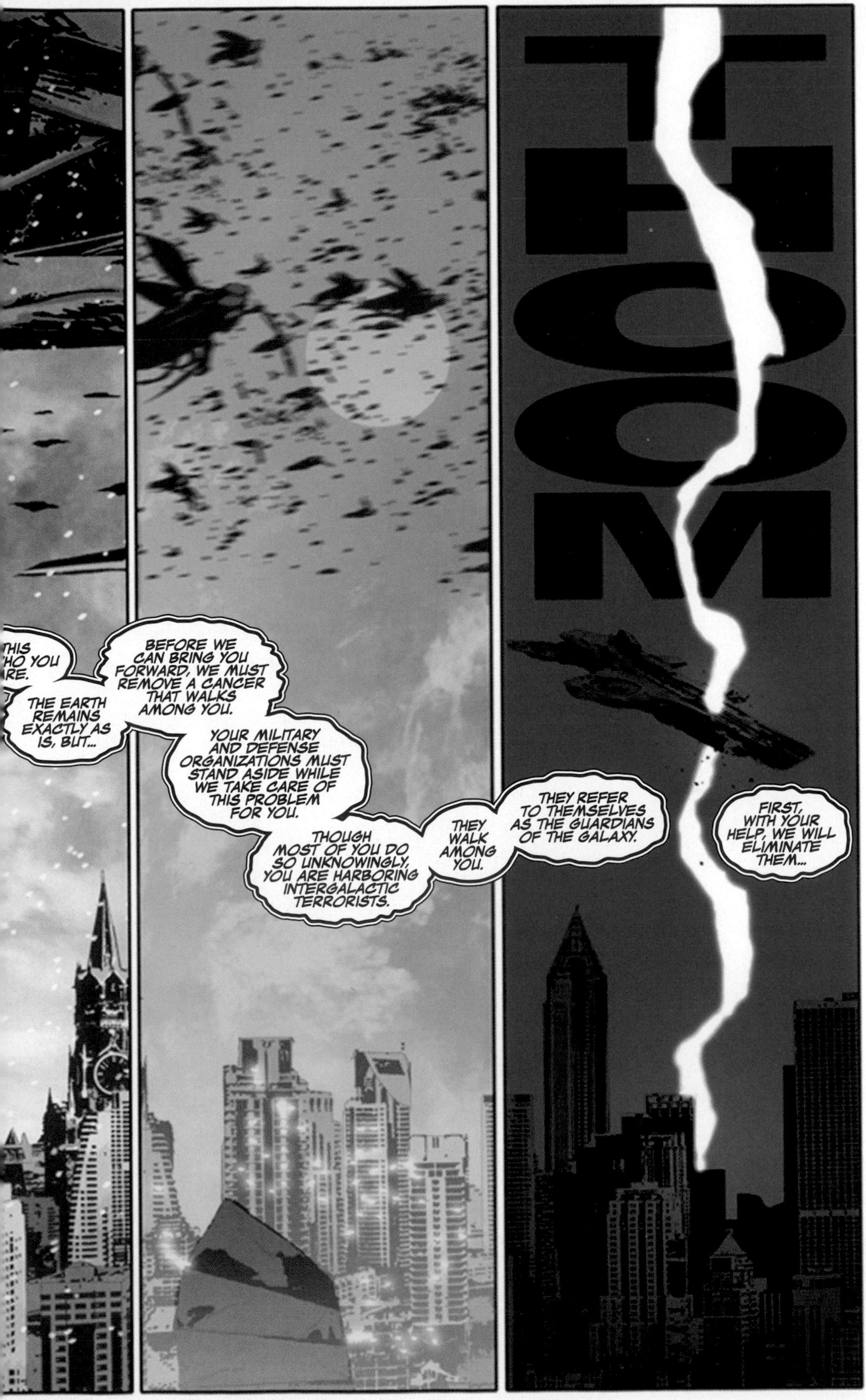
THE EARTH REMAINS EXACTLY AS IS, BUT...
BEFORE WE CAN BRING YOU FORWARD, WE MUST REMOVE A CANCER THAT WALKS AMONG YOU.
YOUR MILITARY AND DEFENSE ORGANIZATIONS MUST STAND ASIDE WHILE WE TAKE CARE OF THIS PROBLEM FOR YOU.
THOUGH MOST OF YOU DO SO UNKNOWINGLY, YOU ARE HARBORING INTERGALACTIC TERRORISTS.
THEY WALK AMONG YOU.
THEY REFER TO THEMSELVES AS THE GUARDIANS OF THE GALAXY.
THOOM
FIRST, WITH YOUR HELP, WE WILL ELIMINATE THEM...

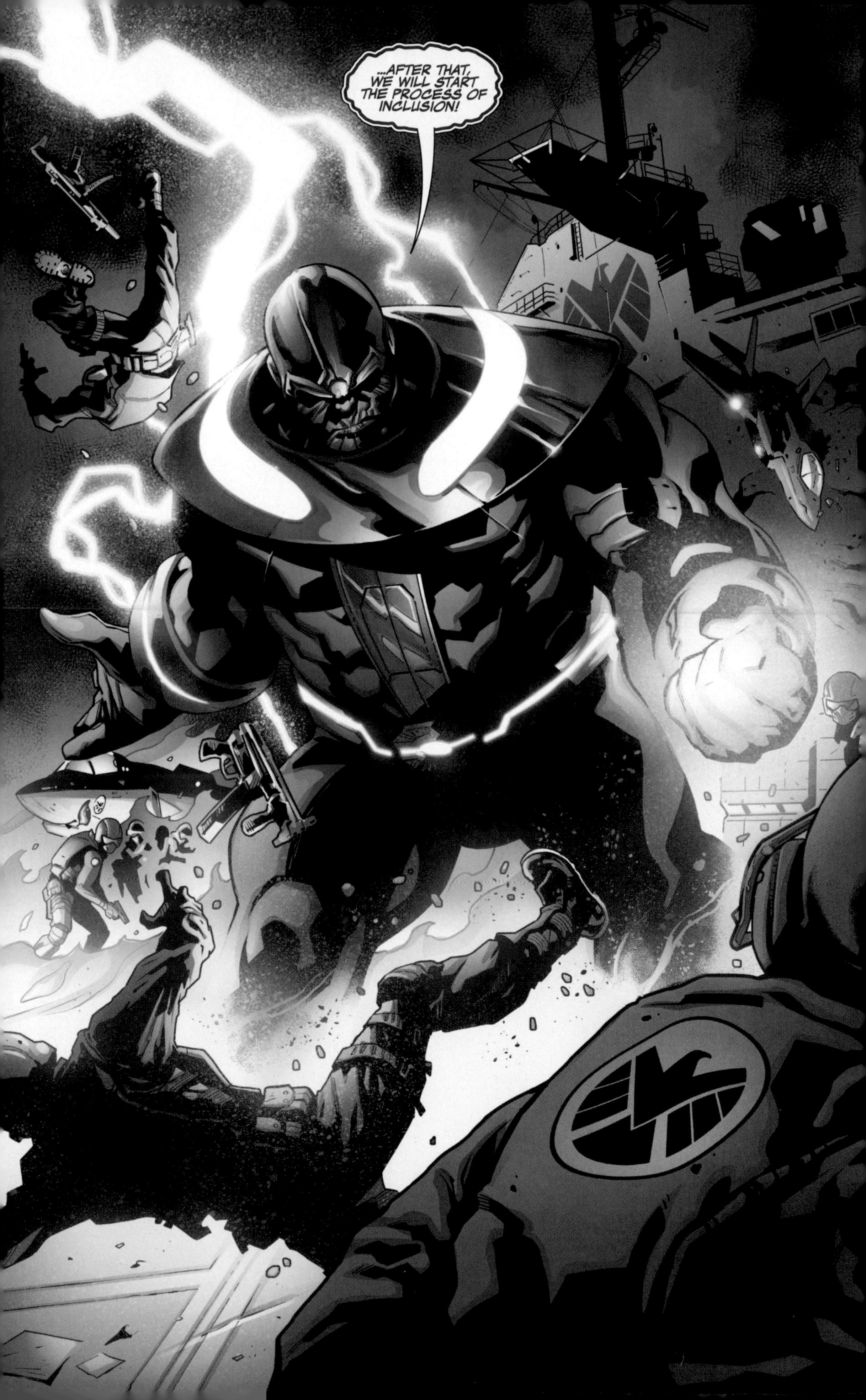
...AFTER THAT, WE WILL START THE PROCESS OF INCLUSION!

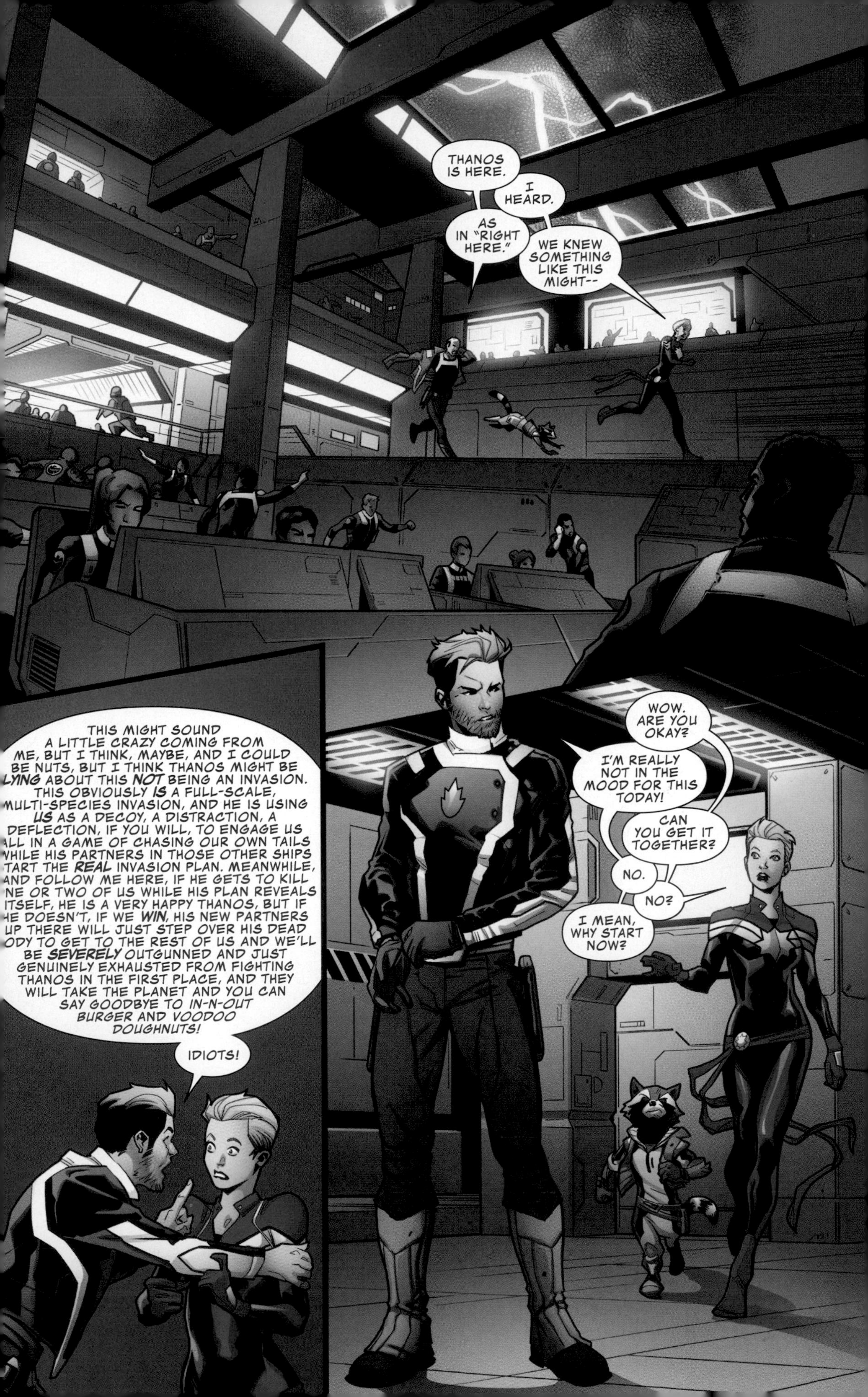

THANOS IS HERE.
I HEARD.
AS IN "RIGHT HERE."
WE KNEW SOMETHING LIKE THIS MIGHT--
THIS MIGHT SOUND A LITTLE CRAZY COMING FROM ME, BUT I THINK, MAYBE, AND I COULD BE NUTS, BUT I THINK THANOS MIGHT BE LYING ABOUT THIS NOT BEING AN INVASION. THIS OBVIOUSLY IS A FULL-SCALE, MULTI-SPECIES INVASION, AND HE IS USING US AS A DECOY, A DISTRACTION, A DEFLECTION, IF YOU WILL, TO ENGAGE US ALL IN A GAME OF CHASING OUR OWN TAILS WHILE HIS PARTNERS IN THOSE OTHER SHIPS START THE REAL INVASION PLAN. MEANWHILE, AND FOLLOW ME HERE, IF HE GETS TO KILL ONE OR TWO OF US WHILE HIS PLAN REVEALS ITSELF, HE IS A VERY HAPPY THANOS, BUT IF HE DOESN'T, IF WE WIN, HIS NEW PARTNERS UP THERE WILL JUST STEP OVER HIS DEAD BODY TO GET TO THE REST OF US AND WE'LL BE SEVERELY OUTGUNNED AND JUST GENUINELY EXHAUSTED FROM FIGHTING THANOS IN THE FIRST PLACE, AND THEY WILL TAKE THE PLANET AND YOU CAN SAY GOODBYE TO IN-N-OUT BURGER AND VOODOO DOUGHNUTS!
IDIOTS!
WOW. ARE YOU OKAY?
I'M REALLY NOT IN THE MOOD FOR THIS TODAY!
CAN YOU GET IT TOGETHER?
NO.
NO?
I MEAN, WHY START NOW?

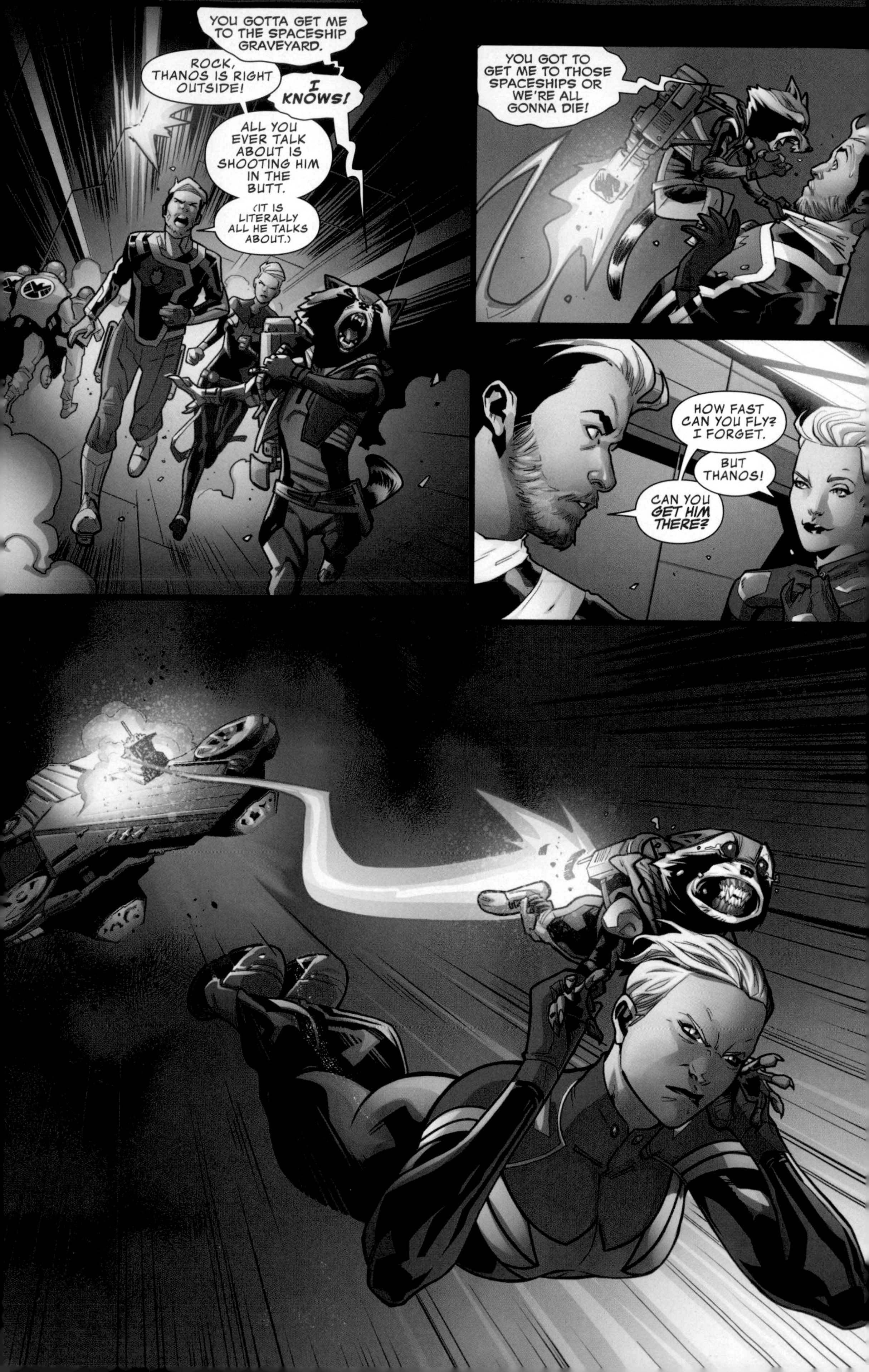
YOU GOTTA GET ME TO THE SPACESHIP GRAVEYARD.
ROCK, THANOS IS RIGHT OUTSIDE!
I KNOWS!
ALL YOU EVER TALK ABOUT IS SHOOTING HIM IN THE BUTT.
(IT IS LITERALLY ALL HE TALKS ABOUT.)
YOU GOT TO GET ME TO THOSE SPACESHIPS OR WE'RE ALL GONNA DIE!
HOW FAST CAN YOU FLY? I FORGET.
BUT THANOS!
CAN YOU GET HIM THERE?

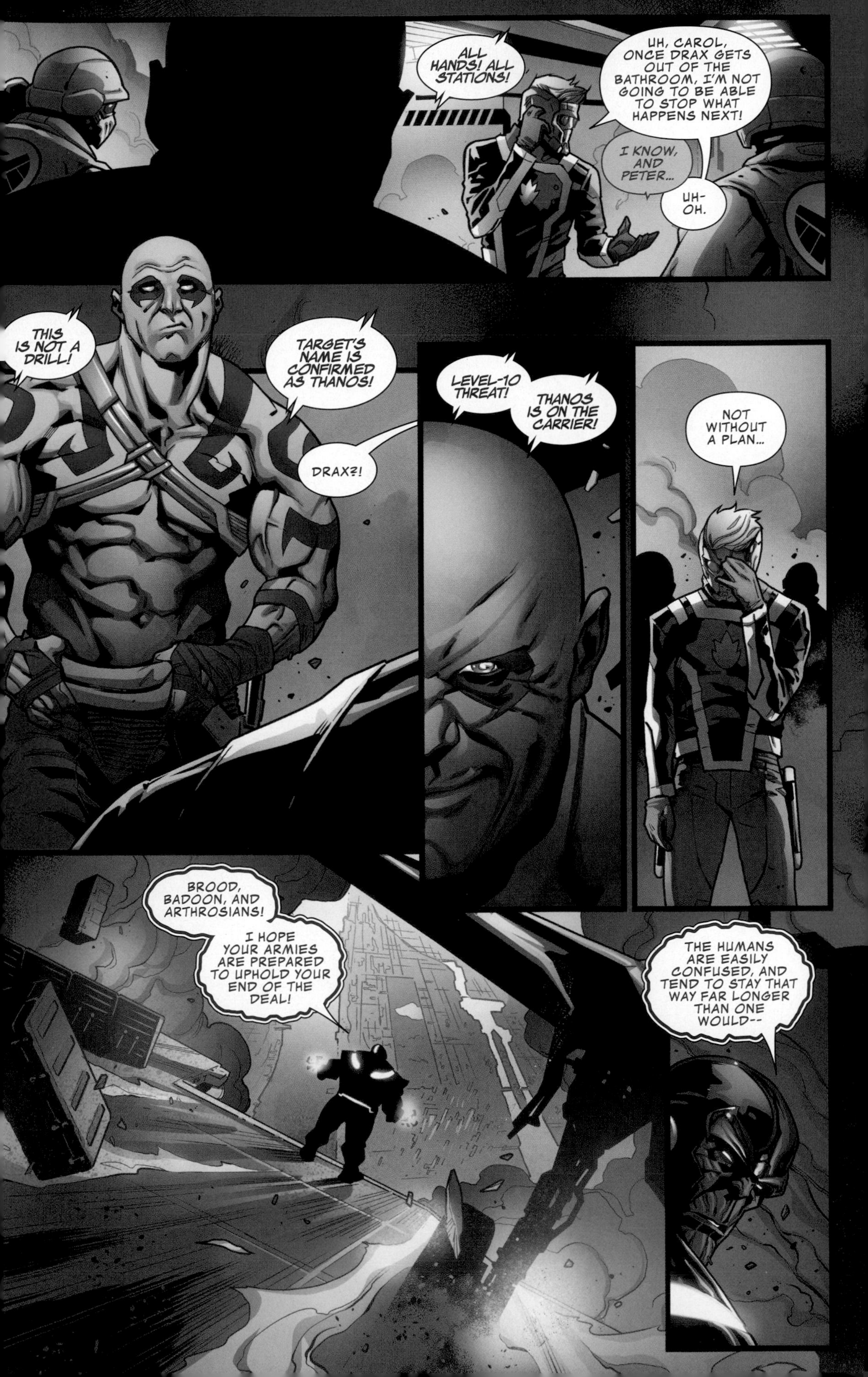
ALL HANDS! ALL STATIONS!
UH, CAROL, ONCE DRAX GETS OUT OF THE BATHROOM, I'M NOT GOING TO BE ABLE TO STOP WHAT HAPPENS NEXT!
I KNOW, AND PETER...
UH-OH.
THIS IS NOT A DRILL!
TARGET'S NAME IS CONFIRMED AS THANOS!
DRAX?!
LEVEL-10 THREAT!
THANOS IS ON THE CARRIER!
NOT WITHOUT A PLAN...
BROOD, BADOON, AND ARTHROSIANS!
I HOPE YOUR ARMIES ARE PREPARED TO UPHOLD YOUR END OF THE DEAL!
THE HUMANS ARE EASILY CONFUSED, AND TEND TO STAY THAT WAY FAR LONGER THAN ONE WOULD--

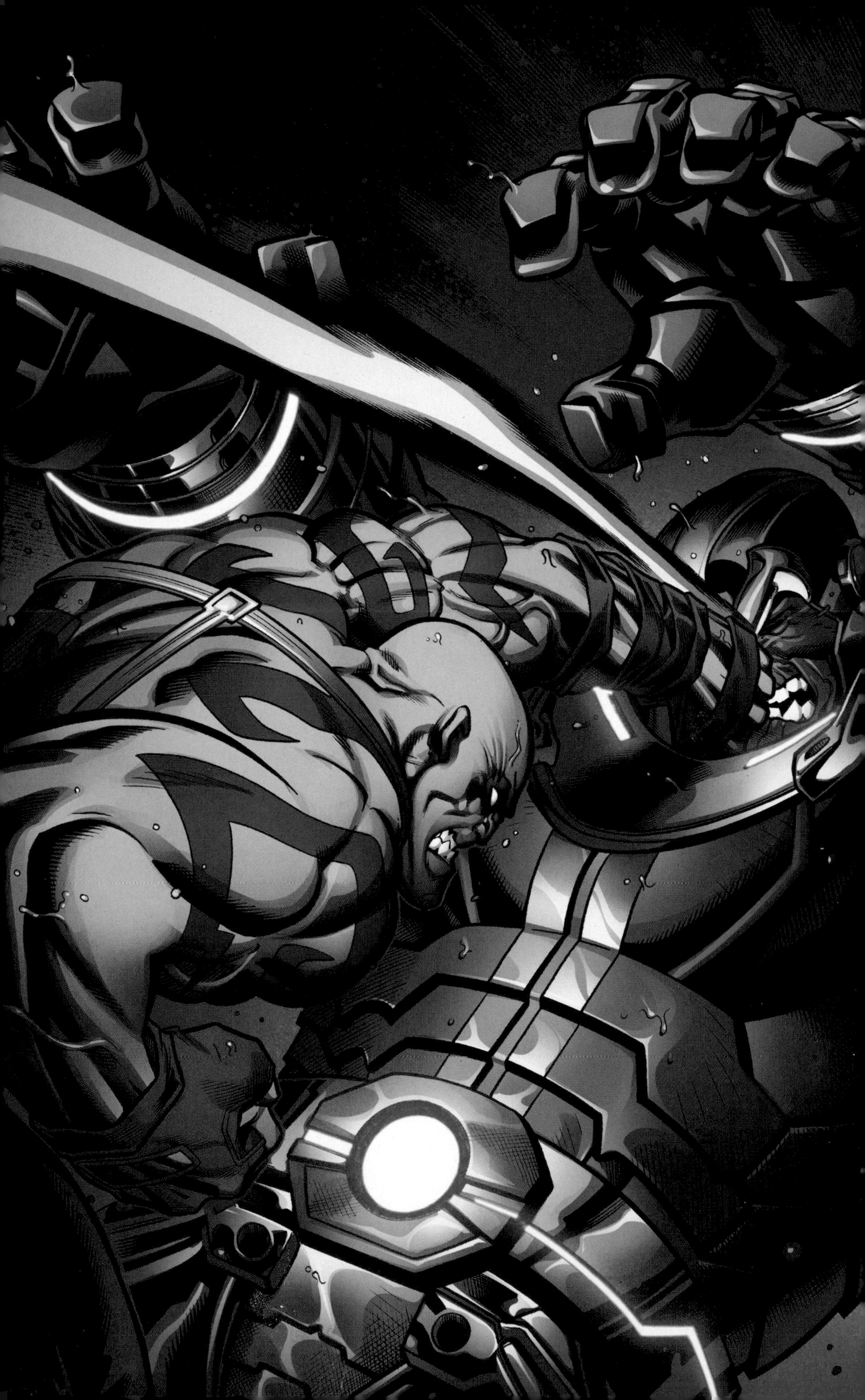

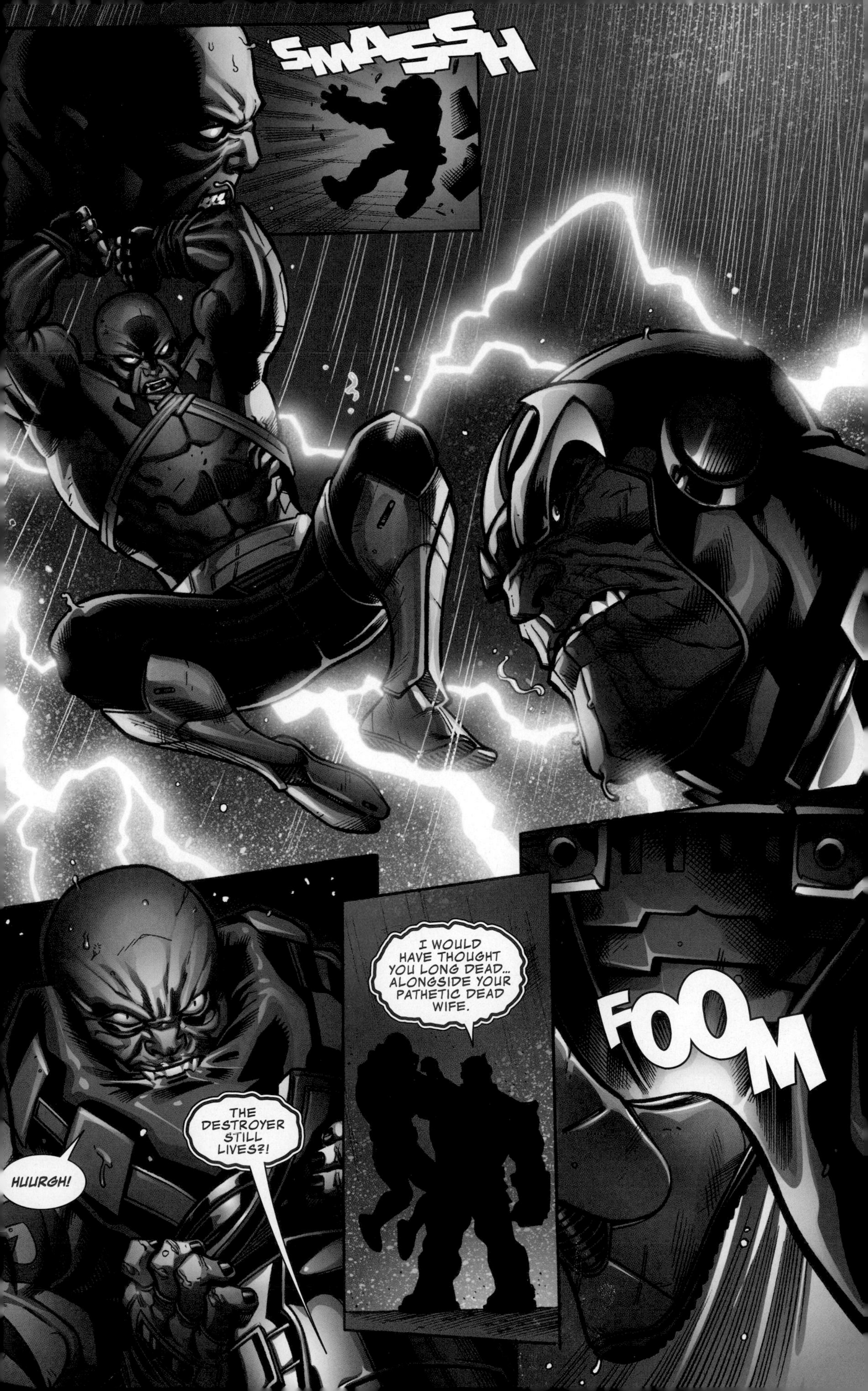
SMASSH
THE DESTROYER STILL LIVES?!
HUURGH!
I WOULD HAVE THOUGHT YOU LONG DEAD... ALONGSIDE YOUR PATHETIC DEAD WIFE.
FOOM

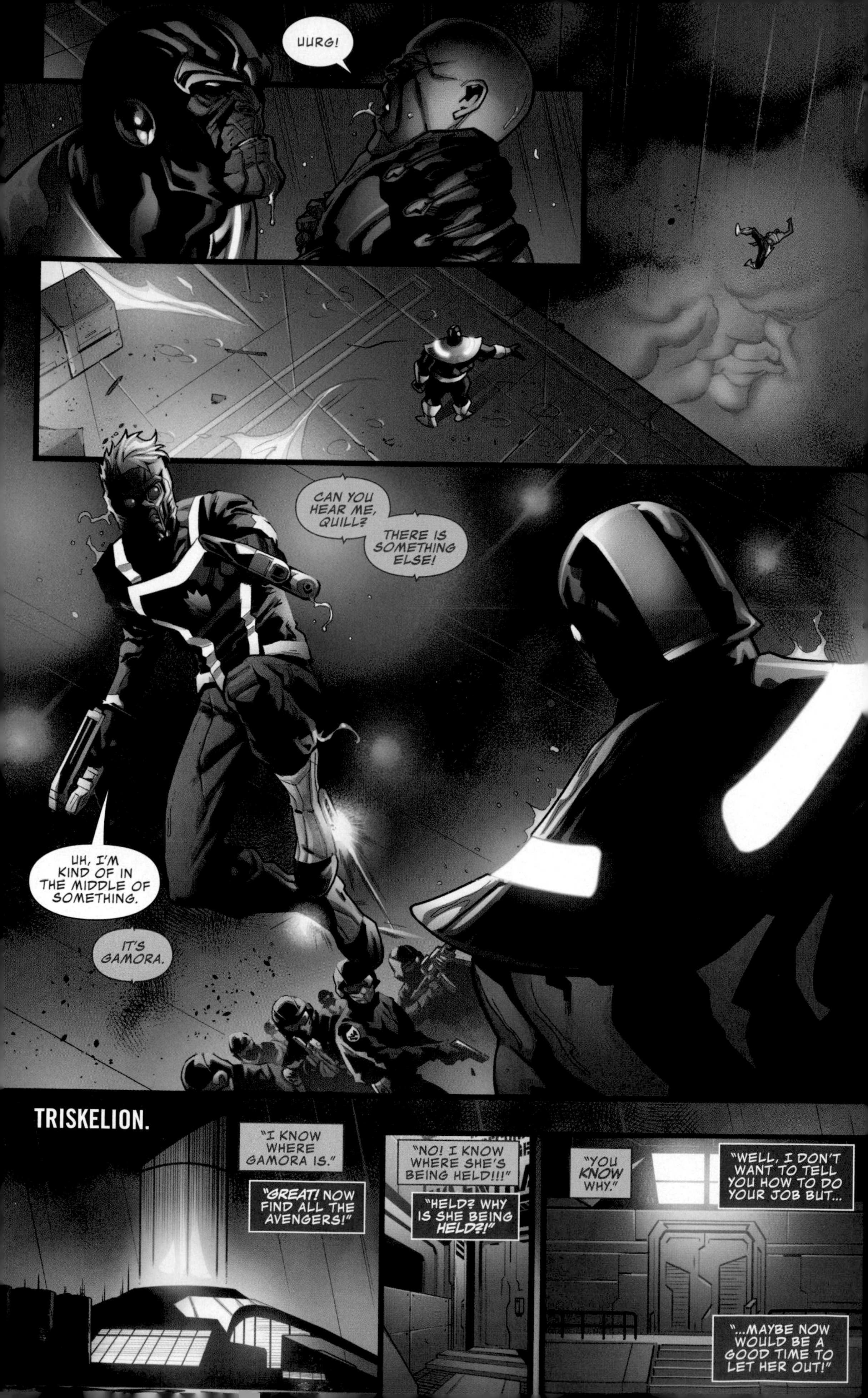
UURG!
CAN YOU HEAR ME, QUILL?
THERE IS SOMETHING ELSE!
UH, I'M KIND OF IN THE MIDDLE OF SOMETHING.
IT'S GAMORA.
TRISKELION.
"I KNOW WHERE GAMORA IS."
"GREAT! NOW FIND ALL THE AVENGERS!"
"NO! I KNOW WHERE SHE'S BEING HELD!!!"
"HELD? WHY IS SHE BEING HELD?!"
"YOU KNOW WHY."
"WELL, I DON'T WANT TO TELL YOU HOW TO DO YOUR JOB BUT...
"...MAYBE NOW WOULD BE A GOOD TIME TO LET HER OUT!"

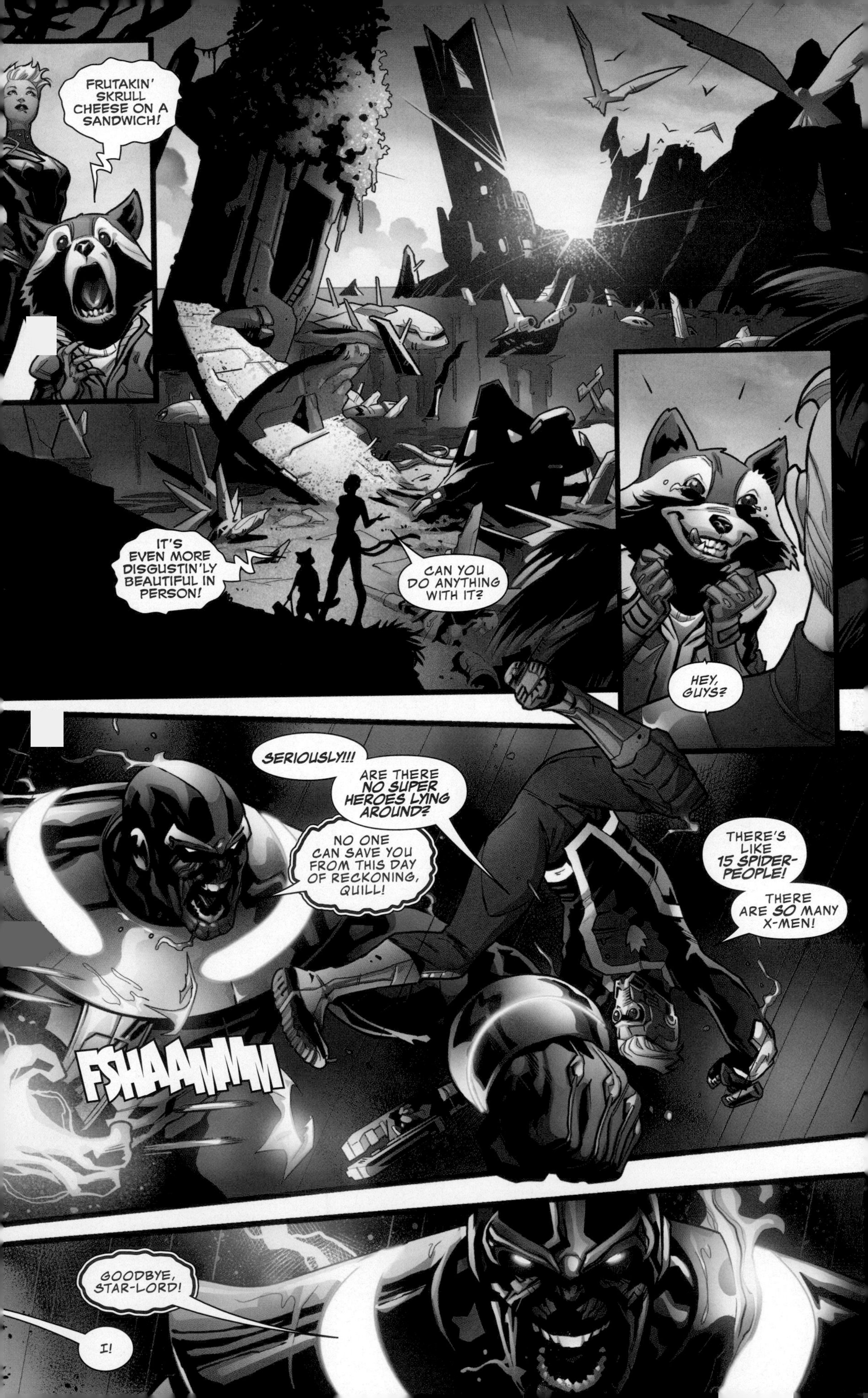
FRUTAKIN' SKRULL CHEESE ON A SANDWICH!
IT'S EVEN MORE DISGUSTIN'LY BEAUTIFUL IN PERSON!
CAN YOU DO ANYTHING WITH IT?
HEY, GUYS?
SERIOUSLY!!!
ARE THERE NO SUPER HEROES LYING AROUND?
NO ONE CAN SAVE YOU FROM THIS DAY OF RECKONING, QUILL!
THERE'S LIKE 15 SPIDER-PEOPLE!
THERE ARE SO MANY X-MEN!
FSHAAMMM
GOODBYE, STAR-LORD!
I!

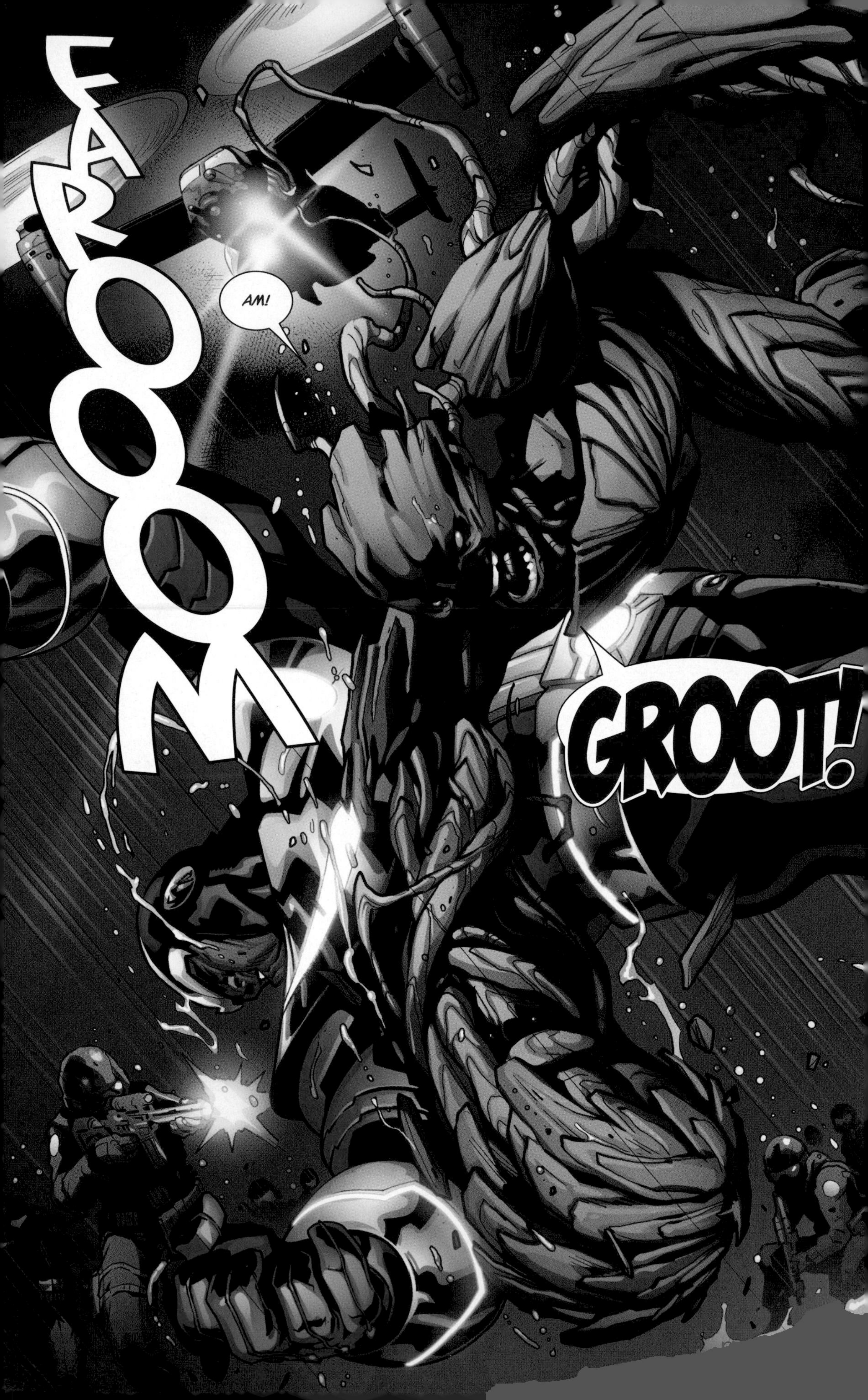
KAROOOOM
AM!
GROOT!

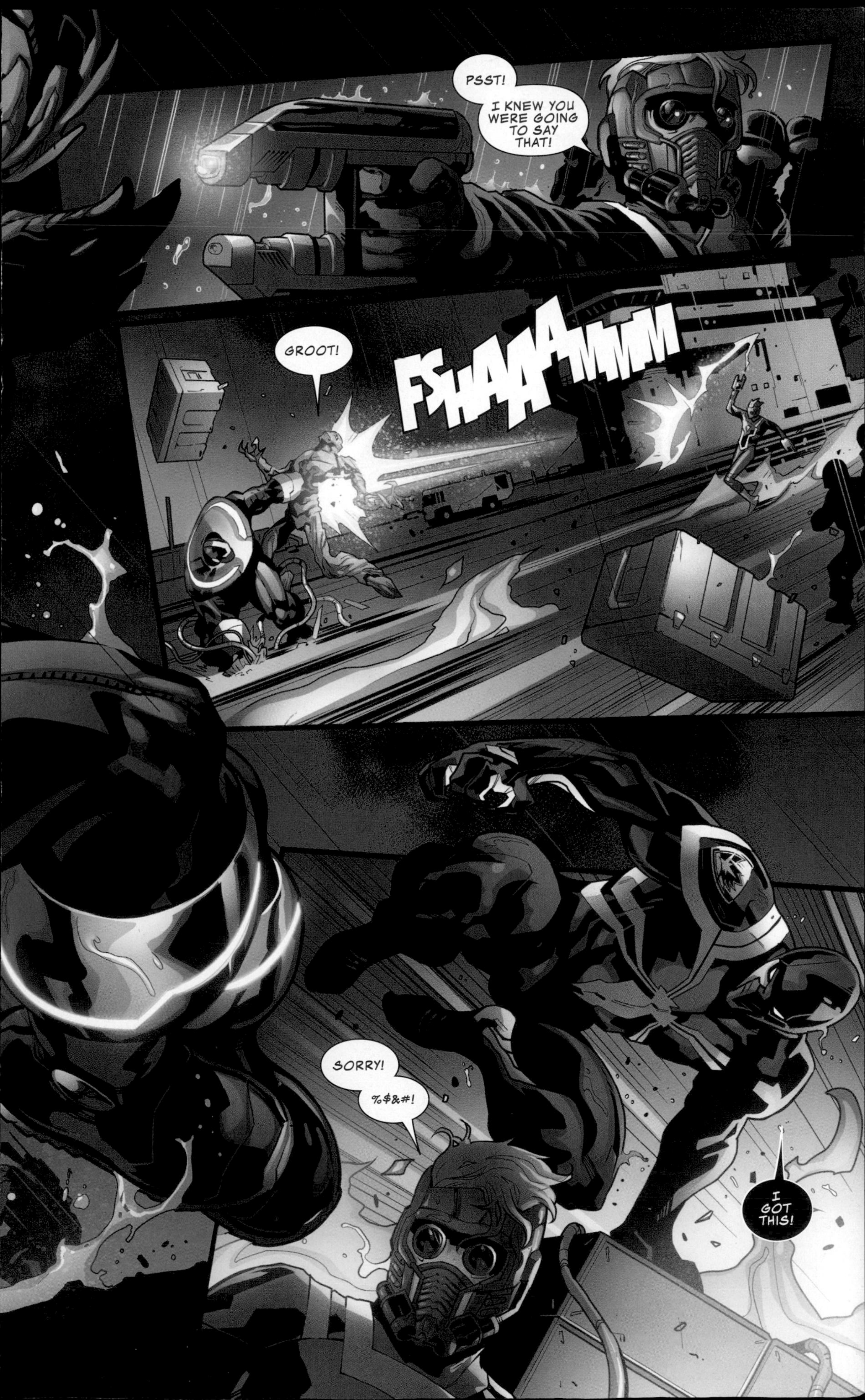
PSST!
I KNEW YOU WERE GOING TO SAY THAT!
GROOT!
FSHAAAMMM
SORRY!
%$&#!
I GOT THIS!

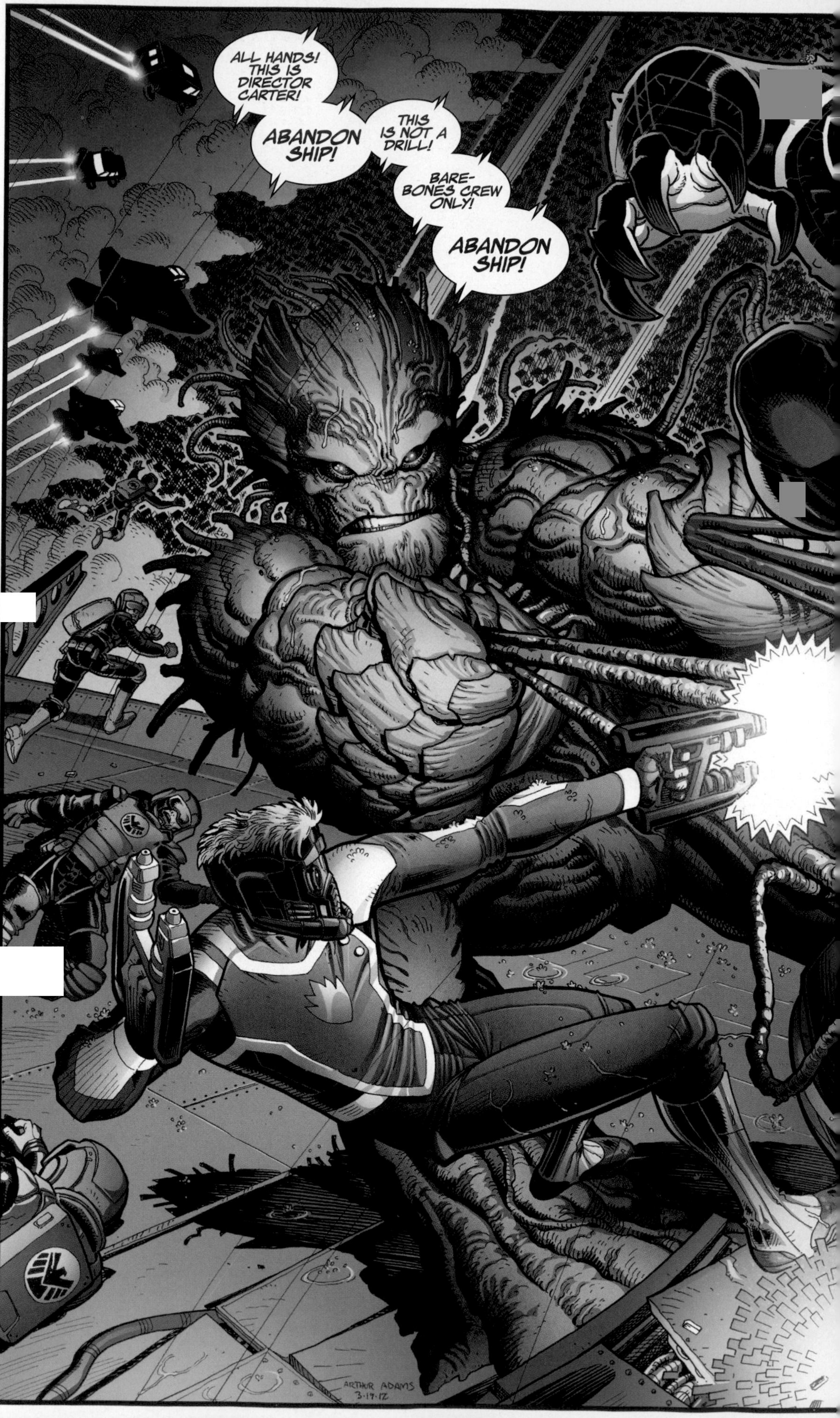
ALL HANDS! THIS IS DIRECTOR CARTER!
ABANDON SHIP!
THIS IS NOT A DRILL!
BARE-BONES CREW ONLY!
ABANDON SHIP!
ARTHUR ADAMS 3-19-12

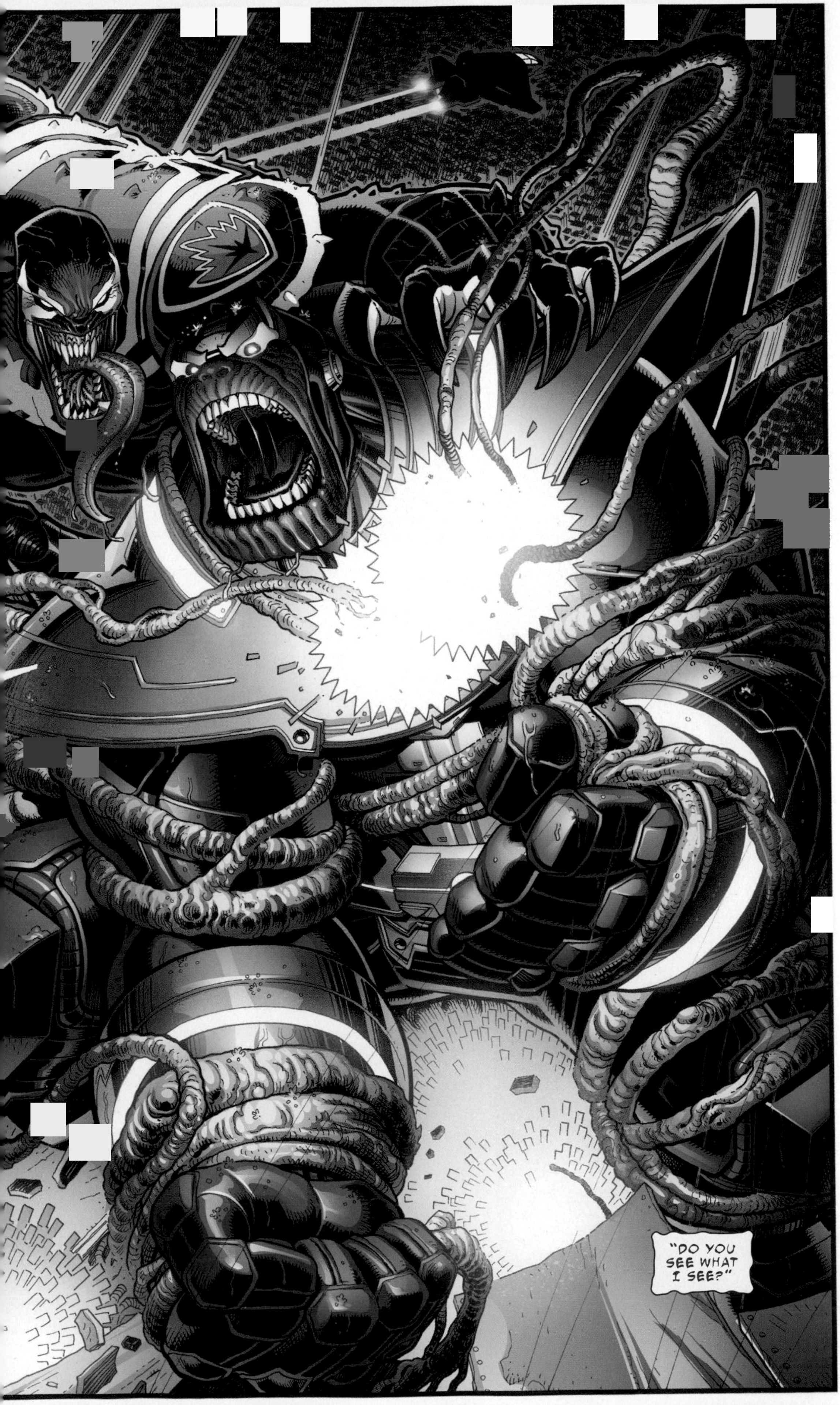
"DO YOU SEE WHAT I SEE?"

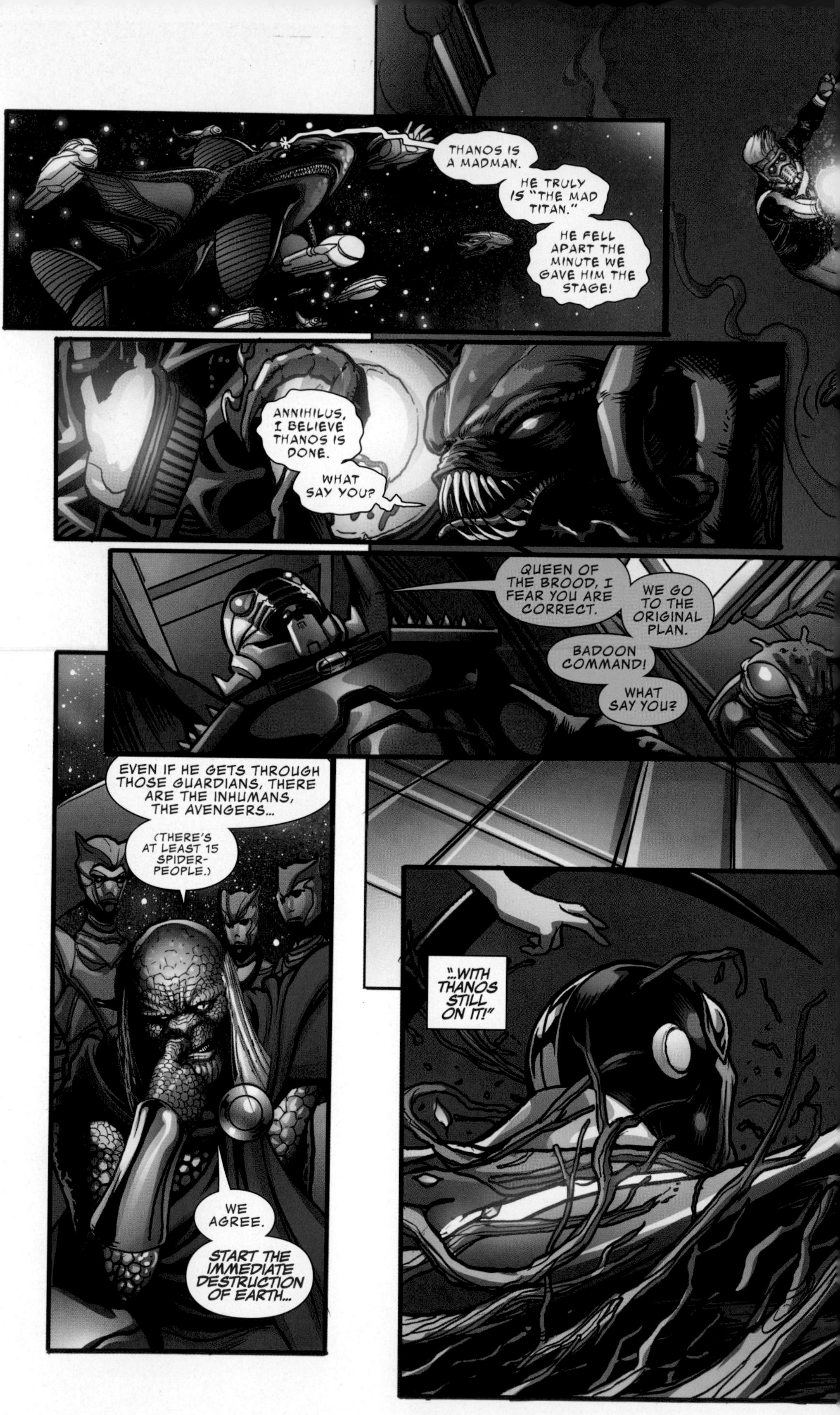
THANOS IS A MADMAN.
HE TRULY IS "THE MAD TITAN."
HE FELL APART THE MINUTE WE GAVE HIM THE STAGE!
ANNIHILUS, I BELIEVE THANOS IS DONE.
WHAT SAY YOU?
QUEEN OF THE BROOD, I FEAR YOU ARE CORRECT.
WE GO TO THE ORIGINAL PLAN.
BADOON COMMAND!
WHAT SAY YOU?
EVEN IF HE GETS THROUGH THOSE GUARDIANS, THERE ARE THE INHUMANS, THE AVENGERS...
(THERE'S AT LEAST 15 SPIDER-PEOPLE.)
WE AGREE.
START THE IMMEDIATE DESTRUCTION OF EARTH...
"...WITH THANOS STILL ON IT!"

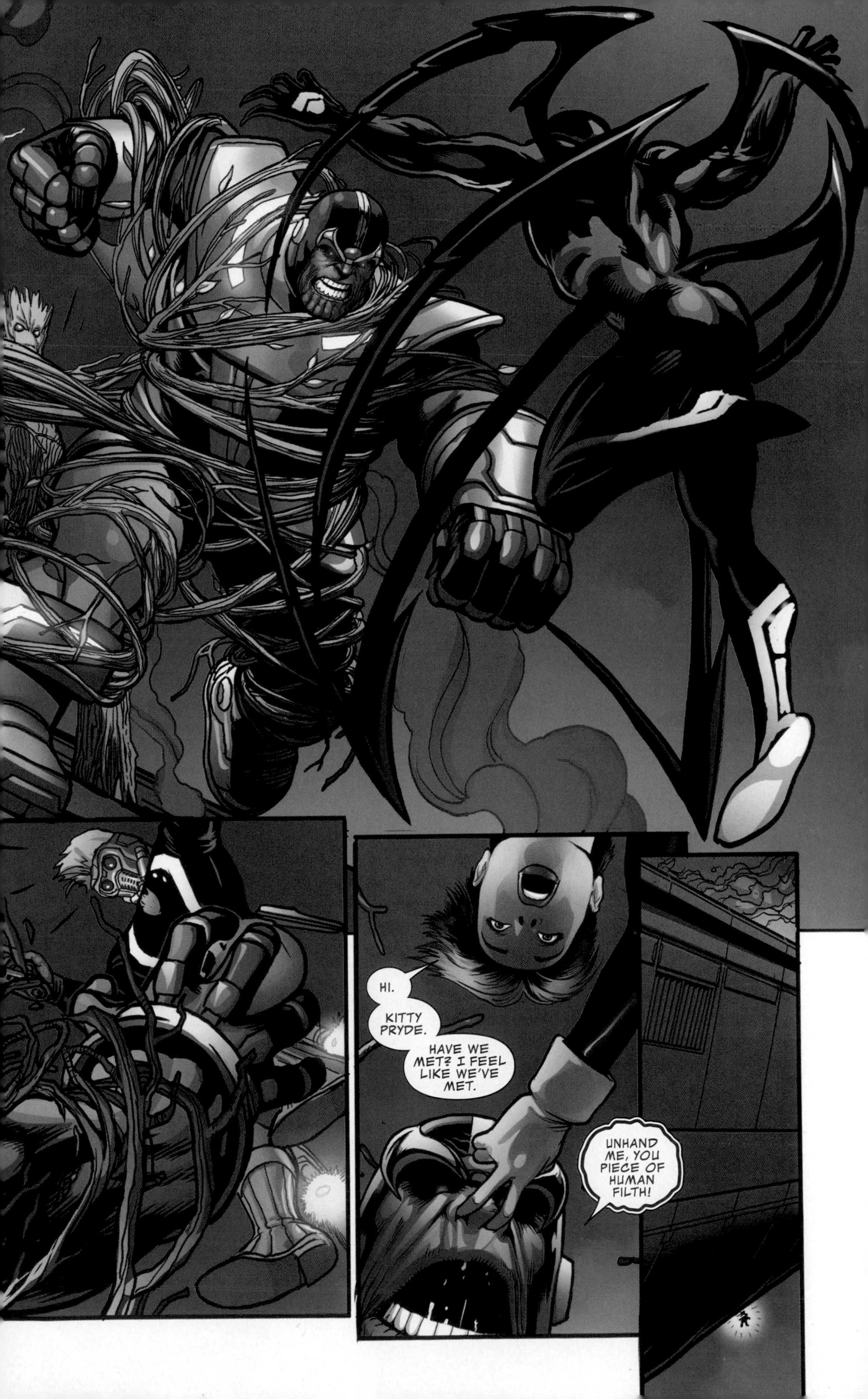
HI.
KITTY PRYDE.
HAVE WE MET? I FEEL LIKE WE'VE MET.
UNHAND ME, YOU PIECE OF HUMAN FILTH!

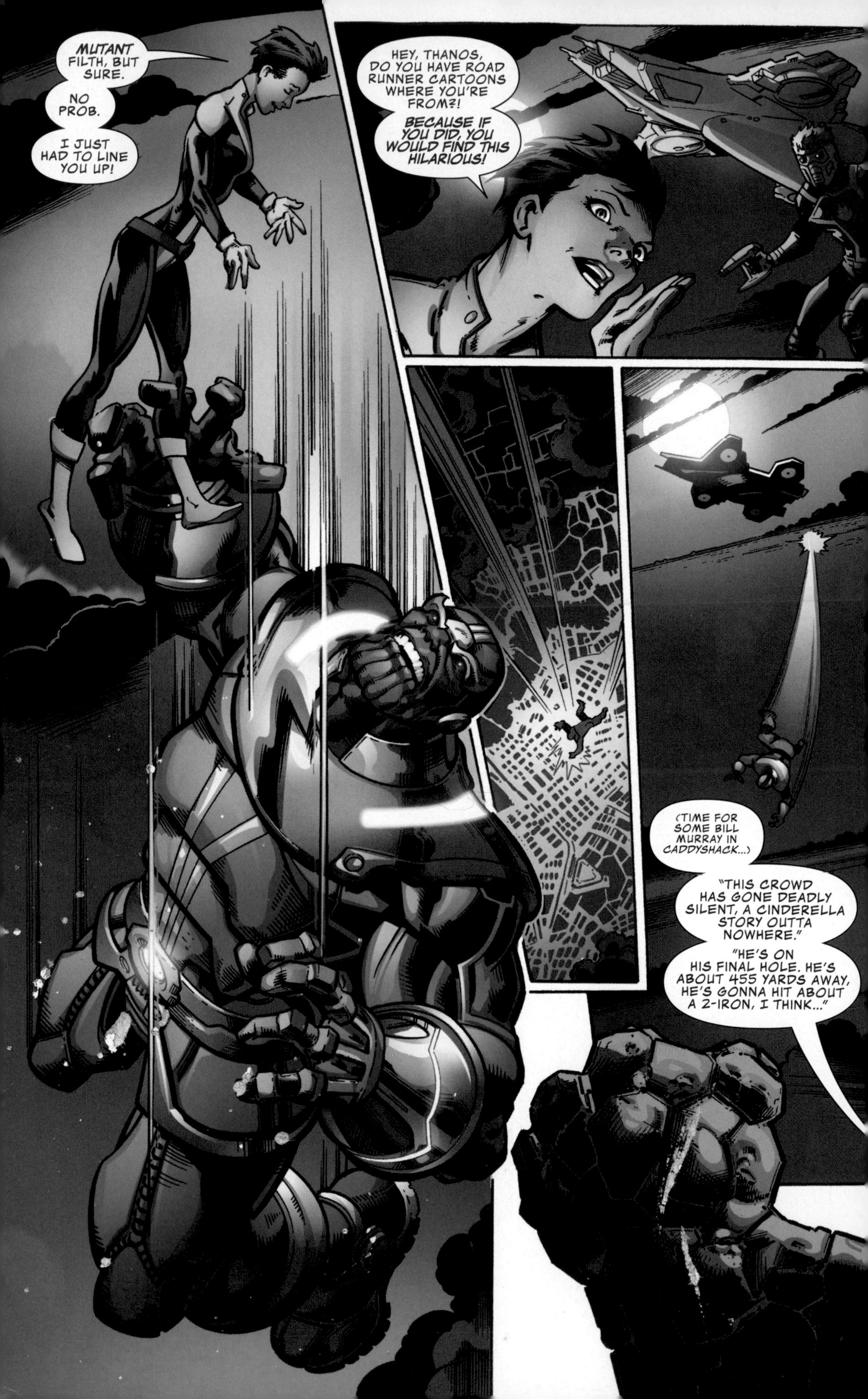
MUTANT FILTH, BUT SURE.
NO PROB.
I JUST HAD TO LINE YOU UP!
HEY, THANOS, DO YOU HAVE ROAD RUNNER CARTOONS WHERE YOU'RE FROM?!
BECAUSE IF YOU DID, YOU WOULD FIND THIS HILARIOUS!
(TIME FOR SOME BILL MURRAY IN CADDYSHACK...)
"THIS CROWD HAS GONE DEADLY SILENT, A CINDERELLA STORY OUTTA NOWHERE."
"HE'S ON HIS FINAL HOLE. HE'S ABOUT 455 YARDS AWAY, HE'S GONNA HIT ABOUT A 2-IRON, I THINK..."

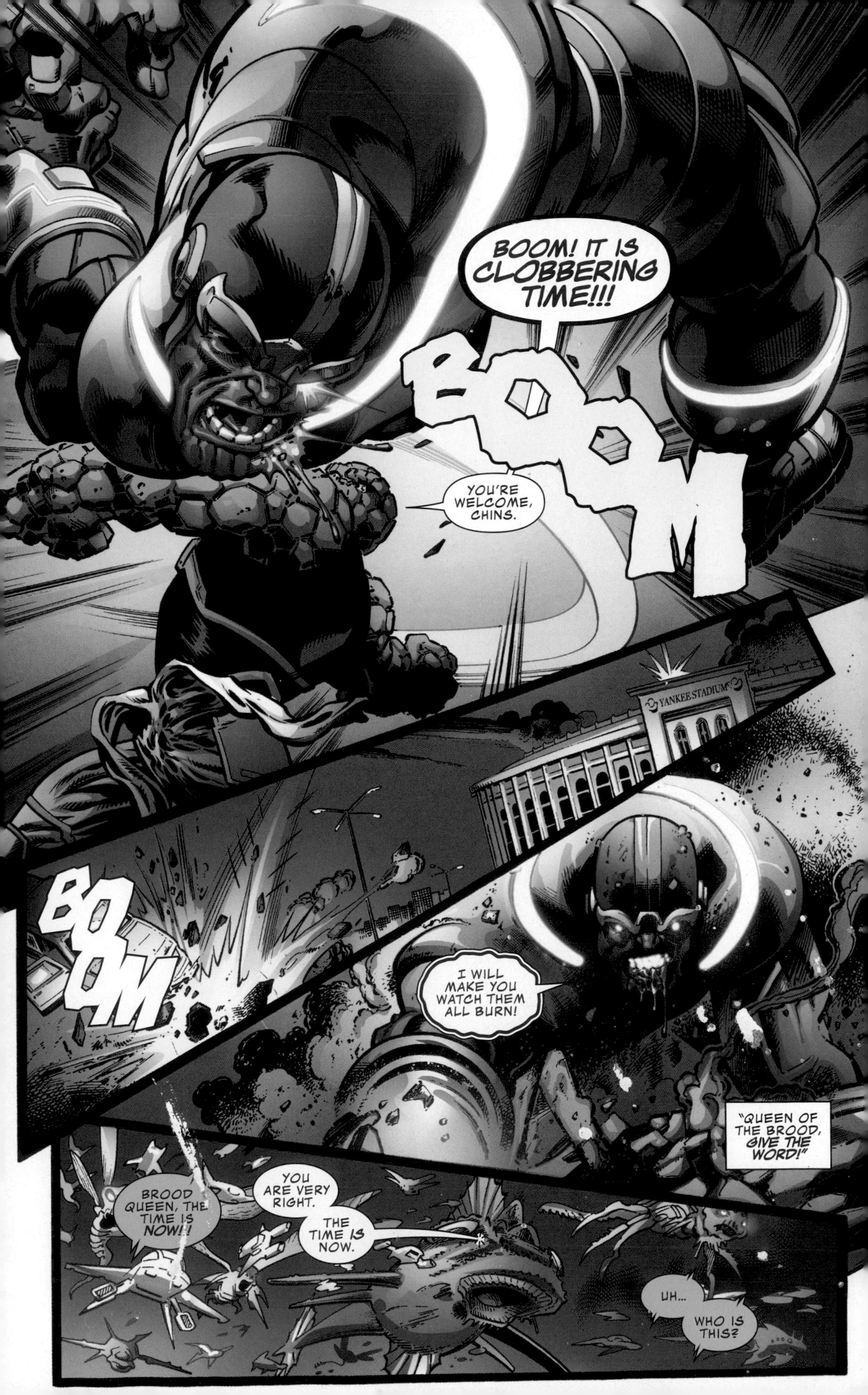
BOOM! IT IS CLOBBERING TIME!!!
BOOM
YOU'RE WELCOME, CHINS.
YANKEE STADIUM
BOOM
I WILL MAKE YOU WATCH THEM ALL BURN!
"QUEEN OF THE BROOD, GIVE THE WORD!"
BROOD QUEEN, THE TIME IS NOW!!
YOU ARE VERY RIGHT.
THE TIME IS NOW.
UH...
WHO IS THIS?

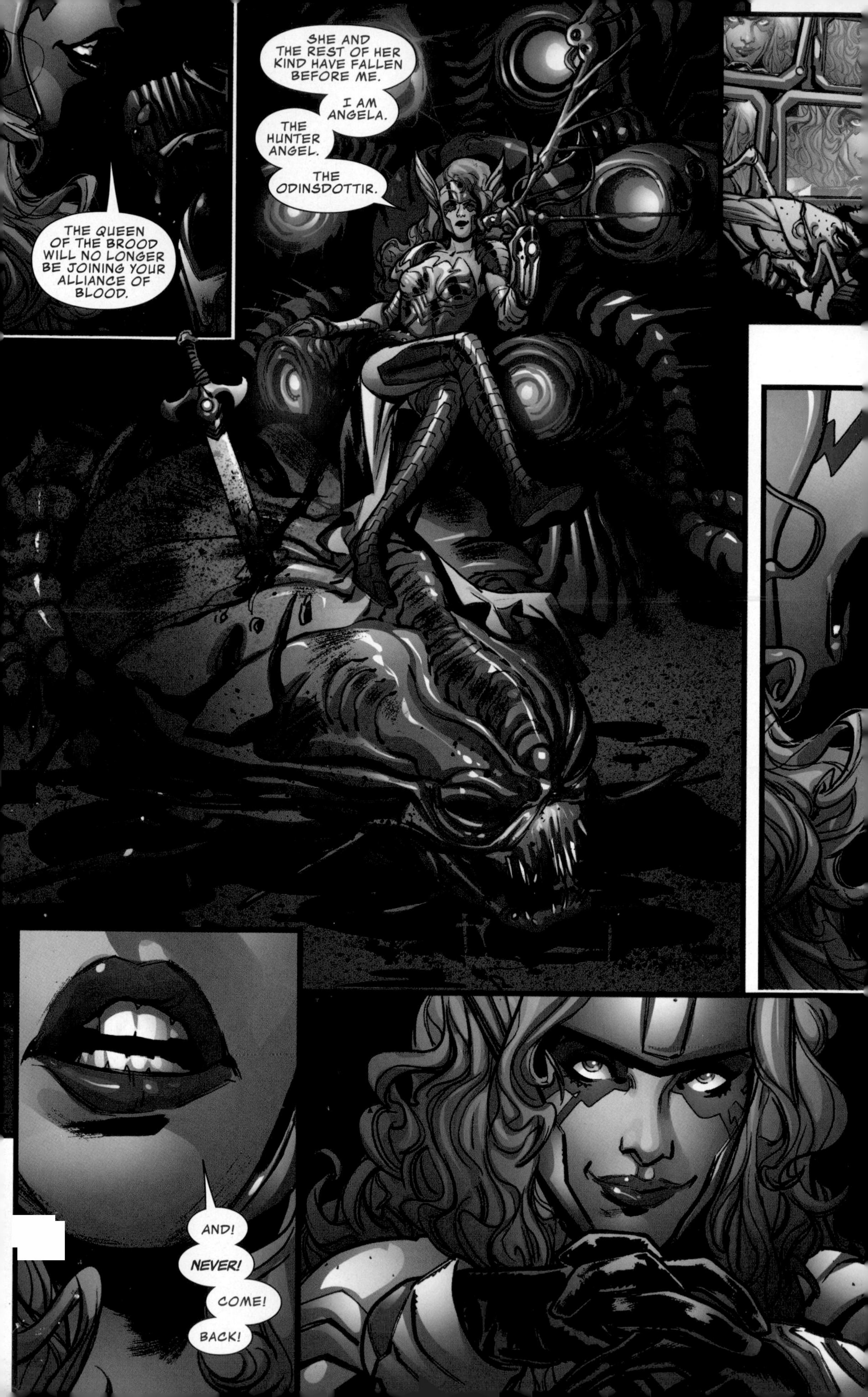
THE QUEEN OF THE BROOD WILL NO LONGER BE JOINING YOUR ALLIANCE OF BLOOD.
SHE AND THE REST OF HER KIND HAVE FALLEN BEFORE ME.
I AM ANGELA.
THE HUNTER ANGEL.
THE ODINSDOTTIR.
AND!
NEVER!
COME!
BACK!

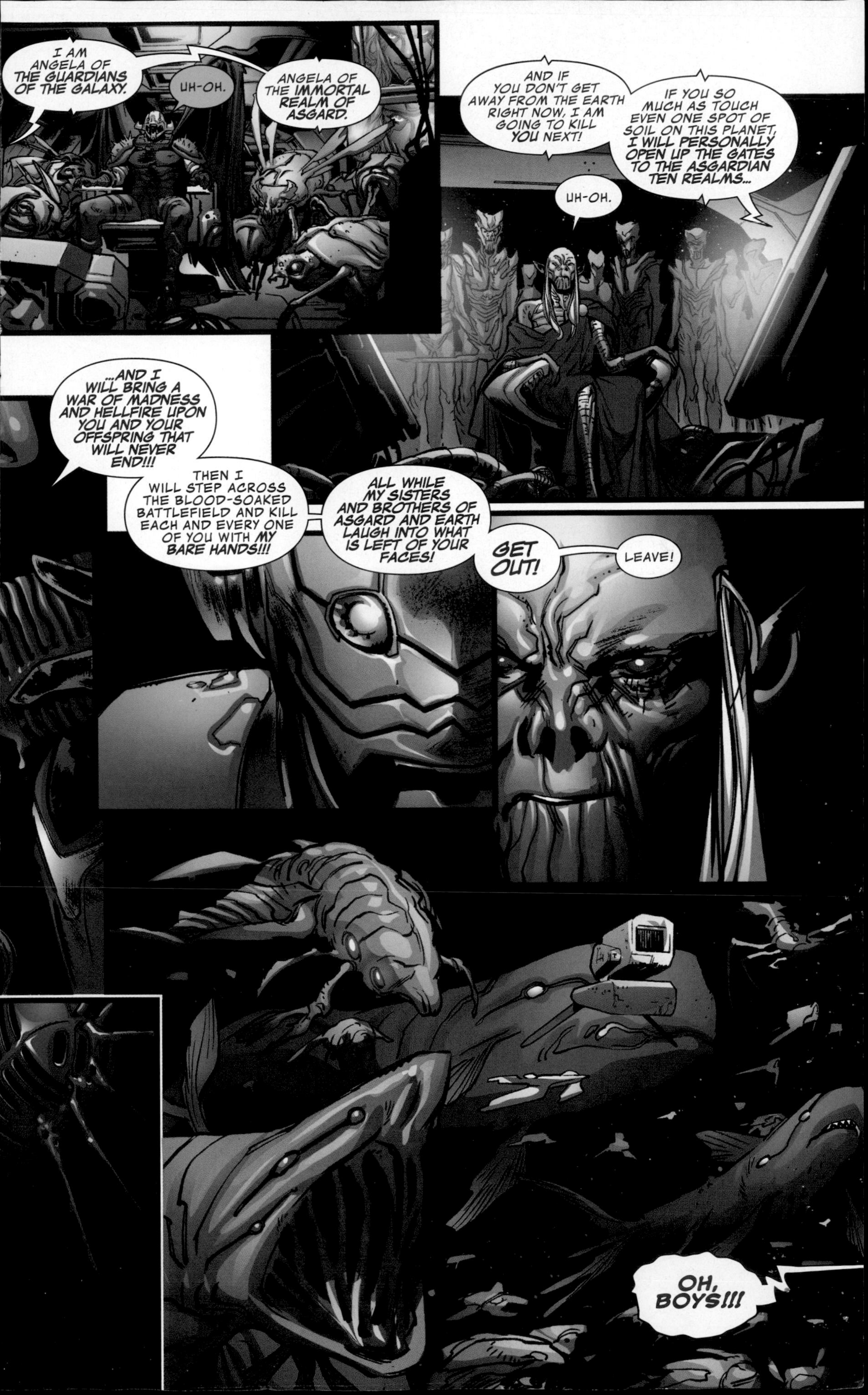
I AM ANGELA OF THE GUARDIANS OF THE GALAXY.
UH-OH.
ANGELA OF THE IMMORTAL REALM OF ASGARD.
AND IF YOU DON'T GET AWAY FROM THE EARTH RIGHT NOW, I AM GOING TO KILL YOU NEXT!
IF YOU SO MUCH AS TOUCH EVEN ONE SPOT OF SOIL ON THIS PLANET, I WILL PERSONALLY OPEN UP THE GATES TO THE ASGARDIAN TEN REALMS...
UH-OH.
...AND I WILL BRING A WAR OF MADNESS AND HELLFIRE UPON YOU AND YOUR OFFSPRING THAT WILL NEVER END!!!
THEN I WILL STEP ACROSS THE BLOOD-SOAKED BATTLEFIELD AND KILL EACH AND EVERY ONE OF YOU WITH MY BARE HANDS!!!
ALL WHILE MY SISTERS AND BROTHERS OF ASGARD AND EARTH LAUGH INTO WHAT IS LEFT OF YOUR FACES!
GET OUT!
LEAVE!
OH, BOYS!!!

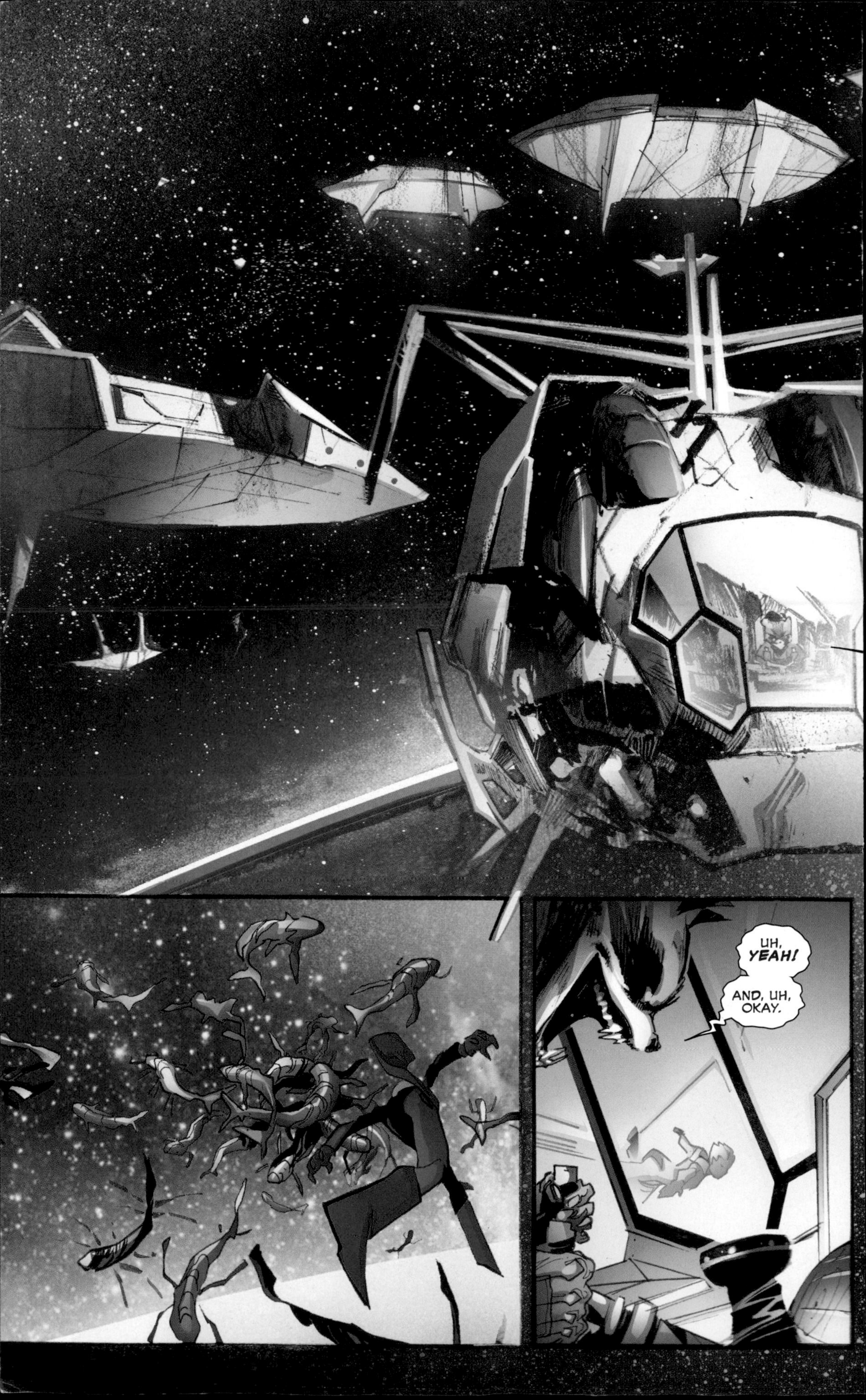
UH, YEAH!
AND, UH, OKAY.

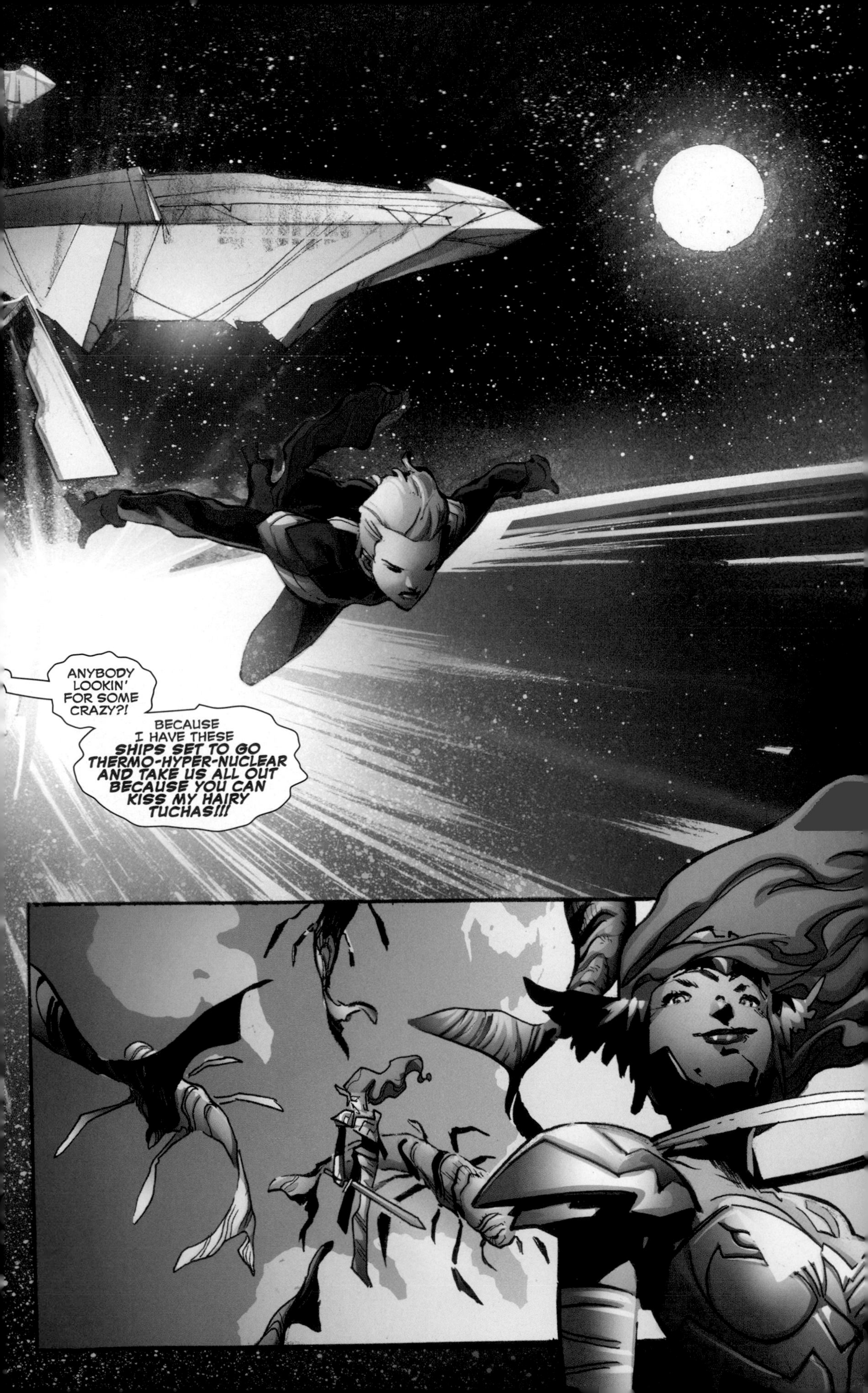
ANYBODY LOOKIN' FOR SOME CRAZY?!
BECAUSE I HAVE THESE SHIPS SET TO GO THERMO-HYPER-NUCLEAR AND TAKE US ALL OUT BECAUSE YOU CAN KISS MY HAIRY TUCHAS!!!

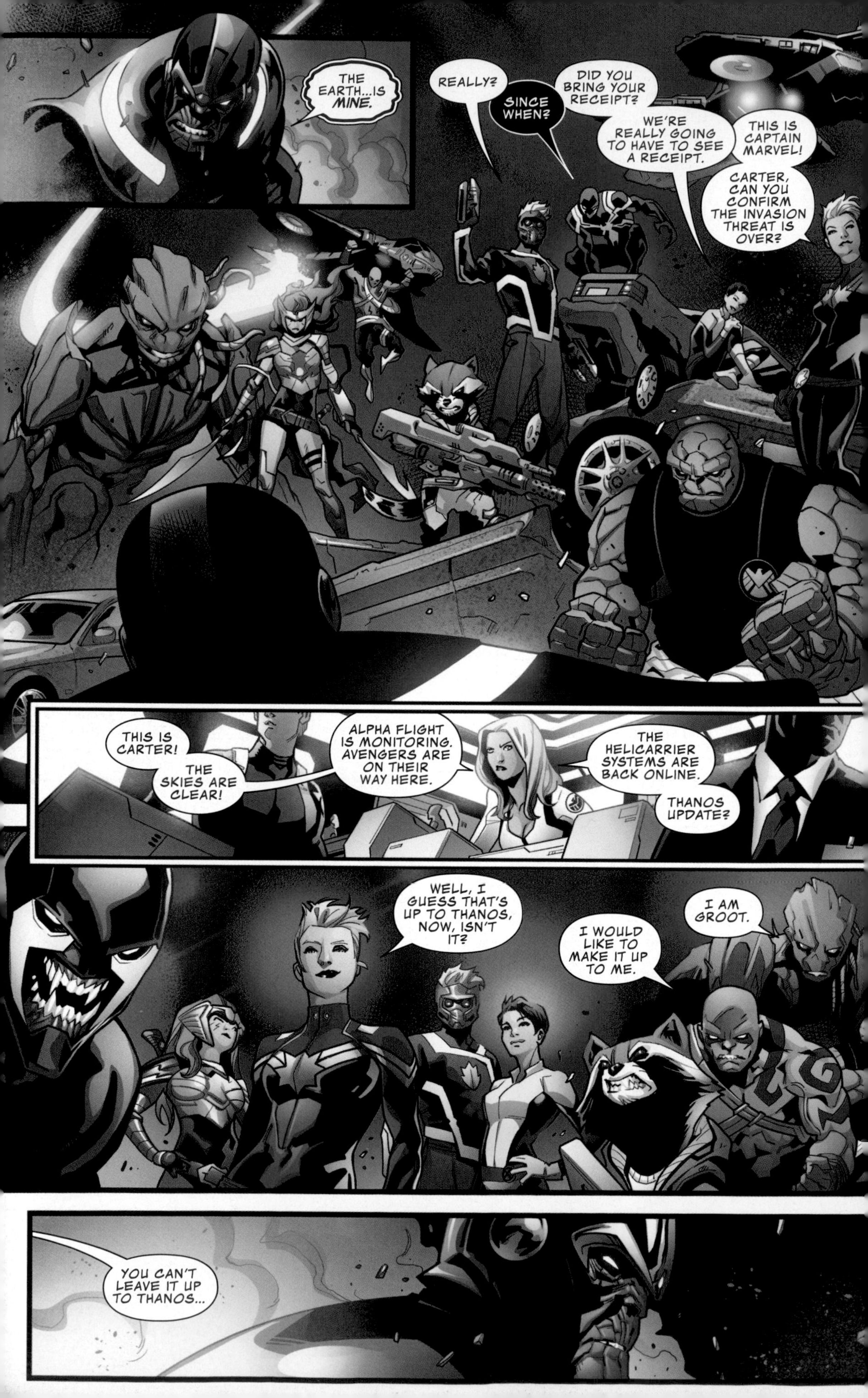
THE EARTH...IS MINE.
REALLY?
SINCE WHEN?
DID YOU BRING YOUR RECEIPT?
WE'RE REALLY GOING TO HAVE TO SEE A RECEIPT.
THIS IS CAPTAIN MARVEL!
CARTER, CAN YOU CONFIRM THE INVASION THREAT IS OVER?
THIS IS CARTER!
THE SKIES ARE CLEAR!
ALPHA FLIGHT IS MONITORING. AVENGERS ARE ON THEIR WAY HERE.
THE HELICARRIER SYSTEMS ARE BACK ONLINE.
THANOS UPDATE?
WELL, I GUESS THAT'S UP TO THANOS, NOW, ISN'T IT?
I AM GROOT.
I WOULD LIKE TO MAKE IT UP TO ME.
YOU CAN'T LEAVE IT UP TO THANOS...

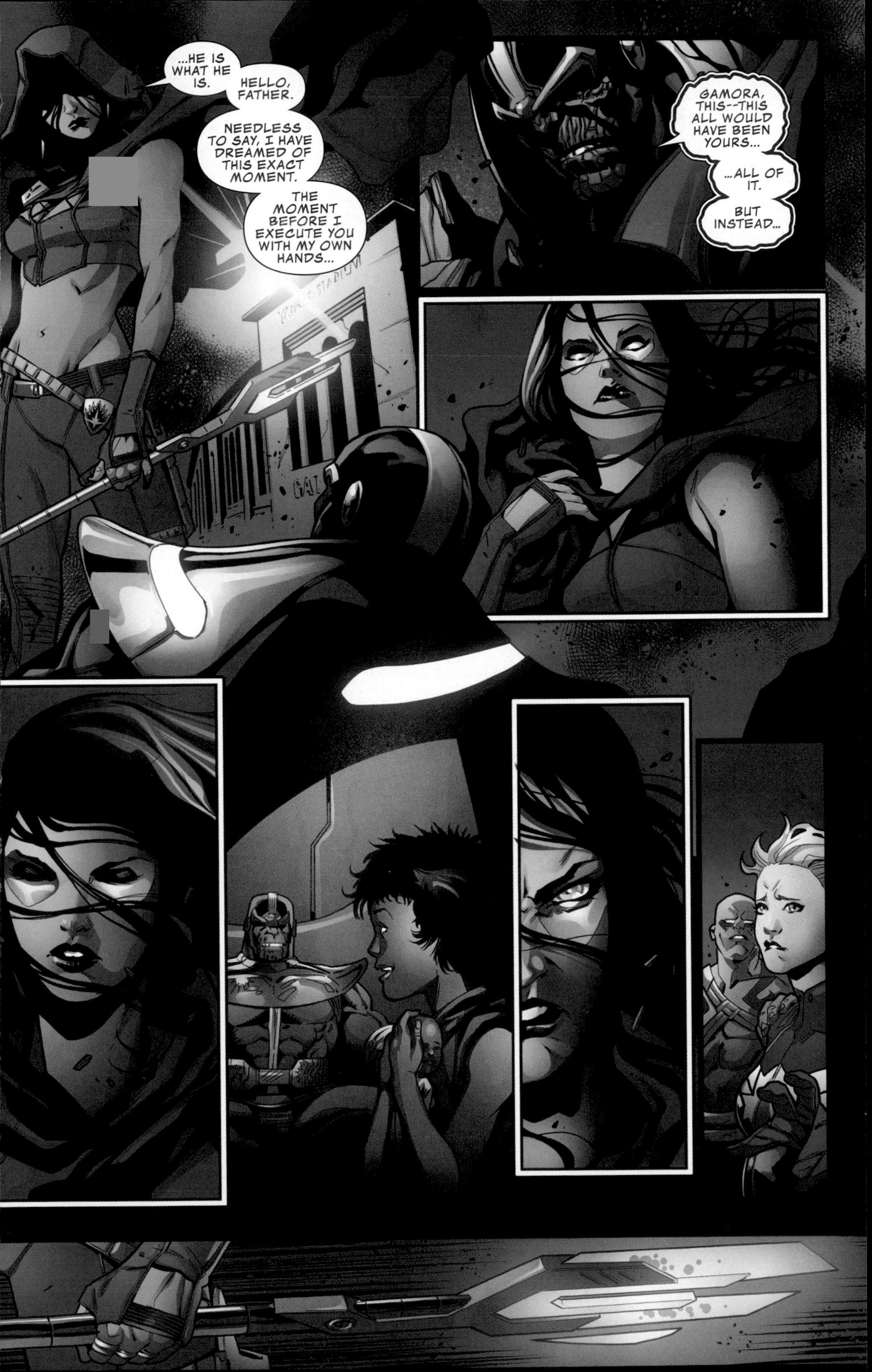
...HE IS WHAT HE IS.
HELLO, FATHER.
NEEDLESS TO SAY, I HAVE DREAMED OF THIS EXACT MOMENT.
THE MOMENT BEFORE I EXECUTE YOU WITH MY OWN HANDS...
GAMORA, THIS--THIS ALL WOULD HAVE BEEN YOURS...
...ALL OF IT.
BUT INSTEAD...

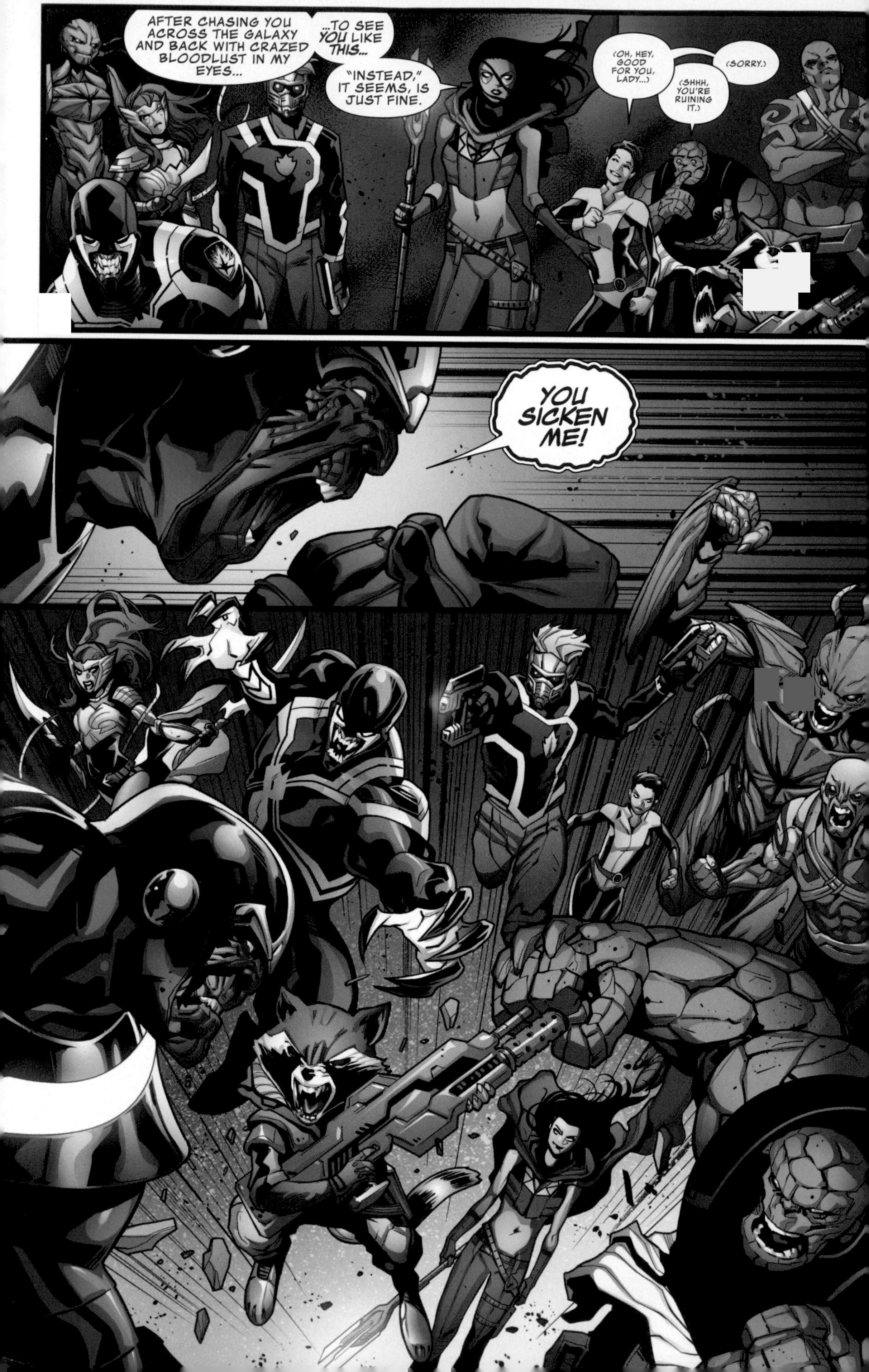
AFTER CHASING YOU ACROSS THE GALAXY AND BACK WITH CRAZED BLOODLUST IN MY EYES...
...TO SEE YOU LIKE THIS...
"INSTEAD," IT SEEMS, IS JUST FINE.
(OH, HEY, GOOD FOR YOU, LADY...)
(SORRY.)
(SHHH, YOU'RE RUINING IT.)
YOU SICKEN ME!

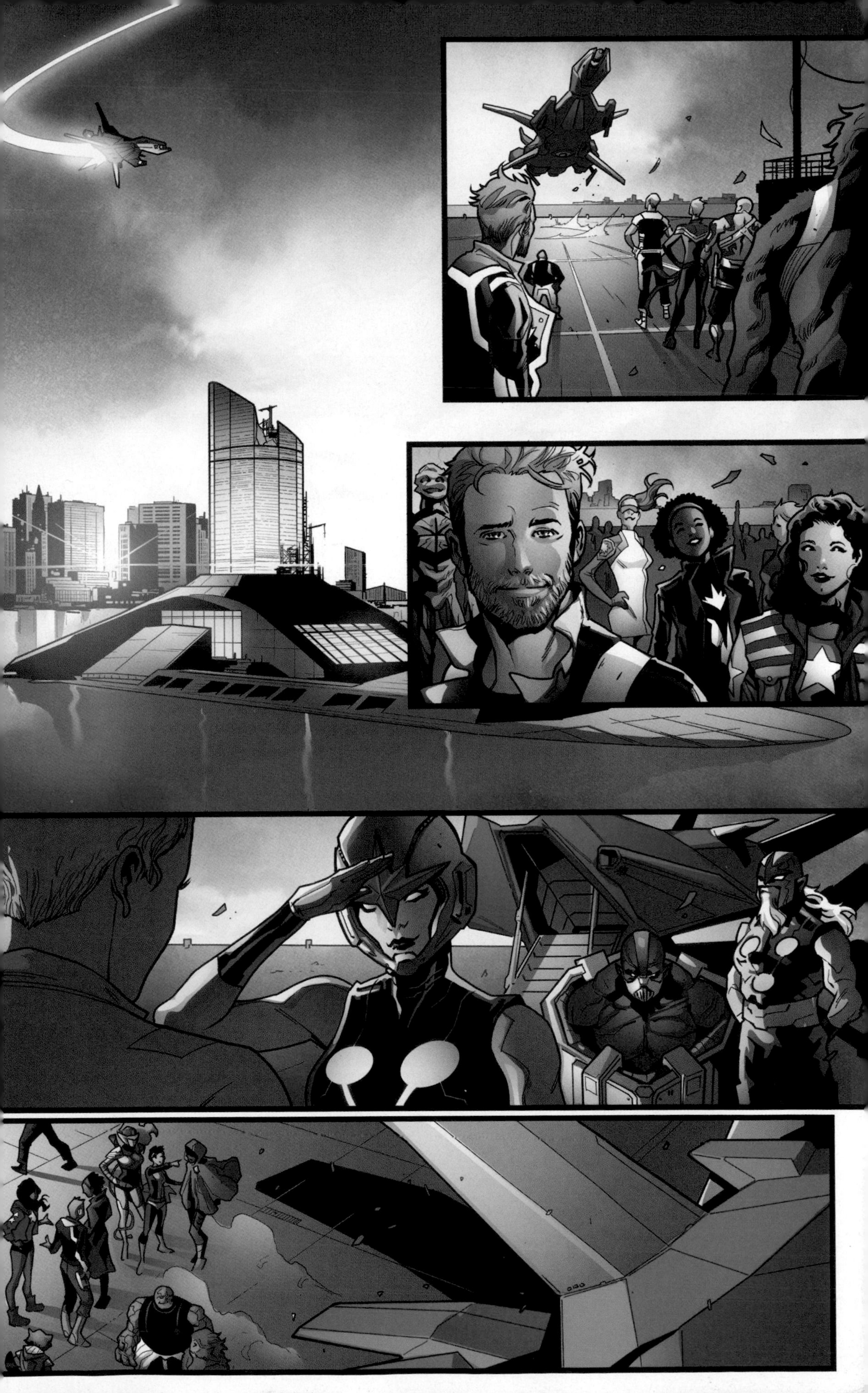

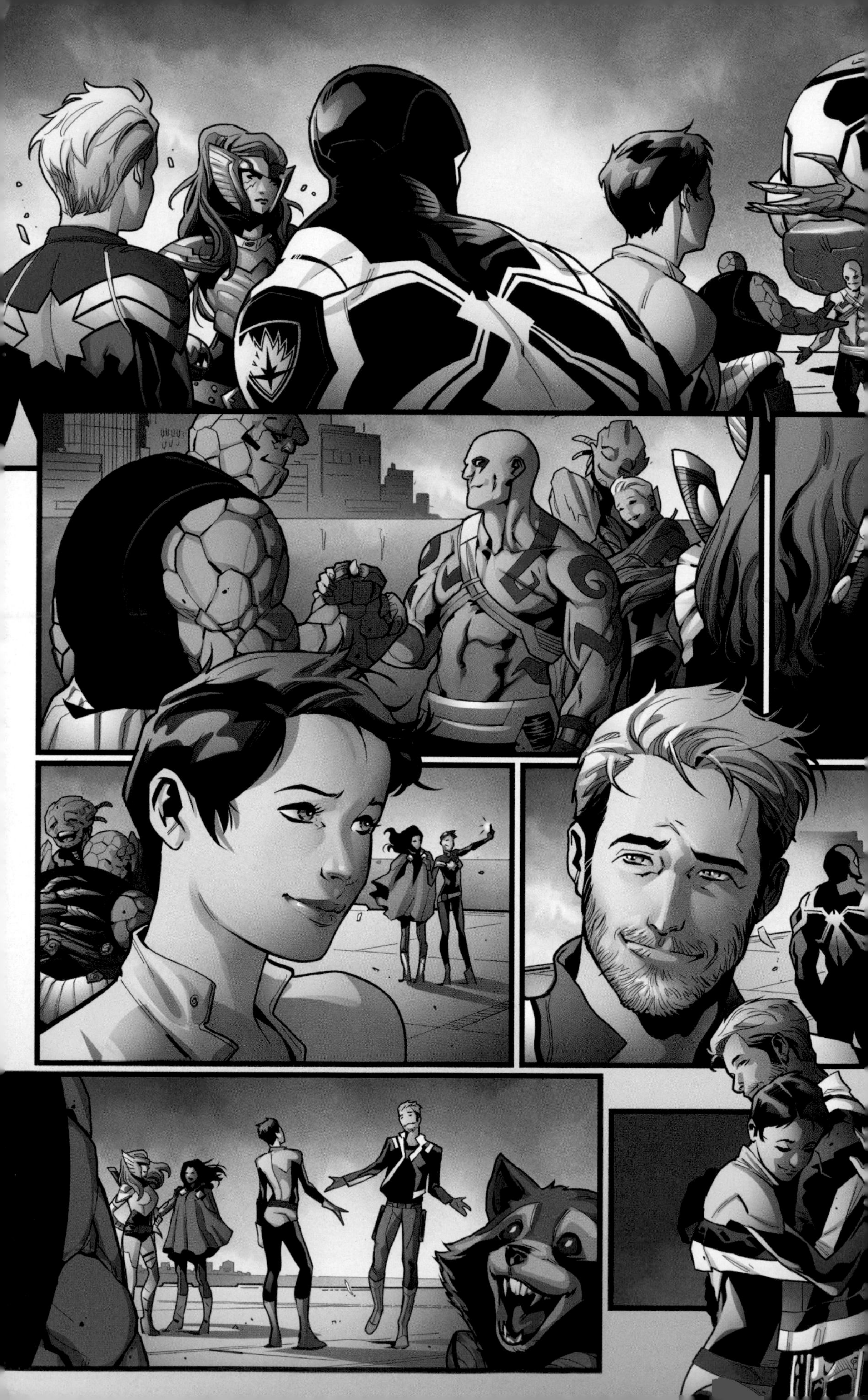

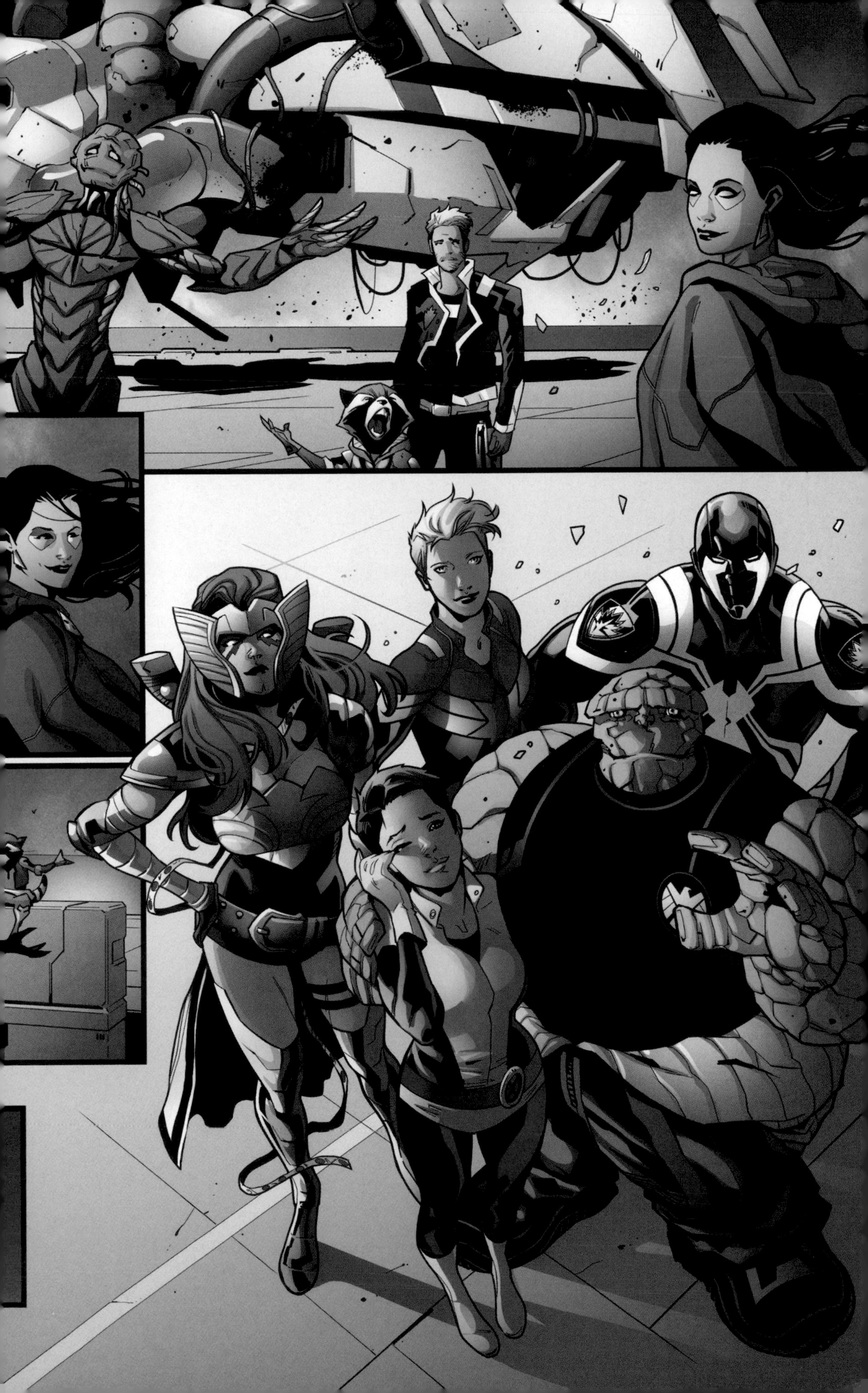

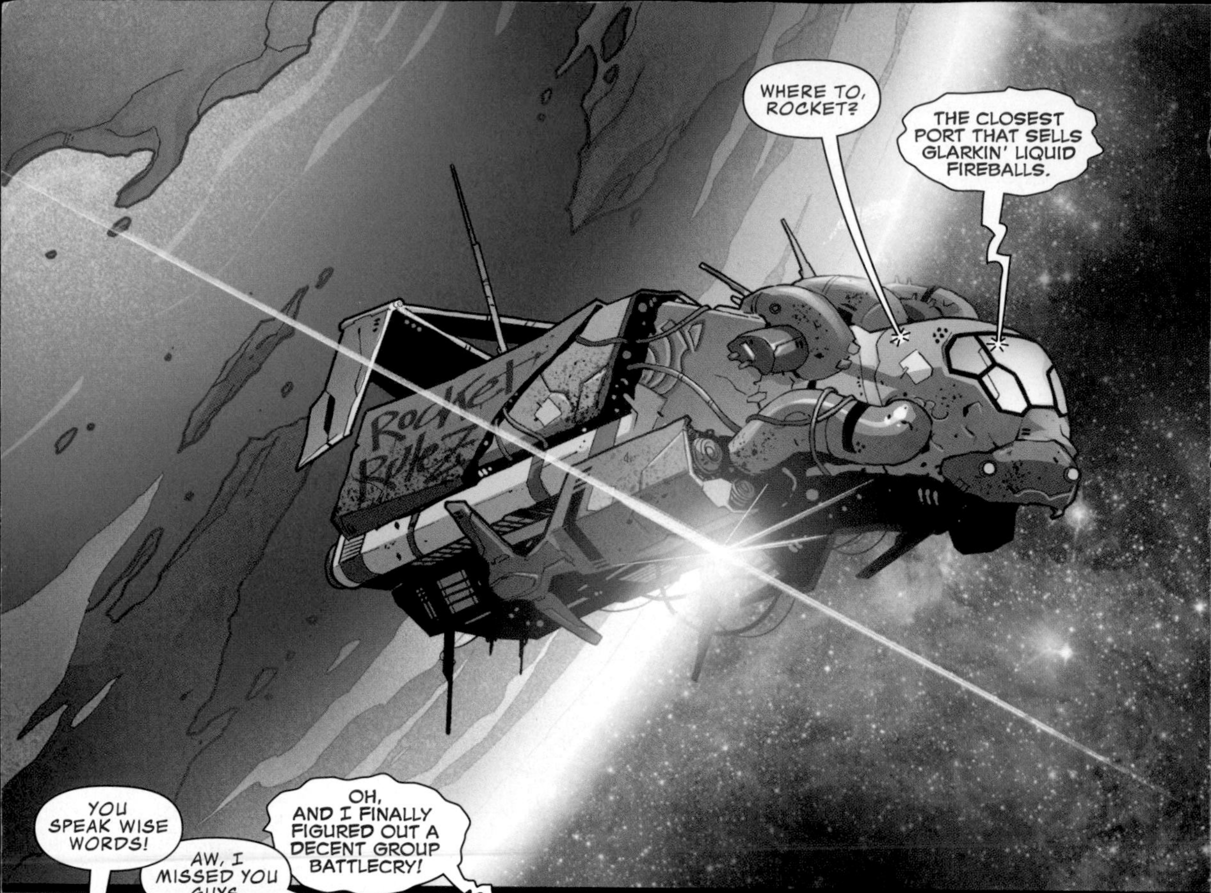
WHERE TO, ROCKET?
THE CLOSEST PORT THAT SELLS GLARKIN' LIQUID FIREBALLS.

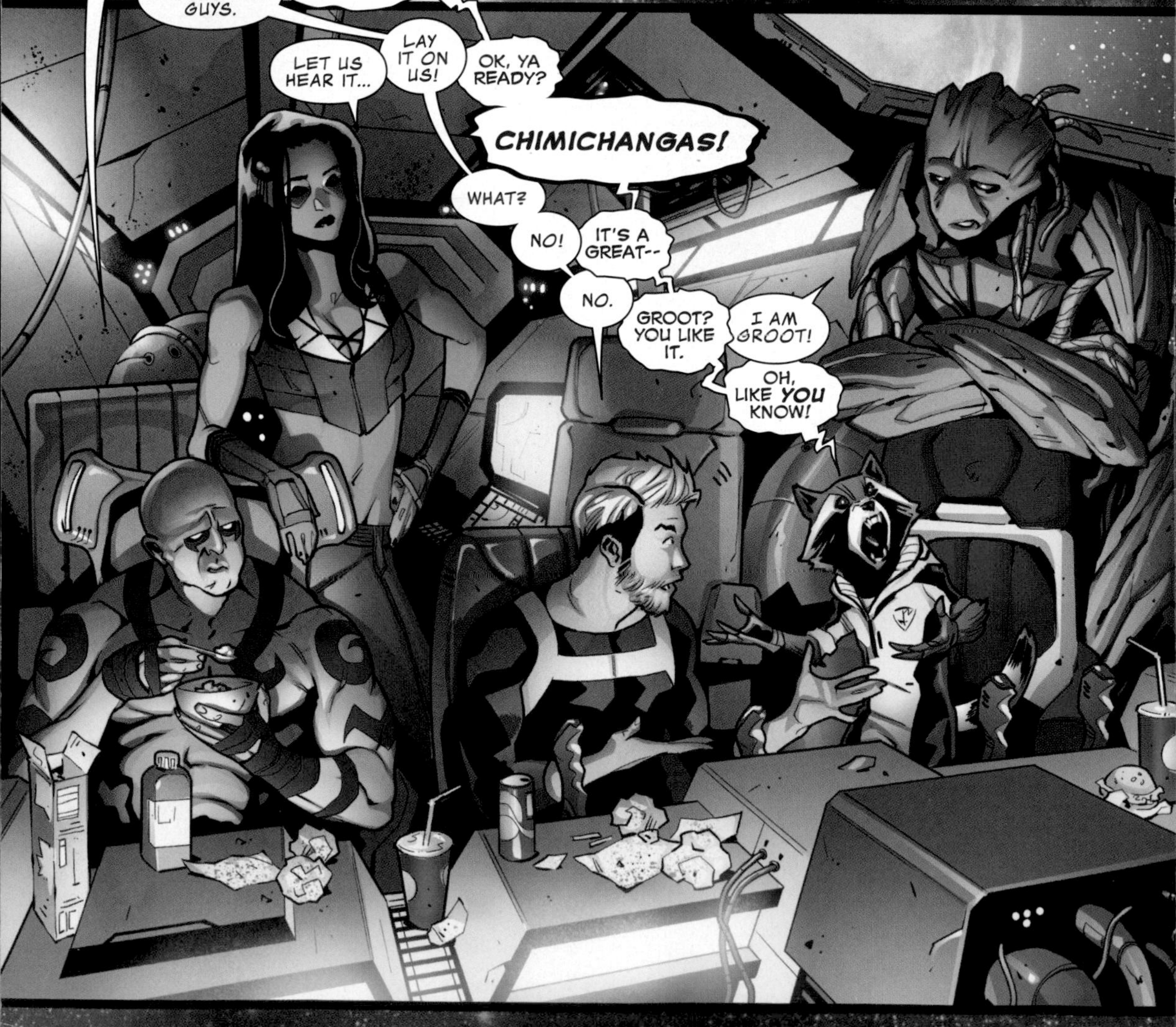
YOU SPEAK WISE WORDS!
AW, I MISSED YOU GUYS.
OH, AND I FINALLY FIGURED OUT A DECENT GROUP BATTLECRY!
LET US HEAR IT...
LAY IT ON US!
OK, YA READY?
CHIMICHANGAS!
WHAT?
NO!
IT'S A GREAT--
NO.
GROOT? YOU LIKE IT.
I AM GROOT!
OH, LIKE YOU KNOW!

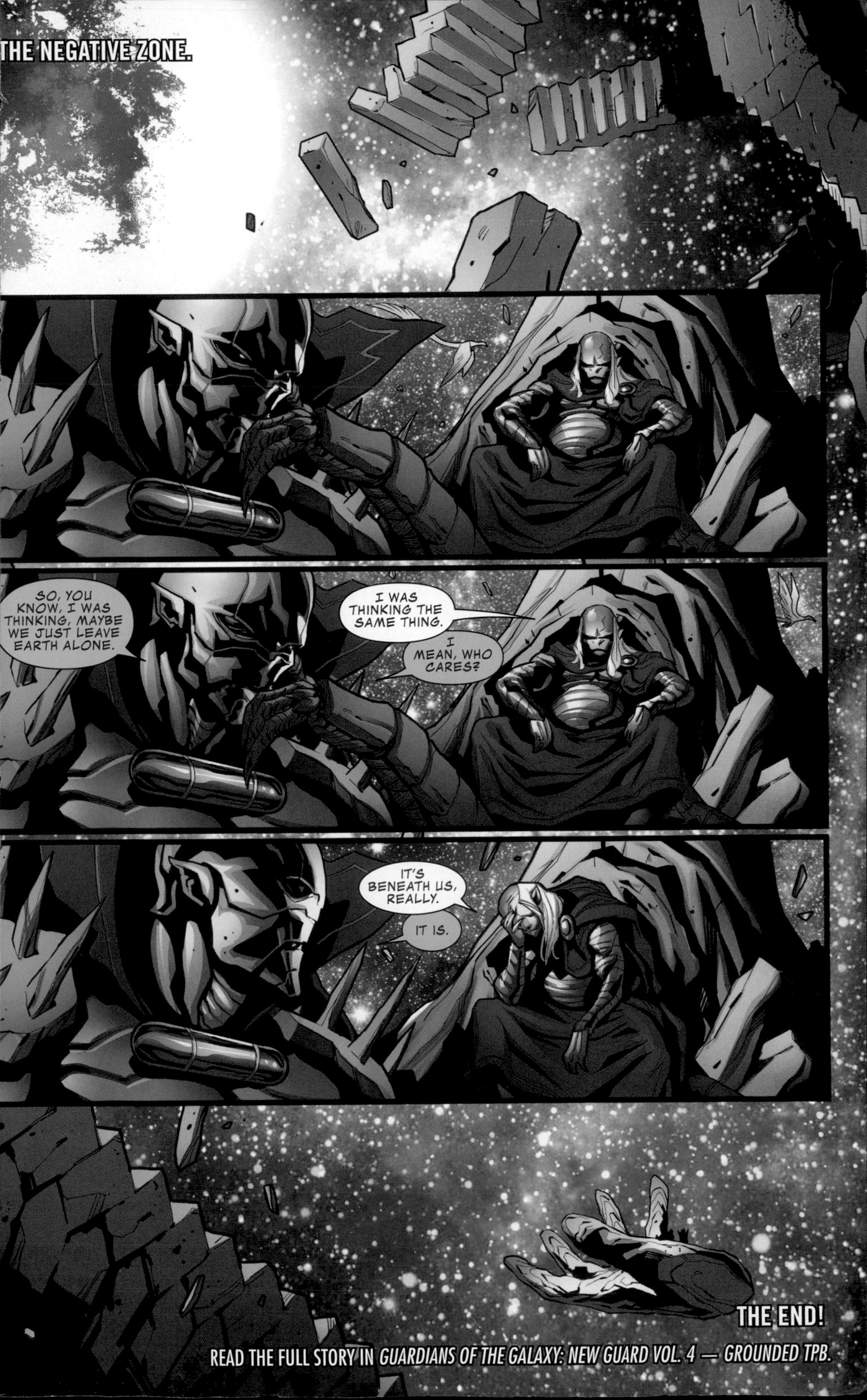
THE NEGATIVE ZONE.
SO, YOU KNOW, I WAS THINKING, MAYBE WE JUST LEAVE EARTH ALONE.
I WAS THINKING THE SAME THING.
I MEAN, WHO CARES?
IT'S BENEATH US, REALLY.
IT IS.
THE END!
READ THE FULL STORY IN *GUARDIANS OF THE GALAXY: NEW GUARD VOL. 4 — GROUNDED TPB.*